MOVING PR

ONE WE

19 DEC 2005

30 M

PEARSON
Education

We work with leading authors to develop the strongest educational materials in Law, bringing cutting-edge thinking and best learning practice to a global market.

Under a range of well-known imprints, including Longman, we craft high quality print and electronic publications which help readers to understand and apply their content, whether studying or at work.

To find out more about the complete range of our publishing, please visit us on the World Wide Web at: www.pearsoneduc.com

MOVING PROBATION FORWARD

EVIDENCE, ARGUMENTS AND PRACTICE

Edited by Wing Hong Chui and
Mike Nellis

PEARSON
Longman

Harlow, England • London • New York • Boston • San Francisco • Toronto
Sydney • Tokyo • Singapore • Hong Kong • Seoul • Taipei • New Delhi
Cape Town • Madrid • Mexico City • Amsterdam • Munich • Paris • Milan

Pearson Education Limited

Edinburgh Gate
Harlow
Essex CM20 2JE
England

and Associated Companies throughout the world

Visit us on the World Wide Web at:
www.pearsoned.co.uk

First edition 2003

ISBN 0 582 47277 6

British Library Cataloguing-in-Publication Data
A catalogue record for this book is available from the British Library

Library of Congress Cataloging-in-Publication Data
Probation : theories, practice, and research / [written and edited by] Wing Hong Chui,
Mike Nellis.—1st ed.
p. cm.
Includes bibliographical references and index.
ISBN 0-582-47277-6 (alk. paper)
1. Probation. 2. Criminals—Rehabilitation. 3. Recidivism—Prevention.
I. Chui, Wing Hong. II. Nellis, Mike.
HV9278.P698 2003
364.6'3—dc21   2002193175

10 9 8 7 6 5 4 3 2
08 07 06 05 04

Typeset in 10/13pt Sabon by 35
Printed in Great Britain by Henry Ling Limited, at the Dorset Press, Dorchester, DT1 1HD

The publisher's policy is to use paper manufactured from sustainable forests.

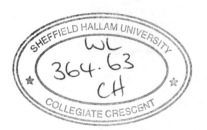

CONTENTS

Preface and Acknowledgements   xi
Notes on Contributors   xii

✳ 1 CREATING THE NATIONAL PROBATION SERVICE –
      NEW WINE, OLD BOTTLES?   Wing Hong Chui and
      Mike Nellis   1
      Introduction   1
      Why (Still) Study Probation?   2
      The Origins and Development of Probation   4
        Creating the Probation Service   4
        Controlling the Probation Service   6
        Modernising the Probation Service   8
        Configuration of the 'new' National Probation Service   10
      Structure of the Book   14
      References   16

  2   THEORIES OF CRIME   Loraine Gelsthorpe   19
      Introduction   19
      Biological Theories   20
        Definition   20
        Early theorists and theories   20
        Contemporary ideas   21
        Comment   22
      Psychological Theories   23
        Definition   23
        Early theorists and theories   23
        Contemporary ideas   25
        Comment   26
      Sociological and Environmental Theories   26
        Definition   26
        Early theorists and theories   27
        Contemporary ideas   28
        Comment   29

Critical and Feminist Theories   29
  Definition   29
  Early theorists and theories   30
  Contemporary ideas   31
  Comment   32
Conclusion   33
Summary of Key Issues   34
References   34

3 WHAT WORKS IN THEORIES OF PUNISHMENT   Sue Rex   38
Introduction   38
Consequentialism   38
  Application to community penalties   39
  What works in consequentialism   41
Retribution   42
  Application to community penalties   44
Does Desert 'Work' in Relation to Community Penalties?   45
Hybrid Theories   46
Beyond Compromise? Punishment as Communication   48
Restorative Justice   50
Summary of Key Issues   52
References   53

4 WHAT WORKS IN REDUCING RE-OFFENDING:
   PRINCIPLES AND PROGRAMMES   Wing Hong Chui   56
Introduction   56
Re-emergence of Rehabilitation in Probation – from
   'Nothing Works' to 'What Works'   57
The 'What Works' Principles   62
What Works: Accreditation of Offending Behaviour
   Programmes   64
Doubts on the 'What Works' Initiative   67
Summary of Key Issues   69
References   70

5 RESEARCH IN PROBATION: FROM 'NOTHING WORKS'
   TO 'WHAT WORKS'   Peter Raynor   74
Introduction   74
Rethinking 'Nothing Works'   75
Influencing Systems Instead of People   77
The Research Behind 'What Works'   78
Applying the Lessons of Research   80

Questions for the Future Probation Research Agenda 82
Summary of Key Issues 87
References 87

6 PRE-TRIAL INVESTIGATION   Mike Nash 92
Introduction 92
Historical Context 93
The Changing Nature of Probation Court Reports 93
Penal Pessimism and Probation Practice 95
The 1991 Criminal Justice Act and National Standards 95
PSRs and National Standards 98
Public Protection, Values and Multi-agency Working 100
Conclusion 104
Key Facts 105
Summary of Key Issues 105
References 105

7 RISK AND RISK ASSESSMENT   Gwen Robinson 108
Introduction 108
Working with Offenders: Dimensions of Risk 109
The Rise of Risk in Probation Practice 110
Approaches to Risk Assessment 112
'Clinical' versus 'actuarial' methods 113
Assessing 'criminogenic needs': the emergence of a
dynamic approach 117
Risk Assessment in Context: Risk-based Decision-making in
Criminal Justice 121
Summary of Key Issues 124
References 125

8 IN SUPPORT OF EFFECTIVENESS: FACILITATING
PARTICIPATION AND SUSTAINING CHANGE
Frances Fleet and Jill Annison 129
The Wider Context 129
Working to Achieve Change 131
Motivational Interviewing 133
Relapse Prevention 136
Crisis Intervention 138
Solution-focused Approaches 140
Concluding Thoughts 141
Summary of Key Issues 142
References 143

9 DESISTANCE-FOCUSED PROBATION PRACTICE
   Fergus McNeill   146
   Introduction   146
   Theoretical Perspectives   147
   Age, Gender and Desistance   149
   Attitudes, Motivation and Desistance   150
   Interventions, Relationships and Desistance   152
   Conclusions: Desistance-focused Practice   156
      Assessment and planning   156
      Engagement, intervention and evaluation   158
   Summary of Key Issues   160
   Acknowledgements   161
   References   161

10 ESSENTIAL SKILLS IN WORKING WITH OFFENDERS
    Jonathan Hopkinson and Sue Rex   163
    Introduction   163
    Responsivity   164
    Aspects of Practice   167
       Assessment   167
       Supervision planning   169
       Case Management   170
    Promoting Change – Techniques   172
       Engaging offenders in change   172
       Promoting Pro-social Behaviour   173
       Promoting compliance   176
    Summary of Key Issues   177
    References   178

11 ENFORCING SUPERVISION AND ENCOURAGING
    COMPLIANCE   Carol Hedderman   181
    A Brief History of Enforcement   181
    Recent Improvements in Enforcement   186
    Forging a Link between Enforcement, Compliance and
       Effective Practice   190
    Summary of Key Issues   192
    References   193

12 PARTNERSHIPS IN THE PROBATION SERVICE
    Judith Rumgay   195
    Introduction   195
    Partnership as Policy   196

Contracting for supervision services 196
Community crime prevention 197
Targeting of special groups 197
Coordinated social planning and provision 198
Theories of Partnership 199
Partnership as redistribution of responsibilities 199
Partnership as system efficiency 201
Partnership as empowerment 203
Successful Partnership 205
Leadership 205
Clarity 206
Process 207
Conflict resolution 208
Conclusion 209
Summary of Key Issues 209
References 210

13 VICTIM WORK IN THE PROBATION SERVICE:
PERPETUATING NOTIONS OF AN 'IDEAL VICTIM'
Basia Spalek 214
Introduction 214
Responding to Victims' Needs: Probation and the Victims'
Movement 215
Probation Practice with Offenders: Incorporating the Victim 220
Restorative Justice and Victim/Offender Probation Work 222
Conclusion 223
Summary of Key Issues 224
References 225

14 HUMAN RIGHTS AND THE PROBATION VALUES
DEBATE Mike Nellis and Loraine Gelsthorpe 227
Introduction 227
Changing Probation Values 228
Values and *A New Choreography* 230
Human Rights: A New Moral Discourse? 233
The Future of Probation Values 237
Summary of Key Issues 241
References 241

15 ELECTRONIC MONITORING AND THE FUTURE OF
PROBATION Mike Nellis 245
Introduction 245
EM and Probation: A Conflict Begins 247

Probation Service Hostility to EM   249
New Labour: Displacing Probation?   251
EM: The Commercial Dimension   254
Popular Punitivism and the Limits to Tagging   255
Conclusion   257
Summary of Key Issues   257
References   258

16 THE END OF PROBATION?   Mike Nellis and
Wing Hong Chui   261
Justice for All: New Sentences   262
  A customised community sentence   263
  Custody Plus   263
  Custody Minus   264
  Intermittent Custody   264
Organisational Change   265
The Central and the Local   267
Victim-centredness and Restorative Justice   268
Image and Language   269
Morale in the Probation Service   273
References   275

Index   277

PREFACE AND ACKNOWLEDGEMENTS

What, in the twenty-first century, is the meaning of probation? In what ways does probation intervention reduce re-offending? How can a probation officer confront, control and monitor offenders in a cost-effective way? What impact has the newly established NPS had on probation officers' day-to-day activities? These are questions commonly asked by trainee probation officers, criminal justice practitioners, managers and policy-makers alike. *Moving Probation Forward* is an edited book that surveys the contemporary development and major work of probation in the context of England and Wales. There were rapid and radical changes in the training of probation officers and the organisation of the criminal justice services at the beginning of the year 2000. The major aims of this book are to provide a much-needed account of issues surrounding probation in a changing context of criminal justice policy and management, to offer practical help to students in probation studies, criminology and law, and to provide information to training officers, managers and practitioners in the field of probation and criminal justice.

This edited book is the fruit of the concerted efforts of a group of practitioners, academics and researchers to examine probation with a view to identifying and promoting effective practice. It has assembled experts and professionals from a wide range of fields to participate in the writing, thus providing manifold perspectives on this specific subject area. It is thus a comprehensive and user-friendly text that covers various key topic areas in probation, and draws on an extensive store of current expertise in the field.

Last but not least, both editors would like to thank all the contributors for their willingness to play a part in writing this book and for their quality work. In addition, we would like to thank Donald Nicolson who proof-read most of the earlier drafts. It should be emphasised that we alone are responsible for what follows.

WING HONG CHUI

MIKE NELLIS

NOTES ON CONTRIBUTORS

Jill Annison

Dr Jill Annison worked as probation officer and specialist social worker in the 1970s and 1980s. After obtaining a First Class Honours Open University degree she undertook postgraduate research, being awarded her PhD in 1998 for her thesis focusing on gender and organisational change in the Probation Service. Since November 1998 she has been Coordinator for the BSc (Hons) Community Justice (Probation Studies) programme at the University of Plymouth, working with the five Probation Areas in the south-west of England.

Wing Hong Chui

Dr Wing Hong Chui has recently been appointed as an Assistant Professor in the School of Law at the City University of Hong Kong. He graduated at the University of Hong Kong with a First Class Honours degree in Social Work, and then worked as leader of an outreach social work team to deal with at-risk youths and young offenders in the community. He completed his master's and doctoral studies in criminology at the University of Cambridge. Before joining the Law School, he held lecturing positions in the Department of Social Work and Probation Studies at the University of Exeter, and in the School of Social Work and Social Policy at the University of Queensland (Australia). His areas of interest include social work with young people, criminology and criminal justice, problem gambling, and human rights issues. Recently he has been appointed as an Associate Fellow of the Centre for Criminology at the University of Hong Kong, and a University Honorary Fellow of the Unit for Research on Community Safety at the University of Exeter.

Frances Fleet

Frances Fleet qualified as a probation officer in 1970 and over the next 30 years gained a wide range of main-grade experience, including practice teaching. She has taught on the academic element of the MA/Diploma in Social Work at the University of Exeter since 1990 and has been involved as a tutor with the Diploma in Probation Studies at the University of Plymouth since its inception in 1998. Her particular interests are translating values, theory and research into professional practice and the teaching of professionally relevant inter-personal skills.

Loraine Gelsthorpe

Dr Loraine Gelsthorpe is a University Senior Lecturer at the Institute of Criminology and Fellow of Pembroke College, University of Cambridge. Her main research and teaching interests revolve around discretion and discrimination in the criminal justice system, gender and justice, youth justice and the links between criminal and social justice. She has published extensively in these fields and in the area of inter-agency aspects of crime prevention and probation and community penalties (especially in relation to social inquiry reports and pre-sentence reports). Among her recent major publications is the co-edited volume: *Community Penalties: Change and Challenges* (Bottoms, Gelsthorpe and Rex, 2001). She has recently completed a Home Office-sponsored major evaluation of community service orders (as part of community punishment) and has plans to develop this work. Dr Gelsthorpe chairs the professional and ethical committee of the British Society of Criminology and is member of the ESRC's national Postgraduate Training Board.

Carol Hedderman

Dr Carol Hedderman was Deputy Director of the Criminal Policy Research Unit, London South Bank University from 1999 to 2002. Research interests include the imposition and enforcement of community penalties, sentencing disparities, parole decision-making, female offending, the treatment of women in the criminal justice system and strategies for improving services for the victims of domestic violence. She was a member of the Parole Board from 2001 to 2002 and has recently been appointed Assistant Director of the Home Office Research and Statistics Directorate with responsibility for research on courts, corrections and offenders.

Jonathan Hopkinson

Jonathan Hopkinson is a Senior Probation Officer working for the Cambridge-shire area of the National Probation Service. He has worked for the Probation Service on and off since 1971. He has a wide experience of Probation Programmes and has recently been responsible for managing the local implementation of several nationally accredited programmes.

Fergus McNeill

Fergus McNeill is a Lecturer in Social Work at the University of Glasgow. After undergraduate studies in philosophy and history, he lived and worked for three years in a residential drug rehabilitation centre before undertaking professional social work education and training. Once qualified, he worked for five years as a criminal justice social worker in the East End of Glasgow until he assumed his current post in 1998. His previous research has focused primarily on front-line workers' perspectives on probation issues, although he has also researched and written about various aspects of youth crime and youth justice. As well as teaching on and developing a number of social work and criminal justice courses, he is involved in several ongoing research projects. These include an exploration of front-line probation ideologies, an ESRC-funded study of social enquiry and sentencing in the Sheriff Courts and the evaluation of the Pathfinder Provider Initiative in Scotland for the Scottish Executive.

Mike Nash

Dr Mike Nash is the Deputy Director of the Institute of Criminal Justice Studies at the University of Portsmouth. He researches and teaches in the areas of dangerousness, probation policy and the politics of criminal justice. He has published widely in his field and Blackstone Press published his first book, *Police, Probation and Protecting the Public*, in 1999. He works with probation and police services to deliver multi-agency dangerousness training and has worked with the Home Office probation and prison departments on a variety of projects. Prior to working in higher education, he was employed by the Probation Service and worked in lifer and maximum security prisons among other locations. He is currently working on a project examining the changing professional culture of the criminal justice sector.

Mike Nellis

Dr Mike Nellis is a Senior Lecturer in Criminal Justice Studies at the University of Birmingham. He has a background in social work with young offenders, and has subsequently been involved in the training of probation officers. He has written widely on community penalties, particularly probation and electronic monitoring, and the values which should underpin their use, as well as the contribution which literature, plays and films can make to public debate on punishment. He is interested in the role of faith-based organisations in the penal reform process and in work with offenders. His most recent research was on yoga teaching in prison. He was a co-founder of the annual Bill McWilliams Memorial Lecture.

Peter Raynor

Peter Raynor is a Professor in the Centre for Applied Social Studies at the University of Wales, Swansea. A former probation officer, he is currently a member of the West Glamorgan Probation Committee and a member designate of the new South Wales Probation Board, as well as of the Joint Prisons and Probation Accreditation Panel for England and Wales. His research over the last 25 years has included work on offenders who misuse drugs, youth justice, Automatic Conditional Release, pre-sentence reports, through-care and resettlement of short-term prisoners, risk and need assessment, and the effectiveness of probation programmes.

Sue Rex

Dr Sue Rex is a Senior Research Associate at the Institute of Criminology, University of Cambridge. Following a PhD in which she examined perceptions of probation in a context of just deserts, completed in 1996, she has developed her research interests in the areas of sentencing principles and practice in the supervision of offenders in the community. She currently holds a fellowship with the Economic and Social Research Council to conduct a research programme to develop community penalties in theory and practice. She has recently completed the evaluation of the Community Service Pathfinder projects (as project manager) under contract to the Home Office, and is currently leading an evaluation of the Joint Accreditation Panel which approves programmes for offenders for use in prison and in the community. She is also undertaking a major piece of research looking at processes of communication in sentencing and punishment, and their application to community penalties.

Gwen Robinson

Dr Gwen Robinson is a Research Associate in the Department of Law at the University of Sheffield, where she is part of a team evaluating Restorative Justice initiatives on behalf of the Home Office. She recently completed her doctorate on risk in probation practice at the University of Wales, Swansea, prior to which she was a researcher at the Probation Studies Unit at the University of Oxford. She obtained a Diploma in Social Work, specialising in social work with offenders, in 1996.

Judith Rumgay

Dr Judith Rumgay is a Senior Lecturer in the Department of Social Policy, London School of Economics (LSE). She was a probation officer prior to her appointment at LSE, where she was responsible for the Home Office-sponsored probation stream on the postgraduate social work programme. More recently her teaching has focused on psychology and crime, rehabilitation of offenders and criminal justice policy. Her research interests have included alcohol- and drug-related offending, the Probation Service, female offenders and voluntary sector involvement in offender rehabilitation. She is the author of *Crime, Punishment and the Drinking Offender* (Macmillan, 1998), and *The Addicted Offender: Developments in British Policy and Practice* (Palgrave, 2000), as well as articles and chapters. She is currently Director of the Griffins Society Visiting Research Fellowship Programme at LSE, book review editor for *Criminal Justice*, and a member of the steering committee for the annual Bill McWilliams Memorial Lecture.

Basia Spalek

Dr Basia Spalek is a Lecturer in Community Justice Studies at the University of Birmingham. Her research interests include victimisation, white-collar crime, and race and religious diversity. She has published on these topics in the *Howard Journal of Criminal Justice*, *International Journal of the Sociology of Law*, and *Criminal Justice Matters*. Her first book *Islam, Crime and Criminal Justice* appeared in 2002.

1

CREATING THE NATIONAL PROBATION SERVICE – NEW WINE, OLD BOTTLES?

Wing Hong Chui and Mike Nellis

INTRODUCTION

There is no issue that touches our citizens more deeply than crime and law and order on our streets, and we need to make the changes so that we have a criminal justice system that punishes the criminal but also offers those convicted the chance to rehabilitate and make their way out of a life of crime. (Prime Minister, Tony Blair, quoted in National Probation Service for England and Wales 2001: 1)

The primary aims of this chapter are to discuss the various processes by which the National Probation Service (NPS) was created in April 2001 and to outline the rationale and structure of the book. The creation of the NPS was the culmination of years of debate and reform, the detail of which is well covered elsewhere (Whitfield 2001; Nellis 2002; Raynor and Vanstone 2002; Ward, Scott and Lacey 2002). Suffice to say that, despite retention of the name 'probation' in the title of the new national service, continuity with the past may be less than meets the eye – hence 'new wine, old bottles' in our title. The Criminal Justice and Court Services Act 2000 and Powers of the Criminal Courts (Sentencing) Act 2000, and the latest version of the *National Standards for the Supervision of Offenders in the Community* (Home Office 2000) have between them had a huge impact on contemporary probation practice. Control over the Service has been centralised, and the number of local areas reduced from 54 to 42. Local Probation Committees have been replaced by smaller Probation Boards. Training has been split from social work. The names of key community penalties have – symbolically – been changed, ostensibly to give the Service a tougher public image. The erstwhile leadership role of the Probation Inspectorate has been reduced by the creation of a National Probation

Director. Once influential probation interest groups such as Association of Chief Probation Officers (ACOP) and the Council of Probation Committees (CPC) have been merged into the Probation Boards Association (PBA), which has yet to secure its place in debates on policy and practice. A former Minister for Prisons and Probation, Paul Boateng, sought to capture the essence of all this change at the beginning of the *National Standards* by saying 'We are a law enforcement agency. It's what we are. It's what we do', presumably to highlight a decisive shift away from probation's former 'social work' identity (although in reality, the post-1948 Service has always had a law-enforcement role).

Exactly what is happening to the Probation Service, and where it is it going? 'Does a national service really improve on the possibilities of crime reduction?' 'Was the inception of the NPS a permanent or a temporary measure, a step towards merger with the prison service'? 'How effective is the prevailing understanding of effective practice?' and 'How far has probation moved away from social work – and how far should it move away?' That change is occurring is obvious, but these questions remain unanswered. The clients of the Probation Service – once understood exclusively as the offenders under supervision – are now understood more broadly to include the courts, crime victims and the public, and indeed, the government itself. There are many constituencies interested in what the Probation Service is now undergoing, some with significant views on what should happen if all the changes still do not bring about the desired results of reduced crime

While it is impossible to answer all these questions in this introductory chapter, an account of how the new NPS originated is necessary here, because it is within and about the framework it has created that most of the contributors in this book have written. Policy changes fast, and even as they wrote new developments were occurring: we will seek to address these in the closing chapter. This present chapter is structured into three parts, i.e. our rationale for editing the book, current developments in probation policy and practice, and key themes in the book.

WHY (STILL) STUDY PROBATION?

Probation has never had as high a profile within the criminal justice system as the police, prisons and law, and its coverage in the mass media has been, and remains, minimal in comparison. Despite its demonstrable value to those under supervision, and to sentencers, it is not surprising that the public has no clear picture of what probation intends to achieve and is seemingly unconcerned about its potential to reduce offending behaviour and achieve offender rehabilitation. In the USA the situation has already become much worse, and some fear that what happened there may happen in the UK. At a conference on probation and parole in the USA in December 1998, one participant commented that '[d]espite a proliferation of outstanding cutting-edge programs, for the most part and in most places public regard for probation is dangerously low, and for the most part in most places what passes for probation supervision is a joke. It's conceptually bankrupt and it's politically not viable' (US Department of Justice 1998).

This edited collection was put together in defiance of that view, in the belief that while traditional probation ideals should never be venerated uncritically, there is definite life in the idea of community supervision of offenders, if it is undertaken in a humanitarian spirit and with due regard to research findings. The collection insists that probation remains an important player in the criminal justice system in England and Wales, and shares with Gill McKenzie (2000), the last chair of the Association of Chief Probation Officers, the belief that its 'future could be greater than its past if it receives proper political support'.

A further reason for editing this book is that practitioners in social services, voluntary agencies, youth offending teams, probation teams and indeed other criminal justice agencies are increasingly required to absorb a distinct body of knowledge, and to prove the effectiveness of their work with explicit evidence. Qualifying training for probation officers and social workers remains linked to universities (albeit on separate courses now) and practitioners are being encouraged to become 'reflective', and to think of themselves as part of 'learning organisations'. After qualifying they are encouraged to adopt personal–professional development strategies, attending workshops and post-qualifying training programmes (now mandatory for all child care staff) in order to keep up with the fast-changing knowledge base. Practitioners therefore need books that relate theory, practice and research to their work, which are written for them, not just as contributions to academic criminology. To that end we have brought together a number of academics, researchers who were formerly probation officers, and some contemporary practitioners to explore both the challenges facing the new service and the nature of effective strategies for working with probationers.

Let us remind ourselves, before embarking on our account of how the NPS came into being, about the contours of the organisation of which we are talking. The contemporary Probation Service is dealing with a large number of offenders sentenced for indictable offences in England and Wales. According to NPS for England and Wales (2001), the caseload on any given day is in excess of 200,000, and approximately 90 per cent are male and 10 per cent are female. *Probation Statistics* shows that the proportion sentenced to community rehabilitation orders (formerly probation orders) or community punishment orders (formerly community service orders) for indictable violence against the person offences has nearly doubled between 1990 and 2000 (Home Office 2002: 1).

Wing Hong Chui and Mike Nellis

Table 1.1   Persons starting criminal supervision by the Probation Service[1]

England and Wales Court orders	Thousands of persons				
	1996	1997	1998	1999	2000
Community rehabilitation order[2]	49.1	51.5	55.5	55.9	53.7
Community punishment order[3, 4]	46.5	47.9	50.3	51.3	52.2
Community punishment and rehabilitation order[5]	17.0	19.1	21.2	20.5	18.5
Children & Young Persons Act 1969	2.9	2.8	2.6	2.2	0.4
Suspended sentence supervision order	0.5	0.6	0.5	0.5	0.5
Money payment supervision order	6.4	4.6	3.0	2.3	1.6
All court orders[6]	115.4	119.8	126.8	126.4	122.0

[1] Each person is counted only once in total even if they started several types of supervision in the year.
[2] Previously known as probation order.
[3] Previously known as community service order.
[4] The 1998, 1999 and 2000 figures include community punishment order for fine defaulters and persistent petty offenders introduced by the Crime (Sentences) Act 1997.
[5] Previously known as combination order.
[6] Includes community punishment orders for breach and Drug Treatment and Testing Orders.

Source: Adapted from the Home Office 2002: 3

As shown in Table 1.1, in 2000 the total number of persons starting criminal supervision by the Probation Service is about 122,000.

THE ORIGINS AND DEVELOPMENT OF PROBATION

Creating the Probation Service

There have arguably been five distinct phases in the development of the Probation Service in England and Wales between 1876 and 2000 – a missionary phase, a welfare phase, a decline of treatment/diversion from custody phase, a punishment in the community phase and, most recently, a public protection phase.

The first phase, in the late nineteenth century, may be called the missionary era of the Probation Service. It came 'about through the pioneering activities of philanthropic individuals rather than as a result of any initiative by the courts or other official bodies' (Brownlee 1998: 64). The Church of England Temperance Society appointed a number of 'police court missionaries' to supervise those conditionally released by the London Police Courts (the forerunner of magistrates' courts) in 1876, most of whom had been charged with either drunkenness or drink-related offences, and whose souls were in need of salvation (May 1994; Mair 1997). The missionaries were chosen more for their Christian character than their professional skills; an ethos of amateurism prevailed. In 1887 the Probation of First Offenders Act gave official recognition to the missionaries' work and marked the formal birth of 'probation', although its administration remained outside the state. The Probation of Offenders Act, enacted in 1907 by a Liberal government committed more broadly to the creation of a welfare state, marked the tentative beginnings of state control. The Act encouraged, without demanding, magistrates' courts to appoint probation officers, and identified the official, legal purpose of probation as being to 'advise, assist and befriend', although it was construed as an *order* of the court, not as a sentence, and therefore not a punishment (Jarvis 1972; Haxby 1978; McWilliams 1983; May 1994).

Gradually, from the 1930s onwards, the ethos of probation officers shifted from the spiritual towards something more recognisable as social work. Under the influence of 'medical', 'welfare' or 'treatment' models (see Crow 2001) they became trained professional experts in diagnosing, assessing and intervening in the social and personal factors assumed to lie behind offending behaviour, and in advising magistrates (and later judges) with social inquiry reports before sentence was passed. Via a trusting officer–offender relationship these officers aimed to cure individuals' offending behaviour rather than save their souls. Garland (1997) usefully summarises what probation became in its second, welfare phase:

> [Probation] was the exemplar, the paradigm, of the welfarist approach to dealing with crime and offenders. It emphasised rehabilitation, resettlement, individualised case-work, re-integration – a social welfare approach to social problems. The problem of crime was understood as a problem of individuals and families in need of help and support, of communities that were disorganised and disadvantaged. (p. 2)

The welfarist conception of probation, reaffirmed and modernised by the Labour government in the Criminal Justice Act 1948, was to last into the 1970s, probation training having formally merged with child care and mental health training in the late 1960s, to signify its place in a unified conception of social work. The 1960s and early 1970s may perhaps be regarded as the heyday of the Probation Service, a time of penological optimism and great confidence about rehabilitation. During this period its responsibilities grew (e.g. for aftercare and resettlement), although some were also reduced (e.g. for juvenile offenders and their families, to local authorities). Caseloads expanded, more staff were recruited, and prestigeous enquiries boosted its reputation with sentencers and policy-makers (McWilliams 1987), although debate on the Service's work was rarely politicised. Among academics and policy-oriented researchers, however, a telling critique of rehabilitative ideals was emerging, aroused by seemingly negative findings on the effectiveness of the usual forms of probation supervision. This began initially in the USA (Martinson 1974) and was followed up in Britain (Brody 1976; Folkard, Smith and Smith 1976).

These mid-1970s developments initiated the third phase of probation's development, the decline of the so-called 'treatment ideal', although in practice this happened more among academics and policy-makers than among practitioners themselves, who continued obstinately believing that individual offenders' behaviour could be changed for the better. Nonetheless, a combination of both empirical and ethical criticisms (i.e. the ease with which rehabilitation, on the grounds of imputed need, could be used to justify intrusive interventions both on probation and in prison) did diminish confidence in rehabilitation and made key observers of the probation scene realise that the community supervision of offenders needed a new rationale if it were to survive as a credible approach in criminal justice. Some thinkers sought a renewal of retributivism (glossed at the time as 'the justice model'; see Bottomley 1980), others began to explore what was later called 'restorative justice' (Christie 1981). In practice, what initially came into being in Britain was simply a more pragmatic approach to dealing with offenders, triggered by ideas about the 'non-treatment' paradigm (Bottoms and McWilliams 1979) which substituted constructive, contractually agreed help and diversion from custody for the treatment ideal. Diversion from Custody – the counterpart and corollary of the decline of treatment's credibility and therefore part of the same phase – grew in importance during the 1980s, as political concern with prison overcrowding grew (Home Office 1984, 1988). The Service was happy to take on some responsibilities in this respect, albeit almost always on its own terms. For a variety of reasons it resisted making community supervision into an onerous and demanding experience, and refused to countenance thinking of its work as punishment (see Raynor 1997).

Controlling the Probation Service

The Conservative government elected in 1979, however, had other ideas. Despite the shift of ethos in probation, it still did not match their law and order ideals, and it politicised debate on probation in a way that had never happened before. The Conservatives erred much more towards retributive thinking, and were alarmed by the great variability of management style and practice in the 54 local probation areas. Each area had considerable local autonomy, being responsible to an unelected probation committee (mostly comprising magistrates) and there was no clear mechanism for exerting central control over the national service as a whole. In 1984 the Home Office sought

How long were Conservatives in power? How 79-97

to persuade the local services to adopt a Statement of National Objectives and Priorities (SNOP), but without success; some services were willing, others were not, and there was a clear element of resistance to this first attempt at centralisation. Growing sentencer demand for Probation's services, coupled with continuing concern about prison overcrowding, meant that the government was continually increasing expenditure on the Service but without having control over it, or being able to guarantee its cost-effectiveness (Statham and Whitehead 1992; Mair 1996). From the perspective of new public management, whose disciplines government was steadily imposing across the public sector, this was an unacceptable state of affairs. The failure of SNOP intensified government desire for greater control over the service, legitimated by a reasonable insistence on financial accountability and geographical consistency, and, eventually, for a more fundamental review of the Service's whole purpose:

> The objective of diverting offenders from custody remained high, but behind [the *Statement of National Objectives and Priorities* (Home Office 1984)] one can see the beginnings of government pressure for the probation service to be more accountable, more aware of how its resources were used, and more managerial – issues which were to take on increasing importance in the 1990s. (Mair 1997: 1202)

The Service's response was mixed, but it undoubtedly began to change (Mair 1996). Youth Justice practice (led by local authorities and voluntary organisations) showed willing, of its own accord, to develop intensive forms of community supervision if this enabled a national reduction in custody for under-18s (Nellis 1988). Probation was reluctant to go down this road, but intense debates occurred as to how intense and intrusive probation supervision needed to be, and also about the very legitimacy of government demands. Magistrates felt they were losing control of 'their' service. The probation union, NAPO, pressed for the development of a service more responsive to class inequality, and to gender and ethnic discrimination in criminal justice. Officers (and academics) more mindful of the Service's individualised, caring traditions sought to revitalise and rebuild a more credible concept of rehabilitation, based on promising insights from cognitive-behavioural psychology. This, as Vanstone (2000) has shown, was the origin of the 'What Works' movement among practitioners, which was later co-opted by government as the Effective Practice initiative. Most tellingly of all in this period, managerialism took root in the Service itself (rather than being imposed from without), producing a cadre of influential staff who were largely responsive to the government's agenda (McWilliams 1987; see also Sparrow, Brooks and Webb 2002).

How far the Service would have gone of its own accord to change its practice and ethos is a moot point. Between 1988 and 1992 government changed the terms of the argument, launching the 'Punishment in the Community' initiative in a succession of Green and White Papers (Home Office 1988; 1990). The Service was in effect told that it must provide intensive community sentences, with new ingredients such as electronic monitoring – the incentive being that its prestige would be enhanced by playing a 'centre-stage' role in the criminal justice system. The term 'punishment' – much disliked in the Service – was emphasised explicitly to enhance the credibility of community-based sentences with sentencers and public alike, and doubt was expressed about the aptness of a social work qualification for probation officers. The resulting Criminal Justice Act 1991 introduced a new framework for community sentencing based on the retributivist principles of 'just deserts' – but in the short period in which it operated it did effectively reduce the use of custody. Nonetheless, probation officers were never comfortable with the Act – the official three-fold purpose of probation (now a sentence in its own right) became the protection of the public, the reduction of offending and – symbolically last – the rehabilitation of the offender. With varying degrees of regret and enthusiasm, criminological commentators noted that the era of 'advise, assist and befriend' was well and truly over (Worrall 1997; Brownlee 1998).

But worse was to come. An internal, rightward shift in the Conservative government in 1993 meant that it repudiated its own late 1980s' ideals on the need to reduce the use of imprisonment. Under a new Home Secretary, the emphasis shifted to 'prison works' (more to incapacitate than rehabilitate) and prison numbers began their seemingly inexorable rise to the present levels. The emphasis for probation remained punitive, but the prospect of a centre-stage role had been taken away. The years 1993–1997 saw the Service at its most marginalised and fearful; the very need for it was being called into question by government neglect. The Probation Inspectorate assumed an important leadership role in this period, working with ACOP and CPC to promote the potential of empirically based effective practice. Government was lukewarm. A 1995 Green Paper (Home Office 1995) mooted the idea of doing away with a distinct probation order, and having a single generic community sentence instead, in which rehabilitation was not an aim at all. The Home Office simultaneously pressed ahead with plans to separate probation training from social work, and indeed to remove to it from universities. Although nothing definite came of these initiatives before the Conservative government lost power in May 1997, a new phase in probation's history was being quietly signalled.

Modernising the Probation Service

There were some who hoped that the advent of a New Labour government in 1997 would restore the fortunes of a much-maligned Probation Service. New Labour, however, who had adopted much of the Conservatives' law and order

rhetoric in order to compete with them, had no qualms about moving probation away from social work, and under the rubric of 'modernisation' and
'joined-up government' pressed ahead with changes that even their predecessors had not envisaged. Using managerial disciplines, they sought to create
what in their terms was a more coherent, unified 'field of corrections', in
particular bringing the work of the prison and probation services, and the
newly created Youth Justice Board, into closer alignment (Nellis 1999; Nellis
and Stephenson 2000):

> In respect of Probation, New Labour's first two moves were to extend the trials of
> electronic monitoring established under Howard, and to authorise new arrange-
> ments for probation training separate from social work, but fortunately still linked
> to higher education. Its third move, quite unexpectedly, was to set up a Prisons/
> Probation Review in June 1997, the aim of which was, ostensibly, to explore
> 'options for closer integration' between the two services. This was a new twist
> in the decade-long attempt of the previous government to find better ways of
> reducing offending and fostering greater public confidence in community penalties.
> (Nellis and Stephenson 2000: 94)

There was huge resistance from magistrates, judges and probation interest
groups to the idea – which the Prisons-Probation review tactfully fell short of
actually proposing – of fully merging the prison and probation services into a
single correctional agency. Nonetheless a degree of *de facto* integration took
place: 'protecting the public' and 'reducing re-offending' became the primary
goals of both services, and joint planning of both services' futures became the
norm within the Home Office. Probation scepticism about these developments
was significantly assuaged by New Labour's clear commitment to the 'What
Works' agenda, which the Inspectorate had skilfully sustained throughout the
Service's 'dark times' prior to 1997 (Chapman and Hough 1998; Underdown
1998). Rehabilitation, albeit firmly in the context of public protection, has
regained some of its former eminence (Raynor 1997). Desirable as this is, it
in no way represents a return to probation's social work roots, as Garland
(1997) recognises:

> Where rehabilitative interventions are undertaken their character is rather differ-
> ent than before. They are now much more focused upon control issues, much more
> concerned to 'address offending behaviour'. There has been a shift from client-
> centredness to offence-centredness. . . . Offence behaviour rather than personality
> or social relations is the target of transformative work. Changing the pattern of
> offending is the primary concern, and this may or may not involve engaging with
> the 'whole person' or any underlying conflicts and difficulties he or she may have.
> (p. 6)

New Labour's rather graceless acceptance that many key interest groups
wished to see probation remain a distinct agency did not deter it from wanting

to exert more control over it, to homogenise its practice and to signal a fundamental change of ethos. In the Criminal Justice and Court Services Bill it proposed centralising the service under a national director, a proposal which it sold to the Service as a way of giving it a stronger voice in government, greater proximity to power. Despite the obvious loss of local autonomy entailed by centralisation – offset, it seemed at the time, by the powers vested in new Probation Boards – probation interest groups accepted this logic. In respect of symbolising a change of ethos, there was no meeting of minds. In the course of parliamentary debate on the Bill the government tried to change the Service's name to the Community Punishment and Rehabilitation Service. This met with vastly greater opposition, and again it was the backroom skills of the Inspectorate, aided by the CPC, which preserved precious continuity with the past (even though the names of key orders were changed).

Such were the circumstances of the NPS's birth. It represented the culmination of government concern with their lack of influence over service practice which goes back to the SNOP in 1984. Centralising trends and shifts of ethos which began under Conservative governments – most notably National Standards – were accelerated dramatically by New Labour as part of a strategy to integrate and streamline the operation of the criminal justice system as a whole. Although in New Labour's terms the NPS may be a political compromise – a merged correctional agency being their probably preferred structure – it is difficult to imagine the present structure coming into being without the underlying disciplines and discourse of the new public management. Like so much in New Labour's modernised public sector, the NPS is a quintessentially managerial achievement, shaped far more by contemporary political styles, and the requirements of accountability and cost-effectiveness than criminological theory or research. The Probation Service entered the twenty-first century in a form that would have been unrecognisable, unimaginable to those who developed it in the late nineteenth and early twentieth centuries, with immensely greater resources and reach, but without, it has to be said, the uplifting moral purpose of its founders. Let us now look in more detail at the framework in which probation practice is developing.

Configuration of the 'new' National Probation Service

What is the new NPS? According to *A New Choreography* (NPS for England and Wales 2001), written by the new Director, Eithne Wallis, a former chief probation officer, it is a key statutory criminal justice service that works closely with police and prison staff, as well as the courts, local authorities, health, housing and education, and other various statutory and non-statutory organisations. More specifically,

The NPS is a law enforcement agency delivering community punishments, super-vising and working with offenders within the terms set by the Court or Parole Board in ways that help offenders to reduce their re-offending and better protects the public. Failure to comply with the supervision requirements elicits breach action through the Courts and can lead to a prison sentence. Where the offender is on early release from custody on statutory licence, the outcome of probation breach action may be recall to prison. (p. iii)

Dick Whitfield, another former chief, sees three 'new' features of probation in the present arrangements under the NPS: new organisation and structure, new national priorities and new names for community penalties. To these may be added a new vision of the role of the NPS and new training arrangements.

New organisation and structure

Bhui (2001: 637) recognises that the NPS replaced the old Probation Unit within the Home Office, and 'is now more clearly associated with other criminal justice agencies' in many respects. Its national director and chief officers are appointed by the Home Secretary, as civil servants rather than employees of Probation Boards (who still appoint lower-grade staff) – by such means will firm control be exerted. The reduction of local areas from 54 to 42, in 10 regions, makes their boundaries coterminous with the police and Crown Prosecution Service areas, and should ease planning and coordination (see Whitfield 2001; Nellis 2002). The Family Court Welfare work of the Probation Service has been completely removed from the new structure, having become anomalous in an organisation so fundamentally concerned with punishment. It has become part of a new organisation, the 'Children and Family Court Advisory and Support Service' (CAFCAS) serving the Family Courts, accountable to the Lord Chancellor's Department (see Bhui 2001).

The new governance of probation has been discussed by the Chief Execut-ive of the Probation Boards' Association (Wargent 2002). Each of the 42 Boards is responsible for performance and financial management, and each Board usually consists of representatives of the local community appointed by the Home Secretary, except for a judge appointed by the Lord Chancellor (Whitfield 2001: ii). The degree of the Board's autonomy was ambivalent in the legisla-tion, but there would be little point to recruiting local community leaders if they were not to have some leeway in implementing policy. Wargent believes, reasonably enough, that Probation Boards have potential for developing good probation practice at both local and national level, and articulates six areas of responsibility for them, these being holding the local service to account for performance; being responsible stewards of the resources of the local service; being advocates for probation(ers); being good employers; being responsible for best practice in governance; and taking responsibility for community justice. Whitfield (2001) warned at the outset that a careful eye would need to be kept on the balance between local implementation and national direction, if the Boards are to maintain the independence that the best of their predecessor Committees had had.

New national priorities

The aims of the NPS are: protecting the public, reducing re-offending, the proper punishment of offenders in the community, ensuring offenders' awareness of the effects of their crime on its victims and the public, and the rehabilitation of offenders (NPS for England and Wales 2001). Judging the order of these aims, it is very clear that the three priorities should be read as public protection, enforcement, and rehabilitation. In addition to this unambiguous remit to make community punishment work, there are two collective aims set for the NPS to achieve, namely 'by 2004 establish itself as a world leader in designing and implementing offender assessment and supervision programmes that effectively reduce re-offending and improve public safety; and by 2006 be recognised as a top performing public service as benchmarked by the European Excellence Model' (NPS for England and Wales 2001: 1). As indicated in Table 1.2, nine specific areas are listed to achieve the above aims between 2001 and 2004.

New names

In order to give probation a new face, but amid some controversy, several key community sentences were renamed by the Home Office. The probation order became a community rehabilitation order; the community service order became a community punishment order, and the combination order became a community punishment and rehabilitation order. Whitfield (2001) – one of many – pointed out that:

Table 1.2   A list of the NPS priorities between 2001 and 2004

- Accurate and effective assessment and management of risk and dangerousness
- More involvement of victims of serious sexual and other violent crime
- Offender programmes that have a track record in reducing re-offending
- Intervening early to take young people away from crime
- Enforcement (the objective is for the Service to fulfil national standards in 90 per cent of cases requiring breach action by staff)
- Providing courts with good information and pre-trial services
- Valuing and achieving diversity in the NPS and the services it provides
- Building an excellent organisation
- Building an effective performance management framework

Source: NPS for England and Wales 2001: 1–3

whether these unwieldy new names will stick (it remains commonplace for courts to use the old terms, which some court legal advisers contend are still valid in that they are descriptive, and on the grounds that no one understands the new) remains to be seen. (p. v)

New vision and values

Another distinctive feature of the NPS is its vision and ethical framework, couched very differently from previous statements of probation's purposes. *A New Choreography* (NPS for England and Wales 2001) outlines a vision which emphasises the concepts of 'justice' and 'protection of the public', and recognises 'preventing victimisation' as an essential probation task:

> At the heart of our vision in a society with fewer new victims and where those who have already been harmed by crime have better protection against re-victimisation, because of the work of the NPS. Victims in direct contact with probation staff will feel that they have been listened to, that the harm done to them has been acknowledged and that they have been given real information and access to the process of justice. (p. 7)

In this context, the NPS then proposes a further 12 values: valuing NP staff and partnership colleagues – seeing them as the organisation's greatest asset; victim awareness and empathy; paramountcy of public protection; law enforcement; rehabilitation of offenders; empiricism based on the evidence of 'What Works'; continuous improvement; openness and transparency; responding and learning to work positively with difference; problem-solving as a way of resolving conflict; partnership; and better quality services (see NPS for England and Wales 2001: 8).

New training arrangements

By the time the NPS became operational (April 2001), new qualifying training arrangements had already been in place for three years, separate from social work training. Before that probation training had been part of generic social work training, under the auspices of the then Central Council for Education and Training in Social Work, created in 1971 (Nellis 2001a, b). We have already noted that it was in the context of 'punishment in the community' that doubts about the aptness of a social work qualification were first raised by the Home Office. While it was recognised and regretted by many practitioners and academics in the 1990s that probation practice was moving away from a social work base, a new form of training was not welcomed by them (Ward 1996; Buchanan and Millar 1997; Aldridge 1999). A hard political battle was fought to retain probation training in social work, and in higher education, and under New Labour, at least the latter was preserved. The new qualification, a Diploma in Probation Studies, comprises an undergraduate degree, usually called Community Justice, and a Level 4 National Vocational Qualification which offers a mixture of academic teaching and employment-based training. The training arrangement is organised regionally, with eight universities contracting to deliver the two-year programmes. The core curriculum is more criminologically focused than the old generic social work curriculum, but as Smith (2001) notes there are also inevitable elements of continuity:

> The reason why the new curriculum resembles the old is not that those who designed and deliver it are indolent, conservative or reluctant to adapt their teaching to make it relevant to practice in the new, modernized, nationally directed probation service. Rather, the similarity derives ultimately from the incoherence of current official thinking on probation. (p. 641)

Many of the readers of this book, we anticipate, will be probation trainees. Let us describe how it is structured, and the topics it covers.

STRUCTURE OF THE BOOK

At the outset, it is important to emphasise that this edited book cannot cover all aspects of probation work and the whole content of a diploma course. Rather it intends to examine some of the key issues surrounding the use of probation in working with offenders in the community by linking theories, research and practice. Chapters 2 and 3 outline the theories of crime and punishment. In Chapter 2, Loraine Gelsthorpe provides an overview of theories of crime, but at the same time offers an annotated resource guide to theories for students and practitioners. A range of theories of crime such as biological theories, psychological theories, sociological and environmental theories, and critical and feminist theories are introduced. Special attention is given to gender differences and pathways into crime for men and women as well as to the need to concentrate on up-to-date theories, and the weight and strength of evidence in relation to those theories. Chapter 3 provides an overview of key theories of punishment such as deterrence, just deserts and rehabilitation, and emphasis is given to the notion of punishment as communication and to the weight and strength of empirical evidence in relation to theories of punishment. Sue Rex examines closely what we know about 'what works' in the context of penal theories, and includes an overview of the relevance and potential impact of contemporary notions of restorative justice.

Attention turns to what probation research has discovered and how we can make sense of existing research findings. In Chapter 4, Wing Hong Chui addresses the question of whether probation works in reducing re-offending behaviour and then emphasis is laid on the principles of effective probation practice which are based upon research evidence. Using a researcher's perspective, Peter Raynor looks at the relationship between probation research, policy and practice, and then discusses how evidence-based practice can be used as a means of reducing re-offending (Chapter 5). In addition, he identifies the gaps and research questions for the future probation research agenda.

Chapters 6–10 examine various aspects of probation practice, and offer insight into what a probation officer should do to achieve the aims of probation and how. In Chapter 6, Mike Nash provides a detailed account of probation pre-sentence work in the past and at present, and discusses how the National Standards influence probation practice during pre-trial investigation. Chapter 7 first defines what 'risk' means and then explains the rise of risk assessment and management in the context of probation. Gwen Robinson also provides an overview of how the assessment of risk has developed and of current approaches and limitations, e.g. in the assessment of 'dynamic' and 'static' risk, combined with the assessment of criminogenic needs. Frances Fleet and Jill Annison recognise the importance of offenders' motivation as a crucial element in effecting change and promoting compliance in Chapter 8, and they further discuss how motivational interviewing, relapse prevention, crisis intervention, and solution-focused approaches can be used in a framework of probation practice. Chapter 9 introduces desistance-focused probation practice in a detailed manner, and Fergus McNeill elaborates how three major perspectives, namely maturational reform theories, social bonds theory and narrative theory, can be used to understand and assess offenders' behaviours, attitudes and motivation to change. He then suggests how desistance-focused probation practice can be applied in day-to-day work with offenders. In Chapter 10, Jonathan Hopkinson and Sue Rex argue that engaging with the offenders is of utmost importance for successful offender intervention. They not only discuss a range of essential skills in working with offenders, but also explore how the concepts of 'legitimacy' and pro-social modelling can be applied in practice in order to promote compliance, cooperation and change. Carol Hedderman further discusses the ways to enforce supervision and encourage compliance in Chapter 11. Developments in policy and practice in the enforcement of community orders are first introduced, and then emphasis is placed on discussing how far the National Standards (Home Office 2000) help promote compliance.

Chapters 12–15 continue to look at other aspects of probation work, including inter-agency cooperation, victim work, anti-discriminatory practice and the use of electronic monitoring. Judith Rumgay, in Chapter 12, points out the importance of partnership and multi-agency work for probation practice and suggests ways of facilitating successful inter-agency work with its statutory and non-statutory partners. In Chapter 13, Basia Spalek investigates how the Probation Service can respond to the victims' needs and how a victim perspective can be incorporated within the work with offenders. Mike Nellis and

Loraine Gelsthorpe, in Chapter 14, address the ongoing debate on probation values, noting the ambivalence that has set in respect of anti-discriminatory practice and questioning whether a 'human rights' perspective will actually have the positive significance that some probation commentators have hoped for. In Chapter 15, Nellis traces the development of electronic monitoring in the criminal justice system and explores the responses of the Probation Service to the introduction of tagging as a part of community sentence.

Finally, the concluding chapter is 'forward-looking' with regard to changes in legislation and the changing functions of the Probation Service, and both editors attempt to identify some key unresolved issues that trainee probation officers, front-line practitioners and academic researchers might engage with if the probation service is to be assured of the future it deserves.

References

Aldridge, M. (1999) 'Probation officer training: Promotional culture and the public sphere', *Public Administration*, 77, 73–90.

Bhui, H. S. (2001) 'New probation: closer to the end of social work?', *British Journal of Social Work*, 31, 637–639.

Bottomley, K. (1980) 'The "Justice Model" in America and Britain: Development and analysis', in A. E. Bottoms and R. H. Preston (eds) *The Coming Penal Crisis: A Criminologoical and Theological Exploration*. Edinburgh: Scottish Academic Press.

Bottoms, A. and McWilliams, W. (1979) 'A non-treatment paradigm for probation practice', *British Journal of Social Work*, 9, 159–202.

Brody, S. (1976) *The Effectiveness of Sentencing: A Review of the Literature* (Home Office Research Study No. 35). London: HMSO.

Brownlee, I. (1998) *Community Punishment: A Critical Introduction*. London: Longman.

Buchanan, J. and Millar, M. (1997) 'Probation: Reclaiming social work identity', *Probation Journal*, 44, 32–36.

Chapman, T. and Hough, M. (1998) *Evidence Based Practice: A Guide to Effective Practice*. London: Home Office.

Christie, N. (1981) *Limits to Pain*. London: Martin Robertson.

Crow, I. (2001) *The Treatment and Rehabilitation of Offenders*. London: Sage.

Folkard, M. S., Smith, D. E. and Smith, D. D. (1976) *IMPACT: Intensive Matched Probation and After-Care Treatment, Volume II – The Results of the Experiment* (Home Office Research Study No. 36). London: HMSO.

Garland, D. (1997) 'Probation and the reconfiguration of crime control', in R. Burnett (ed.) *The Probation Service: Responding to Change* (Probation Studies Unit Report No. 3). Oxford: Centre for Criminological Research, University of Oxford.

Haxby, D. (1978) *Probation: A Changing Service*. London: Constable.

Home Office (1984) *Probation Service in England and Wales: Statement of National Objectives and Priorities*. London: HMSO.

Home Office (1988) *Punishment, Custody and the Community*. London: HMSO.

Home Office (1990) *Crime, Justice and Protecting the Public*. London: HMSO.

Home Office (1995) *Strengthening Punishment in the Community: A Consultation Document* (CM 2780). London: Home Office.

Home Office (2000) *National Standards for the Supervision of Offenders in the Community*. London: Home Office.

Home Office (2002) *Probation Statistics England and Wales 2000*. London: Home Office.

Jarvis, F. V. (1972) *Advise, Assist and Befriend: A History of Probation and Aftercare Service*. London: National Association of Probation Officers.

McKenzie, G. (2000) 'Our future is greater than our past', *Vista: Perspectives on Probation*, 5, 193–199.

McWilliams, W. (1983) 'The mission to the English courts 1876–1936', *Howard Journal of Penology and Crime Prevention*, 22, 129–147.

McWilliams, W. (1987) 'Probation, pragmatism and policy', *Howard Journal of Criminal Justice*, 26, 97–121.

Mair, G. (1996) 'Developments in probation in England and Wales 1984–1993', in G. McIvor (ed.) *Working with Offenders* (Research Highlights in Social Work 26). London: Jessica Kingsley.

Mair, G. (1997) 'Community penalties and the Probation Service', in M. Maguire, R. Morgan and R. Reiner (eds) *The Oxford Handbook of Criminology* (2nd edn). Oxford: Clarendon Press.

Martinson, R. (1974) 'What works? Questions and answers about prison reforms', *Public Interest*, 35, 22–54.

May, T. (1994) 'Probation and community sanctions', in M. Maguire, R. Morgan and R. Reiner (eds) *The Oxford Handbook of Criminology*. Oxford: Clarendon Press.

National Probation Service (NPS) for England and Wales (2001) *A New Choreography: An Integrated Strategy for the National Probation Service for England and Wales – Strategic Framework 2001–2004*. London: Home Office. Available at: www.homeoffice.gov.uk

Nellis, M. (1988) 'Juvenile justice and the voluntary sector', in R. Matthews (ed.) *Privatising Criminal Justice*. London: Sage.

Nellis, M. (1999) 'Towards the "field of corrections": Modernizing the Probation Service in the late 1990s', *Social Policy and Administration*, 33, 302–323.

Nellis, M. (2001a) 'The new probation training in England and Wales: Realising the potential', *Social Work Education*, 20, 416–432.

Nellis, M. (2001b) 'The diploma in probation studies in the Midland region: Celebration and critique after the first two years', *Howard Journal of Criminal Justice*, 40, 377–401.

Nellis, M. (2002) 'Community justice, time and the new National Probation Service', *Howard Journal of Criminal Justice*, 41, 59–86.

Nellis, M. and Stephenson, D. (2000) 'The century of probation: Continuity and change in the Probation Service in England and Wales 1877–1998', in R. Omar and J. Doling (eds) *Issues and Challenges of Social Policy East and West*. Kuala Lumpur, Malaysia: University of Malaya Press.

Raynor, P. (1997) 'Evaluating probation: A moving target', in G. Mair (ed.) *Evaluating the Effectiveness of Community Penalties*. Aldershot: Avebury.

Raynor, P. and Vanstone, M. (2002) *Understanding Community Penalties: Probation, Policy and Social Change*. Buckingham: Open University Press.

Smith, D. (2001) 'Probation and training', *British Journal of Social Work*, 31, 641–642.

Sparrow, P., Brooks, G. and Webb, D. (2002) 'National standards for the probation service: Managing Post-Fordist penality', *Howard Journal of Criminal Justice*, 41, 27–40.

Statham, R. and Whitehead, P. (eds) (1992) *Managing the Probation Service: Issues for the 1990s*. Harlow: Longman.

US Department of Justice (1998) *Rethinking Probation: Community Supervision, Community Safety*. Washington, DC: Office of Justice Programs, Department of Justice. Available at: http://www.ojp.usdoj.gov/probation/welcome.html

Underdown, A. (1998) *Strategies for Effective Supervision: Report of the HMIP What Works Project*. London: Home Office.

Vanstone, M. (2000) 'Cognitive behavioural work with offenders in the UK: A history of influential endeavour', *Howard Journal of Criminal Justice*, 39, 171–83.

Ward, D. (1996) 'Probation training: Celebration or wake?' in S. Jackson and M. Preston-Shoot (eds) *Educating Social Workers in a Changing Policy Context*. London: Whiting and Birch.

Ward, D., Scott, J. and Lacey, M. (eds) (2002) *Probation – Working for Justice* (2nd edn). Oxford: Oxford University Press.

Wargent, M. (2002) 'The new governance of probation', *Howard Journal of Criminal Justice*, 41, 182–200.

Whitfield, D. (2001) *Introduction to the Probation Service* (2nd edn and revised edn). Winchester: Waterside Press.

Worrall, A. (1997) *Punishment in the Community: The Future of Criminal Justice*. Harlow: Longman.

2

THEORIES OF CRIME

Loraine Gelsthorpe

INTRODUCTION

This chapter provides a short overview of key theoretical approaches with regard to pathways into crime. At times, theorists have attempted to construct monolithic, single causal explanations. Most recently, for example, we have learned from scientists at King's College, London, that the link between childhood abuse and anti-social behaviour might be chemical. The scientists have been looking at a 'good behaviour' gene – the one that produces the enzyme that makes all the difference. The enzyme breaks down brain chemicals linked to aggressive behaviour. Twelve per cent of men who had a low active version of the gene committed 44 per cent of the violent crimes (Williams 2002). But the critical reader will immediately understand that there is no general theory here, merely a probability game.

This does not inhibit an apparent faith in a discoverable key to all crime, however. Indeed, Walker (1996) has likened the situation to mediaeval alchemy, by referring to it as the search for the 'criminologists' stone'. But the search for a single theory of criminal behaviour has long been castigated as a vain one. Rather, there is now recognition of huge complexities. Such complexities begin with the very notion of 'crime', for crime is not a self-evident and unitary concept. Its constituent parts are diverse, historically relative and continually contested. Thus 'explanations' of crime depend on the theoretical position taken by those defining crime.

The search for theoretical explanations for crime is not easy. We must acknowledge our biases, learn from the insights and mistakes of predecessors, and give all due consideration to the implications of what might be proposed

as adequate explanations for crime. Some writers have described the challenge
as an adventure (Lilley, Cullen and Ball 1995), but all academic adventures have
their dead ends and cul-de-sacs. We must also think about the social context
in which theories are produced. The erection of particular monoliths at
particular points in history always requires explanation. To search for some
Olympian platform detached from values is illusory: one has to look at the
ideological import of theories and the benefits that accrue to society in their
adoption. In order to help the student of criminal justice to do this, I offer
three questions to ponder in relation to each theoretical perspective outlined:

- What are the origins of new theoretical ideas and what ideas are they
  attempting to replace?
- What is the social and political context in which new theoretical ideas are
  being developed?
- What political purchase might the theoretical perspective have and what is
  the symbolic value of the theoretical ideas being propounded?

BIOLOGICAL THEORIES

Definition

The essential precept underpinning biological explanations for crime is that
certain people are 'born as criminally minded' through the inheritance of a
physiological or genetic predisposition towards crime.

Early theorists and theories

Early criminologists such as Lombroso, Ferri and Garafalo initially defined
the criminal in terms of physical stigmata. Cesare Lombroso's (1836–1909)
early work *L'Uomo Delinquente* (The Delinquent Man), first published in
1876, has become a classic. It contains the idea of the offender as defective
based on the assumption that as humans develop they learn how to adapt to
their environment. Those who do not are atavistic throwbacks to earlier stages
of evolution (and therefore pre-social and more criminally inclined).

This early biological work prompted research on somatotyping, that is, the
diagnosing of the individual's constitution and behaviour by the shape of
their body (Sheldon 1949). His main conclusion was that delinquents were
likely to be mesomorphs – hard, muscular and athletic body types leading
to strong and assertive, if not aggressive personal behaviour. Glueck and
Glueck (1950) attempted to test this conclusion further, with initial support
for Sheldon's finding, but alongside complicating factors which suggested that
really it was a combination of biological, environmental and psychological
factors that characterised delinquents.

Contemporary ideas

The likelihood of some genetic role in the explanation of crime has been made much stronger by recent advances in genetics. In particular twin and adoption studies have made huge contributions to attempts to isolate a genetic factor. Such studies have attempted to test two key propositions: first, that identical (monozygotic or MZ) twins have more similar behaviour patterns than fraternal (dizygotic or DZ) twins, and second, that children's behaviour is more similar to that of their biological parents than to that of their adoptive parents. On the basis of cases occurring between 1929 and 1961, Mednick and Volavka (1980) show a genetic link. A more recent study still upholds the genetic link with crime, but emphasises the importance of social factors too. Rowe (1990) illustrated that twin and sibling *interaction* also play a large part in shaping behavioural patterns.

With regard to findings on genetics and adoption and criminal behaviour, an influential study came from Denmark where Hutchings and Mednick (1977) studied male adoptions where adopting parents were not related to the child. They concluded that boys with criminal biological fathers were more likely to become criminal than those with law-abiding fathers or indeed, than those with criminal adoptive fathers. From such research findings, Mednick, Gabrielli and Hutchings (1987) claimed that criminality is related to genetics, but one critical factor here is that huge efforts are made by adoption agencies to place children in homes similar to those from which they came. The fact that the environment would be relatively unchanged might serve to exaggerate the apparent genetic influences.

A number of writers (see, for example, Wilson and Herrnstein 1985) make claims for a link between crime, race and genetics. This presumes a genetic basis for some of the individual differences in criminality, but this is clearly problematic due to the evident discrimination in the processing of offenders (Bowling and Phillips 2002). Moreover, in a survey of nine countries, Tonry (1997) collated information on the criminal behaviour of immigrant ethnic minority groups as compared with indigenous resident communities, and concluded that while some ethnic minorities are over-represented in the crime statistics in every country, the high-crime groups were not consistently from one ethnic minority group. Thus the claims are not founded in the evidence, though are embraced by an evidently racist 'new right' political group.

Further research within the broad biological perspectives includes research on biochemical factors (levels of testosterone, levels of adrenalin, biochemical imbalances relating to blood-sugar levels, levels of vitamins and minerals within the body, for instance). Most of the researchers working in these fields acknowledge that biochemical effects need to be studied in the context of the effects of the environment and the psychological characteristics of the individual.

Nevertheless, there is some agreement among researchers here that behaviour (including criminal behaviour) is probably linked to biochemical factors, though knowledge of the ways in which this occurs is far from clear.

Other researchers have looked at the role of neurotransmitters (substances such as serotonin and dopamine) which transmit signals between neurons within the brain. In animal studies these kinds of substances have been linked to aggressive behaviour, for instance, with increasing recognition that mechanisms within the brain which affect moods or control behaviour may be impaired – though there is equal recognition that these substances may be produced in inappropriate quantities *by* aggressive behaviour and not the other way round. Electrochemical processes in the brain have also come under scrutiny. Mednick and Volavka (1980), for example, conclude more criminals compared with non-criminals have abnormal brain patterns. Testing for electroencephalograph (EEG) ratings, however, invariably comes *after* a crime has been committed and once an individual is being processed through the criminal justice system; thus it may be the effect of the crime and criminal justice processing that leads to abnormal EEG ratings, rather than the cause of crime.

Comment

Early biological theories have long since been criticised as naïve. Even before Lombroso's death, social anthropologists were questioning the idea of uniform and linear evolution and thus implicitly attacking the notion that atavisms caused criminality. Most of the subsequent criticisms of biological perspectives on pathways into crime have revolved around the need to take into account environmental factors. In other words, it is suggested that while crime may run in families, it may be learned behaviour through poor schooling, unemployment, common residence or cultural transmission of criminal values; it is hard to distinguish between genetic and environmental factors. It is further suggested that many of the theorists have pursued false trails simply because of faulty sampling procedures. Offenders in custody, for example, are by no means representative of the offending population as a whole and yet this population has frequently been used as a basis for theoretical development. Moreover, control groups of 'non-offenders' are likely to include some offenders whose actions have remained undetected.

We are more likely to encounter biological theories as but one element within multiple factor explanations in contemporary perspectives on criminality these days. Recognition of the difficulty of separating out genetic or other biological effects has given way to a new strand of biological theories which come under the heading of socio-biology. But the debates about the relative influence of 'nature' (biology and genetics) as opposed to 'nurture' (environment and social learning) continue. New research in this area carries the possibility of unpalatable research findings that might lead to eugenics, and genetic and DNA fingerprinting carry the potential for misuse. The DNA Databank is to be expanded to hold DNA material from almost anyone connected with the investigation of an offence (Criminal Justice and Police Act 2001 section 82). Thus we need to be alert to the ethical, negative and intrusive consequences of biological research as well as its positive contributions in helping us to understand pathways into crime.

PSYCHOLOGICAL THEORIES

Definition

Insofar as we can discern distinctive psychological theories from biological and sociological theories, they largely revolve around personality, reasoning, thought, intelligence, learning, perception, imagination, memory and creativity. Psychology is the science of the mind. There are three main strands of psychological theories: (i) psychoanalytical and psychodynamic ideas, (ii) behavioural theories, and (iii) cognitive theories which are dealt with here. (For a detailed discussion of mental disorder and criminality, see Blackburn 1993 and Williams 2001.)

Early theorists and theories

(i) Psychoanalytical and psychodynamic ideas have their origins in the work of Sigmund Freud (1856–1939) – especially his notion that the human personality is shaped by three sets of interacting forces: the id (concerning primitive biological drives), the superego or conscience (that operates in the unconscious but is moulded by the internalisation of values through interaction with parents and significant others), and the ego (the conscious personality which interacts with and responds to external influences). According to Freud (1935), arson, shoplifting and some sexual offences reflect a state of mental disturbance relating to psychic development, particularly psychosexual development. His second set of ideas concerning crime reflect the notion of the offender as having a 'weak conscience'. This, in turn, is related to a child's upbringing and the degree to which a person develops the capacity to experience guilt.

Work on maternal deprivation (Bowlby 1951), and on child-rearing techniques (forms of discipline and control), as well as on broken homes, all feature within the broad set of psychoanalytical and psychodynamic ideas.

(ii) Behavioural theories have their origins in the work of Ivan Pavlov (with his work on automatic animal behaviours (conditioning) such as salivation in the presence of food) and B. F. Skinner's work on conditioning extending

Loraine Gelsthorpe

Pavlov's research into *active* learning – where the animal had to do something in order to obtain a reward or avoid punishment). Eysenck built a general theory of criminal behaviour that reflects the notion of conditioning. He argued that individuals are biologically predestined with learning abilities that are conditioned by stimuli in the environment. He premised his theory on the idea that crime can reflect rational choice where individuals maximise pleasure and minimise pain. Thus the notion of what is and what is not acceptable behaviour is learnt.

Eysenck's later contribution was to develop some ideas from the psychoanalyst Carl Jung, and describe three dimensions of personality: extroversion – comprising impulsiveness and sociability; neuroticism, and psychoticism. Jung had suggested that there was a continuance from introversion to extroversion and that each individual could be placed on the continuum. In Eysenck's elaboration of these ideas, a person scoring high on the Extroversion scale would be outgoing, sociable, and impulsive; a high-scoring person on the Neuroticism scale would be anxious, moody and highly sensitive. Those with low scores on these continuums would present the very opposite of these traits: insensitivity to others, sensation seeking and a lack of regard for others are thus associated with Psychoticism (Eysenck 1964). These concepts are sometimes used as an explanation for recidivism, the extrovert and the highly unstable or neurotic personalities being the least able to learn society's norms, and thus most likely to become recidivists.

Criticisms of Eysenck have revolved around the genetic basis of his ideas and the lack of empirical foundation for his claims about recidivism. Notwithstanding these criticisms, however, researchers such as Farrington (1997), who is interested in the development of criminal careers and what distinguishes the person who develops such a career from others, has indicated that this sort of approach seems to identify a link between offending and impulsiveness. One of the drawbacks of learning behaviour theories is the extent to which it ignores cognition, or thinking.

(iii) Some of the key ideas about cognitive theories which revolve around perceptual processes and information processing in particular have their origins in the work of the Gestalt psychologists (Jean Piaget, for instance). The ideas revolve the notion that the developing child builds cognitive structures – mental maps or schema in order to understand and respond to experiences. This is in contrast to the preceding sets of theories that depend on the model of a biologically or genetically predestined actor. It is thus quite radical because it moves thinking away from the idea that criminals have biological or psychological defects. Kohlberg (1976) links moral thinking with cognitive processes. The idea that criminal behaviour is the outcome of a reasoned decision-making process is also central to the rational choice theory (RCT) of crime (Cornish and Clarke 1987) and the idea that the offender will consider the potential benefits (material gain) against the potential costs (effort, getting caught, punishment).

Contemporary ideas

The psychological ideas in vogue at present are mainly to do with risk assessment (with the use of various psychological tests), offender profiling and cognitive-behavioural treatment. Popular media stereotypes of the criminal psychologist being able to 'get inside the head' of the offender are more fiction than reality.

Various psychological tests have been developed (alongside clinical prediction based on case conferences on individuals and social indices) to determine the risks of further crime. Assessments of risk increasingly refer to governing crime through official discourses and techniques of risk management, especially 'actuarial justice' (Feeley and Simon 1994) a term that reflects the centrality of the statistical probability of re-offending alongside individual factors (in other words, prediction). We can see this type of thinking reflected in the Offender Group Reconviction (OGRS) scale and in the new Level of Supervision Inventory-Revised (LSI-R), for instance, the latter capturing more 'dynamic' factors (changeable factors such as drink problems and employment) more than the former (which focus on 'static' factors such as reconvictions). The pattern of scores identifies specific areas of offender need, while the total score can be translated into a risk score for future offending. The empirical evidence supporting the LSI-R as a measure of risk and needs is strong (see also Chapter 7 of this book).

The essence of offender profiling involves teasing out the characteristics of the offender from a detailed knowledge of the offence and other background information (from the scene of crime to the last movements and personality of the victim). It employs psychological principles (relating to cognitive processes, for example) in these explorations. Profiling is controversial not least because even in the most accurate profiles (for example, Cantor's analysis of the railway murderer, Duffy) only a certain number of pointers are accurate (see Williams 2001).

Cognitive behaviouralism has a central position within the government's 'What Works' campaign under the Crime Reduction Programme to address offending behaviour (see Chapter 4 of this book). The rationale underlying cognitive-behavioural programmes (that developing offenders' reasoning skills may accelerate the 'maturing' process by which they abandon crime) fits in with what the criminal careers research tells us about the impulsivity and poor abstract reasoning characteristic of persistent offenders (see Farrington 1997). The programmes include 'Reasoning and Rehabilitation', 'Enhanced Thinking Skills' as well as the renamed 'Think First' programme (McGuire

1995) which was accredited by the Joint Prisons Probation Accreditation Panel in 2000.

Comment

Early psychological explanations for crime are largely rooted in the idea of the predestined actor model of criminal behaviour; here the causes are dysfunctional, abnormal adjustment or deviant personality traits shaped in biology or early socialisation and development. The more recent cognitive learning approach involves a retreat from this model and more emphasis on the social context in which a child is brought up and in which a person lives. Moreover, strong links are drawn in recent research between cognitive learning theories and the rational actor model of behaviour. It should be recognised that there have been criticisms that some of the cognitive psychology theories are not well-founded in research or that the ideas have been based on faulty sampling procedures; the reasoning processes of successful criminals and non-successful offenders may be quite different, for instance, and yet the theories are largely based on unsuccessful criminals (those who have been caught).

Offender profiling has been attacked for its lack of scientific basis (Ainsworth 2000), but it continues to be popular and is certainly employed by the UK police, though generally it might be said that the police prefer to have claimed to have solved crimes via more traditional means. Psychological models of behaviour change have also come under attack, mainly because of the failure to fully address the interconnections between different factors and different levels of analyses. Social, structural and cultural changes, for example, all lie beyond the scope of the cognitive-behavioural programme treatment provider. Additionally, notions of success may have been exaggerated due to methodological problems and biases in measurements of success (Mair 1997), and the programmes, as currently devised, have been criticised for being based on men and possibly inappropriate for women (Gelsthorpe 2001). Leaving such points aside, the evidence from outcome studies suggests that treatment intervention programmes based on cognitive thinking skills provide some modest evidence of the effectiveness of the approach for reducing reconviction for adult offenders.

SOCIOLOGICAL AND ENVIRONMENTAL THEORIES

Definition

Sociological and environmental theories of crime focus on such factors as anomie, social disorganisation, sub-cultures, peer influence and the conditions of particular areas or communities that may cause crime.

Early theorists and theories

Mainstream sociological theories of crime have their origins in the work of nineteenth-century statisticians such as Guerry and Quételet. They analysed crime rates, suicide rates, educational levels, age and sex within certain areas over time and drew out patterns of crime in particular areas. Although regional differences were notable, there were continuities in patterns within areas which led the researchers to conclude that crime was a constant and inevitable feature of social organisation, and not simply to do with individual predisposition or inclination.

Philosophers such as Auguste Comte were also important to the development of a sociological criminology, for Comte argued that society shapes the individual psychologically. Emile Durkheim (1933, 1970) had considerable impact by describing how societies are held together by solidarity and likenesses, and shared aims. Members of society also become interdependent. He argued that the predictability of crime rates mean that they are social facts and thus 'normal'. Increases in crime occur when societies evolve and develop into more complex forms of organisation (producing a state of anomie – normlessness). He also argued that crime and punishment serve a function for society through maintaining social values and social solidarity within a community, and thus can be positive as well as negative.

Subsequent sociological theories have focused on strain between an individual's ability to achieve cultural goals legitimately (relative deprivation), and sub-culture. The idea here being that lower-class culture clashes with middle-class values (such as status or material gain) and that crime may serve as one solution to this conflict. Sociological theories have also focused on peer group pressure, different social mechanisms which produce social conformity, and the effects of particular conditions (for example, unemployment).

Of particular note are the sociological developments in the 1960s which heralded a more 'critical criminology'. These developments included a questioning of positivistic assumptions about the definitions and bases of crime. Within labelling and social interaction perspectives then the focus was on those social processes through which certain individuals and social groups came to be categorised and labelled or deviant or delinquent. The ideas (most closely associated with the work of Howard Becker (1963)) revolve around the premise that, once labelled as delinquents, individuals are bound to act in certain ways and behave accordingly. Recognition of primary and secondary deviance in this way led to the conclusion that social control processes can contribute to deviancy and thus paved the way for the critical criminologies of the 1970s which focused on the state and power of sectional interests.

Turning to environmental or ecological theories now, there were a number of social surveys carried out in the nineteenth century relevant to an understanding of patterns of crime, but failure to adequately theorise the findings meant that they did not gain wide-scale credence and they became overshadowed by individual theories of crime (biological and psychological perspectives). Early ecological theories within criminology thus sprang from the research of sociologists in Chicago in the 1920s and 1930s. They embarked on an in-depth study of all aspects of their local urban environment, likening the organisation of the community to the ecology of plant life whereby individuals would grow together but then social life would be renewed as other individuals came. Sociologists Park and Burgess (1925) in particular noted that the development and organisation of the city of Chicago was patterned and could be understood in terms of areas being invaded by newcomers, there being conflict and then accommodation and assimilation. Burgess's concentric zone theory has received especial interest – with its notion that the city could be divided into zones (ranging from a central business district to leafy commuter suburbs). It was thought that crime was particularly associated with 'zone 2' – the oldest zone and the zone in transition – with business sections expanding, residents being displaced, and generally the area becoming run-down and neglected as a result, being attractive only to the poor, and new immigrants. Later researchers sought to test these ideas by looking at where delinquents lived. The general conclusion was that neighbourhood could play a part in facilitating and sustaining, if not prompting delinquency.

Contemporary ideas

Contemporary sociological research is rich and varied and includes not only a working and reworking of research upon communities and social factors such as unemployment, but of the role of hegemonic masculinity (power, wealth, physical strength) that lends itself to exploitation, risk-taking and aggression. It also includes work on conflict, social exclusion and the exclusive society which is marked by ever wider social inequalities and policies and practices which serve to expel those who trouble us, offenders included (Young 1999). Increasingly, there is recognition of the wider social processes that are relevant to both pathways into and out of crime. (See Critical and Feminist Theories below.)

Recent ecological or environmental theories include a focus on differential access to housing stock and the effects on people of being directed to live in poor housing in 'rough' areas (Bottoms and Wiles 2002). They also include a focus on social class and on differential access to power in localised communities. Thus how individuals recognise space and how they relate to their communities contributes to our understanding of the differential opportunities for crime.

Comment

Despite their important impact in turning attention away from individual biological or psychological defects, towards the effect of social factors, sociological theories have been criticised for two main reasons: the recurring implicit assumption that individuals' behaviour is shaped by external forces as if they have no agency, and second, the assumption that crime is a form of pathology. A third criticism which pertains to early strain and sub-cultural theories in particular is that there is an assumption that there are homogeneous cultural goals in society which all strive to achieve; there is too little recognition of diversity and the assumption of a consensus of legal and moral codes. More recent sociological thinking has addressed some of these criticisms to the point where it is acknowledged that external forces may place constraints on individuals' choice of action, but not determine those actions. Hence the existence of sociological interest in and moves towards integrated theories of crime.

Early ecologists have been criticised for rather assuming that individuals were the product of their environment and had no 'agency' or choice. Moreover, various attempts to test the theories have come under critical scrutiny because of the failure to acknowledge that the official picture of crime is not necessarily an accurate one. Thus studies based on the places of residence of known offenders may lead to inaccurate conclusions. Moreover, studies of public housing indicate that housing authorities themselves are inclined to place 'problem' families together on estates; this rather dilutes any conclusions about the effect of neighbourhood – though recent studies are more sophisticated and have taken such factors into account (Wikstrom 1991; Bottoms and Wiles 2002). The ecological approach certainly has appeal, but it addresses public street crime rather than crime within the home (child abuse or domestic violence); neither does it generally address crimes against businesses in these areas and, until recently, has focused almost exclusively on male criminality and youthful criminality.

CRITICAL AND FEMINIST THEORIES

Definition

Critical criminology involves a broad school of critical ideas applied to criminology and criminal justice. The thrust of these ideas is to place emphasis on social, structural and political contexts in which crime is defined and responded to. Feminist theories revolve around questions relating to the place of sex (biological differences) and gender (the social behaviour associated with sex differences) in criminological theories and criminal justice.

Early theorists and theories

Critical criminology emerged in the 1970s with a marked break from more traditional criminology through the setting up of the National Deviancy Conference (NDC). From the NDC the New Criminology developed. Inspired by Marxist thinking, the New Criminologists (Taylor, Walton and Young 1973) set out a new agenda for the analysis of crime and responses to crime. This involved making connections between the law, the state, the political economy, legal and political relations and the functions of crime. The aim was also to emphasise the crimes of the powerful (corporate criminals, for example) and to shift the gaze of the state from the crimes of the less powerful (street offenders, for example). For the less powerful, the cause of crime is seen to lie in the interplay of marginalisation (separation from mainstream organisations) and criminalisation (intervention by state authorities). The work of critical criminologists has been hugely important in exposing and illuminating a wide range of issues pertaining to less powerful groups: victimisation, immigrant communities, refugees, gay men and lesbians, and working-class young people.

There is some dispute as to whether Left Realist ideas of the 1980s are 'critical'; some would say that Left Realism lends itself to orthodox criminology with all its emphasis on interventionist strategies which reflect powerful, sectional interests. Nevertheless, the architects of Left Realism (Young and Matthews 1990) attempted to respond to some of the criticisms of the New Criminology which revolved around the theorists' resistance to interventionism and distance from official discourses from crime, by 'taking crime seriously'. The Left Realists thus adopted a pragmatic approach and sought to devise a new agenda for understanding crime and its control by holding on to some of the precepts of the New Criminologists regarding the role of the state and the political economy, *but at the same time* recognising that intervention was crucial to address the public's fears about crime. The pragmatic approach promulgated has included local surveys to record public fears about crime in order to inform policing strategies, and emphasis on better accountability in order to ensure more effective policing of those matters which concern the public.

A further important strand of critical criminology concerns the relationship between power and knowledge. Foucault's (1980) notion is that power is not uni-dimensional, but is dispersed throughout society. Official discourses throughout the criminal justice system and related agencies should therefore come under scrutiny. Indeed, this point takes us back to an introductory point about the need to consider theories in their social and political context.

In similar critical vein, early feminist work challenged some of the fundamental precepts of criminology (notably that theories based on men would apply equally to women). It drew attention both to the neglect of women in the study of crime and to the tendency to distort images and understandings of female offenders in the work that did manage to feature women in any shape or form (particularly in early biological and psychological theories). Carol Smart's (1976) *Women, Crime and Criminology* prompted critical perspectives which fundamentally changed the way in which women offenders had been thought about. Feminist studies highlighted the fact that our knowledge of female offenders and their pathways into crime has been beset with myths, muddles and misconceptions which often reflect ideological concerns rather than objective evidence and that even self-consciously 'objective' scientific approaches reflect men's knowledge (Gelsthorpe 2002).

A key theme in feminist theories of crime is the pervasiveness of male dominance in patriarchal society and its impact on crimes committed both by and against women (Naffine 1997). Sexual inequality and the disempowerment of women are thought to be embodied within the legal and criminal justice systems too. Crime against women is regarded as a result of social oppression and economic dependency upon men.

Contemporary ideas

Scraton and Chadwick (1991) have identified a second wave of critical criminology ideas. The initial aim to locate the world of everyday life (including crime) within broader structural relations remains a defining principle, but alongside this there is new emphasis on the relationship between 'structure' (the world of institutions and structural relations) and 'agency' (the experiential, everyday world of diverse social relations and interaction). Also, while early critical criminology focused largely on power and class relations, this second wave of critical criminology includes a focus on related centres of power (neo-colonialism, advanced capitalism and globalisation, and institutionalised racism, for example).

One of the important precepts underpinning feminist perspectives in criminology is that women offenders and victims themselves should be listened to rather than having distant, male-based theories imposed upon them (see Gelsthorpe 2002). In *Criminal Women*, Pat Carlen *et al.* (1985) suggest how the autobiographical accounts of women's criminal careers demonstrate how '... law-breaking may indeed comprise rational and coherent responses to women's awareness of the social disabilities imposed on them by discriminatory and exploitative class and gender relations' (p. 8). Similarly, Chris Tchaikovsky's (2000) *One Hundred Women* highlights, in the words of the women themselves, how social and economic difficulties and histories of abuse characterise the lives of women offenders.

Holding these points in mind, we know from the research literature that a significant number of female offenders have experienced social and economic problems, child sexual abuse, violence from partners and are single parents.

Numerous researchers (feminist and non-feminist alike) have drawn attention to the particular needs of female offenders in terms of child-care responsibilities, drug and/or alcohol abuse, lack of work skills, and low income (Morris *et al.* 1995; Her Majesty's Inspectorate of Prisons 1997). Mair and May's (1997) study of offenders on probation also confirms the picture of female offenders as having distinctive needs which relate to their general poverty and deprivation. Judith Rumgay's (2000) analysis of women on probation in the mid-1990s similarly indicates that women offenders had been abused, had psychological problems, had been in abusive relationships with partners, or had drug and/or alcohol problems, for instance.

A key question, of course, is the degree to which these factors can be said to be offending-related. In particular, there have been relatively few attempts to get to the heart of the relationship between childhood sexual abuse, other social problems experienced by women and routes into crime. The nature of the connections remains under-theorised. The issue of whether or not gender-neutral or gender-specific theories hold most explanatory promise is also unresolved; many men experience the social problems which characterise the lives of female offenders.

Comment

Critical criminology essentially contests and rejects the theoretical assumptions of traditional criminology. It also includes a human rights discourse and agenda. This development reflects the fact that advanced democracies, whatever their claims for upholding principles of equality and liberty, embody and reproduce structural inequalities of global capitalisms, patriarchy and neo-colonialism. Critical criminology further draws attention to the structure and procedures of the criminal justice system, a task which is difficult for those working within it. It is possible that some of the criticisms of the New Criminology for its 'armchair theorising' and reluctance to engage with traditional criminologists and the criminal justice system have been overcome by the intentions and practices of Left Realism. Critical criminology is important in making us reflect on assumed definitions of crime within criminological discourses and criminal justice system interventions. But how much impact such approaches have on policy-making remains open to question.

Feminist criminology cannot be seen as a single perspective or theory (see Gelsthorpe 2002). There are many strands of feminism (socialist, liberal, radical and so on) each having a distinctive voice and aim. Looking at the various feminist contributions together, it is arguable that feminist perspectives have had far-reaching influence on the wider criminological debate (though some researchers maintain that mainstream criminological theories can explain women's crime even if those theories derive from work on men (Gottfredson and Hirschi 1990)). It would also have to be recognised that feminist perspectives have largely been directed towards women's victimisation and their experiences of bias and stereotyping within the law and the criminal justice system, however; there has been relatively little attempt to theorise women's pathways into crime. Another criticism of early feminist contributions concerns essentialist thinking and the lack of attention given to diversity.

Recent attempts to expand thinking in this direction, and to move away from critique, include first, a focus on crime and gender differences and second, a focus on gender theory itself and then possible relationships to crime. In the former the focus is on a gendered understanding of differences in men's and women's involvement in crime (Steffensmeier and Allan 1996). In the latter the interest lies in identifying the different ways in which sex/gender structures men's and women's life-worlds and identities (Chesney-Lind 1997) with concomitant interest into routes into crime.

CONCLUSION

This chapter has covered a lot of ground and it is impossible to pull out one theoretical strand as being more important than another.[1,2] Rather, it is important to emphasise that some contemporary theoretical approaches are characterised by attempts to integrate different levels of explanation (individual, community, structural, for example) and this seems a useful development in theorising. Research on crime and the life course, focusing on adolescence and early adulthood when crime seems to reach a peak (Smith 2002), incorporates such an approach by considering family and parenting, peers, cognitive processes (social information processing), and social structure (neighbourhood and employment, for example).

Moreover, although we might think that we know a lot about gender differences in crime, this is not the case. Not only has there been a great deal of

---

[1] Readers interested in the social and political origins of theories will find Claire Valier's *Theories of Crime and Punishment* (Longman, 2002) and Wayne Morrison's *Theoretical Criminology. From Modernity to Post-modernity* (Cavendish, 1985) of particular interest. Katherine William's *Textbook on Criminology* (Oxford University Press, 2001, 4th edn) provides an in-depth account of key criminological theories, as does Roger Hopkins Burke's *An Introduction to Criminological Theory* (Willan, 2001). *The Oxford Handbook of Criminology* edited by M. Maguire, R. Morgan and R. Reiner (Oxford University Press, 2002, 3rd edn) provides a full and critical account of criminological ideas and research on the application of those ideas.

[2] Contemporary as well as early biological and psychological explanations of crime are described and assessed in David Putwain and Aidan Sammons' *Psychology and Crime* (Routledge, 2002). Sociological theories are explored in *Understanding Deviance* by David Downes and Paul Rock (Oxford University Press, 1998, 3rd edn). This book includes a good commentary on critical and feminist theories too, but recent discussions about critical criminology are encapsulated within *Critical Criminology: Issues, Debates, Challenges* edited by Kerry Carrington and Russell Hogg (Willan, 2002).

research over time on men and boys without recognition that 'masculinity' itself may bear fruit in terms of our understanding the attractions of crime, our picture of the differential involvement of men and women in crime has also been clouded by common assumptions which reflect social attitudes rather than in-depth knowledge of men's and women's pathways into crime (see Jefferson 1997; Moffitt *et al.* 2001; Heidensohn 2002).

Finally, changes in society over the past 50 years or so (a period described as 'late modernity') have led to changes in forms and patterns of crime. The Western world has changed enormously: business and the flows of capital have become increasingly transnational and have created their own transnational orders (Taylor 1999), and recent technologies mean that neither time nor space is the fixed framework of our routines, for instance (e.g. screen-based global trading markets). New theories of crime must take account of all these changes.

SUMMARY OF KEY ISSUES

- It is important to think about the social and political context in which theories emerge and also why fashions in theories change.
- Biological theories, particularly the argument that crime can be explained by genetic inheritance, finds some support in the evidence, but this theory on its own is not wholly persuasive.
- Dominant among psychological theories is the idea that as crime may reflect patterns of learning, it can be unlearnt through cognitive-behavioural approaches.
- Sociological theories are increasingly multi-factorial; environmental criminology in particular is proving to be of interest to policy-makers, especially where individual, cultural and structural factors are integrated.
- Critical theories have not achieved major impact on administrative criminology, but there are signs of an awakening of critical ideas with recognition of the impact of globalisation and shifting modes of social control and criminal justice in late modernity.
- Feminist contributions largely offer a critique of general theories of crime because they are based on men, though new theoretical work is emerging. This work is focused on gendered dimensions of lifestyle and their relation to crime.

References

Ainsworth, P. (2000) *Psychology and Crime: Myths and Reality.* London: Longman.
Becker, H. S. (1963) *Outsiders: Studies in the Sociology of Deviance.* New York: Free Press.
Blackburn, R. (1993) *The Psychology of Criminal Conduct: Theory, Research and Practice.* Chichester: Wiley.

Bottoms, A. E. and Wiles, P. (2002) 'Environmental criminology and crime', in M. Maguire, R. Morgan and R. Reiner (eds) *The Oxford Handbook of Criminology* (3rd edn). Oxford: Oxford University Press.

Bowlby, J. (1951) *Maternal Care and Mental Health*. Geneva: World Health Organisation.

Bowling, B. and Phillips, C. (2002) *Racism, Crime and Justice*. London: Longman.

Carlen, P., Hicks, J., O'Dwyer, J. Christina, D. and Tchaikovsky, C. (1985) *Criminal Women: Autobiographical* Accounts. Cambridge: Polity.

Chesney-Lind, M. (1997) *The Female Offender: Girls, Women and Crime*. Thousand Oaks, CA: Sage.

Cornish, D. and Clarke, R. (1987) 'Understanding crime displacement: the application of rational choice theory', *Criminology*, 25, 933–947.

Durkheim, E. (1933) *The Division of Labor in Society* (first published in 1983). Glencoe, IL: Free Press.

Durkheim, E. (1970) *Suicide* (first published in 1897). London: Routledge & Kegan Paul.

Eysenck, H. (1964) *Crime and Personality*. London: Routledge & Kegan Paul.

Farrington, D. (1997) 'Human development and criminal careers', in M. Maguire, R. Morgan and R. Reiner (eds) *The Oxford Handbook of Criminology* (2nd edn). Oxford: Oxford University Press.

Feeley, M. and Simon, J. (1994) 'Actuarial justice: The emerging new criminal law', in D. Nelkin (ed.) *The Futures of Criminology*. London: Sage.

Foucault, M. (1980) *Power/Knowledge: Selected Interviews and Other Writings 1972–77*, C. Gordon (ed.). Brighton: Harvester Press.

Freud, S. (1935) *A General Introduction to Psychoanalysis* (first published in 1920), translated by Joan Riviere. New York: Liveright.

Gelsthorpe, L. (2001) 'Accountability: difference and diversity in the delivery of community penalties', in A. E. Bottoms, L. Gelsthorpe and S. A. Rex (eds) *Community Penalties: Change and Challenges*. Cullompton: Willan.

Gelsthorpe, L. (2002) 'Feminism and criminology', in M. Maguire, R. Morgan and R. Reiner (eds) *The Oxford Handbook of Criminology* (3rd edn). Oxford: Oxford University Press.

Glueck, S. and Glueck, E. (1950) *Unravelling Juvenile Delinquency*. New York: Commonwealth Fund.

Gottfredson, M. and Hirschi, T. (1990) *A General Theory of Crime*. Palo Alto, CA: Stanford University Press.

Heidensohn, F. (2002) 'Gender and crime', in M. Maguire, R. Morgan and R. Reiner (eds) *The Oxford Handbook of Criminology* (3rd edn). Oxford: Oxford University Press.

Her Majesty's Inspectorate of Prisons (1997) *Women in Prison: A Thematic Review*. London: Home Office.

Hutchings, B. and Mednick, S. (1977) 'Criminality in adoptees and their adoptive and biological parents: A pilot study', in S. Mednick and K. Christiansen (eds) *Biosocial Bases of Criminal Behavior*. New York: Gardner.

Jefferson, T. (1997) 'Masculinities and crimes', in M. Maguire, R. Morgan and R. Reiner (eds) *The Oxford Handbook of Criminology* (2nd edn). Oxford: Oxford University Press.

Kohlberg, L. (1976) 'Moral stages and moralisation: the cognitive developmental approach', in T. Lickona (ed.) *Moral Development and Behavior: Theory, Research and Social Issues*. New York: Holt, Rinehart & Winston.

Lilley, J. R., Cullen, F. and Ball, R. (1995) *Criminological Theory: Context and Consequences*. Thousand Oaks, CA: Sage.

McGuire, J. (ed.) (1995) *What Works: Reducing Reoffending – Guidelines from Research and Practice*. Chichester: Wiley.

Mair, G. (1997) 'Community penalties and the Probation Service', in M. Maguire, R. Morgan and R. Reiner (eds) *The Oxford Handbook of Criminology* (2nd edn). Oxford: Oxford University Press.

Mair, G. and May, C. (1997) *Offenders on Probation* (Home Office Research Study No. 167). London: Home Office.

Mednick, S., Gabrielli, W. and Hutchings, B. (1987) 'Genetic factors in the etiology of criminal behaviour', in S. Mednick, T. Moffit and S. Stack (eds) *The Causes of Crime: New Biological Approaches*. Cambridge: Cambridge University Press.

Mednick, S. and Volavka, J. (1980) 'Biology and crime', in N. Morris and M. Tonry (eds) *Crime and Justice: A Review of Research*, Vol. 2. Chicago: Chicago University Press.

Moffitt, T., Caspi, A., Rutter, M., and Silva, P. (2001) *Sex Differences in Antisocial Behaviour*. Cambridge: Cambridge University Press.

Morris, A., Wilkinson, C., Tisi, A., Woodrow, J. and Rockley, A. (1995) *Managing the Needs of Female Prisoners*. London: Home Office.

Naffine, N. (1997) *Feminism and Criminology*. Cambridge: Polity.

Park, R. and Burgess, E. (eds) (1925) *The City*. Chicago: University of Chicago Press.

Rowe, D. (1990) 'Inherited dispositions toward learning delinquent and criminal behavior: New evidence', in L. Ellis and H. Hoffman (eds) *Crime in Biological, Social and Moral Contexts*. New York: Praeger.

Rumgay, J. (2000) 'Policies of neglect: Female offenders and the probation service', in H. Kemshall and R. Littlechild (eds) *User Involvement and Participation in Social Care: Research Informing Practice*. London: Jessica Kingsley.

Scraton, P. and Chadwick, K. (1991) 'Challenging the new orthodoxies: The theoretical imperatives and political priorities of critical criminology', in K. Stenson and D. Cowell (eds) *The Politics of Crime Control*. London: Sage.

Sheldon, S. (1949) *Varieties of Delinquent Youth*. New York and London: Harper.

Smart, C. (1976) *Women, Crime and Criminology*. London: Routledge & Kegan Paul.

Smith, D. (2002) 'Crime and the life course', in M. Maguire, R. Morgan and R. Reiner (eds) *The Oxford Handbook of Criminology* (3rd edn). Oxford: Oxford University Press.

Steffensmeier, D. and Allan, A. (1996) 'Gender and crime: Toward a gendered theory of female offending', *Annual Review of Sociology*, 22, 459–487.

Taylor, I. (1999) *Crime in Context: A Critical Criminology of Market Economies*. Cambridge: Polity.

Taylor, I., Walton, P. and Young, J. (1973) *The New Criminology*. London: Routledge & Kegan Paul.

Tchaikovsky, C. (2000) *One Hundred Women* (Cropwood Occasional Paper No. 24). Cambridge: Institute of Criminology, University of Cambridge.

Tonry, M. (1997) 'Ethnicity, crime and immigration', in M. Tonry (ed.) *Crime and Justice: A Review of Research*, Vol. 21. Chicago: University of Chicago Press.

Walker, N. (1996) 'A century of causal theory', in H. Klare and D. Haxby (eds) *Frontiers of Criminology*. London: Pergamon.

Wikstrom, P-O. (1991) *Urban Crime, Criminals and Victims*. New York: Springer-Verlag.

Williams, H. (2002) 'Innocent till proven genetically', *The Guardian*, 7 August 2002.

Williams, K. (2001) *Textbook on Criminology* (4th edn). Oxford: Oxford University Press.

Wilson, J. Q. and Herrnstein, R. (1985) *Crime and Human Nature*. New York: Simon & Schuster.

Young, J. (1999) *The Exclusive Society*. London: Sage.

Young, J. and Matthews, R. (eds) (1990) *Rethinking Criminology: The Realist Debate*. London: Sage.

3

WHAT WORKS IN THEORIES OF PUNISHMENT

Sue Rex

INTRODUCTION

This chapter provides an overview of key theories of punishment, beginning with the two classic rival theories: consequentialism and retribution. After summarising the rationale for each theory, and considering its application (or possible application) to non-custodial options, the chapter discusses the weight and strength of the empirical evidence in support of each theory. In other words, it gives particular attention to what we know about 'what works' in the context of penal theory. Following a review of the two main theories, the chapter looks at attempts through 'hybrid' models to compromise between the two, and considers how the idea of 'communication' in punishment has been used to propose a truly integrated penal theory. Finally, it discusses Restorative Justice, whose popularity arises from widespread dissatisfaction with how traditional criminal justice systems deal with victims and the aftermath of crime.

CONSEQUENTIALISM

Consequentialist theories of punishment operate within a utilitarian framework, originally put forward by Jeremy Bentham in his famous work *The Principles of Penal Law* (extracted in von Hirsch and Ashworth 1998), with the aim of maximising the social 'goods' derived from punishment. According to this account, punishment is an evil because it inflicts 'pain' and it must therefore be justified by the perceived benefits to society in the form of crime prevention. There are three 'utilitarian' justifications for punishment which share the forward-looking aim of reducing crime:

1. **Deterrence:** this is the key justification advanced by Bentham, who assumed that human beings are rational and that the role of sentencing is to present them with a disincentive to offend. There are two types of deterrence: special (or individual deterrence) and general deterrence. In the case of special deterrence, the aim is to set the punishment at a level that deters the particular individual from offending again. General deterrence, contrariwise, is addressed to the citizenry as a whole, whom the fear of punishment is assumed to help resist the temptation to offend. Overall, there is agreement that the existence of the criminal justice system, including the institution of punishment, deters people from offending. However, there is considerable disagreement about the extent to which the level at which penalties are set in specific cases will deter either convicted individuals themselves or others.

2. **Incapacitation:** here, the aim is to prevent the individual from offending, not by appealing to his or her rational self-interest or by changing his or her behaviour, but by putting him or her in a position where he or she is physically restrained from offending (usually in prison). Incapacitation is thus more cynical or despairing than deterrence or rehabilitation, which in their different ways assume that offenders' behaviour can be changed. The idea of incapacitation is usually applied to offenders who are deemed dangerous and pursued through predicting offenders' likelihood of reconviction and incapacitating those assessed as more likely to offend. Again, the incapacitative effect of punishment is strongly contested. We will look at the evidence as to whether penalty levels actually achieve any deterrent or incapacitative impact later in this chapter.

3. **Rehabilitation:** in this case, the aim of preventing crime is pursued by changing offenders' social circumstances (for example, their employment situation or misuse of drugs) or their attitudes and behaviour. The availability of new evidence about the effectiveness of rehabilitative techniques has led to a strong revival of this approach, as we shall see below.

Application to community penalties

Of the three consequentialist theories, the one that has undoubtedly had the greatest relevance to community penalties is rehabilitation. Deterrence is rarely considered applicable to community-based options, although some offenders claim that they are discouraged from offending because they do not want to serve another community order or because the order reminds them of the possibility of being caught. For instance, Rex (1997) found that deterrence was perceived as playing a limited role in probationers' thinking about offending. Usually, however, deterrence is seen as operating through the threat of a custodial sentence should the offender fail to comply with the terms of the order or be convicted of a further offence. On this scenario, probation or community service is the 'last chance' to prove oneself able to live legally in the community.[1] Custody, again, dominates thinking about incapacitation, though it is also the case that the person cannot commit offences when he or she is actually serving the requirements of a community order (for example, undertaking community service or being confined to home during a curfew period). However, the complete restraint of a custodial sentence is absent, in the sense that the individual is clearly at liberty to offend outside these formal requirements.

Rehabilitation, through 'help' and 'treatment', by contrast, has featured as one of the main rationales for community penalties. During the first part of the twentieth century, rehabilitationism was seen to be an important aim in sentencing in what has become known as an era of 'penal welfarism'. David Garland (1985) has investigated the origins of penal welfarism at the end of the nineteenth century, and shown that it emerged along with other social changes of the period, such as the development of compulsory school education and the creation of the national insurance system. The dominant theme was the 'inclusion' of the working classes in the social structures of the time, within a normative framework that required educative or corrective measures to be taken to provide appropriate discipline for the individual. However, a penal welfare sanction was not deemed suitable for everyone. A tariff (punishment) approach was applied to hardened criminals or minor offenders, for whom there was not seen to be some reasonable hope of reclamation or some need for individualised treatment. The opposite side of the penal welfare coin was incapacitation, so that 'curable' offenders were treated while dangerous offenders were restrained through measures such as preventive detention.

It is no accident that the probation order emerged during the period of penal welfarism, the Probation of Offenders Act 1907 enabling a court to require a probation officer to 'advise, assist and befriend' an offender as an alternative to sentencing him or her. As McWilliams (1986) records in reviewing the history of the probation service, the focus of probation work moved from a predominantly religious and 'common sense practical' supervisory system in the early twentieth century to a version of psychoanalytically based social casework in the 1960s. Confidence in the efficacy in probation work was at its height, as 'the most significant contribution made by this country to the new penological theory and practice' (Radzinowicz 1958).

By the 1970s, however, treatment became subject to a fundamental critique that caused widespread disenchantment with it as a rationale for sentencing,

---

[1] See Rex (2002) for a discussion of the threat perceived by both magistrates and offenders in a community order that nasty consequences would follow continued offending.

so that Allen (1981) felt able to predict that 'penal rehabilitationism' was likely to be peripheral rather than central to the future administration of criminal justice. Its decline was attributable to two main causes: the first was the lack of a technique that was known to work (encapsulated in the famous dictum 'Nothing Works' following Martinson 1974). This was coupled with the second: growing unease with the vulnerability of treatment to misuse for unintended or unexpressed social ends, its 'manipulation' of offenders, and with the use of indeterminate sentences particularly in the USA. The way was clear for the development of a justice model for sentencing, based on retributive principles, from which the Criminal Justice Act 1991 eventually evolved. As we shall see below, section 6 of the Act applied desert-based sentencing principles to community penalties, representing a quite radical departure from traditional thinking about non-custodial options.

Since the mid-1990s, interest has revived in rehabilitationism, as a result of new evidence about the effectiveness of interventions in reducing offenders' recidivism. We are arguably now in the heyday of a 'What Works' movement. The Joint Prison/Probation (renamed the Correctional Services) Accreditation Panel (JPPAP) has been tasked with approving a core curriculum of demon-strably effective programmes for offenders, and a range of evaluated Pathfinder projects have been funded under the Crime Reduction Programme.[2] A num-ber of advocates of 'New Rehabilitationism' have sought to distinguish its techniques from the discredited earlier model of 'treatment', both in how it is suggested that rehabilitative aims should be pursued in practice and in how it is proposed that they should influence sentencing decisions. Raynor and Vanstone (1994) argue that rehabilitative programmes with the specific object of preventing further offending can respect people's self-determination (their moral agency). Proponents (Hudson 1995; Raynor 1997, 2001) also maintain that rehabilitative goals should be pursued within a framework of sentences proportionate to the gravity of the offence.

What works in consequentialism

What works in rehabilitation is the subject matter of the next chapter, and I will not dwell on it here. Undoubtedly, however, a major research influence has been meta-analysis, which has allowed the findings of a number of different evaluations to be aggregated to achieve statistical significance (see, for example, Lipsey 1992). The application of this technique in reviews of recidivism has

---

[2] This initiative has been the subject of numerous Probation Circulars; for example, see 60/2000 for the Probation Service's 'What Works' Strategy. See http://www.homeoffice.gov.uk/cpd/probu/probu.htm for JPPAP's Second Annual Report.

shown that rehabilitative programmes can be effective, at least among certain types of offenders. McGuire (1995) has drawn together a set of principles about the assembly of effective programmes, which has been highly influential upon publications by Chapman and Hough (1998) and the Home Office (1999). These principles have informed the criteria by which the Accreditation Panel approves offender programmes for use by the prison and probation services. Yet caution is needed in interpreting the claims that can currently be made on the basis of this work, 'our understanding . . . of what works, with which offenders and under what conditions, in reducing offending behaviour' still being 'embryonic' (McIvor 1997: 13). Perhaps the best that can be said is that the evidence is still being accumulated and published in the UK, largely as a result of work under the Pathfinder projects.

As discussed above, deterrence and incapacitation have limited relevance to community penalties. Although space prohibits a full discussion, it is worth summarising the evidence in support of these sentencing aims. Perhaps the most recent authoritative word on the efficacy of deterrence has come from the Halliday Report (Home Office 2001) following the review of the sentencing framework in England and Wales, drawing on an analysis of recent research on 'Criminal Deterrence and Sentence Severity' by von Hirsch *et al.* (1999). According to Halliday, 'the availability of punishment clearly contributes to general deterrence, which undoubtedly exists, but there seems to be no link between marginal changes in punishment levels and changes in crime rates' (Home Office 2001: 8). On incapacitation, too, Halliday pointed to Home Office estimates that suggest that the prison population would need to increase by around 15 per cent to deliver a 1 per cent reduction in crime. The implication was that the cost was simply too high.

RETRIBUTION

In complete contrast to the forward-looking emphasis in consequentialism, retributive theory looks backwards to the offence for which the punishment exacts retribution. This approach has an ancient history as part of the tradition of Judaism, Christianity and Islam. In 'modern' thinking about punishment, retribution dates back to the writings of Immanuel Kant, who objected to Bentham's utilitarianism on the grounds that human beings – as 'moral agents' – should be used as ends in themselves and not as means to an end (or social good). It experienced a strong revival in the 1970s, in the form of the justice model that emerged from the critique of treatment touched on above. According to retributive theory, punishment is justified, not by the benefits it might bring society in preventing crime, but as an intrinsically just response to crime. Retributive writers such as von Hirsch and Ashworth (1998) and Duff (2000) have differing views on the connection between crime and punishment; some argue that punishment removes the 'unfair advantage' that the offender gained in committing the offence, others that it enables society to express its resentment about the offence. However, one principle that they share in common is that of proportionality: that the severity of the punishment should be related to (and therefore restricted by) the gravity of the offence. Thus, although retribution is often equated with a 'punitive' approach to crime, many of its recent proponents have been looking for ways in which to restrict the extent of the power that the state takes over offenders' lives.

The argument that what can legitimately be done to offenders in pursuit of instrumental (crime preventive) goals should be restricted by upper limits was developed initially in the writings of Norval Morris (1982) on 'limiting retributivism'. It has been developed far more fully in desert theory by von Hirsch (1976, 1985, 1993), who argues that proportionality should not merely limit but should actually determine the severity of a sentence. Within Morris's upper limits to what is deserved, von Hirsch asserts that the sentence should be guided by two further principles. One he calls 'ordinal proportionality': offences should be punished according to their rank ordering in terms of seriousness. The other is 'parity': offenders who are similarly culpable should receive punishments that are similarly severe. Other theorists, including consequentialists, dispute the achievability of true 'equality of impact'. For example, Walker (1992) questions the practicality of ensuring that similarly culpable offenders personally suffer the same amount of hardship in view of differences in the particular sensibilities (or perceptions of painfulness) of particular offenders. Morris and Tonry (1990) argue that 'in sentencing, . . . no generic man stands before the court, but countless individuals' (p. 94); therefore, the aim should be the not undeserved, and least intrusive, sanction which was likely to have the desired effect (whether, deterrent, rehabilitative, or incapacitative).

For von Hirsch (1993), the requirement for proportionality arises from the *censuring* function he ascribes to punishment. This is its normative role in simultaneously conveying to the perpetrator that a particular act was wrongful and appealing to other people (and to the offender as a moral agent) to refrain from a proscribed activity. The censure expressed through the penalty should reflect the comparative reprehensibility of the conduct. Von Hirsch does acknowledge that the penalty serves an additional preventive function – of discouraging the illegal conduct – without which it is difficult to justify the 'punitive' element in punishment. He argues, however, that this preventive element should be seen as supplying a prudential reason to refrain from offending that supplements the normative reason conveyed by penal censure. His point is that if the preventive message becomes too prominent, it would amount to treating offenders, not as moral agents, but as 'tigers in a circus' capable of responding only to threats.

Application to community penalties

Arguably, notions of punishment have dominated non-custodial penalties ever since the collapse of the Rehabilitative Ideal in the 1970s, initially as a range of orders were introduced in opposition to the only 'real' punishment of a custodial sentence. However, it was not until the Criminal Justice Act 1991 that community orders were formally presented as punishments in their own right (an idea that has since become intermingled with the aim of public protection). This section traces that development, and reflects on what might be learnt from the experience.

In the immediate aftermath of treatment being discredited, and in the face of a perceived resources crisis over the prison population, the 'alternative to custody' movement arose with the aim of offering judges and magistrates options that avoided the cost and damage of a prison sentence. The first real manifestation of this approach was to provide for a sentence of imprisonment to be suspended in the Criminal Justice Act 1967, followed by the introduction of the community service order in the Criminal Justice Act 1972. In the event, research suggested that both suspended sentences and community service orders replaced terms of imprisonment only in about half the cases in which they were imposed (see Bottoms 1981; Pease 1985). It was widely accepted that such 'alternatives' led to 'net widening' and 'mesh thinning' (Cohen 1985) – that is, the bringing of more and less serious offenders into the penal net than might otherwise have been the case, and the imposition upon them of more severe sanctions (though for an alternative view see McMahon 1990). Whether or not that was so, 'alternatives to custody' clearly failed to have the desired impact on the prison population, which continued an upward trend (see Bottoms 1987). The government realised that a rethink was necessary: judges and magistrates had to be offered sanctions that were more credible if they were to be persuaded to make less use of custody.

For this new thinking, the government turned to the justice model, specifically the desert principles developed by von Hirsch (see above). This formed the central plank in the legislative framework for sentencing in the Criminal Justice Act 1991, which sought to apply desert-based principles to the renamed community orders, as well as to custodial sentences. In order to bring community orders within its overall philosophy of proportionality, section 6 of the 1991 Act defined these personally intrusive measures in terms of restrictions on liberty that should be commensurate with the gravity of the offence, within an overall philosophy of 'punishment in the community'.

The 1991 Act represented a significant departure from the penal-welfare concepts that had predominated in the era of treatment (see above) by making the probation order (the archetypal penal-welfare measure) a sentence of the court. It also created two new orders, the combination order and the electronically monitored curfew order, intended to be sufficiently credible in terms of their restrictions on liberty to offer 'punishment in the community' for offenders who might otherwise receive a custodial sentence.

Section 6 of the 1991 Act appears to be based on suggestions from theorists as to how desert principles might be applied to the sentencing of offenders to community penalties. The first legislative requirement, that a community order can only be imposed where the offence is 'serious enough' for a community sentence yet not 'so serious' that only custody can be justified, adopts the principle of 'limiting retributivism' in the sense that the community order should not be *undeserved* (see sections 6(1) and 1(2) of the 1991 Act respectively). In requiring the sentencer to select the most suitable community order(s) whose restrictions on liberty are commensurate with the seriousness of the offence, the intention seems to be that desert will actually determine the size of the penalty. The model appears close to that recommended by Wasik and von Hirsch (1988), who suggested that, provided the gravity of the offence dictated how severely the offender was punished, it was possible to base the choice between two or more equally 'deserved' sanctions on other grounds – that is crime prevention (for a more detailed discussion of the principles underlying section 6 of the 1991 Act, see Rex 1998). In the case of section 6, the intention seems to be that those other grounds will help the sentencer to decide which deserved community order is suitable for the offender, for example probation if the aim is rehabilitative.

DOES DESERT 'WORK' IN RELATION TO COMMUNITY PENALTIES?

Experience following the 1991 Act suggests that its attempt to apply desert principles to community orders was a failure, at least in achieving the underlying aim of reducing reliance on custodial measures. Initially, the legislation appeared to have the desired effect on sentencing practice. Thus, the proportionate use of custody for indictable offences dropped from 15 per cent immediately before the implementation of the Act in October 1992 to 12 per cent afterwards, while the proportionate use of community penalties rose from 22 per cent to 24 per cent (Home Office 1992). However, closer examination shows that the use of probation orders declined by 19 per cent immediately after the introduction of the Act, and the use of additional requirements increased (Home Office 1996). Community service continued an upward trend, and the new combination order proved popular. Since then, it is well-documented that the use of custody has increased dramatically, and the trend for community penalties has also been upward. Moreover, the statistics suggest that community penalties are being used for less serious offenders with a lower risk of reconviction; the proportions sentenced to probation and community service for indictable offences have dropped over the last decade,[3] and a lower proportion now have prior records.[4] This hardly suggests that the 1991 Act achieved its goal of persuading sentencers that community orders contained credible restrictions on liberty that might displace custodial sentences for a substantial number of offenders.[5] So does this mean that desert principles cannot be applied successfully to community orders?

One factor that needs to be taken into account is the undeniably more punitive climate that has prevailed since 1993, coupled with a focus on public protectionism that seems to have encouraged the imposition of more intensive conditions on offenders, as discussed by a number of commentators (see, for example, Garland 2001 and Nellis 2001). However, the legislative provisions also raised theoretical and practical problems that hampered their effective implementation (Rex 1998). One of these was the difficulty of conceptualising community orders in terms of their restrictions on liberty, and comparing the restrictions imposed by different community orders (for example comparing community service hours with the kinds of restrictions imposed by probation).[6] In practice, following the 1991 Act, this seemed to lead to temptations to increase the easily measurable restrictions by adding requirements to a probation order or combining it with community service to produce a combination order.

HYBRID THEORIES

It will be clear from the above discussion that penal theory has developed considerably in recent decades. Most contemporary theorists now favour a hybrid theory that contains elements of retributive (or desert) theory and consequentialism. As Bottoms (1995) points out, 'no modern version of desert theory completely excludes instrumental considerations in sentencing' (p. 22). It might

---

[3] See Criminal Statistics England and Wales 2000. The proportion of probation orders (now community rehabilitation orders) imposed for indictable offences was 72 per cent in 1990 and 66 per cent in 2000; for CSOs (now community punishment orders) the respective proportions were 69 per cent and 60 per cent.

[4] According to Probation Statistics England and Wales 2000, 25 per cent of those sentenced to probation in 2000 had no previous convictions compared with 12 per cent in 1990; the equivalent proportions for CS were 47 per cent and 14 per cent respectively.

[5] In relation to the combination order, for example, the White Paper setting out the government's legislative proposals expressed the hope that it 'should be particularly suitable for some persistent property offenders' and estimated that it would reduce the number of offenders in prison by up to 1000 (Home Office 1990: paras 4.16 and 9.7).

[6] As argued elsewhere (Rex 1997, cited in Bottoms 1998), a focus on *physical* restrictions such as the number of actual contact hours fails to do justice to the demands that probationers may face in attempting lifestyle changes such as refraining from alcohol or drugs or restraining aggressive reactions to particular situations. Rex and von Hirsch (1998) propose a standard scale for assessing the severity of different community orders to accommodate the more psychological restrictions and loss of privacy entailed in probation supervision.

be argued that this kind of development reflects a wish to have the best of both worlds – to compensate for the weaknesses of the respective model and avoid difficult decisions. But are the backward focus of retributivism and forward-looking consequentialism really reconcilable? Some, like Raynor (1997), would perceive an essential incompatibility between the two approaches. Yet, this perhaps overlooks the fact that elements of one approach are evident in theory based on the other. Von Hirsch's (1993) model entwines censure with crime prevention, although desert – and proportionality – clearly has priority. Similarly, utilitarians (including Bentham) incorporate some notion of 'negative retributivism', in that the gravity of the offence is indeed relevant to the amount of punishment that may be justified to restrain it, but consequentialist goals will always be paramount (von Hirsch and Ashworth 1998; Duff 2000).

A true hybrid is a model where one goal (either desert or crime prevention) will be compromised in pursuit of the other in certain circumstances. Can this ever be achieved without proving fatal to the coherency of the model as a whole? In other words, is it possible to specify clearly when one goal will prevail and when the other? Arguably, one of the weaknesses of section 6 of the 1991 Act (see above) was that it failed to give priority either to proportionality or to suitability in the criteria for community orders. For offenders facing the prospect of multiple demands under a community rehabilitation order with requirements, a combined order or a curfew order (or a custodial sentence long enough to accommodate an offending behaviour programme in prison), this is not a purely academic consideration. Should a given offender receive a condition to attend a programme that might tackle his or her offending behaviour, when 'justice' might demand a lesser community penalty (say, straight community service or probation), or alternatively a 12-month prison sentence that will deny access to rehabilitative resources?

Even von Hirsch (1993) accepts the impracticality of insisting upon a stringent desert criterion that demands unrealistically precise judgements about the relative gravity of offences and severity of punishments, and he therefore espouses a principle of proportionality rather than the stringency of 'commensurability'. However, he doubts that much is to be gained in terms of incapacitation or rehabilitation if one is to preserve a reasonable relationship between the gravity of the offence and the severity of the sentence. By the same token, if large departures are allowed, can the scheme still be said to have any basis in desert? Nonetheless, in relation to non-custodial options, he would support a 'range' model with a modest relaxation in proportionality to allow substitutions between sanctions to be made more easily and enable slightly more severe sanctions to be imposed for breach of a community order. This is the kind of pragmatic compromise on which section 6 of the 1991 Act seems to have been based; unfortunately, it is unclear whether the product is a workable scheme.

BEYOND COMPROMISE? PUNISHMENT AS COMMUNICATION

Another kind of penal theory claims to move beyond mere compromise and towards integration between retribution and consequentialism. This is a communicative theory, developed most fully by Anthony Duff (2000), who accords punishment a forward-looking goal – the reform of the offender through 'moral persuasion'. The idea here is to make material forms of punishment intrinsically appropriate to the aim of bringing offenders to recognise the wrongfulness of their crimes and the need to reform. However, punishment is also retributive in the sense that the communication condemns or censures the crime, requiring a reasonable relationship between the severity of the punishment and the relative gravity of the offence (in other word, proportionality). This is not a purely expressive communication, but one that appeals to the offender as a rational moral agent capable of responding. Indeed, that the punishment should aim to elicit a response from the offender is key to Duff's conceptualisation.

Duff (2000) defines punishment as a 'secular penance', justified as part of a morally communicative process that aims to persuade offenders to repent of their crimes, to communicate their reparative apology to others, and to undertake to reform their future conduct. Others struggle with this somewhat 'religious' terminology; von Hirsch (1999), for example, doubts whether the state is authorised to impose the secular penance envisaged by Duff. It is also questionable whether Duff has resolved the proportionality conundrum: he states that it is more important to achieve a richly communicative penalty than to insist on strict adherence to proportionality, but fails to address what that means in practice. Perhaps it is for others to do so.

Duff (2000) offers a reconceptualisation of community penalties in terms of penal communication. A probation (community rehabilitation) order reminds the offender that the offence cast doubt on the offender's commitment to the community's public values and threatened to undermine the mutual trust on which the community depends. The conditions attached to a probation order aim to bring home to the offender the character and implication of the offences as public wrongs, and to persuade the offender that he or she must (and can) modify his or her future behaviour. Community service (now a community punishment order), as public reparation, enables the offender to express his or her understanding of what he or she has done and his or her renewed commitment to the community, as well as requiring him or her to perform apologetic reparation.

Duff (2000) offers his account as an ideal, and argues that it does not represent criminal justice processes as they operate in practice. However, it seems valid to explore its possible application to how state punishment is actually delivered, or could be delivered, in practice, on the basis that effective thinking about punishment requires a closer relationship between high-level normative thinking and ground-level practical decision-making (Raynor 1997). In other words, theory should be used to help us in making decisions about offenders. Accordingly, I have been investigating the views of victims, offenders, magistrates and probation practitioners about: what punishment communicates; how offenders respond to that communication; and how community orders do or could contribute to the process. I can offer here just a brief summary of my provisional findings so far, based on 65 detailed interviews (Rex 2002).

First, securing a response from the offender – sometimes through deterrence – seemed central to people's understandings of the aims of sentencing. However, although the need for the punishment to reduce offending seemed paramount to most people, this cannot be equated with a purely 'consequentialist' position. Strong elements of retributive thinking were evident – a sense of fairness and cautious endorsement of proportionality, in addition to an almost universal perception of punishment as an expression of censure. It is difficult to disentangle retributive from consequentialist thinking in these accounts, which seem to support a justification for punishment that combines elements of both.

Community orders figured quite prominently in explanations of how particular disposals could be used to convey the expectation of a positive response from the offender. Looking specifically at probation, in keeping with the current vogue for probation programmes to 'confront offending behaviour', probation officers clearly saw their task as to promote offenders' acceptance of responsibility for their offending behaviour. Some also perceived a link between offenders' experiencing remorse and resolving not to offend in the future, and saw their role as helping to stimulate the necessary processes of self-examination. For offenders, although probation supervision might help them realise the harm caused by their offending, they placed considerable emphasis on their own development of a sense of responsibility, and depicted supervision as a morally neutral process in which they received advice or were assisted in their decision-making. Their understandings seemed far short of a conception of probation as aiming to secure their penitent understanding of their wrongs, and therefore their repentance (Duff 2000). However, they could see probation supervision as helping them to develop a better understanding of their offending and its consequences, and as helping them to engage in processes of change and reform.

Clearly, these conclusions are provisional, but they suggest that community orders have rich communicative potential. They seem to provide a basis for work undertaken with offenders supervised in the community to promote constructive responses to the messages communicated in sentencing: that they should take responsibility for what they have done, gain an understanding of the harm it has caused, make amends and move forward in a positive way. One issue that requires further attention is proportionality, where the complex – and apparently contradictory – views expressed by my interviewees reflect the difficulties of the academic debate. That aside, links can be made between the communicative elements in punishment, and an approach that has become prominent recently: Restorative Justice, to which we turn to next.

RESTORATIVE JUSTICE

The current influence of Restorative Justice can be explained, at least partially, by reference to people's growing dissatisfaction with traditional criminal justice systems as neglecting victims and failing to deal with the aftermath of crime. As one early advocate has put it, the aim of Restorative Justice is to restore victims; 'justice' has an obligation to repair the injuries caused by crime, and promote healing and reassurance through a process involving the victim, offender and the community (Zehr 1990). Among restorative theorists, some put more emphasis on the provision of services and compensation for victims, and others on the development of models for conflict resolution (victim–offender mediation, conferencing).[7] Some of the major restorative initiatives, and most ambitious research, for example on conferencing, have taken place in New Zealand and Australia. Restorative Justice has played a minor role in England and Wales since the late 1970s through victim–offender mediation (see Marshall 1996), and has moved to a central role in youth justice over the last five years under the Labour administration (see Dignan 1999; Morris and Gelsthorpe 2000).

There is by now a vast literature on Restorative Justice, a wide range of advocates, and an extensive debate about the exact nature of its underlying principles, enabling detractors to claim that it lacks a sound theoretical basis, or set of unifying concepts (von Hirsch and Ashworth 1998). One important debate concerns the role of the victim – whether this should be restricted to an opportunity to explain the impact that the crime has had on his or her life (perhaps directly to the offender), or whether victims should actually be

---

[7] A classic definition of conferencing is 'a process whereby parties with a stake in a specific offence collectively resolve how to deal with the aftermath of the offence and its implications for the future' (Marshall 1996: 37). In New Zealand, and Australia, and latterly in England and Wales, conferencing has been implemented as an alternative to court proceedings, especially suitable for juvenile offenders, involving the victim and his or her significant other(s), the offender and his or her significant other(s), community representatives, police, social or youth services, and the facilitator or coordinator.

consulted on decisions to prosecute and sentence.[8] Another debate is over its exact relationship with traditional criminal justice, so that some advocates set restorative approaches in opposition to retributive justice (Christie 1982; Zehr 1990). Others argue that these differences have been overstated and suggest that restorative processes and sanctions should be seen as developing or improving more traditional approaches to punishment rather than as an entirely different system of dealing with crime (Duff 2000; Daly 2002).

A third controversy, relevant to this chapter, is the empirical support for Restorative Justice. Daly (2002) overviews the evidence to examine some 'myths' about Restorative Justice, including the one that the experience can produce transformations in people. She cites the 'most robust finding' as being the high levels of procedural justice perceived by victims and offenders alike (who generally view the process and outcomes as fair). However, her own research on the South Australian Juvenile Justice (SAJJ) project found relatively less evidence of 'restorativeness': of offenders' giving sincere apologies, and victims' being able to understand that apologies are sincere.

As Daly (2002) remarks, the conferencing effect everyone asks about is whether it reduces offending.[9] Here, the RISE (Reintegrative Shaming Experiments) project in Canberra found that for one of four major offence categories (violence, but not drink–driving, property offences or shoplifting), those offenders who were assigned to a conference had a significantly reduced rate of re-offending compared with those assigned to court (Sherman, Strang and Woods 2000). In the SAJJ project, and in New Zealand (Maxwell and Morris 2000), links were found between what happened in conferences (for example, expressions of remorse by offenders, agreement over the outcomes) and reduced reconviction during follow-up periods.

Another area of interest explored by some writers is the application of restorative approaches to community-based sanctions. Several commentators have noted the reparative potential of community service, or the opportunity in cognitive behavioural programmes to make offenders more aware of victims' perspectives or even to have contact with victims of offences similar to those they have committed (Duff 2000; Raynor 2001; Johnson and Rex 2002). But there is clearly scope to go further in developing the restorative aspect of community penalties, which might be linked with promoting the communicative potential of community-based supervision. Thus, Duff advocates that

---

[8] Retributive or desert theorists are concerned that the latter would conflict with notions of justice, so that the level of punishment would depend on the preferences of the victim rather than the gravity of the offence (Ashworth 1998).

[9] Here, again, some writers point to the possible exploitation of victims to serve offenders' needs if the emphasis is on reduced recidivism rather than satisfaction with the process and its value to the victim.

victim–offender mediation should be routinely built into probation orders, organised and conducted by the supervising probation officer, so that 'the offender communicates to the wider community, as well as to the victim, his apologetic recognition of the wrong he has done' (2000: 104). Raynor argues for the incorporation of a reparative element in every community sentence, perhaps by involving victims in the choice of rehabilitative work to be carried out by offenders, to 'demonstrate that rehabilitation is itself fundamentally restorative and benefits the community as well as the offender' (Raynor 2001: 197).

SUMMARY OF KEY ISSUES

- This chapter started by looking at the two traditional rival theories of punishment: consequentialism and retribution. Of the three consequentialist forward-looking rationales, rehabilitation has had the greatest salience for community penalties. Shaping probation work during the Penal Welfare Era, rehabilitation has recently enjoyed a revival in the form of the 'What Works' movement. This follows new evidence about the effectiveness of rehabilitative programmes, used to produce a set of principles to govern the design and delivery of effective interventions with offenders. However, caution is needed about the claims that can currently be made on the basis of this work in the UK.

- Doubts about the ethics and efficacy of treatment emerged in the 1970s, leading to the development of the justice model. This relies on a retributive rational for sentencing, looking backwards to the offence to which the punishment should represent a proportionate response (i.e. one that is constrained by the gravity of the offence). This approach, in the form of desert theory, was applied to community penalties in the Criminal Justice Act 1991; the aim was to encourage sentencers to make less use of custody in favour of community sentences presented as credible punishments in their own right. Sentencing trends following the implementation of the 1991 Act hardly suggest that it achieved that goal. In addition to an undeniably more punitive sentencing climate since 1993, theoretical and practical problems that the legislation failed to resolve hampered the successful application of desert principles to community orders.

- Arguably, penal theory has 'matured' over the last two decades in search of compromise between consequentialism and retribution, though with limited success. Recently, a new kind of 'integrated' theory has been developed in which the idea of communication is central and the emphasis is on securing the moral reform of the offender. It is argued that community penalties have rich communicative potential, and can be used to engage offenders in processes which lead them to take responsibility for what they have done, gain an understanding of the harm caused and change their future behaviour.

- Another important development has been the growing influence of Restorative Justice in reaction to the perceived failings of traditional forms of criminal justice. There are uncertainties about the theoretical underpinnings of Restorative Justice, how far it should be developed as an alternative to criminal justice, and the strength of the empirical evidence in support of restorative processes. However, it seems that there is much that traditional systems can nonetheless learn from more restorative approaches, and scope for developing the restorative aspects of community penalties.

References

Allen, F. A. (1981) *The Decline of the Rehabilitative Ideal: Penal Policy and Social Purpose.* New Haven: Yale University Press.

Ashworth, A. (1998) 'Restorative justice', in A. von Hirsch and A. Ashworth (eds) *Principled Sentencing: Readings on Theory and Policy* (2nd edn). Oxford: Hart Publishing.

Bottoms, A. E. (1981) 'The suspended sentence in England 1967–1987', *British Journal of Criminology*, 21, 1–26.

Bottoms, A. E. (1987) 'Limiting prison use in England and Wales', *Howard Journal of Criminal Justice*, 26, 177–202.

Bottoms, A. E. (1995) 'The philosophy and politics of punishment and sentencing', in C. Clarkson and R. Morgan (eds) *The Politics of Sentencing Reform.* Oxford: Clarendon Press.

Bottoms, A. E. (1998) 'Five puzzles in von Hirsch's theory of punishment', in A. Ashworth and M. Wasik (eds) *Fundamentals of Sentencing Theory: Essays in Honour of Andrew von Hirsch.* Oxford: Clarendon Press.

Chapman, T. and Hough, M. (1998) *Evidence-Based Practice: A Guide to Effective Practice.* London: Home Office.

Christie, N. (1982) *Limits to Pain.* Oxford: Martin Robinson.

Cohen, S. (1985) *Visions of Social Control: Crime, Punishment and Classification.* Cambridge: Polity.

Daly, K. (2002) 'Restorative justice: The real story', *Punishment and Society*, 4, 55–79.

Dignan, J. (1999) 'The Crime and Disorder Act and the prospects for restorative justice', *Criminal Law Review*, 48–60.

Duff, R. A. (2000) *Punishment, Communication and Community.* Oxford: Oxford University Press.

Garland, D. (1985) *Punishment and Welfare: A History of Penal Strategies.* Aldershot: Gower.

Garland, D. (2001) *The Culture of Control: Crime and Social Order in Contemporary Society.* Oxford: Oxford University Press.

Home Office (1990) *Crime, Justice and Protecting the Public* (CM 965). London: HMSO.

Home Office (1992) *Criminal Statistics England and Wales, 1992*, London: HMSO.

Home Office (1996) *Probation Statistics England and Wales, 1995*. London: Home Office.

Home Office (1999) *What Works: Reducing Re-offending: Evidence-Based Practice*. London: Home Office Communication Directorate.

Home Office (2001) *Making Punishments Work: Report of a Review of the Sentencing Framework for England and Wales*. London: Home Office.

Hudson, B. (1995) 'Beyond proportionate punishment: Difficult cases and the 1991 Criminal Justice Act', *Crime, Law and Social Change*, 22, 59–78.

Johnson, C. and Rex, S. A. (2002) 'Community service: Rediscovering reintegration', in D. Ward, J. Scott and M. Lacey (eds) *Probation – Working for Justice* (2nd edn). Oxford: Oxford University Press.

Lipsey, M. W. (1992) 'Juvenile delinquency treatment: A meta-analytic inquiry into the variability of effects', in T. Cook, D. Cooper, H. Corday, H. Hartman, L. Hedges, R. Light, T. Louis and F. Mosteller (eds) *Meta-analysis for Explanation: A Casebook*. New York: Russell Sage Foundation.

McGuire, J. (ed.) (1995) *What Works: Reducing Reoffending – Guidelines from Research and Practice*. Chichester: Wiley.

McIvor, G. (1997) 'Evaluative research in probation: Progress and prospects', in G. Mair (ed.) *Evaluating the Effectiveness of Community Penalties*. Aldershot: Avebury.

McMahon, M. W. (1990) ' "Netwidening": Vagaries in the use of a concept', *British Journal of Criminology*, 30, 121–49.

McWilliams, W. (1986) 'The English probation system and the diagnostic ideal', *Howard Journal of Criminal Justice*, 25, 241–60.

Marshall, T. F. (1996) 'The evolution of restorative justice in Britain', *European Journal on Criminal Policy and Research*, 4, 21–43.

Martinson, R. (1974) 'What works? Questions and answers about prison reforms', *Public Interest*, 35, 22–54.

Maxwell, G. M. and Morris, A. (2000) 'Putting restorative justice into practice for adult offenders', *Howard Journal of Criminal Justice*, 40, 55–69.

Morris, A. and Gelsthorpe, L. (2000) 'Something old, something borrowed, something blue, but something new? A comment on the prospects for restorative justice under the Crime and Disorder Act 1998', *Criminal Law Review*, 18–30.

Morris, N. (1982) *Madness and the Criminal Law*. Chicago: Chicago University Press.

Morris, N. and Tonry, M. (1990) *Between Prison and Probation: Intermediate Punishments in a Rational Sentencing System*. New York: Oxford University Press.

Nellis, M. (2001) 'Community penalties in historical perspective', in A. Bottoms, L. Gelsthorpe and S. Rex (eds) *Community Penalties: Change and Challenges*. Cullompton: Willan.

Pease, K. (1985) 'Community service orders', in M. Tonry and N. Morris (eds) *Crime and Justice: A Review of Research, Vol. 6*. Chicago: University of Chicago Press.

Radzinowicz, L. (ed.) (1958) *The Results of Probation: A Report of the Cambridge Department of Criminal Science*. London: Macmillan.

Raynor, P. (1997) 'Some observations on rehabilitation and justice', *Howard Journal of Criminal Justice*, 36, 248–262.

Raynor (2001) 'Community penalties and social integration: "Community" as solution and as problem', in A. Bottoms, L. Gelsthorpe and S. Rex (eds) *Community Penalties: Change and Challenges*. Cullompton: Willan.

Raynor, P. and Vanstone, M. (1994) 'Probation practice, effectiveness and the non-treatment paradigm', *British Journal of Social Work*, 24, 387–404.

Rex, S. (1997) *Perceptions of Probation in a Context of 'Just Deserts'*, PhD thesis. Cambridge: Institute of Criminology, University of Cambridge.

Rex, S. (1998) 'Applying desert principles to community sentences: Lessons from two Criminal Justice Acts', *Criminal Law Review*, 361–380.

Rex, S. (2002) 'Re-inventing community penalties: The role of communication', in S. A. Rex and M. Tonry (eds) *Reform and Punishment: The Future of Sentencing*. Cullompton: Willan.

Rex, S. and von Hirsch, A. (1998) 'Community orders and the assessment of punishment severity', *Federal Sentencing Reporter*, 10, 278.

Sherman, L. W., Strang, H. and Woods, D. J. (2000) *Recidivism Patterns in the Canberra Reintegrative Shaming Experiment (RISE)*. Canberra: Centre for Restorative Justice, Australian National University.
Available at: http://www.aic.gov.au/rjustice/rise/recidivism/index.html

von Hirsch, A. (1976) *Doing Justice: The Choice of Punishments*. New York: Hill and Wang.

von Hirsch, A. (1985) *Past or Future Crimes*. Manchester: Manchester University Press.

von Hirsch, A. (1993) *Censure and Sanctions*. Oxford: Clarendon Press.

von Hirsch, A. (1999) 'Punishment, penance and the state', in M. Matravers (ed.) *Punishment and Political Theory*. Oxford: Hart Publishing.

von Hirsch, A. and Ashworth, A. (eds) (1998) *Principled Sentencing: Readings on Theory and Policy* (2nd edn). Oxford: Hart Publishing.

von Hirsch, A., Bottoms, A. E., Burney, E. and Wikstrom, P. O. (1999) *Criminal Deterrence and Sentence Severity: An Analysis of Recent Research*. Oxford: Hart Publishing.

Walker, N. (1992) 'Legislating the transcendental: von Hirsch's proportionality', *Cambridge Law Journal*, 51, 530–537.

Wasik, M. and von Hirsch, A. (1988) 'Non-custodial penalties and the principles of desert', *Criminal Law Review*, 555–571.

Zehr, H. (1990) *Changing Lenses: A New Focus For Crime and Justice*. Scottdale, PA: Herald Press.

4

WHAT WORKS IN REDUCING RE-OFFENDING: PRINCIPLES AND PROGRAMMES

Wing Hong Chui

INTRODUCTION

As highlighted in Chapter 1, in addition to the protection of the public, 'reducing re-offending' is a major aim of the new National Probation Service (NPS), and this aim also operates within the Home Office's Correctional Policy Framework (Home Office 1999a). Reducing crime, toughening community punishments for those who break the law, and making punishments work have often been used as eye-catching promises by the former Conservative Party and New Labour in order to address the public's fear of crime and moral panic. One of the pressing challenges to probation personnel is to look for ways to reduce offending behaviours by promoting offenders' compliance and enforcing the sentences effectively. The key question among trainee probation officers and practitioners is what can be done to assist offenders in the process of achieving successful re-integration, and the next question is 'how' to facilitate them to change. Likewise, the Prison Service is keen on finding ways to cut rates of re-offending by former prisoners (see Social Exclusion Unit (SEU) 2002).

However, working with offenders is never an easy task, and there is neither 'quick fix' nor 'prescription' to deal with those who experience a wide range of personal and social problems such as drug misuse, poverty, homelessness and unemployment (Drakeford and Vanstone 1996; May and Vass 1996; Williams 1996; Alexander 2000). According to Hans Toch, '[o]ffender recidivism rates are indecently high, and relapse rates for alcohol and drug abusers, sex offenders, and other people with addictive and obsessive dispositions verge on the astronomical' (cited in Maruna 2001: xvi). But does it mean that we should lose our hope for offenders to change, and give up on them? The answer is no. Indeed both the Probation and Prison Services have been looking for innovative and well-designed rehabilitative measures to tackle re-offending behaviour, both in prison and in the community. Several principles for evidence-based practice for rehabilitating offenders have been identified by a number of researchers such as McGuire (1995), Gendreau (1996), Chapman and Hough (1998), and Day and Howells (2002). It is generally believed that some offending behaviour programmes, only if well-planned and implemented, can work to reduce risk of re-offending and address offenders' criminogenic needs (Home Office 1999b). At the time of writing a number of crime-reduction projects are being evaluated though their impact on re-offending is not available in the interim reports (see, for example, Hudson *et al.* 2001; National Probation Directorate 2001; Hollin *et al.* 2002).

The aims of this chapter are two-fold: to revisit the 'What Works' principles that underpin most crime reduction or 'Pathfinder' programmes in England, and to look at some of these initiatives which have been 'accredited' and adopted nationally. At the outset, it should be emphasised that this chapter has been drawn mainly from numerous Home Office reports and other published materials, rather than original research, and readers are recommended to consult other documents for greater detail. This chapter is indeed a summary of the current debates and discussions on the re-emergence of offender rehabilitation and how the 'What Works' initiative or evidence-based practice has been incorporated into mainstream probation work. Finally, while it is vital for probation officers to be aware of 'what works' or otherwise in reducing re-offending behaviour, the importance of reflective probation practice should not be neglected and should be emphasised as a framework to work with the complexities of offending behaviours.

RE-EMERGENCE OF REHABILITATION IN PROBATION – FROM 'NOTHING WORKS' TO 'WHAT WORKS'

Rex, in Chapter 3, highlights rehabilitation – a term sometimes used interchangeably with 'treatment' and 'reformation' – as one of the classical theories of punishment and sentencing, although for most of its century-long existence the Probation Service believed it to be something apart from punishment, an alternative to it (Hudson 1996; Crow 2001). Von Hirsch (1998) provides a clear definition of its usual meaning:

> Rehabilitation is the idea of 'curing' an offender of his or her criminal tendencies. It consists, more precisely, of changing an offender's personality, outlook, habits, or opportunities so as to make him or her less inclined to commit crimes. . . . Traditionally, rehabilitation has consisted in offering counselling, psychological assistance, training, or support – but a variety of other techniques might be used. (p. 1)

Hudson (1996: 26) argues that the aim of reformist or rehabilitative punishment is to induce an offender to refrain from re-offending by 'taking away the desire to offend' (rather than simply refraining out of fear of the consequences). In the era when 'advise, assist and befriend' was the primary objective of probation supervision there was an easy fit with general rehabilitative ideals, especially in the 1950s and 1960s, when casework was influenced predominantly by the medical or psycho-social model. But as Crow (2001: 7) acknowledges (see also Raynor and Vanstone 2002), a wide range of approaches to the treatment has developed within a broad rehabilitative framework, and 'similar types of intervention may go under different titles at different times, depending on the latest thinking in criminal justice policy'. This helps to explain the contested, and sometimes confusing, nature of the term 'rehabilitation'.

For all it was thought of as the moral high ground in the old Probation Service, rehabilitation was never beyond criticism, especially by retributivists. Hudson (1996) reminds us the 'moral integrity objection to rehabilitation', for example, derived from C. S. Lewis's humanitarian theory of punishment:

> . . . he describes the process of rehabilitation as the coerced change of personality according to the edicts of Freud, a process which does not end until either the offender is indeed changed, or has learned to act as if s/he has been changed. (Lewis 1971; cited in Hudson 1996: 29)

Lewis rightly highlights, ahead of his time, the dangers of *coercive* rehabilitation, but perhaps overstates the extent to which rehabilitation, especially in probation, was coercive in his time. Retributivists are perhaps on stronger ground criticising the assumption that the treatment model sees crime as 'determined rather than willed':

> The 'cure' for crime, under the treatment model, is to change the personality of offender, and in taking away the likelihood of choosing to do wrong, taking away the capacity for moral choice at all. (p. 29)

These essentially ethical arguments weakened rehabilitation as a theory, but never fully undermined it. More devastatingly, faith in the treatment of offenders was lost among academics and policy-makers in the latter part of 1960s and the 1970s as a result of US and British research evidence which seemingly showed how ineffective penal measures were in reducing offenders' criminal behaviour (see Martinson 1974; Lipton, Martinson and Wilks 1975; Folkard, Smith and Smith 1976; Raynor's Chapter 5 in this book). The pessimism in the 1970s marked the decline of the rehabilitative ideal and the onset of the 'Nothing Works' era. According to Crow (2001), 'incapacitation', 'alternatives to custody', 'the justice model and just deserts', 'reparation', 'crime prevention' all replaced the treatment model as the central focus of penal policy in England and Wales in the 1980s and 1990s. Emphasis shifted to punishment and retribution in dealing with offenders, and community sentences were seen as 'punishment in the community'. Nonetheless, as Raynor, Smith and Vanstone (1994), McGuire (1995), and lately Crow (2001) rightly argue, rehabilitation did not die out completely in the British criminal justice policy in the 1980s and 1990s, and was stubbornly upheld by a number of probation officers. In this regard, Raynor and Vanstone (2002) note:

> The break with the treatment model has not been total, and in the practitioner literature of the 1980s and 1990s there are numerous examples of work based on a reformulated treatment model predicated on increased collaboration with the offender, the use of contract and a transparent attempt to link a specific theory or theories to practice. The most recent of these, in effect, reinstates rehabilitation as a central goal of community supervision; it can be described, therefore, as 'new rehabilitation'. (p. 45)

Since the mid-1990s there has been a revival of rehabilitationism, on the back of more sophisticated research which has begun to cancel the pessimism of the Nothing Works era (see Chapters 3 and 5 of this book). It has been championed and disseminated by the British 'What Works' conferences, which were initiated by academics, for probation managers and practitioners (see, for example, Rowson and McGuire 1996). Certain research stands out. Vennard and Hedderman (1998) and Crow (2001) recognise that besides the Canadian and North American meta-analytical[1] surveys into effective interventions with offenders, Raynor and Vanstone's (1996, 2001) evaluation of 'Straight Thinking on Probation' (STOP) in Wales clearly demonstrated that some rehabilitative programmes reduced recidivism. STOP was initiated in the Mid-Glamorgan Probation Service in 1991, adapting a Canadian cognitive-behavioural 'Reasoning and Rehabilitation' programme developed by Ross and Fabiano (1985). It showed that when compared with a group of offenders receiving custodial sentences, the STOP programme completers were reconvicted less and self-reported changes in thinking (such as thinking before acting, speaking or offending) and in the level of social and personal problems (Raynor and Vanstone 2001). As a result of such findings, 'cognitively based "what works" programmes gained a growing legitimacy . . . in the UK' (Kemshall 2002: 46) and fed into the growing government interest in constructive approaches to working with offenders and preventing crime. Thus, in

---

[1] According to Dowden and Andrews (2000: 450), 'a meta-analysis is the statistical aggregation of the results from a large collection of independent studies for the purposes of integrating the results. The results from each of these studies are converted into a common metric, termed an effect size, to enable cross study comparison'. For detail, consult Robert Rosenthal's (1991) text on meta-analytic procedures.

the introductory chapter to a Home Office report entitled *Reducing Offending*, Goldblatt and Lewis (1998) concluded that:

> It has become increasingly clear that research evidence produced over the previous 40–50 years indicated that certain approaches to reducing crime would be more effective than others. It was not true that 'nothing works'. (p. 1)

The 'What Works' movement subsequently became the new mission of the Probation Service, a strategy aimed at ensuring the survival of the service in a political climate hostile to soft penalties. The Home Office Probation Unit, the Association of Chief Officers of Probation, Her Majesty's Inspectorate of Probation (HMIP) were determined to show the service's worth, set up the Effective Practice Initiative (currently the 'What Works' Initiative), on the assumption that reputable research showed that 'reductions in offending of between 15 per cent and 20 per cent can be achieved through well-planned supervision of offenders' (Furniss and Nutley 2000: 23). The Home Secretary incorporated this initiative into his Crime Reduction Strategy in July 1998 and supported it with £250 million (Home Office 1999b). Guidance to probation managers and front-line practitioners was given in a number of publications: *Evidence Based Practice: A Guide to Effective Practice* (Chapman and Hough 1998), *Strategies for Effective Offender Supervision* (Underdown 1998), and *A Handbook for Evaluating Probation Work with Offenders* (Merrington and Hine 2001).

It is difficult to overemphasise the amount of change which the Initiative entailed at grassroots level. As Chapman and Hough (1998) indicate, the 'What Works' initiative was not only an attempt to redefine the nature of effectiveness in probation supervision, it was also a response to the many inconsistencies in probation practice highlighted in earlier studies and inspections. These 15 inconsistencies in probation practice show what the promoters of the Initiative were up against:

- supervision programmes for offenders vary depending upon the supervising officer rather than the risk of re-offending and criminogenic needs of the offenders;
- differing views about the purpose of including additional requirements in order;
- variable patterns of referral resulting in inequality of opportunity afforded to offenders and inefficient use of programmes;
- unsatisfactory levels of attendance and completion of programmes;
- inadequate enforcement;
- content of programmes not based upon research into effectiveness;
- staff too often fail either to record or respond to indicators of potential dangerousness in the offenders they supervise;
- weaknesses in the referral process to partnerships;
- poor access to and level of attendance at partnership programmes;

- lack of rigour in targeting and criteria of eligibility for programmes;
- undermining programme integrity by altering manual material;
- over-rigid adherence to manual transcripts;
- more work need on building motivation and sustaining attendance;
- inadequate integration between programme delivery and case management both before and after programmes; and
- most evaluation not comprehensive, timely and sustained.

Source: Chapman and Hough 1998: 3

Chapman and Hough believe that these inconsistencies should be addressed by policy-makers and practitioners by making probation practice more accountable for its practice. Some inconsistences could and should be addressed before effective practice is set in place, but in the light of research, the things to be aimed for are clear. The key principles (which will be fully explained below) relate to risk, need and responsivity, and to programme integrity, and should be used to guide all aspects of probation work: assessment, case management, programme delivery, community re-integration, and monitoring and evaluation.

The service had a huge task ahead if it. Andrew Underdown's (1998) survey of probation programmes in 43 Probation Areas showed clearly that relatively few of them were evaluated properly, or met the demanding effectiveness principles. He too provided guidelines and standards for best practice in effective supervision programmes, attending specifically to issues of design, delivery and evaluation, and also discussed how management arrangements can promote and support them. Simon Merrington and Jean Hine's (2001) later *Handbook for Evaluating Probation Work with Offenders* was a user-friendly guide for probation staff who wished to learn how to evaluate work with offenders in the community. Its key message – again – is that evaluation research is essential to demonstrating outcome effectiveness.

Given its investment in the 'What Works' Initiative, it is not surprising that the Home Office has high hopes of what it will achieve in reducing re-offending. Probation staff, including managers, practitioners and research officers, across the country are expected to work together and achieve specified crime-reduction targets. These were reaffirmed in *A New Choreography*:

The NPS is committed to evidence-based (What Works) practice and Government targets dictate that we should reduce the reconviction rate of those under the supervision of the Service by 5 per cent. For those who misuse drugs the target is 25 per cent.

This will be achieved by roll-out of independently accredited evidencebased programmes that will be consistently available across the country. NPS priorities will lead to more programmes aimed at community reintegration and resettlement and a greater emphasis on the reduction of reoffending in community punishment orders (formerly community service orders). (NPS for England and Wales 2001: 2)

Given that these demands are being made at the same time as a fundamental structural reorganisation is taking place in the Probation Service, it remains to be seen whether these targets are realistic and achievable. Nonetheless, *A New Choreography* was itself optimistic:

> The early results from these new pilot programmes are encouraging. The research evidence only recently made available on aggression replacement training programme piloted in Wiltshire for example, achieved a difference of 14 per cent in one year reconviction rates, against a matched comparison group. The West Midlands sex offender programme has reduced child sexual offences by 7.4 per cent and overall offending by 22 per cent. (p. 19)

In the following sections, the 'What Works' principles which underpin the design, delivery and implementation of various programmes will be presented and followed by an account of some probation offending behaviour programmes which have already implemented and evaluated.

THE 'WHAT WORKS' PRINCIPLES

Drawing from previous research findings on treatment outcome literature, a number of scholars have identified a set of principles of effective intervention with offenders (see, for example, Andrews and Bonta 1994; Losel 1995; McGuire 1995, 2002; Vennard and Hedderman 1998; Day and Howells 2002). These principles not only influence the contemporary probation practice but also form the basis for crime-reduction strategy in the past few years. Furniss and Nutley (2000) stress that 'as part of its response to the government's modernisation programme, the Home Office and the Probation Service in England and Wales are committed to ensuring that by April 2003 all interventions for offenders are consistent with what are known as "what works" principles' (p. 23).

McGuire and Priestley (1995) were among the first in England to articulate guiding principles for more successful rehabilitative programmes. At the time they acknowledged that 'there is hardly any single, outstanding approach that is by itself guaranteed to work as a means of reducing recidivism' (p. 14). Since then, six principles of effective intervention have been identified and refined. They are:

- **Risk classification**: matching between offender risk level based on criminal history and other variables and level of supervision or degree of service intervention (McGuire and Priestley 1995). According to Vennard and Hedderman (1998), intensive programmes should be targeted at high-risk offenders which can be defined on an actuarial basis (see also Robinson's discussion of risk assessment in Chapter 7).

- **Criminogenic needs:** targeting the needs, problems and features of clients' lives that contribute to, or are supportive of, or related directly to offending (McGuire and Priestley 1995). Consistent with Andrew and Bonta's (1994) argument, Day and Howells emphasise that offender rehabilitation should focus on the dynamic risk factors (or criminogenic needs) rather than static factors. Some examples of criminogenic factors are pro-offending attitudes and beliefs, substance abuse, criminal associates and impulsivity whereas examples of non-criminogenic factors are self-esteem, anxiety, depression and psychological distress (Day and Howells 2002: 41). Similarly, drawing on several pieces of social research, nine key factors which influence re-offending among the prisoners have been identified by the Social Exclusion Unit (SEU) (2002). They are education, employment, drug and alcohol misuse, mental and physical health, attitudes and self-control, institution-alisation and life-skills, housing, financial support and debt, and family networks. These factors are not mutually exclusive, and each factor or a combination of them can have a significant impact on the likelihood of a prisoner re-offending. For instance, 'being in employment reduces the risk of re-offending by between a third and a half; having stable accommodation reduces the risk by a fifth' (SEU 2002: 2).
- **Responsivity:** matching learning styles between supervising officers and offenders (McGuire and Priestley 1995). The supervising officers' teaching styles should be responsive to offenders' learning style which may be affected by gender, ethnicity, socio-economic status and mental illness (Day and Howells 2002). In general, more active, participatory methods of working are more desirable than the loose, unstructured and didactic ones.
- **Community base:** locating offender behaviour programmes in the community yields more effective outcomes than those in institutions, seemingly because of their proximity to the home environments (McGuire and Priestley 1995).
- **Treatment modality:** applying a variety of models or approaches such as skills-oriented problem-solving, social skills training, cognitive-behavioural theory to design and implement intervention programmes in order to address attitudes, beliefs, values which support offending behaviour (McGuire and Priestley 1995; Vennard and Hedderman 1998).
- **Programme integrity:** ensuring that the stated aims of programmes are linked to the theories and methods being used, and that well-trained and supported staff deliver the programmes with adequate resources (Hollin 1995; McGuire and Priestley 1995). This pinpoints the importance of quality assurance to effective practice, which must be assessed by close monitoring and evaluation.

Importantly, Day and Howells (2002) add to these six principles the principle of professional discretion. This respects the practice wisdom and professional judgement of the programme staff, and acknowledges the limitations of simply applying static, invariant rules in diverse and sometimes volatile situations:

> [It] allows for professionals to make decisions on the basis of other character-istics and situations not covered by the other principles. It makes sense to build in scope for professional judgement into any rehabilitation system, rather than to rely on the administration of relatively static principles. For example, in working with a child sexual offender, who in other respects may not be identified as high priority for treatment (low risk, low need, low responsivity), a professional may have access to knowledge (e.g. the offender is entering high-risk situations such as babysitting) that would be a concern and indicate further intervention. (p. 43)

To summarise, the principles associated with effective interventions include effective risk management, targeting offending behaviour, addressing the specific factors linked with offenders' offending, relevance to offenders' learning style, promoting community reintegration, and maintaining quality and integrity of programme delivery (see Underdown 1998; Home Office 2001a). These can of course be built on and refined still further. A recent Home Office research study (Powis and Walmsley 2002), for example, concludes that the following factors should be considered by programme developers and deliverers work-ing with the Black and Asian offenders on probation in addition to:

- a good facilitator who is understanding of the needs of this client group and is of minority ethnic background;
- using external experts to develop and evaluate programmes and to act as mentors to participants;
- longer, more intensive programmes (although it has been noted elsewhere that the use of longer programmes may result in unequal treatment of Black and Asian offenders if referral to the programme is not based on an assessment of their criminogenic need); and
- effective targeting which recognises that only some Black or Asian offenders will need separate provision.

Source: Powis and Walmsley 2002: viii

WHAT WORKS: ACCREDITATION OF OFFENDING BEHAVIOUR PROGRAMMES

The 'What Works' principles not only guide the work of practitioners but also inform the Joint Prison/Probation Accreditation Panel in setting its criteria for appraising what makes an 'accredited' programme. The panel is an advisory,

Table 4.1   Eleven criteria for accreditation of programmes – an overview

---

1. A clear model of change backed by research evidence, i.e. the programme has a realistic evidence-based plan for creating change in offenders' future behaviour
2. Selection of offenders, i.e. the programme chooses participants who need to change and whose risk is likely to be reduced by the programme
3. Targeting dynamic risk factors, i.e. the programme chooses the areas of risk which need to be and can be reduced
4. Range of targets, i.e. chooses a range of risk areas to focus upon
5. Effective methods, i.e. uses those proven to work
6. Skills oriented, i.e. teaches skills for offence-free living
7. Sequencing, intensity and duration, i.e. timetables for maximum impact in reducing risk
8. Engagement and motivation, i.e. encourages a positive response
9. Continuity of programmes and services, i.e. coordinates them to maximise the effect of treatment and monitoring
10. Ongoing monitoring, i.e. checks the programme in action
11. Ongoing evaluation, i.e. checks and develops what works

Source: Home Office 2001b

non-departmental public body and consists of a Chair, appointed members who are independent experts such as academics and psychologists and nominated members who represent the Home Office, Prison Service, Probation Service and HMIP (Home Office 2001a). The main purpose of accreditation is making sure that programmes for offenders actually meet the demanding principles and thereby stand a chance of reducing re-offending. The offending behaviour programmes are expected to meet 11 criteria (set out in Table 4.1) before being accredited.

Five supporting manuals must be submitted for accreditation purposes:

- theory manual – describes the rationale for the programme and the model for change;
- programme manual – describes the detail such as aims, objectives, and clear links in each session of the programme;
- assessment and evaluation manual – contains all assessment and evaluation tools used in the programme, guidance on their administration and so on;
- management manual – details the selection, training and performance appraisal of staff, the selection of offenders in the programme, the ways offenders are assessed before, during and after the programme, the roles and responsibilities of managers and staff and so on;
- staff training manual – describe the curriculum and training materials for staff training courses, how staff competence will be assured, how competence will be assessed, and how performance will be evaluated.

Source: Home Office (2001a: 22)

With reference to each criterion, the panel assesses whether the programmes should be (a) accredited, (b) recognised/provisionally accredited, (c) not accredited/promising or not, accredited/no further review warranted, by using the scoring system (zero for criterion not met, one point for each partially met criterion and two points for each fully met criterion).

At the time of writing, various offending behaviour programmes for particular groups of offenders or offences such as sex offenders, drug offenders, drink–drive-related offenders, violent offenders, domestic violence offenders have been accredited or will be considered for accreditation (see Home Office 2002a). For example, two programmes, namely Reasoning and Rehabilitation Programme and Enhanced Thinking Skills Programme, previously accredited by the former General Accreditation for the Prison Service, were accredited for use in the community. Although these two programmes are different in many respects, both of them utilise a collection of methods drawn from the cognitive-behavioural approach to working with offenders. While the former is designed to build thinking or 'cognitive' skills in order to promote change among highly convicted offenders as well as those medium to high-risk offenders within 38 $2^1/_2$-hour sessions (over a period of 9 to 18 weeks), the latter, developed by the Prison Service, aims to change offenders' thinking and behaviour and to improve interpersonal problem-solving skills through structured exercises within $22^1/_2$-hour sessions (over a period of 4 to 10 weeks) (Home Office 2002a).

Other programmes such as Think First, Priestley One-to-one Offending Behaviour, Aggression Replacement Training (ART) Programme and Drink Impaired Drivers Programme were accredited and roll-out has begun, and two programmes for substance misusers, namely Addressing Substance-related Offending (ASRO) and Programme Reducing Individual Substance Misuse (PRISM) are currently recognised/provisionally accredited, according to the Home Office (2002a). Table 4.2 provides a brief description of these programmes.

Hollin and his colleagues (2002) have recently completed the first stage in a 3-year evaluation of the effectiveness of seven offending behaviour programmes which have been introduced in 13 Probation Service areas. By interviewing the probation managers and those delivering the programmes, they found that in general staff were enthusiastic and highly supportive of all seven, especially regarding problems in implementing the programmes such as inappropriate referrals of participants, high dropout rates of participants either before starting the programme or in the early stages, a lack of time and resources to ensure programme integrity, and insufficient levels of administrative support were common. However, the outcome and impact of the programmes on re-offending is not available in Hollin and his colleagues' study and therefore it is too early to say whether the 'What Works' Initiative has achieved its

Table 4.2 A brief description of some offending behaviour programmes

---

- Think First – This cognitive-behavioural programme mainly for medium- or medium-high-risk offenders, which has been designed by James McGuire, teaches problem-solving skills and applies these skills to offending behaviour within 22 2-hour sessions over 11 weeks (Home Office 2002a)
- Priestley One-to-one Offending Behaviour – This one-to-one programme with offenders, based on cognitive-behavioural principles, involves exercises to teach and improve offenders' social skills, problem-solving, empathy and so on within 20 1-hour sessions, delivered once a week (Home Office 2002b)
- Aggression Replacement Training (ART) Programme – This is an adapted version of a programme developed in the USA, and its sessions are 'multi-modal' which combines social skills training, self-control training and training in moral reasoning. It consists of 18 2-hour sessions (Home Office 2002b)
- Drink-impaired Drivers – This employs a combined cognitive-behavioural and educational approach to promote offenders' changes in their problem-solving skills, anti-social attitudes, and knowledge deficits such as lack of knowledge about alcohol and driving which may be associated with their drink–driving behaviour within 12 2-hour weekly sessions (Home Office 2002b)
- Addressing Substance-related Offending (ASRO) – Based on a bio-psychosocial developmental model, this is designed to address issues such as self-control, problem-solving, and maintenance of change among drug offenders within 20 2-hour sessions (Home Office 2002b)
- Programme Reducing Individual Substance Misuse (PRISM) – This is designed for one-to-one work with drug offenders within 20 1- to 2-hour sessions, based on cognitive-behavioural principles, to reduce the use of substances, to promote a healthier lifestyle, and to teach and improve social skills, and the attitudes towards drugs (Home Office 2002b)

---

targets and goals. It is expected that more programmes for working with domestic violence offenders, racially motivated offenders, sex offenders, and female offenders will be developed and accredited in the near future.

DOUBTS ON THE 'WHAT WORKS' INITIATIVE

In the eyes of policy-makers, and now many probation staff, the 'What Works' Initiative advances the claim that 'some things do work' and embodies evidence-based practice in work with offenders, in ways which will almost certainly result in a reduction of offending. Previous research evidence confirms that certain programmes do work when they are well-designed according to a set of effective principles, delivered to consistently high standards, and well-matched to the risks and needs of the offender (Home Office 1999b). Arguments continue about the ways in which programmes can be improved. At the What Works conference in October 2002, for example, James Bonta insisted upon the continuing importance of the supervisory relationship; if offenders do not like their supervisors they are unlikely to learn much from them[2] (see McNeill's Chapter 9 in this book). Intuitively, many probation officers know this. And while recognising the good intentions behind the Effective Practice Initiative, there are those who believe that its principles and criteria are inflexible and rigid, and may undermine professional autonomy and assessment in day-to-day practice with offenders.

Merrington and Stanley (2000) urged a more critical appraisal of the 'What Works' Strategy. They were cautious about its heavy reliance on reconviction data as an outcome measure of the offending behaviour programmes. Doubts have been cast on the accuracy of using this data on its own to measure the changes of offenders (see Mair, Lloyd and Hough 1997). Probation success (or otherwise) can be measured by using various outcome measurements such as rate of compliance, improvements in attitudes related to offending, and reduction in personal and social problems (Raynor 1996). So, there is a danger that the offending behaviour programmes will be deemed failures if reconviction rate is used as the sole indicator of outcome effectiveness. More recently Kemshall (2002) has criticised Chapman and Hough's (1998) narrow, technocratic construction of effective practice, believing that it 'reflected the contemporary preoccupation with evidence epitomised by Blair's statement that "what counts is what works", and neglected searching for evidence which might show that other interventions, not just those based on individualised, rational choice explanations of criminal behaviour, also worked' (p. 47).

As shown in Table 4.2, most of the offending behaviour programmes in one way or another are largely based on cognitive-behavioural approaches. Cognitive-behaviouralism indeed plays a central position within the government's 'What Works' campaign. Three psychological theories underpinning this approach are behaviourism, cognitive theory and social learning theory (Vennard, Sugg and Hedderman 1997, see also Vanstone 2000). Three important features and advantages of using the cognitive-behavioural approach to working with offenders are summarised by McGuire (2000: 13). First, the cognitive-behavioural approach is theory driven and is based on a logically coherent conceptual framework. Second, it is grounded in a considerable volume of empirical research. Third, large-scale reviews of the outcomes of work with offenders have lent significant credence to the view that repeated offending behaviour can be reduced by the application of methods based on the cognitive-behavioural approach. However, Merrington and Stanley (2000) comment that '[w]hilst the international evidence for the impact of cognitive-behavioural programmes is compelling, the published evidence in the UK that these programmes make a substantial impact on re-offending is

---

[2] I am grateful to Sarah Winwin Sein, a senior probation officer, who attended the conference, for this point.

not yet very strong' (p. 274). Also, cognitive-behaviourism assumes that every one is responsible for his or her behaviour, and knows the consequences of the behaviour, thereby putting all blame on the individual. In this respect, while acknowledging the value of teaching social skills, problem-solving skills and cognitive skills, Rex (2001) argues that '[f]or rehabilitative programmes to be effective, . . . there is at least an equally pressing need to pay attention to offenders' social environments, and the normative processes that support non-offending choices' (p. 67). Indeed, Drakeford and Vanstone (1996) and Crow (2001) recognise that promoting offenders' responsibilities for their offending behaviour is only one part of crime-reduction strategy while addressing the social contexts of people's lives and structural issues such as housing and unemployment are central to offender rehabilitation and should never be overlooked.

Finally, the absence of offender perspective research on the 'What Works' Initiative limits our understanding of what offenders make of the programmes they are being put through. A number of probation researchers such as Bailey and Ward (1992), Merrington (1995), Morgan (1995), Rex (1999) and Barry (2000) point out that the real voice of offenders has often been neglected and marginalised in the study of offending and in evaluating probation work, and have stressed the importance of participation by offenders. Allowing offenders to speak not only enables criminal justice personnel to understand the effect of a particular intervention but also recognises the rights of offenders as consumers to give feedback on the delivery and usefulness of the public service. Therefore, the voices of the offenders will be integrated into perspectives on probation and offending behaviour programmes.

SUMMARY OF KEY ISSUES

- This chapter discusses the beginnings of the 'What Works' Initiative in the late 1990s in England and Wales, and then examines various principles of effective intervention to working with offenders and looks at the features of some accredited offending behaviour programmes that have been proved to bring positive outcomes.
- The changes in the roles of treatment and rehabilitation in the criminal justice policy and thinking have been traced since 1960s. During the 1960s, offender rehabilitation was achieved by one-to-one casework counselling. However, the 'Nothing Works' pessimism marked the decline of the rehabilitative ideal, and a 'non-treatment paradigm' was proposed to guide probation practice (see Bottoms and McWilliams 1979). Despite this, rehabilitation was not completely dead in the 1980s and 1990s, and numerous research findings especially in North America and Canada show that 'some things do work' or certain approaches are best working with a

particular group of offenders. The 'What Works' Initiative began in England and Wales in late 1990s after realising the importance of shifting resources to action which will achieve results (Home Office 1999b) and a number of 'What Works' conferences being held.

- The new mission for the contemporary probation practice has become the 'What Works' movement (Raynor 2002).
- Based on a number of meta-analytic reviews, several principles of effective intervention have been identified, namely risk classification, meeting criminogenic needs, responsivity, community base, treatment modality, programme integrity and professional discretion (McGuire and Priestley 1995; Day and Howells 2002).
- The principles of effective supervision have also been translated as the criteria for accrediting offender behaviour programmes in England and Wales since the early 2000s. An accreditation panel was formed to assess whether programmes are well-designed, delivered and implemented based on 11 criteria.
- However, doubts have been cast on the usefulness of 'What Works' strategy in modernising probation practice, and the overemphasis on cognitive-behaviourism in working with offenders in the community and in prisons.

References

Alexander, R. (2000) *Counseling, Treatment, and Intervention Methods with Juvenile and Adult Offenders*. Belmont, CA: Wadsworth/Thomson Learning.

Andrews, D. A. and Bonta, J. (1994) *The Psychology of Criminal Conduct*. Cincinnati, OH: Anderson.

Bailey, R. and Ward, D. (1992) *Probation Supervision – Attitudes to Formalised Helping*. Belfast: Probation Board for Northern Ireland and Nottingham: Centre for Social Action, University of Nottingham.

Barry, M. (2000) 'The mentor/monitor debate in criminal justice: "What works" for offenders', *British Journal of Social Work*, 30, 575–595.

Bottoms, A. and McWilliams, W. (1979) 'A non-treatment paradigm for probation practice', *British Journal of Social Work*, 9, 159–202.

Chapman, T. and Hough, M. (1998) *Evidence-Based Practice: A Guide to Effective Practice*. London: Home Office.

Crow, I. (2001) *The Treatment and Rehabilitation of Offenders*. London: Sage.

Day, A. and Howells, K. (2002) 'Psychological treatments for rehabilitating offenders: Evidence-based practice comes of age', *Australian Psychologist*, 37, 39–47.

Dowden, C. and Andrews, D. A. (2000) 'Effective correctional treatment and violent reoffending: A meta analysis', *Canadian Journal of Criminology*, 42, 449–467.

Drakeford, M. and Vanstone, M. (eds) (1996) *Beyond Offending Behaviour*. Aldershot: Arena.

Folkard, M. S., Smith, D. E. and Smith, D. D. (1976) *IMPACT: Intensive Matched Probation and After-Care Treatment, Volume II – The Results of the Experiment* (Home Office Research Study No. 36). London: HMSO.

Furniss, J. and Nutley, S. (2000) 'Implementing what works with offenders – The Effective Practice Initiative', *Public Money and Management*, 20, 23–28.

Gendreau, P. (1996) 'The principles of effective intervention with offenders', in A. T. Harland (ed.) *Choosing Correctional Options that Work: Defining the Demand and Evaluating the Supply.* Thousand Oaks, CA: Sage.

Goldblatt, P. and Lewis, C. (eds) (1998) *Reducing Offending: An Assessment of Research Evidence on Ways of Dealing with Offending Behaviour* (Home Office Research Study No. 187). London: Home Office.

Hollin, C. R. (1995) 'The meaning and implications of "programme integrity"', in J. McGuire (ed.) *What Works: Reducing Reoffending – Guidelines from Research and Practice.* Chichester: Wiley.

Hollin, C., McGuire, J., Palmer, E., Bilby, C., Hatcher, R. and Holmes, A. (2002) *Introducing Pathfinder Programmes into the Probation Service* (Findings 177). London: Home Office.

Home Office (1999a) *The Correctional Policy Framework.* London: Home Office.

Home Office (1999b) *What Works: Reducing Re-offending: Evidence-based Practice.* London: Home Office.

Home Office (2001a) *What Works Towards Effective Practice – Second Report from the Joint Prison/Probation Accreditation Panel 2000–2001.* London: Home Office.

Home Office (2001b) *Crime Reduction: What Works: Accreditation – A Summary.* London: Home Office.
Available at: www.crimereduction.gov.uk/workingoffenders13.htm

Home Office (2002a) *Crime Reduction: Pathfinders: General Offending Behaviour Programmes.* London: Home Office.
Available at: www.crimereduction.gov.uk/workingoffenders3.htm

Home Office (2002b) *Probation Offending Behaviour Programmes – Effective Practice Guide* (Home Office Development and Practice Report No. 2). London: Home Office.

Hudson, B. A. (1996) *Understanding Justice: An Introduction to Ideas, Perspectives and Controversies in Modern Penal Theory*, Buckingham: Open University Press.

Hudson, C., McMahon, G., Hayward, G., Roberts, C. and Fernandez, R. (2001) *Interim Report of the Evaluation of the Basic Skills Pathfinder Projects – Executive Summary.* London: Home Office.
Available at: www.homeoffice.gov.uk/rds/pdfs/pathfinder.doc

Kemshall, H. (2002) 'Effective practice in probation: An example of "advanced liberal" responsibilisation?', *Howard Journal of Criminal Justice*, 41, 41–58.

Lewis, C. S. (1971) 'The humanitarian theory of punishment', in L. Radzinowicz and M. Wolfgang (eds) *Crime and Punishment* (Volume 2). New York: Basic Books.

Lipton, D., Martinson, R. and Wilks, J. (1975) *The Effectiveness of Correctional Treatment.* New York: Praeger.

Lloyd, C., Mair, G. and Hough, M. (1994) *Explaining Reconviction Rates: A Critical Analysis* (Home Office Research Study No. 136). London: Home Office.

Losel, F. (1995) 'Increasing consensus in the evaluation of offender rehabilitation? Lessons from recent research syntheses', *Psychology, Crime and Law*, 2, 19–39.

McGuire, J. (ed.) (1995) *What Works: Reducing Reoffending – Guidelines from Research and Practice*. Chichester: Wiley.

McGuire, J. (2000) *Cognitive-behavioural Approaches: An Introduction to Theory and Research*. London: Home Office.

McGuire, J. (2002) 'Integrating findings from research reviews', in J. McGuire (ed.) *Offender Rehabilitation and Treatment: Effective Programmes and Policies to Reduce Re-offending*. Chichester: Wiley.

McGuire, J. and Priestley, P. (1995) 'Reviewing "what works": Past, present and future', in J. McGuire (ed.) *What Works: Reducing Reoffending – Guidelines from Research and Practice*. Chichester: Wiley.

Mair, G., Lloyd, C. and Hough, M. (1997) 'The limitations of reconviction rates', in G. Mair (ed.) *Evaluating the Effectiveness of Community Penalties*. Aldershot: Avebury.

Martinson, R. (1974) 'What works? Questions and answers about prison reforms', *Public Interest*, 35, 22–54.

Maruna, S. (2001) *Making Good: How Ex-convicts Reform and Rebuild their Lives*. Washington, DC: American Psychological Association.

May, T. and Vass, A. A. (eds) (1996) *Working with Offenders: Issues, Contexts and Outcomes*. London: Sage.

Merrington, S. (1995) *Offenders on Probation – A Qualitative Study of Offenders' Views on their Probation Orders*. Cambridge: Cambridgeshire Probation Service.

Merrington, S. and Hine, J. (2001) *A Handbook for Evaluating Probation Work with Offenders*. London: Home Office.

Merrington, S. and Stanley, S. (2000) 'Doubts about the what works initiative', *Probation Journal*, 47, 272–275.

Morgan, S. (1995) *Hearing Offenders: Uncredited Voices in Probation Research and Evaluation*. Manchester: Department of Applied Community Studies, The Manchester Metropolitan University.

National Probation Directorate (2001) *Community Punishment Pathfinders: Interim Evaluation Report – Executive Summary*. London: Home Office.

National Probation Service (NPS) for England and Wales (2001) *A New Choreography: An Integrated Strategy for the National Probation Service for England and Wales – Strategic Framework 2001–2004*. London: Home Office.

Powis, B. and Walmsley, R. K. (2002) *Programmes for Black and Asian Offenders on Probation: Lessons for Developing Practice* (Home Office Research Study No. 250). London: Home Office.

Raynor, P. (1996) 'Evaluating probation: The rehabilitation of effectiveness', in T. May and A. A. Vass (eds) *Working with Offenders: Issues, Contexts and Outcomes*. London: Sage.

Raynor, P. (2002) 'Community penalties: Probation, punishment and 'what works', in M. Maguire, R. Morgan and R. Reiner (eds) *The Oxford Handbook of Criminology* (3rd edn). Oxford: Oxford University Press.

Raynor, P., Smith, D. and Vanstone, M. (1994) *Effective Probation Practice*. London: Macmillan.

Raynor, P. and Vanstone, M. (1996) 'Reasoning and rehabilitation in Britain: Results of the STOP programme', *International Journal of Offender Therapy and Comparative Criminology*, 40, 272–284.

Raynor, P. and Vanstone, M. (2001) ' "Straight Thinking On Probation": Evidence-based practice and the culture of curiosity', in G. A. Bernfeld, D. P. Farrington and A. W. Leschied (eds) *Offender Rehabilitation in Practice: Implementing and Evaluating Effective Programs*. Chichester: Wiley.

Raynor, P. and Vanstone, M. (2002) *Understanding Community Penalties: Probation, Policy and Social Change*. Buckingham: Open University Press.

Rex, S. (1999) 'Desistance from offending: Experiences of probation', *Howard Journal of Criminal Justice*, 38, 366–383.

Rex, S. (2001) 'Beyond cognitive-behaviouralism? Reflections on the effectiveness literature', in A. Bottoms, L. Gelsthorpe and S. Rex (eds) *Community Penalties: Change and Challenges*. Cullompton: Willan.

Rosenthal, R. (1991) *Meta-analytic Procedures for Social Research*. Newbury Park, CA: Sage.

Ross, R. R. and Fabiano, E. A. (1985) *Time to Think: A Cognitive Model of Delinquency Prevention and Offender Rehabilitation*. Johnson City, TN: Institute of Social Sciences and Art.

Rowson, B. and McGuire, J. (eds) (1996) *What Works: Making it Happen*. Manchester: What Works Group.

Social Exclusion Unit (SEU) (2002) *Reducing Re-offending by Ex-prisoners*. London: SEU.
Available at: www.cabinet-office.gov.uk/seu/reduce_reoff/reoffending.htm

Underdown, A. (1998) *Strategies for Effective Offender Supervision: Report of the HMIP What Works Project*. London: Home Office.

Vanstone, M. (2000) 'Cognitive-behavioural work with offenders in the UK: A history of influential endeavour', *Howard Journal of Criminal Justice*, 39, 171–183.

Vennard, J. and Hedderman, C. (1998) 'Effective interventions with offenders', in P. Goldblatt and C. Lewis (eds) *Reducing Offending; An Assessment of Research Evidence on Ways of Dealing with Offending Behaviour* (Home Office Research Study No. 187). London: Home Office.

Vennard, J., Sugg, D. and Hedderman, C. (1997) 'The use of cognitive-behavioural approaches with offenders: Messages from the research', in C. Hedderman, D. Sugg and J. Vennard (eds) *Changing Offenders' Attitudes and Behaviour: What Works?* (Home Office Research Study No. 171). London: Home Office.

von Hirsch, A. (1998) 'Rehabilitation', in A. von Hirsch and A. Ashworth (eds) *Principled Sentencing: Readings on Theory and Policy* (2nd edn). Oxford: Hart Publishing.

Williams, B. (1996) *Counselling in Criminal Justice*. Buckingham: Open University Press.

5

RESEARCH IN PROBATION: FROM 'NOTHING WORKS' TO 'WHAT WORKS'

Peter Raynor

INTRODUCTION

People who write today about probation research do so in the knowledge that research can have, and sometimes demonstrably does have, a direct influence on policy and practice. This is a fairly new relationship, which has emerged gradually over a period of about eight years; for the previous nearly 90 years of probation's statutory history in England and Wales, and most of its long previous voluntary history (Vanstone 2001), the relationship was tenuous at best, sometimes antagonistic and sometimes virtually non-existent. This chapter is an attempt to explore these changes from the perspective of a researcher who has been both involved in and surprised by them. Inevitably it takes a provisional view, and some of its conclusions and suggestions may be proved completely wrong over time. However, some attempt to take stock is necessary and timely as the new National Probation Service for England and Wales continues to discover the implications of its courageous commitment to evidence-based practice. Will this new world turn out even approximately to resemble the fragmentary and tentative maps drawn by its early explorers, or is the expedition doomed to sail off the edge of a world which turns out to be flat after all?

This chapter takes a relatively optimistic view which is not shared by some very well-qualified commentators (see, for example, Mair 2000) but also attempts to explore some of the new dilemmas and problems inherent in the emerging closer relationship between research, policy and practice – for example, how far the commitment to evidence-based practice extends beyond identifying successes to its logical but more difficult counterpart, learning

from mistakes. First, however, the recent changes need to be put in the context of the nature and history of research into Probation Service activities,
particularly since for most of the professional lifetime of the managers and
civil servants who run today's Probation Service, research seemed to be telling
them that their activities would have no useful effects.

RETHINKING 'NOTHING WORKS'

Recent writings on probation and criminal justice research, including officially
published accounts summarising the evidence base for new policies (such as
Chapman and Hough 1998, Goldblatt and Lewis 1998, McGuire 2000), trace
an evolutionary path from uncritical optimism about the beneficial effects of
probation (broadly characteristic of the 1950s and 1960s), through extreme
scepticism fuelled by highly negative research findings (a dominant view, at
least in Britain, from the mid-1970s to the early 1990s), to a more realistic
and empirically informed 'What Works' movement which recognises that
evidence-based practice has a better chance of reducing re-offending by people
under various forms of supervision by criminal justice agencies. This evolution
can be traced through the writings of authoritative figures in each stage who
have tried to sum up where research at the time was pointing. The following
quotations encapsulate the views, in turn, of Leon Radzinowicz, founder of
the Cambridge Institute of Criminology and one of the pioneers of probation
research in Britain; John Croft, former director of the Home Office Research
Unit; and finally James McGuire, one of the more recent exponents of 'What
Works'. The direction of development should be clear:

> If I were asked what was the most significant contribution made by this country
> to the new penological theory and practice which struck root in the twentieth
> century – the measure which would endure, while so many of the other methods
> of treatment might well fall into limbo, or be altered beyond recognition – my
> answer would be probation. (Radzinowicz 1958: x)

> Penal treatments, as we significantly describe them, do not have any re-
> formative effect. . . . The dilemma is that a considerable investment has been
> made in various measures and services. . . . Are these services simply to be
> abandoned on the basis of the accumulated research evidence? Will this challenge
> evoke a response . . . by the invention of new approaches and methods? (Croft
> 1978: 4).

> There is now a substantial body of research findings that cut across the 'soft–
> hard' polarity in the criminal justice debate. This evidence demonstrates the
> possibility of reducing offence behaviour not by punishing offenders, nor by being
> indulgent towards them, but by taking constructive action of specific kinds.
> (McGuire 1995: xii)

These quotations, taken together, encapsulate the dominant trends in the history of probation research (summarised in Raynor 2002) and reflect the changing place of probation in penal policy: when few welfare measures were evaluated and good intentions were seen as a guarantee of good results, the climate favoured investment in probation as a way of changing offenders, and the first signs of concern about the effectiveness of social work in America (Powers and Witmer 1951; Meyer, Borgatta and Jones 1965) left the world of probation largely unscathed, in spite of US studies which showed that offenders supervised in small caseloads did no better than those supervised in large caseloads (Adams 1967).

The more sceptical research results and, particularly, research reviews of the 1970s were themselves a reaction to the less than rigorous design of some of the earlier studies (for example, Radzinowicz's 1958 study from which one of my quotations is taken lacked any adequate comparison group to guard against the possibility that similar offenders might do just as well, if not better, if not on probation). Research reviews such as Lipton, Martinson and Wilks (1975) and Brody (1976) aimed to include only studies which met acceptable standards of methodological rigour, but these standards concerned issues such as controlled or comparative design and adequate quantitative measurement of outcomes. Many research studies of that period did not exercise comparable control over inputs, either leaving it to practitioners to determine the detail of the service provided, or attempting to standardise by rather inadequate methods like ensuring that all the practitioners held a qualification. The problem is that if the services provided are not more closely specified they will vary, and the good effects of some may be cancelled out by the bad effects of others, leading to a finding of no overall benefit. The *IMPACT* study of the early 1970s (Folkard, Smith and Smith 1976) suffered from this problem: probationers in the experimental group were assigned to lower caseloads and received more attention, but the nature of the attention was left to the probation officers and consisted largely of more of what they would usually do. This kind of design problem probably contributed to the negative result of a number of the studies which helped to build the 'Nothing Works' consensus, and once the expectation that nothing would work was firmly established studies which contradicted this became less visible. For example, Lipton *et al.*'s actual findings were less consistently negative than the impression given by Martinson's (1974) journalistic summary, and in Britain two Home Office studies (Sinclair 1971 on probation hostels, and Shaw 1974 on prison welfare) produced moderately positive results which, if they emerged now, would be seen as significant contributions to the 'What Works' literature. However, in the context of the 1970s they were largely ignored.

INFLUENCING SYSTEMS INSTEAD OF PEOPLE

What emerged instead during the 1980s was a remarkable and largely constructive alliance between empirical scepticism and political pragmatism. Social work with offenders (of which probation was still seen as the major part) reacted to the deflation of some of its therapeutic ambitions by developing a new mission, the promotion of 'alternatives to custody'. Governments of the 1980s, dedicated to the reduction of unnecessary public expenditure, needed alternatives to costly residential and custodial disposals. If we could not influence offenders, we could at least try to influence the decisions made about them and the forms of punishment or control to which they were subjected. The research which underpinned this approach emerged originally from the juvenile justice system (for example, Thorpe *et al.* 1980) and suggested that over-optimism on the part of social workers about the changes they could produce in offenders could actually be counterproductive, drawing children further up the sentencing tariff without benefiting them, and leading to a situation in which most of the (then) growing number of custodial sentences on young offenders were passed because social workers recommended them. In the light of this kind of research an alternative practice of 'system management' and diversion was developed which aimed to ensure the least damaging interventions so as not to interrupt the presumed natural maturational processes that would lead to 'growing out of crime' (Rutherford 1986). However incomplete a model this may have been in the light of later studies of the variety of ways in which young people start and stop offending (see, for example, Graham and Bowling 1995), it represented a new focus for research and practice on the systems which dealt with offenders and the processes to which criminal justice agencies subjected them, and it emphasised a new kind of goal for practitioners in these systems.

The underpinning research was quantitative, but also informed by a theoretical model of how such systems operated which allowed researchers to make sense of the data they collected: figures represented not just outcomes but also indicators that systems were operating in particular ways. A typical example was that when the Home Office set up evaluative research on the new adult sentencing option of the Community Service Order (which required offenders to make indirect reparation for offences by undertaking unpaid work for the community, and was not designed to have a 'treatment' effect on them) they were primarily interested in whether such orders were being made instead of prison sentences, and the research collected data on a number of indicators of diversion from custody (Pease, Billingham and Earnshaw 1977). Other probation research of this period also looked for information about diversion rather than about effects on offenders, or sometimes found it difficult to get any other information: for example, Mair's (1988) study of day centres, which intended to ascertain re-offending rates, found that such information was not collected because the centres were seen primarily as alternatives to custody.

This combination of system-based research and diversion-based policy served the Probation Service quite well until the early 1990s, when an unpopular Conservative government tried to restore its electoral fortunes with a lurch into populist law-and-order rhetoric. Instead of full implementation of the 1991 Criminal Justice Act (which was intended to reduce custodial punishment and, for a few months, did so very successfully) policy shifted by 1993 to the idea that 'prison works' (starting a rise in prison numbers that at the time of writing is still continuing). The Probation Service, threatened with disappearance through amalgamation with the much larger Prison Service and under fire for supposedly lax enforcement of community sentences, needed a new rationale which emphasised its contribution to reducing crime and protecting the public. It found this in the emerging messages from a new body of research on work with offenders which aimed to document and measure inputs as well as outcomes, with a view to finding out 'what works'.

THE RESEARCH BEHIND 'WHAT WORKS'

There were three main sources for research evidence to underpin the new optimism, and in a short chapter only the briefest summaries can be given: more detailed accounts have been provided in Home Office publications issued to support the Probation Service's development strategy (Chapman and Hough 1998; McGuire 2000), and in Raynor and Vanstone (2002). Basically those studies which have influenced developments in the UK, and in some cases throughout the English-speaking world, fall into three groups, all of which have produced some significant outputs during the late 1980s and 1990s.

The first group of these studies comprises the work of psychological criminologists, many of them Canadian, who have emphasised the role of social learning and of thinking or cognition in the development and maintenance of offending. A feature of the environment in which this work has developed is that a number of key individuals have combined significant academic or research contributions with experience as practitioners within the criminal justice system, in a way which has always proved difficult in Britain. A clear statement of a social learning approach to offending is provided by, among others, Andrews and Bonta's textbook *The Psychology of Criminal Conduct* (1998), which sets out an integrated theory of offending. This connects social disadvantage, personality traits, thinking styles and social strategies into a model of how offending occurs and continues. This kind of model also suggests a process of intervention based on trying to change risk factors which are accessible and likely to make a difference: for example, habits of thinking and patterns of behaviour which can be altered to bring about better results for the individual. A particularly important development was the idea of a 'programme' which put together a series of planned and sequential learning opportunities into a cumulative sequence, covering an appropriate curriculum of skills and allowing plenty of opportunity to reinforce learning through structured practice. Robert Ross, for example, after carrying out research which identified a focus on thinking as a common feature of many successful interventions with offenders (Ross and Fabiano 1985), developed a programme called 'Reasoning and Rehabilitation' (R & R) which systematically adopted a cognitive-behavioural focus (Ross, Fabiano and Ross 1986) and was to exercise a widespread influence on work with offenders both in prisons and in the community.

The second major strand of work which helped to revive rehabilitation as a feasible goal in criminal justice was a series of research reviews which tried to pull together the findings of a substantial body of research in order to draw out general lessons about what approaches were likely to be effective. Some of these were carried out at the request of governments and were traditional narrative reviews which summarised a number of studies and pointed to shared or important findings: for example, McIvor (1990) in Scotland and McLaren (1992) in New Zealand. In general, the narrative research reviews of this period found more studies with positive outcomes than had been available to earlier reviewers such as Lipton *et al.* (1975).

But in addition to this traditional style of review, researchers and practitioners were also beginning to benefit from the new statistical technique of meta-analysis which combines the results from a number of studies by coding them to a common framework and applying a common measure of 'effect size', i.e. the extent to which outcomes for 'treated' groups differ from those for control groups or (in some studies) matched comparison groups. These methods have been criticised (for example, by Mair 1995) and are not perfect: coding a range of rather different studies to a common framework can introduce distortions, and since not all studies record the same variables, some findings may in reality be based on fairly small numbers because few studies have looked at the particular variables concerned. Equally, the evidence base for the meta-analysis will reflect the subjects available for the original research, and we need to avoid over-confidence in drawing conclusions about adults from meta-analyses in which most of the studies have involved juveniles, or conclusions about female or ethnic minority populations from groups of studies which are mainly about white males.

It is clear, however, that meta-analysis has increased our capacity to draw general conclusions by aggregating findings from a number of smaller studies, some of which might carry little weight on their own. Two major meta-analyses in particular have had a large influence on our current understanding of effective practice with offenders, one carried out by Andrews and his colleagues in Canada (Andrews *et al.* 1990) and one by Lipsey in the United States (Lipsey 1992). Others (such as Izzo and Ross 1990) have also made significant contributions, while some researchers have begun to address the problem of groups which are under-represented in the research (for example, Dowden and Andrews 1999).

The third strand of research which prepared the way for the 'What Works' movement was a small group of studies in Britain which provided reasonably convincing evidence for reductions in reconviction among fairly high-risk probationers who had, as part of their probation orders, participated in structured programmes of various kinds designed to address their offending. Such studies were a rarity in Britain after a decade of discouragement, but a few researchers had not completely accepted the 'Nothing Works' agenda and had the opportunity to carry out evaluative studies with local probation services. Examples of this were two studies published in the late 1980s which showed positive results. One, carried out in South Wales (Raynor 1988), showed a group of young adult male probationers achieving a reconviction rate some 13 per cent below comparable offenders sentenced to custody, and another, carried out in Hereford and Worcester (Roberts 1989), also showed substantial reductions both in the numbers reconvicted and in the frequency of reconvictions among those who continued to offend. Also in the late 1980s the first comparative evaluation of the R & R programme (Ross, Fabiano and Ewles 1988) appeared from Canada, which showed particularly encouraging results. Taken together, these three strands of research carried an encouraging message: far from nothing working, it appeared that appropriate forms of supervision were capable of delivering reductions in offending of between 10 per cent and 20 per cent, or even more in some cases. Conversely, the wrong kind of supervision could do harm.

APPLYING THE LESSONS OF RESEARCH

The first fully evaluated attempt in England and Wales to apply these principles to a programme for offenders supervised by the Probation Service was started in the (then) Mid Glamorgan Probation Service in South Wales in 1990. It was known as Straight Thinking On Probation (STOP), a version of Ross's R & R programme, and was subject from the beginning to a comprehensive evaluation study. The study's findings have been widely discussed in Britain, largely because of the shortage of other comparable studies at the time, and the results have often been quoted as lending support to cognitive-behavioural methods of supervision; their impact may even appear disproportionate for what are in reality fairly modest outcomes from a local study carried out with small numbers (59 programme completers, and 655 offenders altogether including comparison groups) and little funding. (For a full account of the findings, readers should refer to Raynor and Vanstone 1996, 1997; Raynor 1998a.) Overall, a fair summary of the findings of the STOP evaluation is that there was some evidence of fairly short-term reductions in offending (35 per cent of programme completers reconvicted in a year, compared to a predicted rate of 42 per cent; in contrast, a custodially sentenced comparison group with the same predicted reconviction rate showed 49 per cent reconvicted within a year of release). There were also more persistent reductions in more serious offending among those who completed the programme. These were associated with reported changes in attitudes, thinking and behaviour consistent with the rationale of a cognitive-behavioural programme. On the whole, STOP appeared to offer a more effective and constructive sentencing option than other likely sentences for this group of relatively serious and persistent offenders. However, the findings also pointed to a need to reinforce what was learned during the programme by appropriate follow-up during the remainder of the period of supervision.

This and other local experiments proceeded hand in hand with policy developments, led largely by the late Graham Smith in his role as Chief Probation Inspector, which were moving the Probation Service in the direction of trying to deliver evidence-based effective practice. An early step was a survey of how far local probation areas were using the new information about effective practice which was becoming available. A research study was set up involving a detailed survey of probation areas by Andrew Underdown, a senior probation manager who was already closely involved in issues around effective practice. The results, eventually published in 1998 (Underdown 1998), were a shock: of the 267 programmes which probation areas claimed they were running based on effective practice principles, only four (one of which was not actually included in the responses to the initial survey) could show actual evidence of positive effects based on methodologically credible evaluation. One of these was the Mid Glamorgan STOP programme; the others were in London, where John Wilkinson played an important role in programme evaluation (Wilkinson 1997, 1998).

These very poor results pointed to the need for a centrally managed initiative to introduce more effective forms of supervision, and the election in 1997 of a new government committed to evidence-based public policy created a climate in which political support could be gained for what eventually became the 'What Works' initiative. Promising programmes were identified for piloting and evaluation as 'Pathfinder' programmes, with support in due course from the government's Crime Reduction Programme, and the ambitious process of rolling out an evidence-based supervision model across the whole Probation Service began. Nobody would pretend that this has been an easy or painless process, and the need to study implementation as an important contributor to effectiveness is discussed further below; however, the process does seem to be bringing about substantial change, and few would argue that the status quo was a realistic option. Evaluations of the Pathfinders are incomplete at the time of writing, but some encouraging interim findings are beginning to emerge (for example, Hatcher and McGuire 2001).

Outcome-based evaluative research has been given huge encouragement by the crime-reduction programme and the associated Probation Pathfinders, and at the time of writing the Home Office has received and is soon likely to publish substantial reports on the resettlement of prisoners, on cognitive-behavioural general offending programmes, on new forms of community punishment and on provision to help probationers to acquire basic skills such as literacy and numeracy. Typically these make substantial use of rigorously quantitative approaches, with measurement of outcomes and relevant com-parisons, and also include more qualitative material drawn from interviews and an organisational focus on the process of implementation (which often presented a number of difficulties). Current 'what works' research is not the simplistic enterprise caricatured by critics such as Gorman (2001): indeed, the fact that any research which uses numbers risks being dismissed as positivist 'bean-counting' seems largely to be an unfortunate consequence of a British system of social science education which has trained sizeable numbers of people to undertake a critical deconstruction of anything but a measurement of nothing.

QUESTIONS FOR THE FUTURE PROBATION RESEARCH AGENDA

This seems an opportune point at which to consider some of the gaps in current probation research which future studies might usefully address. These suggestions are not in any particular priority order, but some are concerned with implementation and policy and others are concerned with understanding basic social processes with which probation services must work. I start with some examples of the latter.

First, it would be helpful to be able to draw on a wider range of research on recidivism and desistance. Probation services presumably try to reduce the former and promote the latter, but we know more about how often they happen, and to whom, than we know about the actual processes involved. Two recent attempts to get to grips with these areas (Zamble and Quinsey 1997; Maruna 2001) have begun to show how useful they might prove to be. However, there has been little work so far which tries to bring together what we know about desistance with the messages of the 'What Works' research: we do not often connect our studies of what practitioners can effectively do with an understanding of the offender's own experience of the process. Two recent exceptions (Rex 1997; Farrall 2002) have begun to make these connections by comparing offenders' experience of supervision with officers' views and accounts. This kind of qualitative study adds depth and texture to our understanding of the impact of supervision, but the supervision experienced by their subjects was simply what was available at the time in the study areas rather than a product of more recent attempts to apply new knowledge. Farrall's research at least includes the salutary reminder that most of the life-changes that probationers thought were important had little to do with the activities of their supervisors.

These activities themselves could usefully be the subject of a slightly different kind of research scrutiny in addition to that which they currently receive as components of effective programmes. A number of researchers have begun to point out that programmes are only part of a process of supervision which also draws on the personal and professional skills of individual supervisors or 'case managers': Rod Morgan, who moved from a distinguished career in criminological research to the post of Chief Inspector of Probation, suggested in his first annual report that 'programme fetishism' was diverting attention from other important aspects of the supervision process, without which programmes would be less effective (Her Majesty's Inspectorate of Probation (HMIP) 2002). Future research in this territory could build on the work of Trotter (1993, 2000) who showed some years ago that probation officers who showed a higher level of pro-social modelling in their supervision, and also consciously reinforced pro-social attitudes and behaviour, had a more positive impact on their probationers' risk of reconviction than officers who were poor models or colluded with anti-social attitudes. This work has been picked up in Britain particularly by Susan Rex and her colleagues in Cambridge (Rex and Matravers 1998) who have applied it to the development and evaluation of a model of Community Punishment (formerly Community Service) which is intended to influence offenders' behaviour and attitudes.

Other resources for thinking about the effective use and development of supervisors' personal skills can be found in the substantial literature (of admittedly varied quality) on effective helping which researchers have built up in the fields of social work, counselling and psychotherapy, going right back to the pioneering work of psychologists in the 1960s (see, for example, Truax and Carkhuff 1967). Applying this kind of research to probation requires some care (for example, what makes a good counsellor may not be exactly the same as what makes a good probation officer, given the relatively poor impact of counselling techniques on re-offending – see McLaren 1992) but the qualities of empathy, concern and genuineness which it identifies are among those consistently highly valued by probationers in consumer studies (for example, Bailey and Ward 1992). The social work literature also contains some useful ideas about structuring the supervision process (for example, Reid and Epstein

1972) and research on their application in settings which include probation work (Goldberg, Gibbons and Sinclair 1985). Such material used to form part of the curriculum for trainee probation officers until the social work heritage came to be seen as an embarrassment rather than an asset. However, the search for effective practice cannot afford to ignore relevant research just because it goes under a currently disparaged label. Another obstacle to research on individual skills and qualities might be staff resistance, but the contribution of individual staff skills to effective practice is likely to be so substantial that its importance should not be overlooked.

Moving on from these fundamental issues to questions of implementation and policy, research so far has told us more about what ways of working might be effective than it has about how to ensure that they are actually used, either at the level of individual case management or at the level of the organisations as a whole. The praiseworthy ambition to roll out effective programmes as widely and as fast as possible is certainly producing experience of implementation problems and of rapid problem-solving, but as a subject of systematic research it has lagged behind the development of effective methods. The research literature is now beginning to engage with these questions of implementation (Gendreau, Goggin and Smith 1999, Bernfeld, Farrington and Leschied 2001; Porporino 2002) but the volume of material is small so far. For example, we need a better understanding of what happens when initiatives which originally grew from enthusiastic local experiment become parts of a directively managed national programme.

At the level of individual case management there are plans for some Home Office-led research to identify good-practice models, and again it is to be hoped that good material in the social work literature (such as Reid and Epstein 1972; Goldberg and Warburton 1979) will not be overlooked in this process. When probation programmes were first developed in Britain they were seen as additions to the normal processes of supervision rather than being in themselves the whole supervision 'package', but some probation managers seem currently to talk as if there is little to the case management process beyond assessment, assignment to the appropriate programme and enforcement of attendance. Some available evidence points in a rather different direction: some very high programme-completion rates are reported where programme attendance is supported by close contact with probation officers in the case management role (for example, Raynor and Miles 2001). Recent research on Home Office pilot projects for the resettlement of short-term prisoners (Lewis *et al.* 2002) suggests that the more effective projects were those which combined programmes intended to influence thinking and motivation with individual work on problems of access to resources and opportunities. Such problems would have been the typical focus of social work with this target group in an earlier era of probation practice. Clearly much more work is needed on issues around implementation and case management, if only to throw light on the widely varying degrees of success enjoyed by different probation areas in implementing the new programmes (HMIP 2002).

Other issues which call particularly clearly for more research attention include the development of appropriate methods of work with offenders whose risk of re-offending is so high that they lie outside current guidelines for admission to programmes. Some of these offenders will fall within the target group of 'prolific offender' initiatives based on very frequent supervisory contact and close collaboration with the police service (such as the work in Staffordshire described by Walton 2001), and more piloting and research is planned. There may be a group of offenders who combine high levels of risk with low levels of (or recognition of) the kinds of needs which might be addressed in programmes within the time boundaries of a community rehabilitation order. Appropriate forms of supervision for such offenders will need to be developed, although at the moment the delay in implementing national arrangements for risk/needs assessment will make such offenders harder to identify. Other modes of supervision which can be applied with or without programmes and need more research include hostels (now the focus of a new evaluated Pathfinder project) and electronic tagging (the focus of a number of Home Office evaluations including Mair and Nee (1990) and Mortimer (2001), but not yet assessed in the form which has been most successful in some other countries, as an adjunct to more personal forms of supervision).

Other new research agendas are being created by the new policy interest in the resettlement of prisoners, particularly short-sentence adult prisoners who are often persistent offenders with a high risk of reconviction (Maguire *et al.* 2000; Home Office 2001) but have received, since the mid-1980s, little or no supervision or assistance on release. This group has been the focus of one set of evaluated 'pathfinder' projects (Lewis *et al.* 2002) and new projects are being launched at the time of writing. Evaluation of the projects has required attention not simply to prisoners' thinking, beliefs and attitudes but also to their social exclusion and their access to basic resources such as accommodation. The clear overlap between criminal justice concerns and social policy issues, once denied by Conservative politicians who insisted there was no connection between unemployment and crime, has been made explicit by a Social Exclusion Unit report on the resettlement of prisoners (Social Exclusion Unit 2002). In this context, we can expect at least some probation research to be informed by a broader range of social policy concerns.

Some similar issues are beginning to emerge in other areas of probation research: for example, a current survey of minority ethnic offenders on probation is having to engage with experiences of social exclusion and limited opportunity rooted in the wider social experience of minority groups in Britain. In these and other ways the probation research agenda is broadening and becoming concerned with a wider range of social issues, without abandoning its recent and productive focus on 'what works'. The next few years are likely to see a renewed focus on how to mobilise community resources to support the resettlement process, and on how to promote new community sentences in the Courts. The recent White Paper *Justice for All* (Home Office 2002), together with continued behind-the-scenes official concern about how to control the rising prison population, point to a new era of 'alternatives to custody', albeit wrapped in a new rhetoric of 'custody minus' and 'custody plus'. In this context we may begin to see a new synthesis of 'diversion' research and 'what works' research, and an approach to evaluation which will be broad enough to engage with a more community-based vision of justice as well as specific enough to measure the impacts of policy and practice changes. At least we might see some move away from the current tendency to make more and more first offenders subject to Community Rehabilitation Orders when not only diversion theory but also long-established outcome research indicates that this is likely to be damaging (Walker, Farrington and Tucker 1981; Raynor 1998b).

This relatively optimistic vision of the future depends, of course, on continued official commitment to evidence-based policy and practice, and here a note of caution must be sounded. At the beginning of this chapter I pointed out that research is only one influence on policy, and seldom the most important. Future policies may be *informed* by research, but they will be *shaped* by politics and by a political perception of public sentiment. A high-profile case, a newspaper campaign or a focus group will sometimes matter more than years of painstaking research. Research is, however, now a serious influence alongside these others: one sign of this is the appointment of senior university-based criminologists to head the Home Office's Research, Development and Statistics Directorate and HMIP. Another sign is that, at least in the probation field, new projects and new initiatives are now routinely accompanied by the funding of an evaluation study, often undertaken by researchers external to the Home Office. The next two or three years will produce a mass of information on the new probation projects rolled out as part of the 'What Works' initiative, including eventually reconviction studies, and it is likely that some of them will turn out to have been more successful than others. This will be the next major test for evidence-based probation: will projects and programmes which by then will represent significant investment, and will have acquired their own staff and supporters, be discontinued or changed in the light of research findings? This echoes the quarter-century-old question from John Croft (1978) which I quoted near the beginning of this chapter. This time can we be a little more optimistic about the answer?

SUMMARY OF KEY ISSUES

- Over the last eight or nine years we have seen the development in Britain of a new and more optimistic approach to the rehabilitation of offenders, based largely on new research findings.
- The shifts which have taken place in the research consensus, from over-optimism via overstated pessimism to the realistic promotion of effectiveness, reflect gradual improvements in research methods.
- Early optimistic studies tended to lack adequate comparative designs; later research of the 1970s which reached more pessimistic conclusions was better designed for the measurement of outcomes, but often lacked adequate specification of inputs and did not concentrate on methods which were *designed to be* effective.
- Not all the consequences of 'Nothing Works' were negative: for example, in the 1980s an interest in alternatives to custody produced some significant successes.
- The new guarded optimism of the 1990s stems from three main sources: psychological criminology based on social learning theory; meta-analytic reviews of large groups of evaluative studies; and a handful of well-evaluated projects in Britain which showed good results for structured and programmed supervision.
- Current research on the probation 'Pathfinder' projects is likely to add significantly to our knowledge, but the research agenda should also include attention to the processes of recidivism and desistance; effective pro-social case management; the rich but neglected social work research literature on effective helping; and the problems of effective implementation.
- We also need to focus on the needs of particular groups which have not been central to 'What Works' research so far, such as prolific offenders, short-term prisoners and minority ethnic offenders, and on the likely emergence of new forms of 'alternative to custody' in response to an urgent need to limit prison numbers.
- Finally we have to remember that research is only one of many influences on policy. The next few years will be a critical test of how much difference an evidence-based approach can make.

References

Adams, S. (1967) 'Some findings from correctional caseload research', *Federal Probation*, 31, 48–57.

Andrews, D. A. and Bonta, J. (1998) *The Psychology of Criminal Conduct*. Cincinnati, OH: Anderson.

Andrews, D. D., Zinger, I., Hoge, R. D., Bonta, J., Gendreau, P. and Cullen, F. T. (1990) 'Does correctional treatment work? A clinically relevant and psychologically informed meta-analysis', *Criminology*, 28, 369–404.

Bailey, R. and Ward, D. (1992) *Probation Supervision: Attitudes to Formalised Helping*. Belfast: Probation Board for Northern Ireland.

Bernfeld, G. A., Farrington, D. P. and Leschied, A. W. (eds) (2001) *Offender Rehabilitation in Practice: Implementing and Evaluating Effective* Programs. New York: Wiley.

Brody, S. (1976) *The Effectiveness of Sentencing: A Review of the Literature* (Home Office Research Study No. 35). London: HMSO.

Chapman, T. and Hough, M. (1998) *Evidence-Based Practice: A Guide to Effective Practice*. London: Home Office.

Croft, J. (1978) *Research in Criminal Justice*. London: HMSO.

Dowden, C. and Andrews, D. (1999) 'What works for female offenders: A meta-analytic review', *Crime and Delinquency*, 45, 438–452.

Farrall, S. (2002) *Rethinking What Works with Offenders: Probation, Social Context and Desistance from Crime*. Cullompton: Willan.

Folkard, M. S., Smith, D. E. and Smith, D. D. (1976) *IMPACT: Intensive Matched Probation and After-Care Treatment, Volume II – The Results of the Experiment* (Home Office Research Study No. 36). London: HMSO.

Gendreau, P., Goggin, C. and Smith, P. (1999) 'The forgotten issue in effective correctional treatment: program implementation', *International Journal of Offender Therapy and Comparative Criminology*, 43, 180–187.

Goldberg, E. M. and Warburton, R. W. (1979) *Ends and Means in Social Work*. London: Allen & Unwin.

Goldberg, E. M., Gibbons, J. and Sinclair, I. (1985) *Problems, Tasks and Outcomes*. London: Allen & Unwin.

Goldblatt, P. and Lewis, C. (eds) (1998) *Reducing Offending: An Assessment of Research Evidence on Ways of Dealing with Offending Behaviour* (Home Office Research Study No. 187). London: Home Office.

Gorman, K. (2001) 'Cognitive behaviourism and the holy grail: The quest for a universal means of managing offender risk', *Probation Journal*, 48 (1), 3–9.

Graham, J. and Bowling, B. (1995) *Young People and Crime* (Home Office Research Study No. 145). London: Home Office.

Hatcher, R. and McGuire, J. (2001) *Report on the Psychometric Evaluation of the Think-First Programme in Community Settings*. Liverpool: Department of Clinical Psychology, University of Liverpool.

Her Majesty's Inspectorate of Probation (HMIP) (2002) *Annual Report 2001–2002*. London: Home Office.

Home Office (2001) *Making Punishments Work: Report of a Review of the Sentencing Framework for England and Wales*. London: Home Office.

Home Office (2002) *Justice for All* (CM 5563) London: Home Office.

Izzo, R. and Ross, R. (1990) 'Meta-analysis of rehabilitation programs for juvenile delinquents', *Criminal Justice and Behaviour* 17, 134–142.

Lewis, S., Vennard, J., Maguire, M., Raynor, P., Vanstone, M., Raybould, S. and Rix, A. (2002) *The Resettlement of Short-Term Prisoners: An Evaluation of Seven*

Pathfinders. A Report to the Home Office Research, Development and Statistics Directorate.

Lipsey, M. (1992) 'Juvenile delinquency treatment: a meta-analytic enquiry into the variability of effects', in T. Cook, H. Cooper, D. S. Cordray, H. Hartmann, L. V. Hedges, R. L. Light, T. A. Louis and F. Mosteller (eds) *Meta-Analysis for Explanation: A Case-book*. New York: Russell Sage Foundation.

Lipton, D., Martinson, R. and Wilks, J. (1975) *The Effectiveness of Correctional Treatment*. New York: Praeger.

McGuire, J. (ed.) (1995) *What Works: Reducing Reoffending – Guidelines from Research and Practice*. Chichester: Wiley.

McGuire, J. (2000) *Cognitive-Behavioural Approaches: An Introduction to Theory and Research*. London: Home Office.

McIvor, G. (1990) *Sanctions for Serious or Persistent Offenders*. Stirling: Social Work Research Centre, University of Stirling.

McLaren, K. (1992) *Reducing Reoffending: What Works Now?* Wellington, NZ: Department of Justice.

Maguire, M., Raynor, P., Vanstone, M. and Kynch, J. (2000) 'Voluntary after-care and the Probation Service: A case of diminishing responsibility', *Howard Journal of Criminal Justice*, 39, 234–248.

Mair, G. (1988) *Probation Day Centres* (Home Office Research Study No. 100). London: HMSO.

Mair, G. (1995) 'Standing at the crossroads: What works in community penalties', in *Managing What Works Conference Programme*, London: Home Office.

Mair, G. (2000) 'Credible accreditation?', *Probation Journal*, 47, 268–271.

Mair, G. and Nee, C. (1990) *Electronic Monitoring: The Trials and Their Results* (Home Office Research Study No. 120). London: Home Office.

Martinson, R. (1974) 'What works? Questions and answers about prison reform', *The Public Interest*, 35, 22–54.

Maruna, S. (2001) *Making Good: How Ex-convicts Reform and Rebuild their Lives*. Washington: American Psychological Association.

Meyer, H. J., Borgatta, E. F. and Jones, W. C. (1965) *Girls at Vocational High: An Experiment in Social Work Intervention*. New York: Russell Sage Foundation.

Mortimer, E. (2001) *Electronic Monitoring of Released Prisoners: An Evaluation of the Home Detention Curfew Scheme* (Research Findings 139). London: Home Office.

Pease, K., Billingham, S. and Earnshaw, I. (1977) *Community Service Assessed in 1976* (Home Office Research Study No. 39). London: HMSO.

Porporino, F. (2002) 'Considerations for programme implementation', *What Works News*, 7.

Powers, E. and Witmer, H. (1951) *An Experiment in the Treatment of Delinquency*. New York: Columbia University Press.

Radzinowicz, L. (ed.) (1958) *The Results of Probation: A Report of the Cambridge Department of Criminal Science*. London: Macmillan.

Raynor, P. (1988) *Probation as an Alternative to Custody*. Aldershot: Avebury.

Raynor, P. (1998a) 'Attitudes, social problems and reconvictions in the STOP probation experiment', *Howard Journal of Criminal Justice*, 37, 1–15.

Raynor, P. (1998b) 'Reading probation statistics: A critical comment', *Vista: Perspectives on Probation*, 3, 181–185.

Raynor, P. (2002) 'Community penalties: probation, punishment and What Works', in M. Maguire, R. Morgan and R. Reiner (eds) *The Oxford Handbook of Criminology* (3rd edn). Oxford: Oxford University Press.

Raynor, P. and Miles, M. (2001) *Risks, Needs and Reoffending: Evaluating the Impact of Community Sentences in Jersey*. A Report to the Jersey Probation Service. Swansea: Swansea and Cognitive Centre Foundation, University of Wales.

Raynor, P. and Vanstone, M. (1996) 'Reasoning and Rehabilitation in Britain: The results of the Straight Thinking On Probation (STOP) programme', *International Journal of Offender Therapy and Comparative Criminology*, 40, 272–284.

Raynor, P. and Vanstone, M. (1997) *Straight Thinking On Probation (STOP): The Mid Glamorgan* Experiment (Probation Studies Unit Report No. 4). Oxford: Centre for Criminological Research, University of Oxford.

Raynor, P. and Vanstone, M. (2002) *Understanding Community Penalties: Probation, Policy and Social Change*. Buckingham: Open University Press.

Reid, W. J. and Epstein, L. (1972) *Task Centred Casework*. New York: Columbia University Press.

Rex, S. (1997) *Perceptions of Probation in a Context of 'Just Deserts'*, PhD thesis. Cambridge: Institute of Criminology, University of Cambridge.

Rex, S. and Matravers, A. (eds) (1998) *Pro-Social Modelling and Legitimacy*. Cambridge: Institute of Criminology, University of Cambridge.

Roberts, C. (1989) *Hereford and Worcester Probation Service Young Offender Project: First Evaluation Report*. Oxford: Department of Social and Administrative Studies, University of Oxford.

Ross, R. R. and Fabiano, E. A. (1985) *Time to Think: A Cognitive Model of Delinquency Prevention and Offender Rehabilitation*. Johnson City, TN: Institute of Social Sciences and Arts.

Ross, R. R., Fabiano, E. A. and Ewles, C. D. (1988) 'Reasoning and rehabilitation', *International Journal of Offender Therapy and Comparative Criminology*, 32, 29–35.

Ross, R. R., Fabiano, E. A. and Ross, R. D. (1986) *Reasoning and Rehabilitation: A Handbook for Teaching Cognitive Skills*. Ottawa: University of Ottawa.

Rutherford, A. (1986) *Growing Out of Crime*. Harmondsworth: Penguin.

Shaw, M. (1974) *Social Work in Prison* (Home Office Research Study No. 22). London: HMSO.

Sinclair, I. (1971) *Hostels for Probationers* (Home Office Research Study No. 6). London: HMSO.

Social Exclusion Unit (SEU) (2002) *Reducing Re-offending by Ex-prisoners*. London: SEU.

Thorpe, D. H., Smith, D., Green, C. J. and Paley, J. (1980) *Out of Care: The Community Support of Juvenile Offenders*. London: Allen & Unwin.

Trotter, C. (1993) *The Supervision of Offenders – What Works: A Study Undertaken in Community Based Corrections*. Melbourne: Social Work Department, Monash University and the Victorian Department of Justice.

Trotter, C. (2000) 'Social work education, pro-social modelling and effective probation practice', *Probation Journal*, 47, 256–261.

Truax, C. C. and Carkhuff, R. R. (1967) *Toward Effective Counselling and Psychotherapy*. Chicago: Aldine.

Underdown, A. (1998) *Strategies for Effective Supervision: Report of the HMIP What Works Project*. London: Home Office.

Vanstone, M. (2001) *Making Sense of Probation: A History of Professional Discourse*, PhD thesis. Wales: University of Wales.

Walker, N., Farrington, D. and Tucker, G. (1981) 'Reconviction rates of adult males after different sentences', *British Journal of Criminology*, 21, 357–360.

Walton, D. (2001) 'When the carrot meets the stick', *What Works*, 6, 6.

Wilkinson, J. (1997) 'The impact of Ilderton motor project on motor vehicle crime and offending', *British Journal of Criminology*, 37, 568–581.

Wilkinson, J. (1998) *Developing the Evidence-base for Probation Programmes*, PhD thesis. Guildford: University of Surrey.

Zamble, E. and Quinsey, V. L. (1997) *The Criminal Recidivism Process*, Cambridge: Cambridge University Press.

6

PRE-TRIAL INVESTIGATION

Mike Nash

INTRODUCTION

The origins of the Probation Service have placed it at something of an inter-face within the criminal justice process. As McWilliams (1983) indicates, it was the concept of 'mercy' which best explains its historical central place within the courts, its role in the delivery of embryonic criminal justice object-ives and defined its early social enquiry practice (p. 137). We will discuss the development of pre-trial enquiries in greater depth below but at this point it is worth an attempt to contextualise how those enquiries might change or be influenced over time. If we accept McWilliams' view, it is obvious that practice which is based on a belief in the importance of dispensing mercy (to the deserving) as an aspect of sentencing practice, is likely to have to change as that quality or ethos increases or decreases in importance. The interface is historically that between mercy and punishment and it is therefore clear where the concept of probation as an alternative to punishment originates. As the nature of punishment itself is defined and re-defined, to include probation supervision within the definition, then it is likely that the nature of social or pre-trial enquiries will also change. Clearly associated with these changes is a public view of, or attitude towards, the offender – any shift in public sympathy likely to determine both the amount of mercy shown and the nature of the relationship between offender and probation officer. Traditional probation pre-sentence work therefore has a singular origin in a distinctive style of criminal justice. If that style or ethos changes then so must the nature of probation work. Failure to change in this way is likely to lead to greater marginalisation or even the disappearance of its role. This chapter will note these historical developments before describing current pre-trial practice in the Probation Service.

HISTORICAL CONTEXT

McWilliams' quartet of articles (1983, 1985, 1986, 1987) provide an invaluable chronology of the Probation Service with a focus on pre-trial enquiries acting as a connecting thread. In its early work with defendants the Probation Service was operating in a climate where the public were beginning to feel less afraid of offenders and where feelings of safety and security were increasing (McWilliams 1983: 131) – in marked contrast to today's risk society (Beck 1992). In its 'pleas' to the courts the Probation Service began to mediate on behalf of defendants who indicated, during enquiries, that they had the capacity to change and improve. The Victorian legacy of self-improvement is evident in this style of work and is a clear demonstration of the philanthropic origins of the Probation Service. It is obvious from this that probation officers were likely to try to present the offender in as good a light as possible – in other words be 'on their side'. It is equally obvious that for this situation to develop it must have reflected a mood within criminal justice circles and the public more widely. To understand the nature of pre-trial enquiries today, and how they have changed since those early days, the 'changing representation of the criminal' (Melossi 2000) has to be a consideration of central importance.

Before examining this revision of the offender's status, however, it is important to understand the place of pre-trial enquiry within the dominant mode of justice in the UK for most of the twentieth century. By this we mean a style of justice predicated on a belief in reform, change and rehabilitation – a focus on the individual and their circumstances, in other words, individualised justice. This can be described as a 'modern' or positivist view, absorbed into a strategy that Garland (1996, 2001) has described as 'penal welfare'. As this belief gained ground it coincided with the 'growing professionalisation' of those who saw themselves as the new 'experts' in criminal justice. Probation officers were to be a major part of this new approach and their reports were to become the medium by which their quest for professional status was to be pursued. As Garland (1996) reminds us, however, the status of the criminal justice expert has become increasingly marginalised in late modern society and this process can be detected in the changing nature of probation reports which will be discussed below.

THE CHANGING NATURE OF PROBATION COURT REPORTS

As the scientific and rational approach to offending gained ground, so did the development of the probation report as a diagnostic tool. In moving from a plea for mercy for deserving offenders, it increasingly became a medium for probation officers to make assessments based on a form of psychosocial case-work. The Probation Handbook of 1958 emphasised this point: 'Probation, like other forms of casework, should begin with social diagnosis. In many instances the first stage of such diagnosis occurs when the probation officer is required to prepare a report for the court . . .' (McWilliams 1986: 255). The report therefore afforded the probation officer an opportunity to display their skills in assessment and prediction, a matching of 'need' and 'provision' with a view to correcting (or 'normalising', Foucault 1977) behaviour. Indeed, so established a part of the court process did this become, that probation officers almost reached a stage of expertise which required no more than an 'in my opinion' judgement to secure agreement to, for example, the making of a probation order.

On reaching this high point, however (see King and Jarvis 1976 for a discussion on the influence of probation in wider criminal justice policies) a change in direction set in almost immediately. The Streatfield Report of 1961 witnessed a gradual shift from a backward-looking philosophy to one that looked ahead to a concern with influencing future behaviour. Reports were to be professional documents concerned with the assessment of culpability and risk. By the time of the Morrison Report (1962) the now newly named social enquiry report (SER) was to provide three forms of information:

- That regarding the social and domestic background of the offender that is relevant to the court's assessment of culpability
- That regarding the offender and his surroundings relevant to a consideration of how a criminal career might be checked
- Opinion concerning the effect of probation and other disposals on criminal careers (cited in Worrall 1997: 80).

The change in emphasis of social enquiry practice gathered pace as doubts began to spread concerning the effectiveness of what Garland (2001) has described as the 'penal welfare' strategy. If the strategy itself were increasingly under question then so naturally would be the mechanism for conveying its message – the SER. Not only was the effectiveness of the method under scrutiny from without but also increasingly from within. The ability of probation officers to engage in the type of assessments they undertook was questioned by critical authors such as Walker and Beaumont (1981) and increasingly radical movements within the National Association of Probation Officers (NAPO) queried the departure from probation's traditional roots. The tide of criminal justice was turning and with it the Probation Service – that change was to escalate from the 1970s onwards.

PENAL PESSIMISM AND PROBATION PRACTICE

Probation officers had worked hard at achieving professional status and clearly had secured a position of influence within the criminal justice process (King and Jarvis 1976). Yet several broad developments were set to challenge that position and significantly impact upon probation practice. These developments would include the general pessimism that flowed following the work of Martinson (1974) and Brody (1976), the internal critique following the work of authors such as Walker and Beaumont (1981) and the rise of a New Right philosophy on both sides of the Atlantic. This in turn would see a rational choice view of offending begin to supplant the positivist explanations which had seen the probation service's role become so important and the diagnostic SER a key tool.

In this newly fashionable philosophy crime was increasingly viewed as a matter of offender choice rather than a result of circumstances driving the offender to a certain course of action. The result of this shift in direction was a new focus on crime prevention (particularly situational) at the expense of diagnosis and a search for a 'cure' for offending behaviour. Feeley and Simon (1992, 1994) dubbed this movement as 'New Penology' with its emphasis on attempting to manage the problem of crime rather than seek a solution to its occurrence. Risk reduction and risk management would supplant notions of treatment and proportionality, leading some commentators such as Hudson (2001a) to talk more in terms of 'risk control'. It is clear that if this view of offending and offenders becomes widespread then probation practice in terms of pre-trial investigation would have to change by default. In crude terms, rather than the probation officer looking for where 'things went wrong' in the offender's life history, the search was now on for an identification of the risk factors which might trigger further offending and the proposal of a solution by which these factors might best be managed. As Hudson (2001a) notes, 'needs factors' have now become 'risk factors'. Although much previous probation practice could be brought forward into this new world of risk assessment, it is clear that a fundamental shift was underway because the focus and perhaps rationale for intervention were also changing.

THE 1991 CRIMINAL JUSTICE ACT AND
NATIONAL STANDARDS

By the 1980s the Probation Service, in common with the rest of the public sector, was to be subjected to a wave of 'new public management reforms', which were characterised by a reduction of professional discretion and an increase in central direction of practice. For probation officers this would result in a set of National Standards, first published by the Home Office (1992), which aimed to set minimum standards of practice for all aspects of probation work including social enquiry practice. The impact of these standards, and the 1991 Criminal Justice Act (CJA) which laid the ground for them, will be discussed below. However, we should also note that there were ongoing problems within social enquiry practice before this point was reached, notably around women offenders. As Mair and Brockington (1988) observed, women's offending tended to be 'problematised' more than that of male offenders, leading to proportionately more recommendations for probation orders to help sort out their 'emotional problems'. Inconsistency in practice was therefore perhaps a wider issue than that envisaged by the new managerial critics of the probation service, and indeed in terms of assessing crime seriousness continues to be problematic (Nash 1995, 1999).

The managerialist reforms of the 1980s were essentially concerned with bringing private market discipline to the state sector. They appeared to be based on a fundamental mistrust of professionals to deliver both an efficient and a cost-effective service and to implement government policies. As Garland (1996) noted, so-called criminal justice experts and their body of knowledge were increasingly doubted by government and the public alike as the problem of crime continued to grow. In practice terms this was to set in train a process where probation officers were to lose the 'in my opinion' status described above to one where they would increasingly have to state their sources and detail what they would seek to achieve in supervision.[1] This was very much tied up with the drive to give the courts the confidence to make more community sentences as provided for in the 1991 CJA and increase the effectiveness of targeting practice as suggested by the Audit Commission (1989). At stake was the independence of the probation officer, once regarded as the hallmark of the profession. Where poor practice was a feature of that independence then few would have argued at an increase in openness and accountability. If, however, the result of this process was a diminution of standards then professional concern might be viewed as justified (see Butler 1996 for a comment on similar developments in the police service and Caulkin 1995 for the National Health Service).

The 1991 CJA epitomised the 'justice' or 'just deserts' movement that had evolved throughout the 1980s. Its implementation was to offer the probation

---

[1] To a certain extent it could be argued that this 'status' has at least been partially retained in the specific sentence report (SSR). Here the court will adjourn the case, maybe for a few hours only, so that the probation officer can comment on the court's consideration of imposing a straightforward community sentence. These reports may be delivered verbally and are meant to save time. The use of these reports, vigorously promoted by the Home Office (see HO Circular 85/99), fits squarely with the present government's drive to reduce delay in the criminal justice system.

service a renewed opportunity to move centre-stage in criminal justice delivery after the worries and doubts of the previous decade. Yet it would also entail a considerable increase in the powers of the centre to direct probation practice – a process that has continued almost unabated since. For the purposes of this chapter the 1991 CJA made a considerable impact upon the pre-trial practice of the probation service and it is to this that we will now turn.

The 1991 CJA had been described in *The Times* as the most enlightened criminal justice Act ever (*The Times*, Leader, 21 August 1990). Despite denials by the then Home Secretary David Waddington, it did appear to have a clear intent to reduce the use of custody in the UK (and indeed succeeded in this purpose in the year immediately following its implementation). By developing the idea of 'punishment in the community' and the concept of a 'graduated restriction of liberty', the government hoped that courts would have more faith in community-based disposals. As a part of the process of rebuilding that confidence, SER practice was to be radically overhauled. An immediate and basic change was to the name, moving from social enquiry to pre-sentence report (PSR). National Standards for PSRs would determine the structure, content and purpose in a determined shift to move reports away from the 'special pleading' culture or what a former Home Secretary, Douglas Hurd, had once described as a flabby approach to crime. In future, reports would pay less attention to the offender's social background and more to an assessment of the risk of re-offending. Background information would be included only if relevant to the crime committed and offence-reduction strategies. The offender's attitude to the crime would be a central feature of the reports. Another significant development would be the ending of the probation officer's 'recommendation' and its replacement by a 'proposal'. At the time probation staff worried over what appeared to be a fundamental shift in report-writing practice but by including a requirement for report authors to comment on the 'suitability' of offenders to community disposals, there did appear to be a continuation of a more traditional role. The 1991 CJA also offered hope for the continued future of the probation service by stating that PSRs should be prepared in every case where custody or a community sentence was being considered by the court (sections 3(1) and 7(3)). Yet by February 1995 schedule 9 of the 1994 Criminal Justice and Public Order Act (CJPOA) had introduced wide discretion to courts to sentence adults without a PSR if they felt it to be appropriate. Life for the probation service throughout the 1990s was undoubtedly something of a roller-coaster ride, one minute being centre-stage and the next under threat. The changing nature and importance of pre-trial enquiries perhaps demonstrates this very well.

Nonetheless there had been a significant change in probation practice in terms of the nature of the enquiries undertaken on a routine basis. From a time when SERs were in essence about looking for the best and most positive aspects of offenders' lives, there was now expected to be a decidedly more neutral stance. In assisting the court to find the most 'suitable' way in which to deal with the offender it was likely that reports might develop into documents that were less 'sympathetic' than they might have been previously. A focus on the crime, its impact upon the victim and the offender's attitude to offending had begun the shift of concentrating probation practice increasingly upon the concept of 'risk' – in this case of re-offending. Instead of being a mechanism by which an appraisal was undertaken of past and present events in the offender's life to assess how future crime might be avoided (by tackling the problems), PSRs would instead focus on the future, and needs factors would now be recast as risk factors.

To assist in this process predictive scales began to be developed which aimed to assist decision-making and reduce subjectivity and potential discriminatory practice. These tools have become increasingly sophisticated and have developed from crude 'risk of custody' scales through to devices such as the LSI-R (Level of Service Inventory – revised), ACE (Assessment, Case Recording and Evaluation) and OASys (Offender Assessment System). In essence these devices assist probation officers to assess risk, based not only on static factors such as age and criminal record but also on examining dynamic risk factors, or 'criminogenic' factors based on offenders' circumstances, resources, behaviour, attitudes etc. (see also Robinson's Chapter 7 in this book). These tools fit well with the actuarial approaches to offending which are a key feature of New Penology. They enable information extrapolated from offender sub-groups to be generalised into prediction scales that aim to assess the risk of further offending. Although many people argue that such devices do qualitatively inform practice (Clear and Cadora 2001) it should be noted that they are more likely to be effective with 'ordinary' rather than unusual or potentially dangerous offenders (Scott 1977; Floud and Young 1981; Floud 1982).

PSRS AND NATIONAL STANDARDS

The nature of pre-trial investigation has therefore changed. It is now risk oriented with public protection and crime prevention as key indicators of effectiveness. The most recent version of national standards makes clear the purpose of PSRs, 'to provide information to the sentencing court about the offender and offence(s) committed and to assist the court to decide on suitable sentence'. In many ways this is not so very different from the older SERs; however, once what the report *should* contain is considered it is possible to detect the change in emphasis and focus which has developed since the 1991 CJA. For example, a detailed analysis of the offence has to be undertaken focusing on issues such as circumstances, premeditation, culpability, impact on victim, offender's attitude and any reparation or positive action to address offending since the crime was committed. It is of course more than likely that good probation officers have undertaken such enquiries for years, but it is equally likely that such an analysis would not have been *included* in the old SER. Similarly in assessing the offender, the attention is drawn towards assessing 'needs' which have or may become criminogenic factors. Readers are directed towards National Standards 2000 for the latest detailed guidance on PSR writing, but for the purpose of this chapter a summary will suffice to indicate general purpose and intent. According to the National Standards (Home Office 2000: B1), a PSR shall:

- be objective, impartial, free from discriminatory language and stereotype, balanced, verified and factually accurate;
- be based on the use of the Offender Assessment System (OASys), when implemented, to provide a systematic assessment of the nature and the causes of the defendant's offending behaviour, the risk the defendant poses to the public and the action which can be taken to reduce the likelihood of re-offending;
- be based on at least one face-to-face interview with the offender;
- specify information available from the Crown Prosecution Service, any hostel placement or from any relevant source;
- be written, and a copy provided to the court, the defence, the offender and (where required by the Crime (Sentences) Act 1997) the prosecution;
- be prepared within, at most, 15 working days of request; or such shorter timescale as has been agreed in protocols with the court.

It is therefore clear that the purpose of PSRs and their intended focus has been refined by the government with a determined attempt to reduce the inclusion of what may be viewed as unnecessary and irrelevant background information. However, it could be argued that it is perhaps the end of the report, rather than the beginning and middle that has seen the most significant change in recent years. The situation described above, during the heyday of probation influence, was one where very few details of the supervisory process would be given to the courts. It was seemingly sufficient for courts to believe that offenders would receive help and have an eye kept on them. The change in attitude away from a welfare-based penal strategy, outlined briefly above, has however altered the perception of expert advice and led to demands that it be more detailed, more focused, more explicit of what would happen in any given situation. The latest version of National Standards (Home Office 2000: B3) does indeed make it abundantly clear that every PSR shall contain a conclusion which:

- evaluates the offender's motivation and ability to change and identifies, where relevant, action required to improve motivation;

- explicitly states whether or not an offender is suitable for a community sentence;
- makes a clear and realistic proposal for sentence designed to protect the public and reduce re-offending, including for custody where this is necessary;
- where the proposal is for a probation order or combination order, includes an outline supervision plan containing:
  - a description of the purposes and desired outcomes of the proposed sentence;
  - the methods envisaged and interventions likely to be undertaken, including attendance at accredited programmes where appropriate;
  - the level of supervision envisaged (which for offenders at high risk of causing serious harm to the public is likely to be higher than the minimum required by the Standards).

The Standards also require specific detail on conditions, suitability of addresses for curfew orders, comments on extended supervision in serious sexual and violent offences and finally the impact of a custodial sentence on the offender's circumstances. The inclusion of more specific detail than that included in the old SERs is obvious. The intention is clearly to be more open about what the supervision process involves, to increase the confidence of the courts in the probation service and indeed to make its role and purpose more clear to the general public. Those who are familiar with older probation pre-trial practice will also note the substantial departure from the past with the expectation that report authors comment on *and propose* a custodial sentence where appropriate. Such an activity was almost taboo in the probation service of not so long ago and almost in this one development can be seen the decidedly more neutral position that the probation service has come to adopt within the sentencing process, with public protection now a significant factor.

PUBLIC PROTECTION, VALUES AND MULTI-AGENCY WORKING

Therefore a key component of pre-trial investigation and report writing is the assessment of risk of harm to the public. Public protection has been a major feature on the criminal justice agenda since the mid-1990s and has had a significant impact upon the working practices of the probation service, especially its collaboration with other partners (Nash 1999, 2001). Public protection has accelerated a shift in probation pre-trial work that has been evident for a few years now. This shift has been the formalising of work with other agencies and a diversification of task, and it is to this that the chapter will now turn.

In many ways one of the simplest ways to conceptualise the recent change is to focus on a shift from post- to pre-conviction work with offenders. In the past, as now, court reports followed on from a finding of guilt. There are, however, now many ways in which the probation service is involved in pre-trial work with offenders, some of which signal a significant change in ethos and will be discussed below. However, other pre-trial work, such as the provision of bail information reports, would fall squarely in line with a long probation tradition of trying to avoid the unnecessary use of custody. Begun at the Vera Institute of Justice in New York in the 1970s, the scheme was piloted in 16 magistrates' courts as a result of Home Office Circular 155/75, although it should be noted that this initiative was to come from within existing resources. The aim of the scheme was to provide verified information to the court to avoid, if possible, unnecessary remands in custody. Members of the Probation Service (probation officers and probation ancillaries/Probation Service officers) would interview defendants in police cells and seek to obtain information concerning accommodation, which might alter the original recommendation for a remand in custody. However, initial interest in the scheme waned as a result of the Bail Act 1976 and the 1975 Home Office circular both of which led to a temporary reduction in the remand population. Drakeford *et al.* (2001) also note that the probation service might have been ambivalent over this area of work due to civil rights concerns and defence lawyers felt that their territory was being invaded (p. 13). The remand crisis of the 1980s re-ignited interest in bail information and support schemes and by 1995 over 100 first appearance and a number of second appearance (prison-based) schemes were in existence.

As might be expected, such a sizeable and important aspect of Probation Service work is covered by National Standards states:

> The purpose of Bail Information by probation services is to assist the court by providing to the Crown Prosecution Service (CPS) verified information to add to their factual knowledge of the defendant, including risk of harm to the public, and hence contributing to their representations on bail. (Home Office 2000: B1)

National Standards have moved these reports on from a position of providing only positive information and this is undoubtedly one means by which to increase credibility with courts and the CPS. The Standards (Home Office 2000: B2) state that reports shall:

- be objective, factual and impartial;
- contain a front sheet which sets out the factual information on the defendant and list the sources used to prepare the report;
- include reference to any ongoing supervision or licence where the offender is currently subject to supervision;

- clearly indicate the author, the date on which the report is written, the court and the date of hearing for which the information is intended and basic details about the defendant;
- include details of relevant information such as accommodation and employment;
- be presented as a written report whenever possible;
- be made orally when a written report cannot be prepared in time, and then be written up as soon as possible thereafter;
- in cases where risk of serious harm to the public is apparent, be copied to the police, social services or health authority as appropriate; and
- be made available to the court duty officer where the writer is unable to be in court.

The effectiveness of these schemes is reviewed by Drakeford *et al.* (2001: 27–29) and it is evident that they do make a significant impact by diverting offenders away from unnecessary remands. Indeed the same authors conclude that pre-trial work should be at the heart of probation practice, becoming a defining and central strategy for the criminal justice system as a whole.

Such a fundamental shift in philosophy would, Drakeford *et al.* (2001) argue, produce significant humanitarian and financial benefits as unnecessary remands would be avoided and the prison population would fall considerably. An increased emphasis on work in this area does represent a shift in approach for the probation service but does offer an opportunity to spread its 'values' further into the wider criminal justice field. Of course this subject has been debated for some time (see Nellis 1995; Harding 2000 for examples of the arguments examining a 'new' set of values for the probation service), and yet it is unclear which values the service would bring to an extended sphere of pre-trial work. Despite their calls for a more integrated and central pre-trial strategy, Drakeford *et al.* (2001) also offer words of caution for the probation service. In considering evidence from the United States they find that pre-trial services have moved to become a more central feature of the overall criminal justice strategy, but in so doing have adopted the values of that strategy rather than 'espousing and practising its own humanitarian ideal' (p. 50). In other words care needs to be taken that each opportunity does not come at a cost. If it does then organisations such as the Probation Service have to decide if that cost is too high or if they are to adapt to the new scenario and change their values and ethos fundamentally.

Pre-trial work therefore affords an opportunity to work with other organisations but it is important that the unique and distinctive qualities of probation practice are not lost in the process. The second Labour government have launched a major initiative to 'join-up' government and as part of this process the criminal justice process itself is to become joined-up. Targets will be set across the sector with the intention of improving efficiency and effectiveness. Implicit in the nature of greater inter-agency collaboration will be an expectation that information will be shared more readily than in the past (see Rumgay's Chapter 12 in this book). This sharing will not only take place with agencies which might loosely be described as within the 'care' sector, but increasingly with the prison and perhaps more significantly, the police service. The move to greater information-sharing has not been easy (see Home Office 1995) but is a process that has considerably developed with the increase in importance attached to public protection issues (Home Office 1998; Nash 2000; Kemshall and Maguire 2001).

As noted above, it is the recent rise of public protection issues within the criminal justice agenda which has spurred the drive to greater inter-agency working. The protection of the public has become the number-one priority for criminal justice agencies and as a result there have developed significant changes to probation work, pre- and post-trial. At the pre-trial stage work in what have become known as multi-agency public protection panels (MAPPPs) means that probation officers will be involved with individuals who may not yet have committed or been convicted of a crime but are giving 'cause for concern'. Although most of those considered by panels will be subject of post-custody release arrangements, or indeed subject of PSR enquiries, some will undoubtedly not fit into either category. The potential outcomes of MAPPP decisions could of course be the surveillance of individuals by the police service or an application for a sex offender order. Either of these issues has significant implications for the rights and freedoms of the individual under consideration. The 'penal marking' of sex offenders (Garland 2000) represents another shift from the way in which probation officers have traditionally worked with this group (Worrall 1997). Nonetheless the opportunity remains for probation staff to make a major contribution to this process based on its experience of assessing risk and supervising sex offenders and other high-risk individuals. It is important that the organisation does not relinquish its distinctive contribution in a rush to avoid the blame for failure, which is so much a part of the public protection agenda (Douglas 1992).

As noted above, joined-up working is very much seen as the most effective way forward for criminal justice agencies. Government announcements constantly refer to the message that the problem of crime cannot be solved by one agency working alone (normally the police) and that not only should agencies engage in partnerships with each other but engage with the community. Activating the community as a crime-prevention entity in itself is seen as the only solution to crime and has been warmly adopted in the policies of Tony Blair's 'Third Way' approach to politics (Giddens 1998) and builds on the ideas of Etzioni (1997) in aiming to re-moralise communities. This broad, partnership approach to crime attempts to remove agency barriers based on culture and notions of confidentiality. The essence of effective inter-agency working is information-sharing and of course trust becomes a very important commodity. By producing cross-sector targets the government intends that agencies become more homogenised in their approach to crime and less concerned with single-agency issues. At the pre-trial phase this has led to much greater involvement on the part of the probation service with a variety of public and private sector agencies. These can range from drugs agencies to housing departments, education services to voluntary advice centres. Once again, however, it should be noted for readers that this is not necessarily 'new' practice for probation officers. Good probation practice has always been concerned to make the best use of available community resources. Recent developments appear to formalise this involvement much more and perhaps aim to ensure that practice that might have slipped from the agenda in recent years is resurrected.

CONCLUSION

The aim of this chapter has been to review the origins, development and current state of probation pre-trial practice. From voluntaristic beginnings where 'deserving' offenders were the subjects of special pleading, the medium of conveying the message, the court report, has changed significantly. The growth in use of the old SER coincided with a period in penal history when it was believed that the right sort of intervention at the right time could 'cure' the problem of crime. To find the cure it was of course necessary to diagnose the problem and hence the SER became the medium of social casework diagnosis. The increased use of pseudo-scientific diagnostic tools also reflected the quest for probation officers to attain professional status. However, having achieved the hallmark of professional status – independence of practice – this was soon followed by increasing attempts at controlling professional discretion using guidance and rules emanating from the Home Office. Pre-trial practice and in particular the writing of reports to the court subject to growing direction and re-definition. This naturally did not occur in isolation and can be viewed as a broader attempt to re-focus the work of the probation service in general.

Court reports today, in PSR guise, are documents that seek to offer objective, verified and very specific information to the court to assist in the sentencing process. Although they continue to assist courts to consider the most suitable community disposal they also now have to realistically consider whether custody is a necessary sentence and propose it if appropriate. This has shifted practice away from an 'offender focus' to one that is more victim-oriented, with crime reduction and public protection at the core. Just as report writing has taken on a wider crime prevention and reduction focus, so has much of probation work. It is now firmly embedded in practice that pre-trial practice means more than writing reports. It now involves utilising the resources of other agencies, forming partnerships with them and, through agreed protocols, sharing often-confidential information. What was once good, but usually informal practice, has become formalised through agreements and legislation. The probation service no longer works in isolation and its reports are used by other agencies. Its skills in assessment and supervision remain intact and should continue to form a distinctive feature of the criminal justice agenda. It retains an important place in the delivery of criminal justice objectives, but needs, as Harding (2000) and Hudson (2001b) have commented, to ensure that its values, even if reconfigured, continue to inform those objectives at every stage of the process.

KEY FACTS

In the year 2000 the probation service completed 241,253 pre-sentence reports of which 21,255 were no contact (no interview). Of these 139,325 reports were prepared for the adult magistrates' courts and 2740 for the youth court and 51,067 for the Crown Court; 14,801 reports came under the specific sentence category described in footnote 1. Over the ten years from 1990 to 2000, the number of bail information reports prepared increased from 4458 to 13,976 but this latter figure shows a considerable decrease from a high of 24,779 in 1997. However, as an indication of the changing nature of probation report practice, the number of means enquiries fell from 20,960 in 1992 to 1402 in 2000. The number of reports prepared for an 'average' workload is approximately 69.3 (to include PSRs, bail information, inquiries for institutions etc.) according to *Probation Statistics 2000* (Home Office 2002).

SUMMARY OF KEY ISSUES

- This chapter describes the changing nature of probation practice in the pre-trial phase of the criminal justice process.
- There is a particular focus on the developments arising from the changes to social enquiry practice, contextualised by the wider transformations of penal policy in recent years.
- The growing extent and diversity of probation pre-trial work is used to illustrate and underline the way in which the Probation Service as a whole has significantly altered its focus in recent years.

References

Audit Commission (1989) *The Probation Service: Promoting Value for Money*. London: HMSO.

Beck, U. (1992) *Risk Society: Towards a New Modernity*. London: Sage.

Brody, S. (1976) *The Effectiveness of Sentencing: A Review of the Literature* (Home Office Research Study No. 35). London: HMSO.

Butler, A. J. P. (1996) 'Managing the future: A chief constable's view', in F. Leishman, B. Loveday and S. P. Savage (eds) *Core Issues in Policing*. London: Longman.

Caukin, S. (1995) 'The measure principle', *Observer*, 30 July.

Clear, T. R. and Cadora, E. (2001) 'Risk and correctional practice', in K. Stenson and R. R. Sullivan (eds) *Crime, Risk and Justice: The Politics of Crime Control in Liberal Democracies*. Cullompton: Willan.

Drakeford, M., Haines, K., Cotton, B. and Octigan, M. (2001) *Pre-trial Services and the Future of Probation*. Cardiff: University of Wales Press.

Douglas, M. (1992) *Risk and Blame: Essays in Cultural Theory*. London: Routledge.

Etzioni, A. (1997) *The New Golden Rule: Community and Morality in a Democratic Society*. New York: HarperCollins.

Feeley, M. and Simon, J. (1992) 'The new penology: Notes on the emerging strategy of corrections', *Criminology*, 30, 449–474.

Feeley, M. and Simon, J. (1994) 'Actuarial justice: The emerging new criminal law', in D. Nelkin (ed.) *The Futures of Criminology*. London: Sage.

Floud, J. (1982) 'Dangerousness and criminal justice', *British Journal of Criminology*, 22, 213–228.

Floud, J. and Young, W. (1981) *Dangerousness and Criminal Justice*. London: Heinemann.

Foucault, M. (1977) *Discipline and Punish*. London: Macmillan.

Garland, D. (1996) 'The limits of the sovereign state: Strategies of crime control in contemporary society', *British Journal of Criminology*, 36, 445–471.

Garland, D. (2000) 'The culture of high crime societies: Some preconditions of recent "law and order" policies', *British Journal of Criminology*, 40, 347–375.

Garland, D. (2001) *The Culture of Control: Crime and Social Order in Contemporary Society*. Oxford: Oxford University Press.

Giddens, A. (1998) *The Third Way: The Renewal of Social Democracy*. Cambridge: Polity.

Harding, J. (2000) 'A community justice dimension to effective probation practice', *Howard Journal of Criminal Justice*, 39, 132–149.

Home Office (1992) *National Standards for the Supervision of Offenders in the Community*. London: Home Office.

Home Office (1995) *Dealing with Dangerous People: The Probation Service and Public Protection* (Report of a Thematic Inspection HMIP). London: Home Office.

Home Office (1998) *Exercising Constant Vigilance: The Role of the Probation Service in Protecting the Public from Sex Offenders* (Report of a Thematic Inspection HMIP). London: Home Office.

Home Office (2000) *National Standards for the Supervision of Offenders in the Community*. London: Home Office.

Home Office (2002) *Probation Statistics England and Wales 2000*. London: Home Office.

Hudson, B. (2001a) 'Punishment, rights and difference: Defending justice in the risk society', in K. Stenson and R. R. Sullivan (eds) *Crime, Risk and Justice: The Politics of Crime Control in Liberal Democracies*. Cullompton: Willan.

Hudson, B. (2001b) 'Human rights, public safety and the Probation Service: Defending justice in the risk society', *Howard Journal of Criminal Justice*, 40, 103–113.

Kemshall, H. and Maguire, M. (2001) 'Public protection, partnership and risk penality: The multi-agency risk management of sexual and violent offenders', *Punishment and* Society, 1, 237–264.

King, J. F. S. and Jarvis, F. V. (1976) 'The influence of the probation and after-care service', in N. Walker and H. Giller (eds) *Policy-making in England*, Papers presented to the Cropwood Round-Table Conference December 1976. Cambridge: Institute of Criminology, University of Cambridge.

McWilliams, W. (1983) 'The mission to the English Police Courts 1876–1936', *Howard Journal of Penology and Crime Prevention*, 22, 129–147.

McWilliams, W. (1985) 'The mission transformed: Professionalisation of probation between the wars', *Howard Journal of Criminal Justice*, 24, 257–274.

McWilliams, W. (1986) 'The English probation system and the diagnostic ideal', *Howard Journal of Criminal Justice*, 25, 241–260.

McWilliams, W. (1987) 'Probation, pragmatism and policy', *Howard Journal of Criminal Justice*, 26, 97–121.

Mair, G. and Brockington, N. (1988) 'Female offenders and the probation service', *Howard Journal of Criminal Justice*, 27, 117–126.

Martinson, R. (1974) 'What works? Questions and answers about prison reform', *The Public Interest*, 35, 22–54.

Melossi, D. (2000) 'Changing representations of the criminal', in D. Garland and R. Sparks (eds) *Criminology and Social Theory*. Oxford: Oxford University Press.

Nash, M. (1995) 'Aggravation, mitigation and the gender of probation officers', *Howard Journal of Criminal Justice*, 34, 250–258.

Nash, M. (1999) *Police, Probation and Protecting the Public*. London: Blackstone.

Nash, M. (2000) 'Deconstructing the probation service – The Trojan Horse of public protection', *International Journal of the Sociology of Law*, 28, 201–213.

Nash, M. (2001) 'Influencing or influenced? – The probation service and criminal justice policy', in M. Ryan, S. P. Savage and D. S. Wall (eds) *Policy Networks in Criminal* Justice. Basingstoke: Palgrave.

Nellis, M. (1995) 'Probation values for the 1990s', *Howard Journal for Criminal Justice*, 34, 19–44.

Scott, P. (1977) 'Assessing dangerousness in criminals', *British Journal of Psychiatry*, 131, 127–42.

Walker, H. and Beaumont, B. (1981) *Probation Work: Critical Theory and Socialist Practice*. Oxford: Blackwell.

Worrall, A. (1997) *Punishment in the Community: The Future of Criminal Justice*. Harlow: Longman.

7

RISK AND RISK ASSESSMENT

Gwen Robinson

INTRODUCTION

During the last decade, the Probation Service has come to think about and respond to offenders primarily in terms of categories of risk. Correspondingly, risk assessment has assumed the status of a 'core task'. An assessment of the risks posed by the offender is now a mandatory requirement in all pre-sentence reports (Home Office 1995, 2000); it is also the starting point for all of the service's work with the offenders for whom it has a statutory responsibility. For those offenders subject to supervision, risk assessments increasingly form the basis of decisions about the type and intensity of the supervision which they receive. As Garland (1997) has explained, offenders have:

> come to be risks to be assessed and then managed, characterised by high risk or low risk profiles, and treated accordingly. The nature of the risk indicates how resources are to be allocated or targeted. (p. 4)

As the Probation Service has become more focused on risk, so the attention of researchers has come to focus on the processes through which practitioners arrive at assessments of risk and, increasingly, on improving the quality and reliability of the Service's risk assessments (see, for example, Kemshall 1996a, 1998a). Since the mid-1990s, there has been a proliferation of training materials on risk (Home Office 1997) and an unprecedented level of investment in the development of risk-assessment technology, such that the Probation Service now has at its disposal a range of instruments to assist in the process of assessing risk.

This chapter is organised into four main sections. The first, brief section attempts to clarify what is meant by the concept of risk in the context of probation practice. The second sets the rise of risk assessment in context and argues that the probation service's current preoccupation with risk is largely attributable to the convergence of the agendas of 'public protection' and 'effective practice' (or 'what works') during the 1990s. The third and most substantial section outlines and evaluates the main approaches to risk assessment, and reviews recent developments in risk-assessment technology. The final section looks more broadly at some of the implications of – and problems with – an increasingly risk-based approach to decision-making in criminal justice. The chapter closes with a summary of the key issues covered.

WORKING WITH OFFENDERS: DIMENSIONS OF RISK

Although the rise of the concept of risk in probation practice has been rapid – some might say meteoric – it has also been somewhat confused. A major source of confusion, both in 'official' literature and at the level of practice, has been the plurality of meaning inherent in the concept of risk. During the 1980s, the concept of 'risk of custody' was central to probation discourse: it was those offenders for whom a custodial sentence was a likely option who were targeted for a community-based 'alternative' (Raynor 1997). In this context, the offender was not generally considered to be a *source of* risk, but rather *subject to* it.

However, legislative and other changes in the early 1990s (see below) brought about a fundamental reconceptualisation of risk, such that it increasingly came to be understood *as an attribute of* offenders. This was to herald further confusion because, in the context of offending, the notion of risk relates to both the probability or likelihood of offending *per se*; and to the potential gravity or seriousness of any future offending behaviour. This has led to a lack of clarity about, for example, whether a 'high-risk offender' is someone who is very likely to commit further offences, possibly of a routine nature; or someone whose next offence is likely to be very serious if it occurs (Raynor *et al.* 2000). In fact, neither interpretation of 'high risk' is incorrect, but the example serves to illustrate the importance of conceptual clarity in risk assessment. In the absence of reference to the dimension(s) of risk in question, labels such as 'high risk' and 'low risk' are unhelpful at best.

The practice of risk assessment, then, involves making judgements or predictions about the likely future behaviour of an individual (or group) and this involves thinking about future behaviour on a number of levels. Hazel Kemshall (1996b), a leading authority on risk in probation practice, helpfully defines risk assessment as:

> a probability calculation that a harmful behaviour or event will occur, [which] involves an assessment about the frequency of the behaviour/event, its likely impact and who it will affect. (p. v)

According to Kemshall's definition, then, a thorough risk assessment should consider both the *gravity or seriousness* of any future offending behaviour and the *probability or likelihood* of such a behaviour occurring. These two dimensions of risk are commonly referred to as *risk of harm* and *risk of re-offending* respectively. A further important dimension of risk assessment concerns the likely target(s) or victim(s) of the individual's offending (or other harmful) behaviour. Thus, the practitioner should take into account both the risk(s) posed by the offender to him- or herself (i.e. risk of self-harming behaviour), as well as the likely risks to others: that is, to the public at large, to particular communities (e.g. children; ethnic minority groups), and/or to specific individuals (e.g. a former partner; a known associate).

THE RISE OF RISK IN PROBATION PRACTICE

In recent social-theoretical work, risk emerges as a central cultural theme in contemporary society (Giddens 1990, 1991; Beck 1992). For theorists of the 'risk society', late modernity is characterised by dangers which are wholly man-made, which affect everyone, and which cannot be converted into 'certainties', even by the expert systems on which we normally rely. While considerations of risk in recent social theory focus in particular on low-probability, high-consequence risks such as the threat of nuclear war, the risk profile of late modern society is thought to permeate society generally, such that the identification and management of risks have become structuring principles of contemporary life. For example, Giddens (1991) notes that a significant part of 'expert' thinking today is made up of *risk profiling*: that is,

> analysing what, in the current state of knowledge and in current conditions, is the distribution of risks in given milieux of action. (p. 119)

While social theory goes some way towards explaining the contemporary prominence of the practice of 'risk profiling' across a broad spectrum of institutions, the rise of risk in the context of probation practice is largely attributable to two more local developments, both of which assumed prominence in the 1990s. These are, first, the emergence of an explicit 'public protection' agenda in criminal justice; and, second, the parallel emergence of a body of knowledge about 'what works' in reducing re-offending.

Since the early 1990s, the criminal justice system has witnessed a growing preoccupation with the principle of 'public protection', such that a number of recent legislative provisions have defined sex offenders and those who have committed offences of serious violence as distinct groups requiring increased levels of control and/or surveillance (Kemshall 2001; Maguire *et al.* 2001). These legislative provisions have placed new responsibilities on the criminal justice agencies – not least the Probation Service – in respect of identifying and effectively managing those individuals who pose a particular risk of harm to the public. For example, although largely based on principles of 'desert' and 'proportionality' in sentencing, the 1991 Criminal Justice Act enabled courts to impose sentences of 'preventative' imprisonment in cases of sexual and violent offences. The Act also included provisions for extended periods of post-release community supervision for sex offenders, also on the grounds of preventing 'serious harm' in the future. These provisions placed a new onus on the Probation Service to provide the courts, where appropriate, with 'evidence of risk to the public of serious harm from the offender' (Home Office 1992: 2). This new focus on the assessment of *risk of serious harm* was further reinforced in a position statement on risk from the Association of Chief Officers of Probation (ACOP) and in the report of a thematic inspection of the Service's work with 'dangerous' offenders (ACOP 1994; HM Inspectorate of Probation (HMIP) 1995). The latter set out an expectation that all area services should hold a central register of offenders assessed as potentially dangerous; it also conveyed a clear message that, in terms of resourcing, the supervision of potentially dangerous offenders should take priority over that of 'other' categories of offender.

More recently, the Sex Offenders Act 1997, which requires people convicted of most forms of sexual offence to register their name and address with the police, has encouraged the establishment of Multi-agency Public Protection Panels, in which probation services play an active role (Nash 1999; Maguire *et al.* 2001). These panels exist to assess registered offenders and, where the level of risk is assessed as high enough to warrant it, to draw up a plan to 'manage' the risk in the community. Under the Criminal Justice and Court Services Act 2000, the establishment and operation of these multi-agency panels have been placed on a statutory footing: the Act requires police and probation services to establish joint arrangements to assess and manage the risks posed by sexual and violent offenders and others who may cause serious harm to the public.

The early evolution of risk as a way of thinking about offenders in the probation context, then, was clearly focused on one dimension of offender risk: namely, risk of serious harm, and it was in relation to work with risk of serious harm that the notion of 'risk management' first entered probation discourse (Robinson 2002). Meanwhile, however, as the Service's new 'public protection' role was being fostered, the lessons of a new body of research were also starting to filter into probation practice. This 'What Works' research, which was associated with renewed optimism about probation's rehabilitative effects, was to play a key role in promoting and extending risk-assessment practice in the latter part of the decade (for an account of this developing agenda, see McGuire and Priestley 1995; Vanstone 2000; Robinson 2001; Chui's Chapter 4 of this book).

'What Works' research impacted on risk-assessment practice through its promotion of a *principle of risk classification*. Risk in this context referred not to the potential for harm, but to the likelihood of reconviction. The 'risk principle' was derived from Canadian research which indicated not only that intensive cognitive-behavioural programmes tended to be most effective for higher-risk offenders, but also that subjecting lower-risk offenders to intensive programmes could actually be counter-productive (Andrews, Bonta and Hoge 1990). The risk principle thus dictated that, in order to maximise the rehabilitative potential of the service's work, there should be:

> a matching between offender risk level and degree of service intervention, such that higher-risk individuals receive more intensive services, while those at lower risk receive lower or minimal intervention. (McGuire and Priestley 1995: 14)

The Service's ability to routinely assess risk of re-offending in the offender population thus came to be an accepted prerequisite of effective probation practice.

The extension of risk-assessment practice in line with the risk principle was quickly endorsed in revised National Standards, which introduced a new requirement to include an explicit risk assessment in all pre-sentence reports (PSRs), not just those addressing violent or sexual offences. This was to comprise:

> a concise statement of the report writer's professional judgement of the risk of re-offending *and* the risk of harm to the public which the offender who is the subject of the report now poses. (Home Office 1995: 11, emphasis added)

The new National Standards also emphasised risk assessment as a regular requirement in relation to all offenders under supervision, stating that such assessments 'should be undertaken systematically at regular intervals' (Home Office 1995: 18).

By the late 1990s, then, risk assessment had been confirmed as a core task, and the Service's assessments of risk were increasingly encompassing both risk of harm *and* risk of re-offending. Further, the Service's risk assessments were increasingly forming the basis of decisions about the rationing of its resources. In short, the greater the level of assessed risk, the greater the input of probation resources.

APPROACHES TO RISK ASSESSMENT

As a prediction of future events, risk assessment is not an exact science, and the achievement of certainty in risk assessment is acknowledged to be an unrealistic goal. As Kemshall (1998b) has explained:

> Whilst risk decisions are almost entirely about the prediction and control of the future, the future is highly contingent and risk, whilst often translated into the language of probabilities, is still an attempt to predict the unpredictable. (pp. 67–68)

In recognition of the inherent unpredictability of future behaviour, it is generally accepted that 'defensibility' rather than 'certainty' is the goal of risk assessment practice. A 'defensible' risk assessment is one which is judged to be as accurate as possible and which would stand up to scrutiny if the handling of the case were to be investigated (HMIP 1995; Carson 1996; Kemshall 1998b).

In its pursuit of 'defensible' risk assessments the Probation Service has, in the last decade or so, paid increasing attention to issues of quality, consistency and accuracy in risk-assessment practice. This section describes the move toward more 'formalised' risk assessment methods and considers the relative merits and limitations of the main approaches toward the assessment of risk.

'Clinical' versus 'actuarial' methods

A key debate in contemporary probation practice concerns the relative merits of 'clinical' and more formalised ('actuarial') approaches to risk assessment. The notion of 'clinical' assessment derives from the tradition of one-to-one casework in medical, social work and probation contexts, and refers to the practitioner's use of experience, interviewing skills, observation and professional judgement to arrive at an assessment of the individual. Bonta (1996) has characterised the clinical approach as the 'first generation' of assessment practice. Actuarial risk assessment is derived from the methods used in the insurance industry, and is based upon statistical calculations of probability. In contrast to the clinical method, actuarial – or 'second generation' (Bonta 1996) – assessment is based on a set of identified factors or items, each of which has been empirically demonstrated to correlate with reconviction.

The mid-1990s witnessed a growing critique of the clinical approach, which centred on the lack of consistency between assessments conducted by different practitioners, and on the questionable accuracy of assessments which could not be shown to have taken on board contemporary knowledge about known risk factors (e.g. Roberts 1993; Burnett 1996). For Bonta (1996) the most serious weakness of the clinical approach is that the rules for collecting and interpreting information about the individual are subject to considerable personal discretion: for example, the practitioner is free to ask questions that he or she considers important, which makes fairness problematic. The subjectivity of a purely clinical approach was illustrated in Burnett's (1996) research on assessment practice. In the course of this research over 100 probation officers and senior probation officers in ten probation areas were interviewed, and it was found that over half thought that the assessment of the offender and/or the proposal in a pre-sentence report was likely to differ according to the particular experience or skills of the report writer.

The development of actuarial or so-called 'objective' risk assessment technology can be traced back to the work of Burgess in the 1920s. In a study of over 3000 parolees, Burgess (1928) identified 21 factors which differentiated parole successes from parole failures and these factors were used to construct a 'risk scale'. In assessing the parolee, the presence of a factor merited a score of '1' such that the higher the parolee's score, the greater the likelihood of failure while on parole. The next major step in the development of actuarial risk assessment was the work of Glueck and Glueck (1950), who developed a system for predicting the probability of (male) delinquent behaviour. The Gluecks' system marked a departure from Burgess's in that the variables or 'risk factors' were 'weighted' according to their predictive validity: that is, their relative importance as a predictor of delinquency.

Kemshall's (1996b) review of actuarial risk assessment methods identifies the prediction of reconviction for known offenders – including those on probation – as the main area in which actuarial prediction methods have been utilised in the criminological arena.

Actuarial risk assessment in the probation context: assessing risk of reconviction

The development of an actuarial tool to aid assessments of risk of reconviction in the probation context dates back to the early 1990s (Humphrey, Carter and Pease 1992; Copas, Ditchfield and Marshall 1994). The 'reconviction predictor scale' developed by Copas was subsequently refined and, in 1996, the Home Office launched the 'Offender Group Reconviction Scale' (OGRS), a Windows-based computer program for use by probation personnel (Home Office 1996; Copas and Marshall 1998; Taylor 1999).

OGRS was developed on the basis of a national Home Office database consisting of information about the demographic characteristics and offending histories of a large sample of offenders, and was designed for the assessment of male and female offenders aged 17 and over. The instrument provides an estimate of the statistical likelihood of one or more reconvictions within two years of release from custody or from the beginning of a community sentence. The key variables which OGRS considers in calculating the statistical likelihood of reconviction are as follows:

- Age
- Sex
- Offence
- Number of custodial sentences while aged under 21
- Number of previous convictions
- Age at first conviction

OGRS was designed with two purposes in mind. First, it was intended as an aid to practitioners' risk assessments, particularly in pre-sentence reports. Second, it was designed as an aid to evaluating the effectiveness of supervision programmes. Using an actuarial tool such as OGRS as an evaluation instrument involves calculating an *expected reconviction rate* for each of a group of offenders and then calculating an average, which may be compared to the *actual reconviction rate* for the same group of offenders when the two-year follow-up period has elapsed. A lower observed or actual rate of reconviction than that which was expected indicates, in principle, that the intervention has been effective in reducing the risk of reconviction (for example, see Wilkinson 1994; Raynor and Vanstone 1997).

Evaluating actuarial methods

The main strength of actuarial methods lies in their reliance on clearly articulated risk factors or indicators which are grounded in empirical data. This means that they can offer high levels of predictive validity or accuracy. However, despite their proven predictive validity, actuarial methods suffer from a number of limitations in the context of predicting the risks posed by individual offenders (for a review of the limitations of actuarial methods in evaluating the effectiveness of interventions, see Lloyd, Mair and Hough 1994).

First, while actuarial methods are commonly associated with objectivity, recent research has raised questions about their reliability in practice: that is, the extent to which such tools produce the same or similar scores when applied by different practitioners. Stephens and Brown (2001) have demonstrated the significant scope for error in reading and interpreting information about offenders and their criminal convictions from Police National Computer (PNC) print-outs, which form the basis of OGRS calculations. Their research points clearly to the need for training to ensure the reliability of such tools.

Second, it is important to remember that the probability of reconviction, which actuarial tools such as OGRS measure, is not synonymous with the probability of *re-offending*. In general terms, the probability of re-offending is likely to exceed the probability of reconviction, since a great deal of offending goes undetected. This disparity between rates of re-offending and reconviction is greater for some types of offending than for others, due to differential rates of reporting, detection and prosecution for different types of crime. For example, offenders who are convicted of burglary are likely to be reconvicted more quickly than those who commit a sexual offence (Taylor 1999). A related point is that actuarially based tools can increase the likelihood of 'consistently discriminatory assessments' (Bhui 1999), because the data on which such assessments are based may to a large extent be a reflection of discriminatory processes in the criminal justice system, such as the overpolicing of Black communities (see also Daley and Lane 1999).

Third, while actuarial instruments such as OGRS offer a useful means of predicting the likelihood of *any reconviction*, they generally tell the practitioner nothing about the *type or seriousness* of any future offence for which the individual may be reconvicted. This means that a high risk of reconviction score may in fact mask a reduction in the seriousness of an individual's offending over time. It also means that actuarial instruments are of limited use in relation to the prediction of serious harm.

Indeed, actuarial methods have not been extensively utilised to predict risk of serious harm because far less is known about the factors which are predictive of serious harm than is known about those which are predictive of reconviction generally. This is principally because behaviours which cause serious harm have a relatively low *base rate*: that is, they are relatively rare (Milner and Campbell 1995).[1] This low base rate makes it difficult to identify factors which can reliably distinguish between those who will and those who will not commit further acts causing serious harm. Although a revised version of OGRS (OGRS 2) *does* offer a means of predicting reconvictions for sexual and violent offences, a number of limitations of the instrument are acknowledged (Taylor 1999). Reflecting the limited utility of actuarial methods in respect of assessing risk of serious harm, one recent research study found that offence type and/or length of (custodial) sentence were the main criteria against which risk of harm status was initially judged by practitioners in two area probation services. It was also found that, while the assessment of sex offenders was assisted by practitioners' use of a psychometric instrument developed by the Home Office, staff were otherwise reliant upon locally developed, non-actuarial procedures for assessing risk of harm (Robinson 2002).[2] Notwithstanding attempts to 'formalise' or structure the assessment of risk of harm, then, this area of assessment was acknowledged, by both practitioners and managers, to be reliant mainly upon professional judgement (see also Maguire *et al.* 2001: 28–31).

A fourth limitation of actuarial methods derives from the fact that they are both based on and designed for use with groups or *populations* of offenders. This means that they cannot provide accurate predictions of risk in respect of individuals. For example, OGRS can do no more than provide an estimate of the probability that *an* offender with a particular set of characteristics will be reconvicted within two years; it does not purport to make an accurate prediction for a specific individual. Thus, if an offender has an OGRS score of 75 per cent, this indicates that three-quarters of offenders of this age and sex and with a comparable criminal record are likely to be reconvicted within two

---

[1] Other problems of prediction in respect of risk of harm are discussed in depth elsewhere (e.g. Kemshall 1997b; Prins 1999).

[2] For a review of specialist assessment instruments for the assessment of sexual and violent offenders, see Kemshall 2001.

years. The score cannot tell the assessor whether this particular individual will be one of the 75 per cent of offenders with this profile who *will* be reconvicted, or one of the 25 per cent who *will not.*

Finally, tools such as OGRS tend to rely on a particular type of information about offenders: namely *static* factors. These factors are static in the sense that they cannot be altered or modified: for example, an offender can do nothing to change his or her age, sex or offending history. While these static factors are strongly predictive of reconviction, they provide little direction for the practitioner who wishes to know what kind of intervention might *reduce* the individual's risk of re-offending. The reliance on static factors also makes actuarial tools relatively ineffective when it comes to evaluating changes in levels of risk over time, because they take no account of changes in the offender's personal circumstances, behaviour or attitudes.

Assessing 'criminogenic needs': the emergence of a dynamic approach

It is principally in the light of some of these limitations that researchers have, in the last decade or so, begun to explore alternative approaches to the assessment of risk. In particular researchers have been keen to explore the possibility of incorporating *non-static* factors into the risk prediction process. By the mid-1990s, 'What Works' research had begun to identify a number of non-static factors pertaining to the lifestyles and attributes of offenders which could be shown to be linked with offending behaviour (e.g. Andrews *et al.* 1990; Andrews and Bonta 1994, 1995). These factors have come to be known as *dynamic risk factors*, or *criminogenic needs*. As Bonta (1996) has explained,

> Criminogenic needs are linked to criminal behaviour. If we alter these needs, then we change the likelihood of criminal behaviour. Thus criminogenic needs are actually risk predictors, but they are *dynamic* in nature rather than static. (p. 23)

In terms of assessing risk, criminogenic needs are a crucial 'discovery' in that they contribute to a more *individualised* assessment of risk which can usefully point to the areas of the offender's life – such as his or her accommodation or employment situation, drug or alcohol use, or attitudes – which, if subject to intervention and help, are likely to reduce his or her risk of further offending. Although much of the research on criminogenic needs has been conducted in North America, a recent UK study by May (1999) lends support to the role of dynamic – or 'social' – risk factors in contributing to offending behaviour.

Risk/needs-assessment instruments

Since the mid-1990s, a number of assessment instruments incorporating dynamic risk factors or criminogenic needs have been available to UK probation areas. These are commonly referred to as 'risk/needs'-assessment instruments and, according to Bonta's (1996) typology, these constitute the 'third generation' of offender assessment.

Risk/needs-assessment instruments tend to blur the traditional distinction between clinical and actuarial methods. While based on items which have been shown to be predictive of reconviction, these instruments cannot be completed on the basis of paper records (e.g. PNC print-outs) alone, although such records usually contribute to the assessment. Rather, they are reliant on the practitioner's ability to elicit the relevant information, through interviewing the offender and, where appropriate, consultation with other persons and/or sources.

To date, the most popular risk/needs-assessment instruments have been the *Assessment, Case Recording/Management and Evaluation* (ACE) system (Roberts *et al.* 1996; Gibbs 1999), and the *Level of Service Inventory – Revised* (LSI-R) (Andrews and Bonta 1995). The ACE instrument, initially commissioned in 1994 by the Warwickshire probation area, was developed over a number of years by researchers at the University of Oxford, in collaboration with practitioners. ACE consists entirely of 'dynamic' factors and was designed to be used alongside an actuarial predictor such as OGRS. LSI-R, developed by Canadian psychologists and correctional practitioners since the early 1980s and imported to the UK in 1996, combines both static and dynamic factors which are organised into ten sub-components. The ten sub-components cover areas such as criminal history, education/employment, accommodation and alcohol/drug use, all of which have been statistically proven to be related to risk of reconviction. By 1998 the majority of area probation services were using either ACE or LSI-R (Raynor *et al.* 2000).

In the context of its *Effective Practice Initiative*, the Home Office announced in 1999 its intention to develop a new risk/needs-assessment instrument, for use by all UK prison and probation services (Home Office 1999). The resulting *Offender Assessment System* (OASys) was designed by a multi-disciplinary team including researchers, managers and practitioners from both probation and prison services (OASys Development Team 2001). Its development was informed by the findings of a number of research studies, such that OASys would combine the best features of existing instruments, in terms of both predictive accuracy and user-friendliness (Aubrey and Hough 1997; Aye-Maung and Hammond 2000; Raynor *et al.* 2000). During the development stage, the instrument was extensively piloted in both probation and prison contexts, and subject to amendments in the light of feedback received. At the time of writing, OASys is in the process of being 'rolled out' to probation and prison services nationally and is likely to be subject to further refinements in the future. At present, it is a paper-based system, but it is hoped that an IT version will soon be available.

OASys was designed to meet a comprehensive specification, such that it includes both an assessment of reconviction (incorporating both static and dynamic factors) and a structured format for the assessment of risk of harm. OASys also triggers other, more specialist assessments in relevant cases (e.g. basic skills; sexual and violent offender assessments). Finally, it also provides a system for translating the OASys assessment(s) into a supervision or sentence plan.

Risk/needs assessment: problems and potential

Risk/needs-assessment instruments boast a number of useful applications. Not only have they been shown to be effective in predicting risk of reconviction (e.g. Raynor *et al.* 2000), but their inclusion of dynamic variables also enables users to identify the areas of an offender's life which, if tackled in probation supervision, are likely to lead to a reduction in the level of risk posed. Such instruments can also provide a measure of the effectiveness of probation intervention, via the comparison of scores at the start and at the end of a period of supervision. Thanks to their inclusion of dynamic variables, risk/ needs-assessment instruments – in contrast to 'pure' actuarial instruments such as OGRS – are as valid for gauging the progress of individual offenders as they are for measuring effectiveness at the level of aggregates (i.e. groups of offenders) (Aye-Maung and Hammond 2000). Finally, in the context of effective information systems, risk/needs-assessment instruments can be used to inform service managers about the spread of criminogenic needs in local and/ or national offender populations. This information can be extremely valuable in informing spending on specific services, such as treatment for drug and alcohol users, many of which are provided by agencies funded through partnership agreements.

Although it is too soon to evaluate OASys, a number of studies of users' views have found that practitioners have broadly welcomed the introduction of risk/needs-assessment instruments such as ACE and LSI-R (Roberts *et al.* 1996; Roberts and Robinson 1998; Gibbs 1999; Aye-Maung and Hammond 2000; Robinson forthcoming). In particular, practitioners have welcomed the move towards greater consistency in assessment practice, and have acknowledged a positive impact on the quality of other areas of practice, such as PSR writing and supervision planning. By virtue of their grounding in 'scientific' evidence, risk/needs-assessment instruments have also been viewed as contributing significantly to the credibility or 'defensibility' of the service's risk assessments, particularly in the eyes of external audiences, such as the courts (Aye-Maung and Hammond 2000; Robinson 2003).

However, research has also revealed a number of problems in respect of the implementation of risk/needs-assessment instruments. For users, the incorporation of these instruments into everyday practice has entailed considerable demands, in terms of both additional paperwork and the time required to gather the relevant information and complete a thorough assessment. In one study, the most common complaint among ACE users was that the forms were a burden to complete (Aye-Maung and Hammond 2000). A separate study found that LSI-R completion was linked with managerial oversight: that is, practitioners avoided using LSI-R except in conjunction with PSR preparation, when they knew that their use of the instrument was routinely monitored (Robinson 2003). Findings such as these raise questions about the reliability of such instruments: that is, the extent to which 'completion fatigue' among users may compromise the quality of assessments.

Indeed, one of the main problems in the design of risk/needs-assessment instruments has been achieving a balance between comprehensiveness and user-friendliness. The development and piloting of both ACE and OASys have demonstrated the difficulties in achieving such a balance, in that the tendency towards the inclusion of ever-greater numbers of items in the interests of comprehensiveness in the assessment process has been tempered by users' demands for brevity and relative simplicity. The developers of OASys have attempted a compromise on this issue by producing two versions of OASys: both a full assessment and a briefer, 'screening' version for use in the context of time-limited work (OASys Development Team 2001).

A further problem has been achieving a balance between, on the one hand, the pursuit of consistency and standardisation in the assessment process; and, on the other, the discretion or professional judgement of the user. There are two paradoxical aspects to this. First, because risk/needs-assessment instruments rely on the assessor's ability to elicit and interpret a range of information, there are clearly limits to the reliability of such instruments. Although one study of inter-rater reliability in relation to ACE and LSI-R assessments has reported satisfactory findings, the sample was small and further research in this area is needed (Raynor *et al.* 2000). Second, while practitioners have welcomed the notion of consistency in the interest of greater equity for offenders, concern has also been expressed about potential 'de-skilling' and/or de-professionalisation as a result of the increasing standardisation of assessment practice (Roberts *et al.* 1996; Colombo and Neary 1998; Gibbs 1999; Robinson 2003). Indeed, this kind of resistance to structured forms of assessment can be traced back to the introduction of an early version of OGRS in the mid-1990s, which provoked a defensive response from the National Association of Probation Officers (NAPO) (Fletcher 1995) and a subsequent campaign against its introduction. At that time NAPO's concerns were expressed as follows:

> Such predictive methods are no substitute for sound professional assessment of risk, formed during full interviews with defendants . . . Further, they invite assessment by staff who do not have the appropriate training and experience. (*NAPO News* February 1996: 4)

More recently, a study of LSI-R implementation in two probation areas revealed concerns among users about the potentially de-professionalising impact of structured assessment instruments which, it was feared, might eventually render professional experience and/or qualifications redundant. As a consequence, practitioners tended to emphasise the amount of discretion and skill required to complete the assessment and commonly referred to LSI-R as an assessment in its own right or as a *supplement* to a professional clinical assessment, rather than an alternative to it (Robinson 2003).

Finally, some researchers have questioned the degree to which actuarially based risk/needs-assessment instruments, designed with reference to (largely white) male offender populations, are applicable to women and other minority groups of offenders. Shaw and Hannah-Moffatt (2000) argue that the notion of 'criminogenic' (i.e. offending related) need is not necessarily the same for minority groups as it is for white men. This, they argue, may mean that the specific needs of these groups are being overlooked in assessments. Alternatively, it is argued, there is a danger that the blurring of 'needs' and 'risks' will result in inflated estimates of risk in respect of minority and/or disadvantaged groups and justify greater than necessary levels of intervention and control (Hannah-Moffatt 1999; Hudson 2001). For Hudson (2001),

> Risk assessment sounds rational and non-blaming, but there is surely an echo of the euphemisms of 'old style' rehabilitation, where rights and liberties were trampled upon in the name of 'help' and 'treatment'. (p. 109)

The tendency towards 'consistently discriminatory assessments' which was noted in relation to actuarial methods has also been registered in relation to risk/needs assessment. For Hudson (2001), risk/needs-assessment instruments pose a threat to racial equality because some of the data which they take into account reflect discriminatory processes in wider society (e.g. employment status) and/or measures of 'lifestyle' which treat patterns among white populations as the 'norm' (e.g. family relationship/residency patterns).

RISK ASSESSMENT IN CONTEXT: RISK-BASED DECISION-MAKING IN CRIMINAL JUSTICE

In recent years, the rise if risk in probation practice has been rapid, and the main questions about risk assessment have tended to be 'technical' ones, relating to the refinement of risk assessment technology and the predictive validity of the various assessment instruments available. However, as questions about punishment come to be increasingly linked with questions of risk, it is important that practitioners are encouraged to think about some of the broader issues and problems which are thrown up by an approach toward offenders which increasingly accords risk assessment a central role.

In the context of criminal justice, a risk assessment is a powerful statement. Risk assessments composed by criminal justice personnel, including probation officers and, increasingly, police and prison officers, affect decisions about the liberty of individual offenders. By the same token, risk assessments impact on public safety. For example, risk assessments in pre-sentence reports play a pivotal role in sentencing decisions, and those contained in reports to the Parole Board affect decisions about the release of offenders serving lengthy custodial sentences (Hood and Shute 2000). Risk-based decision-making, then, involves weighing up the community's right to protection from the offender, against the offender's right to liberty, or to the least necessary restrictions (Hudson 2001).

However, a number of problems arise when information about risk dominates decisions about punishment. First, as we have seen, risk assessment is not associated with certainty: even the most advanced risk-assessment technology cannot guarantee 100 per cent accuracy. Errors, then, are inevitable. In any risk assessment there is the potential for two basic types of error: these are known as *false positives* and *false negatives*. False positive predictions refer to the erroneous identification of low-risk offenders as high risk. In contrast, false negative predictions refer to the erroneous identification of high-risk offenders as low risk. In the context of risk-based decision-making, both types of error can have far-reaching consequences. False positives are likely to result in stigmatising labels and/or the unnecessary loss of liberty for the offender, while false negatives potentially compromise public safety and the credibility of both risk assessors and the agencies in which they work (Kemshall 1997a).

Further, the objectivity of risk assessment is influenced by the social and political context, as a number of commentators have pointed out. As the social and political climate changes, society's tolerance of different types of error tends to change in tandem, and those charged with assessing risk are arguably inclined further toward one or other type of error. For example, in the present political climate, where the principles of 'public protection' and the rights of victims are prioritised (e.g. see National Probation Service for England and Wales 2001), society's tolerance of false negative predictions is low. As a consequence, the assessment of risk – particularly risk of harm – tends toward 'precautionary' or 'defensive' practice, and the generation of a high proportion of false positives (Kemshall 1998b; Tuddenham 2000). This tendency towards extreme caution in risk-assessment practice has been noted recently in respect of the decisions of the Parole Board (Hood and Shute 2000) and the risk classifications of some multi-agency Public Protection Panels (Tuddenham 2000; Maguire *et al.* 2001). As Tuddenham (2000) has recently argued, 'there are few prizes for taking risks with offenders, only penalties' (p. 175).

In relation to sentencing decisions, a more fundamental question concerns the relationship between a risk-based approach and notions of justice and fairness. Proponents of desert theory argue that punishment should be limited to offences which people have actually committed, rather than offences which they might commit in the future (e.g. von Hirsch 1985). While the principle of desert essentially looks back at and punishes the offence(s) committed, a preoccupation with risk and risk assessment indicates an approach which is essentially forward-looking or future-oriented. American criminologists Feeley and Simon (1994) refer to this as *actuarial* justice. This tendency to look toward future rather than (or as well as) past offending undermines the connection between crimes and punishment and, taken to an extreme, dispenses with this connection altogether. Hudson (2001) offers the example of recent proposals to introduce preventative incarceration, in the absence of a criminal conviction, for persons diagnosed as having severe, untreatable personality disorders, on the basis that they conform to the 'profile' of a dangerous offender.

A second important principle which is undermined by an emphasis on risk, Hudson notes, is that of *proportionality* of punishment to offence. Proportionality, she argues, is rendered particularly problematic when recidivism risk is taken into account by sentencers, as in US-style 'Three Strikes' legislation, which justifies disproportionate sentences for repeated non-violent offences such as burglary. As we saw in the discussion of risk-assessment technology, Hudson also draws attention to the potential conflict between a risk-based approach and the principle of *equality*: that is, the treatment of like offences with similar punishments.

Turning to the context of community penalties, it has been explained that risk assessments now play a major role in informing decisions about the type and/or intensity of supervision appropriate to individual offenders. However, using risk information to determine resource allocation decisions has proven problematic in practice. In a recent research study, two probation areas were found to be experiencing significant difficulties when it came to defining offenders' suitability for different types of supervision in purely actuarial or numerical terms: that is, on the basis of their scores on a risk/needs-assessment instrument (Robinson 2002). For example, many of those offenders deemed suitable for intensive probation programmes by virtue of high-risk scores proved not to be good candidates in view of issues such as mental health, drug use or a history of failure to complete programmes. Practitioners and managers in the two probation areas studied quickly learned that risk scores by themselves were not an adequate basis for decisions about the type of supervision which offenders should receive, and that a more nuanced understanding of the particular needs and circumstances of individual offenders was in fact necessary. Increasingly, practitioners were falling back on clinical judgement as a guide to decision-making. The consensus among practitioners in the two probation areas was summarised by one officer's comment, that 'it's not always as simple as a figure'. She continued:

> you can't sort of simply say that a score of 30 odd needs this help [...]. It *is* more complicated than that. But as *part* of that, I don't think there's anything *wrong* with that, you know, to *guide* us, but to recognise that it's not the be all and end all of working out what should be done with people. (Quoted in Robinson 2002: 16)

There are a number of reasons, then, why risk assessment alone is not an adequate basis for decision-making in criminal justice contexts. While risk assessment has a valid and useful contribution to make, it is best regarded as a starting point, or as one of a number of factors to be considered in the decision-making process.

SUMMARY OF KEY ISSUES

- During the 1990s, risk assessment assumed the status of a core task in probation practice. This was largely due to the rise of 'public protection' and 'effective practice' agendas, both of which encouraged the Service to think about offenders in terms of risk and legitimised the concept of risk as a basis for the rationing of the service's resources. In the context of probation practice, the concept of risk has a number of dimensions, and it is important that practitioners are clear about the dimension(s) of risk addressed in any risk assessment. As a prediction about future behaviour, risk assessment is not and never will be an exact science and for this reason 'defensibility' rather than 'certainty' is acknowledged to be a realistic goal of risk-assessment practice.
- In its pursuit of more defensible risk assessments, the Probation Service has played an active role in the developing 'science' of risk assessment. In general terms, risk-assessment practice has moved away from an approach based purely on clinical judgement towards an approach that utilises actuarial (i.e. statistical) methods alongside clinical judgement. However, advances in respect of assessing risk of re-offending have significantly over-taken developments in respect of risk of harm assessment, where actuarial methods have only limited utility. In recent years, actuarially-based risk assessment technology has developed rapidly and the probation service has been particularly keen to adopt 'risk/needs' assessment instruments, which combine the prediction of reconviction with an assessment of the offender's criminogenic needs. The Offender Assessment System (OASys) developed by the Home Office heralds the beginning of a unified approach toward the assessment of offender risk across both probation and prison services.

- It is predicted that the coming decade will witness continued investment and research activity around the development of actuarially based risk assessment technology. However, as the technology becomes increasingly sophisticated, it will be important that the Service, its masters and the public do not lose sight of the fact that the assessment of risk is not a 'perfectible' practice.
- As a guide to decision-making in criminal justice settings, risk assessments are both relevant and valuable. However, information about risk is best regarded as a starting point, or as one of a number of factors to be considered in the decision-making process.

References

Andrews, D., Bonta, J. and Hoge, R. (1990) 'Classification for effective rehabilitation', *Criminal Justice and Behavior*, 17, 19–52.

Andrews, D. A., Zinger, I., Hoge, R. D., Bonta, J., Gendreau, P. and Cullen, F. T. (1990) 'Does correctional treatment work? A clinically relevant and psychologically informed meta-analysis', *Criminology*, 28, 369–404.

Andrews, D. and Bonta, J. (1994) *The Psychology of Criminal Conduct*. Cincinnati, OH: Anderson.

Andrews, D. and Bonta, J. (1995) *The Level of Service Inventory – Revised: Manual*. New York: Multi-Health Systems Inc.

Association of Chief Officers of Probation (ACOP) (1994) *Guidance on Management of Risk and Public Protection*. London: ACOP.

Aubrey, R. and Hough, M. (1997) *Assessing Offenders' Needs: Assessment Scales for the Probation Service* (Home Office Research Study No. 166). London: Home Office.

Aye-Maung, N. and Hammond, N. (2000) *Risk of Re-offending and Needs Assessments: The User's Perspective* (Home Office Research Study No. 216). London: Home Office.

Beck, U. (1992) *Risk Society: Towards a New Modernity*. London: Sage.

Bhui, H. S. (1999) 'Race, racism and risk assessment', *Probation Journal*, 46, 171–181.

Bonta, J. (1996) 'Risk-needs assessment and treatment', in A. T. Harland (ed.) *Choosing Correctional Options That Work: Defining the Demand and Evaluating the Supply*. Thousand Oaks, CA: Sage.

Burgess, E. W. (1928) 'Factors making for success or failure on parole', *Journal of Criminal Law and Criminology*, 19, 239–306.

Burnett, R. (1996) *Fitting Supervision to Offenders: Assessment and Allocation Decisions in the Probation Service* (Home Office Research Study No. 153). London: Home Office.

Carson, D. (1996) 'Risking legal repercussions', in H. Kemshall and J. Pritchard (eds) *Good Practice in Risk Assessment and Risk Management*. London: Jessica Kingsley.

Colombo, A. and Neary, M. (1998) 'Square roots and algebra': Understanding perceptions of combined risk/needs assessment measures', *Probation Journal*, 45, 213–219.

Copas, J., Ditchfield, J. and Marshall, P. (1994) 'Development of a new reconviction prediction score', *Home Office Research Bulletin*, 36, 30–37.

Copas, J. and Marshall, P. (1998) 'The Offender Group Reconviction Scale: A statistical reconviction score for use by probation officers', *Applied Statistics*, 47, 159–171.

Daley, D. and Lane, R. (1999) 'Actuarially-based "on-line" risk assessment in Western Australia', *Probation Journal*, 46, 164–170.

Feeley, M. and Simon, J. (1994) 'Actuarial justice: the emerging new criminal law', in D. Nelken (ed.) *The Futures of Criminology*. London: Sage.

Fletcher, H. (1995) 'New reconviction scale', *NAPO News*, 72, 1.

Garland, D. (1997) 'Probation and the reconfiguration of crime control', in R. Burnett (ed.) *The Probation Service: Responding to Change* (Probation Studies Unit Report No. 3). Oxford: University of Oxford Centre for Criminological Research.

Gibbs, A. (1999) 'The assessment, case management and evaluation system', *Probation Journal*, 46, 182–186.

Giddens, A. (1990) *The Consequences of Modernity*. Cambridge: Polity.

Giddens, A. (1991) *Modernity and Self-Identity*. Cambridge: Polity.

Glueck, S. and Glueck, E. (1950) *Unravelling Juvenile Delinquency*. New York: Commonwealth Fund.

Hannah-Moffatt, K. (1999) 'Moral agent or actuarial subject: risk and Canadian women's imprisonment', *Theoretical Criminology*, 3, 71–94.

HM Inspectorate of Probation (HMIP) (1995) *Dealing with Dangerous People: The Probation Service and Public Protection*. London: Home Office.

Home Office (1992) *National Standards for the Supervision of Offenders in the Community*. London: Home Office.

Home Office (1995) *National Standards for the Supervision of Offenders in the Community*. London: Home Office.

Home Office (1996) *Guidance for the Probation Service on the Offender Group Reconviction Scale (OGRS)* (Probation Circular 63/1996). London: Home Office.

Home Office (1997) *Management and Assessment of Risk in the Probation Service*. London: Home Office.

Home Office (1999) *Effective Practice Initiative: A Joint Risk/Needs Assessment System for the Prison and Probation Services* (Probation Circular 16/1999). London: Home Office.

Home Office (2000) *National Standards for the Supervision of Offenders in the Community*. London: Home Office.

Hood, R. and Shute, S. (2000) *The Parole System at Work: A Study of Risk Based Decision-Making* (Home Office Research Study No. 202). London: Home Office.

Hudson, B. (2001) 'Human rights, public safety and the probation service: Defending justice in the risk society', *Howard Journal of Criminal Justice*, 40, 103–113.

Humphrey, C., Carter, P. and Pease, K. (1992) 'A reconviction predictor for probationers', *British Journal of Social Work*, 22, 33–46.

Kemshall, H. (1996a) 'Risk assessment: Fuzzy thinking or "decisions in action"?', *Probation Journal*, 43, 2–7.

Kemshall, H. (1996b) *Reviewing Risk*. London: Home Office.

Kemshall, H. (1997a) 'Training materials for risk assessment and risk management', in Home Office (ed.) *Management and Assessment of Risk in the Probation Service*. London: Home Office.

Kemshall, H. (1997b) 'The dangerous are always with us: Dangerousness and the role of the probation service', *Vista: Perspectives on Probation*, 2, 136–153.

Kemshall, H. (1998a) *Risk in Probation Practice*. Aldershot: Ashgate.

Kemshall, H. (1998b) 'Defensible decisions for risk: or "it's the doers wot get the blame"', *Probation* Journal, 45, 67–72.

Kemshall, H. (2001) *Risk Assessment and Management of Known Sexual and Violent Offenders: A Review of Current Issues* (Police Research Series Paper No. 140). London: Home Office.

Lloyd, C., Mair, G. and Hough, M. (1994) *Explaining Reconviction Rates: A Critical Analysis* (Home Office Research Study No. 136). London: HMSO.

Maguire, M., Kemshall, H., Noaks, L. and Wincup, E. (2001) *Risk Management of Sexual and Violent Offenders: The Work of Public Protection Panels* (Police Research Series Paper No. 139). London: Home Office.

May, C. (1999) *Explaining Reconviction Following a Community Sentence: The Role of Social Factors* (Home Office Research Study No.192). London: Home Office.

McGuire, J. and Priestley, P. (1995) 'Reviewing "what works": past, present and future', in J. McGuire (ed.) *What Works: Reducing Reoffending – Guidelines from Research and Practice*. Chichester: Wiley.

Milner, J. and Campbell, J. (1995) 'Prediction issues for practitioners', in J. Campbell (ed.) *Assessing Dangerousness*. London: Sage.

Nash, M. (1999) *Police, Probation and Protecting the Public*. London: Blackstone.

National Probation Service for England and Wales (2001) *A New Choreography: An Integrated Strategy for the National Probation Service for England and Wales – Strategic Framework 2001–2004*. London: Home Office.

OASys Development Team (2001) *The Offender Assessment System: User Manual*. London: Home Office.

Prins, H. (1999) *Will They Do It Again?* London: Routledge.

Raynor, P. (1997) 'Evaluating probation: a moving target', in G. Mair (ed.) *Evaluating the Effectiveness of Community Penalties*. Aldershot: Avebury.

Raynor, P. and Vanstone, M. (1997) *Straight Thinking on Probation (STOP): The Mid Glamorgan Experiment* (Probation Studies Unit Report No. 4). Oxford: Centre for Criminological Research, University of Oxford.

Raynor, P., Kynch, J., Roberts, C. and Merrington, S. (2000) *Risk and Need Assessment in Probation Services: An Evaluation* (Home Office Research Study No. 211). London: Home Office.

Roberts, C. (1993) 'How to improve practice', in *Improving Practice: Towards a Partnership Between Information, Research and Practice*, Proceedings of the Ninth Annual Conference of the National Probation Research and Information Exchange. University of Warwick, 30 March–2 April 1993, NPRIE.

Roberts, C., Burnett, R., Kirby, A. and Hamill, H. (1996) *A System for Evaluating Probation Practice* (Probation Studies Unit Report No. 1). Oxford: Centre for Criminological Research, University of Oxford.

Roberts, C. and Robinson, G. (1998) 'Improving practice through pilot studies: The case of pre-sentence reports', *Vista: Perspectives on Probation* 3, 186–195.

Robinson, G. (2001) 'Power, knowledge and "what works" in probation', *Howard Journal of Criminal Justice*, 40, 235–254.

Robinson, G. (2002) 'Exploring risk management in the probation service: Contemporary developments in England and Wales', *Punishment & Society*, 4, 5–25.

Robinson, G. (2003) 'Implementing OASys: Lessons from research into LSI-R and ACE', *Probation Journal*, 50(1), 30–40.

Shaw, M. and Hannah-Moffatt, K. (2000) 'Gender, diversity and risk assessment in Canadian corrections', *Probation Journal*, 47, 163–172.

Stephens, K. and Brown, I. (2001) 'OGRS2 in practice: An elastic ruler?', *Probation Journal*, 48, 179–187.

Taylor, R. (1999) *Predicting Reconvictions for Sexual and Violent Offences Using the Revised Offender Group Reconviction Scale* (Home Office Research Findings No. 104). London: Home Office.

Tuddenham, R. (2000) 'Beyond defensible decision-making: Towards reflexive assessment of risk and dangerousness', *Probation Journal*, 47, 173–183.

Vanstone, M. (2000) 'Cognitive-behavioural work with offenders in the UK: A history of influential endeavour', *Howard Journal of Criminal Justice*, 39, 171–183.

von Hirsch, A. (1985) *Past or Future Crimes*. Manchester: Manchester University Press.

Wilkinson, J. (1994) 'Using a reconviction predictor to make sense of reconviction rates in the probation service', *British Journal of Social Work*, 24, 461–473.

8

IN SUPPORT OF EFFECTIVENESS: FACILITATING PARTICIPATION AND SUSTAINING CHANGE

Frances Fleet and Jill Annison

THE WIDER CONTEXT

The changing practice base of the Probation Service in England and Wales provides an overarching context for the issues and approaches that are discussed in this chapter. After a lengthy period of turbulence and uncertainty stemming from the negative legacy of 'Nothing Works' (Martinson 1974), professional practice in the Probation Service moved into the new millennium with a focus on effectiveness and 'What Works' (Chapman and Hough 1998; Underdown 1998). This transformation has taken place on many fronts: new organisational structures have been put in place that extend still further managerial oversight of probation work (Raine and Wilson 1993; Raine 2002). Moreover, legislative changes have brought in new, and newly named, community orders, with resources being directed to the implementation of a range of accredited programmes incorporating new methods of work (Wallis 2002). This coalescence of political imperatives, policy and practice directives, alongside public punitiveness towards offenders, has driven an effectiveness agenda for probation that primarily concentrates on outcomes measured in terms of reduction in re-offending (see Chapman and Hough 1998). This is clearly a relevant and laudable aim for the individual offender and for the community – but one that we will argue needs to be placed within a practice environment that encourages and fosters a range of interventions that are based on 'communication, dialogue, a recognition of common humanity and common human rights' (Raynor 2002: 184).

We are therefore acknowledging the centrality of cognitive-behavioural approaches within accredited programmes and the importance of evaluation within a framework of evidence-led practice in work with offenders. This is accepted on two levels. First, a pragmatic response to the situation where probation staff are responsible for implementing and running an expanding range of groupwork and one-to-one accredited programmes. Moreover, clear targets have been put in place that link future resourcing of the Probation Service with the reduction of the reconviction rate of offenders subject to probation supervision (National Probation Service for England and Wales 2001).

Our second level of response relates to probation's accountability as a public service (see, for instance, HM Inspectorate of Probation 1998), and to ethical practice in work with offenders. There is a danger that the 'What Works' and effectiveness agendas may lead to narrow, mechanistic responses, which overlook the interactive nature of work towards personal change with offenders (Matthews and Pitts 2000). An empirical approach to practice can encourage clarity of intervention objectives, and well-planned and systematic evaluation and research of such work. Nevertheless, this framework for practice needs to be placed in a working environment where recognition of diversity and the complex nature of offenders' situations is recognised and responded to (Trotter 1999). Thus, while recent research (McGuire 1995, 2000) indicates that cognitive-behavioural methods are the most likely to produce the desired outcomes with the highest number of offenders, questions have been raised as to whether they are adequate to meet all the factors underpinning offending behaviour (Rex 2001). Moreover, critical scrutiny of the research evidence for such approaches leads to a much more tentative acceptance of their applicability and effectiveness in probation settings with adult offenders. As Mark Oldfield (2002) points out, these uncertainties 'render problematic the evangelical zeal with which "What Works" has been promoted as offering a universal template for practice' (p. 88).

This chapter therefore holds on to a wider contextual view and advocates a more holistic foundation for probation work (Eadie 2000). This draws on a value base articulated by Brian Williams (1995) that proposes that probation intervention with offenders can bring about change, can reduce levels of re-offending, and can be based on professional working relationships that are influential. Within the current context of evidence-based practice, we acknowledge that proposals for the interventions and practice methods that we outline here will need to be accompanied by thorough, ongoing evaluation and the compilation of an evidence base. At this point, however, we are reasserting that professionally trained probation officers hold a unique range of knowledge and skills. This provides a professional 'tool box' that has the potential to underpin the reflective application of a repertoire of interventions. These can assist with the identification, assessment and subsequent work with individuals to reduce their level and frequency of offending (Boswell 2002).

In this respect we are urging the professional development and retention of a range of practice skills and methods. We are also suggesting that such interventions may be needed with some offenders to pave the way to successful compliance with community orders, to prepare for participation in accredited programmes, or to achieve sustained change. Such an approach builds on the recent repositioning of probation practice and probation officer training within a criminologically informed training base, but also seeks to retain and reinforce practice methods from a wide spectrum of theoretical and practice perspectives. The methods we have chosen to explore within this chapter are currently being applied in many probation areas as part of case management models, where they underpin the crucial importance of the relationship between the supervising officer and the offender (Holt 2002). Moreover, these methods acknowledge and extend the repertoire of practice interventions and can act as constructive links between different elements of individual supervision plans over the course of community orders. We are thus drawing on existing practices and pointing to their continuing relevance and applicability for probation work with a range of offenders.

We will be looking first at issues of working with offenders to develop motivation to change, specifically motivational interviewing and then at methods which aim to reduce relapse into previous behaviours (relapse prevention). Later in the chapter we will explore the potential impact of personal crises on compliance and participation. Through an examination of this body of theory, usually known as crisis intervention, practice approaches are identified which may help us to prevent such events undermining effectiveness. Finally, we will recognise that in some instances offending behaviour is one symptom of the multi-faceted problems faced by some individuals and we will again look for interventions which may enable probation's work to achieve some impact on the ensuing chaos. This section will focus particularly on the solution-focused approach. It will not be possible within the scope of this chapter to outline any of these highly complex methods in complete detail. We shall therefore simply seek to identify the core principles of each and then explore key issues in their application in the context of current probation practice. Beyond that we will hope that readers will feel inspired to follow up further reading and opportunities for training.

WORKING TO ACHIEVE CHANGE

In order to achieve its core objectives of protection of the public and rehabilitation of offenders (National Probation Service for England and Wales 2001) the Probation Service in its intervention with offenders is working primarily to achieve behavioural and attitudinal change. While the evidence from meta-analysis currently supports cognitive-behavioural methods as the most effective (see, for instance, Lipsey 1995; Lösel 1995), the old adage about taking a horse to water reminds us that success will only be achieved if the individual is committed to change in the desired direction. Our starting point is therefore what we know about how people change. The model developed by Prochaska and DiClemente (1982, 1983) demonstrates that change is a process. This 'cycle' model is explored extensively in a number of key sources for current probation practice (Chapman and Hough 1998; McGuire 2000). It will therefore only be briefly summarised here.

The model recognises that any major change involves an initial process of moving from a state of not even recognising that a change could be considered ('precontemplation') to one in which serious thought is given to the possibility. This period of 'contemplation' will eventually either lead to rejection of the notion of change or to a 'decision' to take some form of 'action'. This is followed by a period of 'maintenance' when the individual is trying to sustain the changed behaviour and consolidate it into an adapted lifestyle. If this is successfully achieved then the model would suggest that the cycle of change has been completed. Alternatively the individual may experience one or more episodes of 'relapse' into previous patterns of behaviour. Figure 8.1

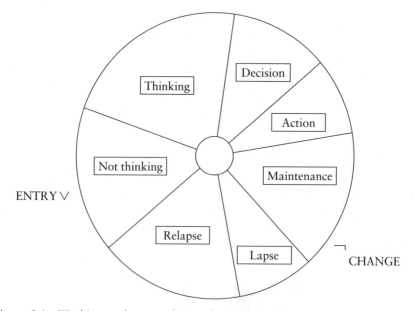

Figure 8.1 Working tool encapsulating the stages of change model (adapted by Fleet 1999 from Prochaska and DiClemente 1983)

was a working tool developed by Frances Fleet and incorporates what was felt to be more practitioner-friendly language. It was deliberately drawn with a hollow centre to enable the worker to demonstrate that any instances of relapse do not have to mean abandoning the process of change or starting back at the beginning. Instead it is possible to return to any of the stages and continue the process from there.

One of the key uses of this model for probation practice is that if we can identify which point on the cycle most closely reflects the offender's position in relation to offending, it can provide useful guidance as to what we need to be doing. While cognitive-behavioural programmes are clearly applicable to the 'contemplation', 'decision', or 'maintenance' stages of this model, the offender's level of participation in such interventions, including actual attendance, will depend on the degree to which he or she feels motivated towards the intervention's objective – reduction of offending behaviour. It is therefore hardly a quantum leap to assume that work to increase appropriate motivation is in many instances an essential precursor to committed engagement with, and the effective implementation of community penalties.

MOTIVATIONAL INTERVIEWING

National Standards (Home Office 2000a) recognise the importance of both the offender's motivation and ability to change by making an assessment of these factors part of every pre-sentence report (PSR). The assessment of motivation is also an essential part in the referral process for accredited programmes such as Think First, not least because 'research indicates that offenders who do not complete programmes are more likely to re-offend than those who do not start' (Home Office 2000b). It is therefore essential that we have an understanding of how motivation is developed, sustained and influenced. To date, the study of these factors which appears to be most relevant to the work of the Probation Service rests with the development by Miller and Rollnick (1991) of motivational interviewing. This is recognised by HM Inspectorate of Probation who state that while the method, which was developed in the field of addictions and compulsive behaviours, is not yet 'specifically validated in the treatment of offenders' there are 'sufficient similarities and overlaps' between the two groups for it to be 'worth testing for effectiveness' (1998: 60). This theme of the similarities between offending and other compulsive behaviours has been explored in detail in Hodge, McMurran and Hollin (1997). However, even without this link, personal experience would probably tell all of us that sustaining motivation in the face of any major life change is a complex and at times fraught procedure.

So what is motivational interviewing? Miller and Rollnick (1991) describe it as a particular way to help people to recognise and address problems. They see it as especially useful with people who are reluctant to change and are ambivalent about changing. This perhaps immediately suggests its applicability for probation since 'equivocation' about desisting from offending has been identified as a significant response (Rex 2001). The method focuses on ambivalence, seeing it as a normal reaction. It is, after all, difficult to conceive of any change that does not involve some element of loss as well as gain. This will be as true for offending as for any other behaviour. A method that works actively with ambivalence and its resulting resistance is therefore likely to have some relevance for work with offenders.

Motivation is, however, an immensely complicated issue. According to Parkinson and Colman (1995) it encompasses a range of 'interlocking processes' including biology, acquired affinities and aversions and conscious intentions and learning as well as external factors. Miller and Rollnick (1991) challenge the view that motivation is a personality trait which individuals either do or do not possess. For them motivation is a state of readiness that fluctuates and can be influenced.

A key issue has to be whether an intervention developed in another field can match the current values and objectives of the Probation Service. There is no doubt that work with offenders needs to convey consistent messages about the harm caused by offending, issues of individual responsibility and the punishment element of all community penalties. Any contradiction of this ethos would be confusing to offenders and staff alike and potentially counter-productive. Although motivational interviewing has its roots in non-directive counselling it is in fact quite focused. The authors observe that the worker will typically have a clear goal, and will pursue systematic strategies to achieve that goal (Miller and Rollnick 1991). The objective, however, is to facilitate the development of intrinsic motivation, that is, motivation which arises from within the individual, rather than being the result of pressure from external factors. This means that the strategies have to be 'more persuasive than coercive' (Miller and Rollnick 1991: 52). This might at first sight suggest a clash with a system that puts such emphasis on compliance, but any practitioner in the criminal justice field will not have to look far to find an instance of extrinsic motivation fading as soon as the external pressure, such as the court hearing, is released. Given the immensity of the changes which desistence from offending requires from some offenders, it is clear that only intrinsic, internally owned motivation will be effective in achieving any sustainable progress.

The objective of motivational interviewing is therefore to get individuals to recognise for themselves that they need to make specific changes and then to make a commitment to act on this recognition. This commitment needs to be expressed in the form of 'self-motivating statements' (Miller and Rollnick 1991). The individual needs to make the case for changing in his or her own words so that the commitment is owned. Professional experiences of one of us (Frances Fleet) in using motivational interviewing in practice have demonstrated that such overt expressions of intent are extremely powerful in work with offenders. The spoken word, particularly when spoken in the context of a respectful relationship, has a kind of durability – it cannot be unsaid and any future retraction or deviation will have to be precisely that. It is probably also true that in order to articulate something to another person we have to process an idea in a particularly clear way for ourselves. This is encapsulated by McMurran's (1994) reference to the phrase 'I learn what I believe as I hear myself talk' (p. 105).

There are five key principles underlying motivational interviewing. The first is that the intervention needs to be delivered in a style that is empathic and accepting of the individual. Miller and Rollnick (1991) are very clear, however, that empathy and acceptance do not necessarily mean agreeing with or approving of an individual's perspective or actions. They mean an in-depth and non-judgemental understanding of that perspective but without collusive support for it. The 'acceptance' referred to above is thus very clearly about accepting the person, not the behaviour; a distinction which is essential in all work with offenders (Williams 1995).

The next key principle is to develop discrepancy between 'present behaviour and broader goals', that is, between 'where one is and where one wants to be' (Miller and Rollnick 1991: 56–57). This discrepancy was originally described by Miller (1983) as 'cognitive dissonance', that is, a conflict of thought processes. This is an idea that harmonises well with the cognitive-behavioural models of other probation interventions. The task of the motivational interviewer in developing discrepancy may need to be confrontational and persistent in facing the individual with the reality of the situation. Miller and Rollnick acknowledge this, but their method utilises a style of confrontation which is powerful, without risking the alienation that can result from heavy-handed or aggressive challenge. This approach aligns well with the recognition that some offenders may respond poorly to 'highly confrontational services' (McGuire 1995: 43). For Miller and Rollnick confrontation is a goal rather than an intervention and it involves asking 'evocative' (disturbing) questions which result in the individual having to draw his or her own challenging conclusions about the repercussions of present behaviours.

This leads inevitably to the third principle, which is to avoid argumentation. Arguing, according to Miller and Rollnick (1991), is more likely to result in resistance and denial of the problem than in movement in the desired direction. Similarly what Miller and Rollnick call 'roll with resistance' is another key principle. They see resistance as a normal reaction to the discomfort of ambivalence and cognitive dissonance and therefore as something to be worked with rather than seen as a problem. There are some interesting points inherent in these principles that are important to reflect on in relation to many aspects of supervisory work with offenders.

The final principle of motivational interviewing is one of supporting self-efficacy. This term relates to a person's belief in their ability to carry out and succeed in a particular activity (Miller and Rollnick 1991, Bandura 1997). Without it self-doubt will be liable to undermine any motivation to make and certainly to sustain change. One way to achieve this sits particularly comfortably with current probation aims about instilling personal responsibility (Home Office 2000a):

> The person not only *can* but *must* make the change, in the sense that no one else can do it for him or her. (Miller and Rollnick 1991: 61, italics in original)

Motivational interviewing is widely used with offenders in partner agencies, particularly addiction partnerships, and is included by James McGuire (2000) in the 'change processes' section as relevant for probation practice. It has also been explored in relation to use with sex offenders (Garland and Dougher 1991) and has been suggested as potentially useful with joy-riders (Kilpatrick 1997). In our view it has considerable potential in probation practice at PSR stage for eliciting commitment to a community penalty, in the early weeks of supervision to strengthen commitment to compliance and participation in planned interventions and as a 'rescue' intervention at signs of decreasing motivation or diminishing sense of self-efficacy. While we recognise the constraints of time, particularly at the PSR stage, one of the most encouraging factors relating to this method is the clear recognition by the originators that it can be delivered effectively, in the right circumstances as a brief, even a single session intervention (Miller and Rollnick 1991).

RELAPSE PREVENTION

The techniques systematised under this heading were again originally designed for use with addictive behaviours. Nevertheless, they have already been incorporated into some areas of work with offenders, such as sex offenders (Chapman and Hough 1998; Laws 1989 [as cited in McGuire 1995]), and in the post-group sessions in the Think First Accredited Programme Manual (Home Office 2000c). McGuire (2000) also refers briefly to the method in his publication *Cognitive-Behavioural Approaches*. While acknowledging its use with offending behaviour he still places it in a section relating to addictions. It is our contention however that consideration should be given to the application of this method to the broad range of offenders.

In relation to the cycle of change these interventions are likely to be most relevant with individuals in the maintenance stage, that is struggling to sustain change. The theory was first formulated by Marlatt and Gordon in 1985 and was then developed into a practice manual by Wanigaratne *et al.* (1990). According to the latter, the method can be summed up as a 'self-control programme that combines behavioural skills training, cognitive interventions and life-style change procedures' (Wanigaratne *et al.* 1990: 1). In theory it should therefore accord well with the mainly cognitive-behavioural methods currently in use in probation.

Central to all relapse prevention work is the concept of the 'high-risk situation'. The individual is encouraged to identify for him- or herself the precise details of situations that will most jeopardise the changes achieved and to plan, with similar individuality, coping strategies to avoid relapse. Marlatt and Gordon (1985) identified that high-risk situations may be intrapersonal, such as negative, or sometimes enhanced emotional states, or interpersonal. The two most obvious examples of the latter would be conflicts or social pressure. Marlatt and Gordon liken the maintenance of change to a journey which is characterised by a number of hazards to be negotiated. These need to be foreseen as far as possible and the size of the challenge rated against the individual's perceived coping ability. Advanced journey planning is then possible including such techniques as rehearsal, self-talk or the development of an 'emergency drill' to enable an 'escape route'.

Among the hazards which Marlatt and Gordon identified are 'seemingly irrelevant decisions' in which a series of small decisions lead the individual into a situation in which lapse is almost inevitable. The person will either be unaware or only partially aware of this happening but with guidance can learn to identify the process as one of self-deception (Wanigaratne *et al.* 1990). This puts the individual in the position of having choice.

Marlatt and Gordon's work distinguishes between lapse and relapse; seeing the former as a 'one-off' slip by the individual which may, but essentially does not have to lead to full relapse back into the previous behaviour (the earlier diagram illustrates this point). Marlatt and Gordon's theory identified a process which they called the abstinence violation effect, (subsequently adapted to rule violation effect by Wangaratne *et al.* 1990), in which a lapse leads to giving up on the grounds that success is beyond the person's capabilities. Relapse-prevention work aims to reduce the likelihood of this happening and encourages lapse to be seen as predictable, given the difficulty of major change. It is also reframed as a learning opportunity which informs the individual about their particular vulnerabilities. In probation interventions this aspect of the model clearly has to be handled with care. It would not be appropriate to give any collusive message about the acceptability of lapses into further offending, but encouragement not to give up can still be incorporated. The concept of developing a sense of self-efficacy referred to above is again significant here.

Wanigaratne *et al.*'s (1990) manual makes it clear that the work can be done either individually or in groups. Experience of utilising this approach with offenders (by Frances Fleet), which drew on the principles of the manual during 1999–2000, confirmed the usefulness of these techniques in addressing the avoidance of further offending. Within the Think First accredited programme (Home Office 2000c) this aspect of post-group work is referred to as self-risk management (drawing on Bush 1995). While it is recognised that a high percentage of offenders are to some extent involved with addictive substances, for others concepts such as high-risk situations or seemingly irrelevant decisions have been relevant to instances of poor problem-solving, social or emotional pressure, impulsiveness or sheer habit. Although relapse-prevention approaches do not address many of the factors underlying such triggers to offending, their use may enable offenders to desist from the behaviour long enough for other interventions, particularly accredited programmes, to be applied. It would also appear to have considerable potential as follow-up intervention prior to the end of supervision.

CRISIS INTERVENTION

This is a method with which all staff trained generically alongside social workers will be familiar and we will be drawing on the literature of social work in order to explore this type of intervention. We do not intend to suggest that it is a method which is directly applicable to addressing offending behaviour but it is our contention that it may have considerable relevance to removing obstacles to compliance and participation.

A number of authors have outlined this method (Payne 1991; Thompson 1991; Coulshed and Orme 1998; Chui and Ford 2000). They all identify that the concept of crisis in this context refers to the individual's reaction to a situation, rather than to the situation itself. A crisis reaction is one in which the person's coping capacity, their equilibrium, is temporarily overwhelmed, leaving them emotionally vulnerable and unable to achieve their normal level of functioning. The individual is precipitated into a state of helplessness in which habitual coping strategies are no longer successful.

It is not always dramatic or tragic events which result in this kind of crisis situation. The loss of equilibrium may be triggered by something quite small which, in a cumulative situation, becomes the 'last straw' for the individual. Definition of crisis therefore depends on the impact on the person rather than the nature of the event. This is an important point because often what is experienced as a crisis by the individual may seem quite easily resolved to the worker. If, however, it precipitates the kind of disabling loss of coping capacity described above, it needs to be responded to as a crisis.

Coping capacity varies with every individual but psychological theory would suggest that it is related to emotional maturity, ego strength, social learning, cognition and the sense of self-efficacy that is becoming a recurring theme of this chapter (Hollin 1989). Research into offenders would equally suggest that these are characteristics which are often poorly developed in this group (Andrews 1995). Couple this with the precarious social and personal circumstances of many offenders, such as unstable accommodation, employment and finances, insecure relationships and chaotic lifestyles, and it can be seen that many of the people under probation supervision will present quite regularly in the state of crisis defined above. If they do then it is equally predictable that faced with such a breakdown of equilibrium they will be unable to participate constructively (if at all) in interventions which are demanding in terms of both commitment and concentration. Probation staff therefore need to be able to reduce the impact of such crisis reactions and the first steps in this direction may be to have some understanding of what has been identified as the crisis process and what responses may be most effective.

Three stages have been recognised (Caplan 1961, cited in Thompson 1991). The first is the 'period of impact'. Tension rises in the face of some kind of event that is perceived as a threat to the 'steady state'. Habitual problem-solving mechanisms are deployed. If they fail tension rises further to a breaking point and major (internal) disorganisation becomes apparent. Perception may become distorted, thinking becomes confused. This may be followed by a 'period of recoil'. More extreme problem-solving devices are activated such as freezing, denial or flight. If the situation is not resolved at this stage the person may move into a 'post-traumatic period' in which an apparent adjustment to the crisis may be reached but this may be maladaptive and accompanied by somatic and/or psychiatric symptoms.

The objective of crisis intervention is to facilitate the individual in returning as soon as possible to a state of autonomous functioning. Again thinking of three stages may be helpful (Coulshed and Orme 1998). In the initial disorganisation stage it is important to keep the focus on the crisis event – what actually happened – in order to encourage 'cognitive grasp' and to draw out the affective responses which may be blocking thinking. It may also be relevant in terms of restoring a sense of self-efficacy to ask how he or she has coped with crises before. The theory then suggests moving on to outline the next step, finding out what is most pressing for the individual, taking account of safety factors and breaking the target area into manageable chunks. As the person's thinking clarifies, it is important to re-establish a sense of coping by giving him or her something concrete to do and as much control as possible over the decisions about the intervention. An important recognition within the theory, however, is that at this stage it may be necessary to 'do for' the person, if the sense of helplessness is overwhelming.

In the third stage, once there are signs of recovering functioning, the emphasis needs to be on restoring the individual's autonomy. This may be advanced by exploring the crisis situation in more detail, identifying any cognitive distortions which are adding to the sense of helplessness and starting to search for achievable solutions through harnessing personal strengths.

In the short term the benefits for probation practice would be avoiding the breakdown of supervision plans and possible breach action. A capacity to respond effectively to an individual in crisis may also be a major factor in developing the elements of trust and confidence which remain crucial to effective supervision (Boswell 1996). In the longer term crisis intervention work may be able to help the individual to develop increased coping resources which may reduce the likelihood of further offending of the kind which stems from short-term panic responses to problems. The method is one which in our opinion remains viable within the boundaries of current practice. It is presented by all its exponents as an intentionally structured short-term intervention. Many crises however stem from unresolved, deep-rooted underlying problems. In these instances the worker will need to be careful to ensure that appropriate operational boundaries are not breached, and that referrals are made to the requisite agencies for ongoing social work or therapeutic interventions, particularly in relation to non-criminogenic needs.

SOLUTION-FOCUSED APPROACHES

These potentially offer probation staff a further approach to working with the kind of intractable personal problems which constantly threaten to undermine offenders' responses to supervision and maintenance of progress towards change. They are again intended to be short-term and to involve minimum intervention. Although originally developed from the counselling modality of brief therapy, the method has been specifically identified as appropriate for use in social work and criminal justice settings and to be adaptable to involuntary clients (O'Connell 1998). Although research evidence to effectiveness is still limited, George, Iveson and Ratner (1999) list a series of follow-up studies suggesting positive applications, including one in a prison setting.

The key tenet of the method is to work with the person rather than the problem. This suggests that lengthy in-depth exploration of the roots of the problem is unnecessary. The objective instead is to identify what would constitute an achievable solution for the individual. This is explored in great detail. Very precise information is elicited about how the person would know that the problem had been solved. What would be the identifiable differences? Who else would perceive the changes and what would they notice? From this wealth of detail it is then possible to identify whether there are any signs that elements of the solution may already be in place. If exceptions to the problem can be found then these are searched for clues as to what may be enabling their existence. In this way an attainable route to the 'preferred future' may be discovered by cooperative effort between the person concerned and the worker.

As with all the other methods which we have examined in this chapter, the individual's own view of their competence is crucial. The solution-focused method therefore makes interesting use of scales on which the individual can identify their own perception of their current position in relation to any number of relevant issues. The most obvious would be how far he or she feels from achieving the solution but others might be confidence about achieving a solution, commitment to doing so or current sense of safety. These can be used later as reference points to plot progress. As with the quest for solutions this work also involves encouraging the person to identify in minute detail what are the factors which are being used to select the position on the scale. These then provide identifiable criteria against which perceived changes can be traced.

While there is a strong emphasis on the individual setting his or her own goals, there is recognition that the work has to remain within strict legal and ethical boundaries (George, Iveson and Ratner 1999). Work by Lethem (1994) in the field of domestic violence demonstrates how this can be achieved. Her emphasis is on restricting the use of authority to those behaviours for which there is a statutory or ethical requirement for control, while leaving the individual the maximum autonomy over his or her day-to-day life. This has obvious implications for work in probation settings. Given those boundaries it should be possible to accommodate the solution-focused approach's emphasis on the individual taking the lead in setting both the agenda and the methods by which change is to be achieved.

Although the model was designed as a coherent whole the literature suggests that practitioners in other fields can successfully adapt specific elements of it. It is this flexibility, combined with its very focused approach to finding solutions to specific difficulties, which in our opinion means that this approach has considerable potential for practitioners in probation.

CONCLUDING THOUGHTS

The different types of interventions which have been explored within this chapter are presented as practice methods that can be utilised in probation work with offenders. The current emphasis on accredited programmes puts in place a framework of structured, time-limited interventions that can be implemented with targeted offenders who fit into the appropriate profile in terms of level of risk and relevant criminogenic needs (Home Office 2000b). However, these recent developments have a tendency to overlook the complexity of the problems affecting many offenders and the fluctuating levels of response and chaotic lifestyles that many of them experience. It is this reality that the approaches considered here address: motivational interviewing and relapse prevention can both be seen as complementary to, and supportive of, the work that is undertaken in cognitive-behavioural programmes. More specifically, the crisis intervention method and solution-focused approaches can be utilised to address difficulties surrounding compliance with the requirements of community orders for, as George Mair (2002) points out,

> there is a real tension between the requirements for breach action in National Standards and the need to get offenders through accredited programmes. (p. 7)

The practice methods outlined here offer the possibility of addressing this tension by recognising that many offenders will need a range of interventions, at different times, over the (possibly lengthy) period of probation supervision. We advocate that these short-term, structured approaches should be subjected to evaluation, thus opening up to wider review issues about 'why a particular intervention works, for whom, and in what circumstances' (Gorman 2001: 8). This portrayal of practice skills also demonstrates the scope and need for continuing professional development and effective intervention by probation staff within a case management model (Chapman and Hough 1998). Most of all, these approaches suggest the extension and consolidation of the repertoire of interventions currently operated within the Probation Service, by drawing on the training, expertise and practice experience of many probation officers working within this area. This undoubtedly lacks some of the evangelical zeal that often accompanies the roll-out of the accredited programmes, but is intended to present a more grounded and reflective approach to the range of probation work with offenders.

SUMMARY OF KEY ISSUES

- The discussion within this chapter advocates the crucial need for probation staff to engage with offenders via a range of practice skills throughout community sentences or post-release supervision. While acknowledging the current centrality of cognitive-behavioural approaches in accredited programmes, it is suggested here that case management models have the potential to incorporate a range of relatively short-term interventions which can be applied to prepare offenders for successful compliance with an order and community supervision; to prepare for participation in accredited programmes, and to support and achieve sustained change.
- The different types of interventions which are considered are Motivational Interviewing, Relapse Prevention Crisis Intervention, and Solution-focused Approaches. The core principles for each approach are briefly discussed, together with a review of the applicability for work at different points with individual offenders. A case is made for a repertoire of professional skills to be developed and applied by probation staff. This is considered to be essential given the complex range of problems and disruptive life events that are experienced by many offenders. In this way proactive approaches

are promoted in order to address and resolve difficulties that may arise during the supervision period. These are intended to facilitate constructive links between different elements of probation interventions. These proposals point to a further evolution of the effectiveness agenda and to the development and integration of an extended 'tool box' of practice interventions and skills within probation.

References

Andrews, D. (1995) 'The psychology of criminal conduct and effective treatment', in J. McGuire (ed.) *What Works: Reducing Reoffending – Guidelines from Research and Practice*. Chichester: Wiley.

Bandura, A. (1997) *Self-Efficacy: The Exercise of Control*. New York: W. H. Freeman.

Boswell, G. (1996) 'The essential skills of probation work', in T. May and A. A. Vass (eds) *Working with Offenders: Issues, Contexts and Outcomes*. London: Sage.

Boswell, G. (2002) 'Deconstructing dangerousness for safer practice', in D. Ward, J. Scott and M. Lacey (eds) *Probation: Working for Justice* (2nd edn). Oxford: Oxford University Press.

Bush, J. (1995) 'Teaching self-risk management to violent offenders', in J. McGuire (ed.) *What Works: Reducing Reoffending – Guidelines from Research and Practice*. Chichester: Wiley.

Chapman, T. and Hough, M. (1998) *Evidence Based Practice: A Guide to Effective Practice*. London: Home Office.

Chui, W. H. and Ford, D. (2000) 'Crisis intervention as common practice', in P. Stepney and D. Ford (eds) *Social Work Models, Methods and Theories: A Framework for Practice*. Lyme Regis: Russell House.

Coulshed, V. and Orme, J. (1998) *Social Work Practice: An Introduction* (3rd edn). Basingstoke: Macmillan.

Eadie, T. (2000) 'From befriending to punishing: Changing boundaries in the Probation Service', in N. Malin (ed.) *Professionalism, Boundaries and the Workplace*. London: Routledge.

Fleet, F. (1999) *CJP 2005 – Assessing and Addressing Offending Behaviour in Probation Settings*, University of Plymouth Stage 2 Module Material for BSc (Hons) Community Justice (Probation Studies). Plymouth: University of Plymouth.

Garland, R. J. and Dougher, M. J. (1991) 'Motivational intervention in the treatment of sex offenders', in R. Miller and S. Rollnick (eds) *Motivational Interviewing: Preparing People to Change Addictive Behavior*. New York: Guilford Press.

George, E., Iveson, C. and Ratner, H. (1999) *Problem to Solution: Brief Therapy with Individuals and Families* (2nd edn). London: Brief Therapy Press.

Gorman, K. (2001) 'Cognitive behaviourism and the holy grail: The quest for a universal means of managing offender risk', *Probation Journal*, 48 (1), 3–9.

HM Inspectorate of Probation (1998) *Exercising Constant Vigilance: The Role of the Probation Service in Protecting the Public from Sex Offenders* (Report of a Thematic Inspection). London: Home Office.

Hodge, J. E., McMurran, M. and Hollin, C. R. (eds) (1997) *Addicted to Crime*. Chichester: Wiley.

Hollin, C. R. (1989) *Psychology and Crime: An Introduction to Criminological Psychology*. London: Routledge.

Holt, P. (2002) 'Case management evaluation: Pathways to progress', *VISTA: Perspectives on Probation*, 7 (1), 16–25.

Home Office (2000a) *National Standards for the Supervision of Offenders in the Community*. London: Home Office.

Home Office (2000b) *Think First Programme Outline*. London: Home Office Communication Directorate.

Home Office (2000c) *Think First Programme Manual*. London: Home Office Communication Directorate.

Kilpatrick, R. (1997) 'Joy-riding: An addictive behaviour?', in J. E. Hodge, M. McMurran and C. R. Hollin (eds) *Addicted to Crime*. Chichester: Wiley.

Laws, D. R. (ed.) (1989) *Relapse Prevention with Sex Offenders*. New York: Guilford Press.

Lethem, J. (1994) *Moved to Tears, Moved to Action: Solution Focused Brief Therapy with Women and Children*. London: Brief Therapy Press.

Lipsey, M. W. (1995) 'What do we learn from 400 research studies on the effectiveness of treatment with juvenile delinquents?', in J. McGuire (ed.) *What Works: Reducing Reoffending – Guidelines from Research and Practice*. Chichester: Wiley.

Lösel, F. (1995) 'The efficacy of correctional treatment: A review and synthesis of meta-evaluations', in J. McGuire (ed.) *What Works: Reducing Reoffending – Guidelines from Research and Practice*. Chichester: Wiley.

McGuire, J. (ed.) (1995) *What Works: Reducing Reoffending – Guidelines from Research and Practice*. Chichester: Wiley.

McGuire, J. (2000) *Cognitive-Behavioural Approaches: An Introduction to Theory and Research*. London: Home Office.

McMurran, M. (1994) *The Psychology of Addiction*. London: Taylor & Francis.

Mair, G. (2002) 'Potential problems in rolling out accredited programmes', *NAPO News*, 137, 7.

Marlatt, G. A. and Gordon, J. R. (1985) *Relapse Prevention: Maintenance Strategies in the Treatment of Addictive Behaviours*. New York: Guilford Press.

Martinson, R. (1974) 'What works? Questions and answers about prison reform', *The Public Interest*, 35, 22–54.

Matthews, R. and Pitts, J. (2000) 'Rehabilitation, recidivism and realism: Evaluating violence reduction programmes in prison', in V. Jupp, P. Davies and P. Francis (eds) *Doing Criminological Research*. London: Sage.

Miller, R. (1983) 'Motivational interviewing with problem drinkers', *Behavioural Psychotherapy*, 1, 147–172.

Miller, R. and Rollnick, S. (1991) *Motivational Interviewing: Preparing People to Change Addictive Behavior*. New York: Guilford Press.

National Probation Service for England and Wales (2001) *A New Choreography: An Integrated Strategy for the National Probation Service for England and Wales – Strategic Framework 2001–2004*. London: Home Office.

O'Connell, B. (1998) *Solution-Focused Therapy*. London: Sage.

Oldfield, M. (2002) 'What works and the conjunctural politics of probation: Effectiveness, managerialism and neo-liberalism', *British Journal of Community Justice*, 1, 79–97.

Parkinson, B. and Colman, A. M. (eds) (1995) *Emotion and Motivation*. New York: Longman.

Payne, M. (1991) *Modern Social Work Theory: A Critical Introduction*. Basingstoke: Macmillan.

Prochaska, J. O. and DiClemente, C. C. (1982) 'Transtheoretical therapy: Towards a more integrative model of change', *Psychotherapy: Theory, Research and Practice*, 19, 276–288.

Prochaska, J. O. and DiClemente, C. C. (1983) 'Stages and processes of self-change of smoking: Toward an integrative model of change', *Journal of Consulting and Clinical Psychology*, 51, 390–395.

Raine, J. (2002) 'Modernisation and criminal justice', in D. Ward, J. Scott and M. Lacey (eds) *Probation: Working for Justice* (2nd edn). Oxford: Oxford University Press.

Raine, J. and Wilson, M. (1993) *Managing Criminal Justice*. Hemel Hempstead: Harvester Wheatsheaf.

Raynor, P. (2002) 'What works: Have we moved on?', in D. Ward, J. Scott and M. Lacey (eds) *Probation: Working for Justice* (2nd edn). Oxford: Oxford University Press.

Rex, S. (2001) 'Beyond cognitive-behaviouralism? Reflections on the effectiveness literature', in A. Bottoms, L. Gelsthorpe, and S. Rex (eds) *Community Penalties: Change and Challenge*. Cullompton: Willan.

Thompson, N. (1991) *Crisis Intervention Revisited*. Birmingham: PEPAR Publications.

Trotter, C. (1999) *Working with Involuntary Clients*. London: Sage.

Underdown, A. (1998) *Strategies for Effective Supervision: Report of the HMIP What Works Project*. London: Home Office.

Wallis, E. (2002) 'Foreword', in D. Ward, J. Scott and M. Lacey (eds) *Probation: Working for Justice* (2nd edn). Oxford: Oxford University Press.

Wanigaratne, S., Wallace, W., Pullin, J., Keaney, F. and Farmer, R. (1990) *Relapse Prevention for Addictive Behaviours: A Manual for Therapists*. Oxford: Blackwell Scientific Publications.

Williams, B. (ed.) (1995) *Probation Values*. Birmingham: Venture Press.

9

DESISTANCE-FOCUSED PROBATION PRACTICE

Fergus McNeill

INTRODUCTION

Increasingly, policy-makers, managers and practitioners in adult and youth justice have come to recognise that understanding the needs, deeds and characteristics of people involved in persistent offending is vital in responding to the challenges that their behaviour and their problems represent. However, while 'criminal careers' research around persistent offending has become increasingly well-known, the related research around 'desistance' – that is, ceasing offending – has emerged only more recently and, as yet, has had a more muted impact on policy and practice. Given that desistance is such an important aspect of what probation and, in Scotland, social work agencies are increasingly charged with achieving, this might seem like something of a paradox.

Part of the reason for this apparent paradox may be that, until recently, the desistance literature has tended to address 'the wider social processes by which people *themselves* come to stop offending' (Rex 1999: 366, my emphasis). Thus, it has not been necessarily or indeed primarily a literature about criminal justice interventions. Indeed, Maruna (2000, also see Maruna 2001) points out that some of the research focuses on 'spontaneous desistance' – which is achieved without 'assistance' from or through the criminal justice system. By implication, this focus challenges the 'medical model of corrections' in which an appropriate remedy is systematically administered, at the right 'dosage', to 'treat' or 'cure' a well-defined symptom. Maruna (2000) recognises that few of those who work in the field of rehabilitative intervention would wholeheartedly endorse such a model. Rather, they might stress the complex

146

personal, inter-personal and social factors that form the contexts of their work. Bearing this in mind, he argues that, in theory and in practice, the boundaries between desistance and rehabilitation blur. For example, *processes* of change (Prochaska 1984) towards desistance may share similarities whether they are spontaneous or professionally assisted. It therefore becomes critical to understand not just 'what works' in terms of interventions but also *how and why* ex-offenders come to change their behaviours. Rex (1999) has similarly argued in connection with probation that:

> The knowledge we are beginning to acquire about the type of probation services which are more likely to succeed could surely be enhanced by an understanding of the personal and social changes and developments associated with desistance from crime. (p. 366)

With that purpose in mind, this chapter aims to make some of this emerging research evidence more accessible to readers. It begins with a brief review of related theoretical perspectives before exploring some of the relationships between desistance, age and gender, motivation and attitudes, relationships and interventions. Finally, in conclusion, it offers some ideas about the practical implications of the literature reviewed.

THEORETICAL PERSPECTIVES

Maruna (2000) identifies three broad theoretical perspectives in the desistance literature:

- Maturational reform
- Social bonds theory
- Narrative theory

Maturational reform theories have the longest history and are based on the established links between age and certain criminal behaviours, particularly street crime. Critics, however, point out that chronological age has little or no inherent meaning. Rather the term 'age' indexes a range of different biological, social and experiential variables. Maruna (2000) claims that 'none of the usual suspects of the biological literature on development (for example, hormonal changes, physical strength or intellect) seem causally linked to changes in criminal behavior in anything like a direct fashion' (p. 11). Further, the ages at which people who offend desist show great variations.

Social bonds theories suggest that ties to family, employment or educational programmes in early adulthood explain changes in criminal behaviour across the life course. Where these ties exist, they create a stake in conformity, a reason to 'go straight'. Where they are absent, people who offend have less to lose from continuing to offend. However, critics argue that such theories present human subjects as passive objects on which social forces prevail. Clearly, individual agency is also at play in our decisions about relationships, work and education and so it becomes difficult to disentangle whether, for example, people stop offending because of their job, or whether they keep their job because they have stopped offending.

Narrative theories have emerged from more qualitative research which stresses the significance of subjective changes in the person's sense of self and identity, reflected in changing motivations, greater concern for others and more consideration of the future. Maruna (2000) notes that critics complain that such theories 'are too difficult to measure scientifically, tend towards circularity and do not answer the question of "why?"' (p. 12). While narrative theories give accounts of *how* the person's motivation or sense of self has altered, they do not explain *why* it has changed.

Maruna (2000) argues that none of the more general desistance theories has offered much specific assistance to practitioners as to what they should actually do. Evidently those who work with children, young people and adults involved in offending cannot afford to wait until their clients get older, find job and relationships, or change their sense of self.

The same problem of seeking to find ways to interpret and use research in driving policy and practice arises in connection with the better-known 'What Works' research concerning effective rehabilitative programmes, since:

> ... such research tells us little about individual differences among client experiences in the process ... Every individual encounters and interprets unique social inter-actions within a program setting ... every intervention consists of thousands of different micro-mechanisms of change ... By concentrating almost exclusively on the question of 'what works', offender rehabilitation research has largely ignored questions about *how* rehabilitation works, *why* it works with some clients and why it fails with others. (Maruna 2000: 12)

Maruna (2000) argues that desistance research can and should redress these deficits in the 'What Works' research by identifying processes of reform and helping in the design of interventions that can enhance or complement spontaneous change efforts. Such research could assist practitioners with the challenge of helping people progress towards the point of being ready and able to make changes, perhaps by accelerating processes that appear to have slowed or stalled for a variety of reasons. Recognising the limitations of each form of research (desistance and rehabilitation) on its own, Maruna (2000) proposes a marriage of the two; with the desistance research's focus on the success stories of those that desist offering an 'individual-level view' that, in partnership with the rehabilitation literature's identification of general practices that seem successful, can better inform understandings of the change processes involved.

The desistance research studies reviewed below begin to explore some key aspects of this 'individual-level view' and, in so doing, appear to have much to offer practitioners and managers in criminal justice social work and youth justice.

AGE, GENDER AND DESISTANCE

Jamieson, McIvor and Murray (1999) and McIvor, Jamieson and Murray (2000) explored desistance and persistence among three groups of young people aged 14–15 (the peak age for recruitment into offending for boys), 18–19 (the peak age of offending) and 22–25 (the age by which many would be expected to grow out of crime). They paid particular attention to gender differences in their study which was based on interviews with a total of 75 'desisters' (43 male and 32 female) and 109 young people (59 male and 50 female) who were still offending or had done so recently.

McIvor, Jamieson and Murray (2000) discovered some age-related differences concerning desistance. In the youngest age group, desistance for both boys and girls was associated with the real or potential consequences of offending and with growing recognition that offending was pointless or wrong. Young people in the middle age group similarly related their changing behaviour to increasing maturity. This was often linked to the transition to adulthood and related events like securing a job or a place at college or university, or entering into a relationship with a partner or leaving home. For the oldest group, 'desistance was encouraged by the assumption of family responsibilities, especially among young women, or by a conscious lifestyle change' (p. 9).

In general, the young women tended to attribute their decisions to desist to the assumption of parental responsibilities, whereas the young men focused on personal choice and agency. Among persisters, girls and young women were more often keen to be seen as desisters, perhaps reflecting societal disapproval of female offending. McIvor, Jamieson and Murray (2000) speculate that:

> Assigning the offending to the past rather than acknowledging it as a current or future reality may enable young women to better cope with the tensions that may arise when, on the one hand, society encourages gender equality and, on the other, continues to double condemn young women who step beyond their traditional gender roles. (p. 9)

Graham and Bowling's (1995) earlier study of young people aged 14–25 had found similar gender differences. They noted a clear association between the life transition from adolescence to adulthood and desistance from offending among young women. Young men, in contrast were less likely to achieve independence and those that did leave home, formed partnerships and had children, were no more likely to desist than those that did not. Failure to desist among young men seemed to be best explained by three sets of risk factors: a high frequency of prior offending, continued contact with delinquent peers and heavy drinking and controlled drug use. Graham and Bowling (1995) speculate that life transitions:

> only provide *opportunities* for change to occur; its realisation is mediated by individual contingencies. Males may be less inclined to grasp, or be able to take advantage of such opportunities, as females. (p. 65)

More recent studies have revised this conclusion to some extent; suggesting that similar processes of change do indeed occur for (some) males but that they seem to take longer to 'kick-in'; the assumption of responsibilities in and through intimate relationships and employment does make a difference but this difference is more notable in men aged 25 and over (Uggen and Kruttschnitt, 1998; Farrall and Bowling 1999; Flood-Page *et al.* 2000). Thus, it seems that young men take longer to grasp the opportunities for change that these life transitions provide.

In Graham and Bowling's (1995) study, only two factors seemed to be positively associated with desistance for males in the 16–25 age range: first, their perception that their school work was above average, and, second, continuing to live at home. It may be that continuing to live at home is associated with desistance because of relatively positive relationships with parents and, as a result, spending less time with delinquent peers.

ATTITUDES, MOTIVATION AND DESISTANCE

Returning to McIvor, Jamieson and Murray's (2000) study, it is also important to note that 'persisters' in the youngest age group were more optimistic about their ability to desist whereas:

> for older respondents, who may have become more entrenched in patterns of offending and drug use, desistance was rarely considered to be an immediate or achievable goal. (p. 9)

The significance of this finding is underlined by Burnett's (1992, 2000) study of efforts to desist among 130 adult property offenders released from custody. She noted that while most, when interviewed pre-release, wanted to 'go straight' (8 out of 10), 6 out of 10 subsequently reported re-offending post-release. Burnett (2000) noted that, for many, the intention to be law-abiding was provisional in the sense that it did not represent a confident prediction; only 1 in 4 reported that they would definitely be able to desist. Importantly, Burnett discovered that those who were most confident and optimistic about desisting had greatest success in doing so. For the others, the 'provisional nature of intentions reflected social difficulties and personal problems that the men faced' (p. 14).

On the basis of her interviews, Burnett (2000) delineates three categories of *persisters*, though she notes that these categories are neither fixed nor mutually exclusive. 'Hedonists' were attracted by the feelings of well-being gained through criminal involvement, whether in terms of the 'buzz' at the time, the emotional high afterwards or the place of the financial rewards of crime in funding lifestyles sometimes associated with alcohol and drugs. The 'earners' varied in their enthusiasm for crime, but regarded it as a viable money-making enterprise. The 'survivors' were generally dependent on substances and unhappily committed to persistent property offending to fund their substance misuse.

The *desisters* also fell into three broad categories. The 'non-starters' adamantly denied that they were 'real criminals' and, in fact, had fewer previous convictions than the others. For the 'avoiders', keeping out of prison was the key issue. They appeared to have decided that the costs of crime outweighed the benefits. The 'converts', however, were:

> the most resolute and certain among the desisters. They had found new interests that were all-preoccupying and overturned their value system: a partner, a child, a good job, a new vocation. These were attainments that they were not prepared to jeopardize or which over-rode any interest in or need for property crime. (Burnett 2000: 14)

Burnett (2000) notes that simply classifying the men as persisters or desisters 'misrepresents the switching, vacillating nature of desisting from offending' (p. 15). Most were ambivalent towards crime and, in consequence, desisting seemed like a protracted 'back and forth' or 'zigzag' process.

Bringing these studies together, the research on factors associated with desistance is neatly summarised in Farrall's (2002: 11) account, which stresses the significance of the relationships between what we might term 'objective' changes in the offender's life and his or her 'subjective' assessment of the value or significance of these changes:

> ... the desistance literature has pointed to a range of factors associated with the ending of active involvement in offending. Most of these factors are related to acquiring 'something' (most commonly employment, a life partner or a family) which the desister values in some way and which initiates a re-evaluation of his or her own life ...

In some senses, this characterisation of desistance marries the three theoretical perspectives above; desistance resides somewhere in the interfaces between developing personal maturity, changing social bonds associated with certain life transitions, and the individual subjective narrative constructions which offenders build around these key events and changes. It is not just the events and changes that matter; it is what these events and changes *mean* to the people involved. Some of the existing research studies exploring the relationships between intervention and desistance offer some important insights concerning how practitioners can work with and through these critical interfaces to support change.

INTERVENTIONS, RELATIONSHIPS AND DESISTANCE

Burnett (2000) suggests that identifying the mind-set of offenders could assist practitioners in reinforcing or shifting offenders' views and intentions. Although she does not make the point, her work also redirects intervention towards addressing the attendant social and personal problems that might hinder efforts at desistance (a theme addressed further below). This is the context of the ambivalence that she suggests practitioners need to work with and through. Crucially, Burnett (2000) notes that '... for influence to be exerted in interventions, good communication built on empathy and the establishment of trust are needed' (p. 15).

While Burnett's (2000) suggestions about intervention approaches are necessarily speculative, some more recent research studies have directly examined desistance among those who have been the subject of probation interventions. Such studies have produced further evidence both about processes of change and about the characteristics of effective working relationships with people involved in offending behaviour. Evidently, listening to what those previously involved in offending tell us about 'assisted desistance' seems essential in seeking better ways of working to promote such desistance.

Rex's (1999) research addresses the features of probation relationships and how they come to exert positive influence. Her research involved interviews with 21 probation officers and 60 of their probationers, 11 of whom were aged under 21. One-quarter of the sample was women. While her research methodology did not enable her to determine whether the offenders that she interviewed had, in fact, desisted, they provided considerable insights into the role of probation in their reported processes of change.

Those who attributed changes in their behaviour to probation supervision described it as *active* and *participative*. Probationers conveyed the sense of being engaged through negotiation in a partnership. Given their recognition both of the need to *sustain* a decision to desist and of the possibility of relapse, probationers seemed more willing to 'embark' on desistance where they felt committed to and engaged in the supervisory relationship. In turn, '[t]his engagement seemed to be generated by the commitment, both personal and professional, shown by workers' (Rex 1999: 371). The 'mechanism' by which some probationers come to accept probation officers as role models, Rex (1999) suggests, may rely on 'the sense of obligation which the probation officers' support and encouragement seem to generate in probationers' (p. 378). She found that as many as half of the probationers she interviewed revealed feelings of *personal* loyalty and accountability towards their supervisors.

In their experiences of supervision, probationers could discern and appreciate efforts to improve their *reasoning and decision-making*. However, attempts to exert influence through cognitive approaches had to 'carry conviction in their eyes if they were to be effective' (p. 373). This conviction depended on the personal and professional commitment from workers discussed above. Furthermore, attempts to address cognitive skills seemed likely to be insufficient alone. Probationers also valued guidance in their personal and social problems at least as often. Rex (1999) summarises this aspect of work as *strengthening social ties*. Significantly in this context, younger men trying to establish independence also sought practical help, whereas women and other male probationers were keen to receive problem-solving advice so that they *themselves* could resolve such difficulties.

Reinforcing pro-social behaviour was another prominent feature of probationers' accounts of positive supervision. Probationers could identify advice in this regard as evidence of concern for them *as people*, and 'were motivated by what they saw as a display of interest in their well-being' (Rex 1999: 375). Notably in this context, such encouragement seemed especially important for younger people involved in recidivist offending. Previous research in Scotland by Ditton and Ford (1994) has similarly suggested that persistent young offenders might need to be 'won over' by persistent workers to change their behaviour. In this regard, Rex (1999) found some evidence that probationers were more willing to accept guidance than probation officers were to be directive, so long as the former could understand the latter's direction as evidence of concern expressed within an engaging relationship.

Though it does not draw directly on desistance research, perhaps the best-known model of intervention focused on the supervisory relationship, rather than on the features of a given intervention programme, is that developed in Australia by Chris Trotter (1999). Many aspects of Trotter's (1999) 'pro-social modelling' will be familiar to social work staff from other related methods. Its central principles include:

- **Role clarification**: involving frequent and open discussions about roles, purposes, expectations, the use of authority, negotiable and non-negotiable aspects of intervention and confidentiality
- **Pro-social modelling and reinforcement**: involving the identification, reward and modelling of behaviours to be promoted and the identification, discouragement and confrontation of behaviours to be changed
- **Problem-solving**: involving the survey, ranking and exploration of problems, goal-setting and contracting, the development of strategies and ongoing monitoring

- **Relationship**: involving the worker being open and honest, empathic, able to challenge and not minimise rationalisations, non-blaming, optimistic, able to articulate the client's and family members' feelings and problems, using appropriate self-disclosure and humour.

Trotter's (1996) empirical research tested the hypotheses (formed on the basis of earlier research) that clients of probation officers who made use of these principles would be more likely to experience reductions in their problems and would be less likely to offend. Trotter (1996) trained 12 probation officers in the approach and followed up 104 of their clients. He compared the outcomes for this experimental group with outcomes for a control group of 157 probation clients. Clients in the experimental group were subsequently significantly more likely to report that their problems were reduced and their re-offence rates were also significantly lower than those in the control group. Among the principles, the use of pro-social modelling was most consistently, strongly and significantly correlated with lower offence and imprisonment rates. The model was *most* effective with young, high-risk, violent and drug-using offenders.

Despite the familiarity of the principles described above, Trotter's (1999) model is important for three reasons. First, although it would be possible to conceive of pro-social modelling as a form of individualised programme, it is perhaps better described as a style of or approach to practice. He demonstrates therefore that we can conceive of styles and approaches and not merely specific programmes as being evidence-based and effective. Second, Trotter's (1999) research and his model direct attention to workers' qualities as well as being about the characteristics of specific programmes. Recently, Trotter (2000) has produced evidence to suggest that among staff working in community corrections in Australia, those with a social work background were more likely to learn and make use of pro-social modelling and, in turn, to produce lower rates of reconviction. In line with Rex's (1999) findings, Trotter (1996, 2000) suggests that this might be about possession of the social work skills and qualities required to achieve genuinely collaborative problem-solving.[1] The third reason for the importance of Trotter's (1999) model is that, perhaps by accident, through its focus on effective relationships and processes, it represents work at the interface of the rehabilitation and desistance literatures and attests to the value of exploring this interface.

However, these findings about desistance and suggestions about developing effective probation and social work interventions need to be seen within the wider social contexts both of offending and of desistance. In this regard,

---

[1] These findings seem particularly ironic given developments in England and Wales which have divorced probation from social work in terms of professional education.

it is salutary to review the conclusions of the most recent and perhaps most thorough study of probation and desistance. Farrall (2002) explored the progress or lack of progress towards desistance achieved by a group of 199 probationers. Over half of the sample evidenced progress towards desistance.

Farrall (2002) found that desistance could be attributed to specific interventions by the probation officer in only a few cases, although help with finding work and mending damaged family relationships appeared particularly important. Desistance seemed to relate more clearly to the probationers' motivations and to the social and personal contexts in which various obstacles to desistance were addressed. Importantly, Farrall does not conclude that probation does not work:

> The answer to the question of whether probation works is a qualified 'yes'. In many cases the work undertaken whilst on probation was of little *direct* help to many of the probationers, however the *indirect* impact of probation (i.e. naturally occurring changes in employment, accommodation and personal relationships) was of greater significance. (Farrall, 2002: 213, emphasis in original)

Farrall (2002) is surely right in going on to argue that interventions themselves and evaluations of them must pay greater heed to the community, social and personal contexts in which they are situated. After all, 'social circumstances and relationships with others are *both* the object of the intervention *and* the medium through which . . . change can be achieved' (p. 212, emphasis added). Necessarily, this requires that interventions be focused not solely on the individual person and his or her perceived 'deficits'. As Farrall (2002) notes, the problem with interventions based on such shaky criminological foundations is that while they can build *human capital*, for example, in terms of enhanced cognitive skills or improved employability, they cannot generate that *social capital* which resides necessarily in the relationships through which we achieve participation and inclusion. Vitally, it is social capital that is necessary to encourage desistance. It is not enough to build *capacities* for change where change depends on *opportunities* to exercise capacities:

> . . . the process of desistance is one that is produced through an interplay between individual choices, and a range of wider social forces, institutional and societal practices which are beyond the control of the individual. (Farrall and Bowling 1999: 261)

For Farrall, this necessitates a rethinking both of 'what works' and of practice. He suggests that practice should be focused not on 'offence-related factors' but on 'desistance-related factors'. An offence focus must, of course, be necessary and appropriate given that, within any justice context, it is offending which occasions and justifies intervention. However, being offence-focused might in some senses tend to accentuate precisely those aspects of an offender's history, behaviour and attitudes which intervention aims to diminish. It may also tend towards identifying the problem as one of individual 'malfunctioning'. Being desistance-focused, by contrast, implies a focus on the purpose and aspiration of the intervention rather than on the 'problem' that precipitates it. It tends towards recognising the broader social contexts and conditions required to support change. Thus, where being offence-focused encourages practice to be retrospective and individualised, being desistance-focused allows practice to become prospective and contextualised.

The nature of the difference between the two approaches is well-captured by one of the probationers in Farrall's (2002) study, in response to a question about what would prevent him from re-offending:

> Something to do with self progression. Something to show people what they are capable of doing. I thought that was what [my Officer] should be about. It's finding people's abilities and nourishing and making them work for those things. Not very consistent with going back on what they have done wrong and trying to work out why – 'cause it's all going around on what's *happened* – what you've already been punished for – why not go forward into something . . . For instance, you might be good at writing – push that forward, progress that, rather than saying 'well look, why did you kick that bloke's head in? Do you think we should go back into anger management courses?' when all you want to do is be a writer. Does that make any sense to you at all? *Yeah, yeah. To sum it up, you're saying you should look forwards not back.* Yeah. I know that you have to look back to a certain extent to make sure that you don't end up like that [again]. The whole order seems to be about going back and back and back. There doesn't seem to be much 'forward'. (p. 225)

CONCLUSIONS: DESISTANCE-FOCUSED PRACTICE

So, what might desistance-focused practice look like? This concluding section briefly suggests how such practice might be developed, first, in terms of assessment and planning, and second, in terms of engagement, intervention and evaluation.

Assessment and planning

One of the general messages from the research is that desistance-focused assessment (and intervention) would, of necessity, be thoroughly individualised. The age and gender related differences in both persistence and desistance reported above attest to the need for practice that sensitively and thoughtfully *individualises* generalised messages about effective interventions. This need is unsurprising since although there are certain commonalities, for example, among young people involved in persistent offending, the categorisation of their characteristics, needs and deeds in large-scale studies tends to conceal their differences (McNeill and Batchelor 2002). From the outset in desistance-focused assessment and intervention, employing approaches to and styles of practice that not only accommodate but also value and exploit that diversity seems necessary. Only where risk- and needs-assessment instruments promote and support thorough and properly argued professional analyses, and where they include resources for engaging people in the process (Roberts *et al.* 2001), can they assist in enhancing the quality, credibility and consistency of individualised assessments. The qualities and skills of workers remain vital in developing the relationships within which information is gathered and analysed.

What might be some of the parameters of this individualised assessment? We noted above that the reasons for desistance seem to reside somewhere in the interfaces between developing personal maturity, changing social bonds associated with certain life transitions, and the individual subjective narrative constructions which offenders build around these key events and changes. If this interpretation of the research is correct, then it suggests that practitioners should engage in mapping out these differing interfaces on a case-by-case basis; exploring the three dimensions of maturity and age, life transitions and social bonds, and subjective narratives of change associated with attitudes and motivation. Figure 9.1 indicates the range of issues and relationships to be addressed.

In terms of assessment, what this might mean is, first, an exploration, in partnership with the probationer, of each of these three discrete areas; their levels of maturity, their personal history and current social circumstances, and their narratives around change, motivation, views and attitudes. While such work will sound very familiar to practitioners, the difference might be that, in each of the three areas, the worker and the probationer would work to make

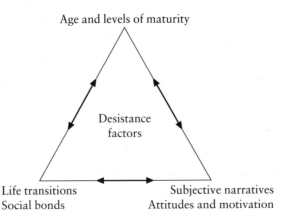

Figure 9.1   Constructing desistance

explicit how, in what ways and to what extents the three factors would serve to support or hinder desistance.

Taking the narrative, subjective aspects of desistance as an example, both Burnett's (1992, 2000) findings about attitudes, motivation and desistance and Prochaska's (1984) familiar model of change suggest the need to assess and understand at which stage of the change process workers encounter individuals. The appropriate practical strategies (and the measures of effectiveness employed) would differ depending on whether the work is with 'pre-contemplative' or 'contemplative' individuals as opposed to those who are ready for action in securing change or requiring assistance to prevent or address relapse (McNeill 2000).

Once the three points of the triangle had been explored, the more complex and important task, in the second stage of the assessment, would be elaborating the inter-relationships between the three areas (represented by the arrows in Figure 9.1). If there were consonance between the three areas such that all are 'pulling together' in the direction of desistance, then a reinforcing support plan might be relatively straightforward to construct. If all aspects were consonant in the direction of continued offending, by contrast, this would suggest both implications for risk assessment and, if community supervision is appropriate, the need for an intensive and multi-faceted intervention. If, as is perhaps likely in most cases, there were some dissonance within and between the three areas, then the task becomes one of reinforcing the 'positives' and challenging the 'negatives'.

Hence, for example, an offender might have secured work and shown some signs of seeking to reconstruct his or her identity through that work, but may seem to lack the personal maturity required to sustain the employment in the meantime. In such a case, the focus of support might be on strategies aimed at accelerating the maturing process (perhaps via motivational work, pro-social modelling, cognitive techniques or problem-solving). Similarly, an offender might have formed a positive relationship with a supportive partner who discourages offending, but remain wedded to aspects of his or her identity as an offender (perhaps within a peer group). In such a case, the worker might work with both partners to build on the strengths of the relationship (reinforcing its pull towards desistance), while working with the offender on issues of motivation, identity and dissociating from the peer group.

Engagement, intervention and evaluation

The message from the studies above concerning desistance and intervention seems clear with regard to engagement. The works of Burnett (1992, 2000), Rex (1999) and Trotter (1996, 1999, 2000) direct us towards the crucial significance of worker–client relationships. Clearly, working to promote change within the context of the ambivalent and shifting nature of 'commitments' to desistance, particularly among young men involved with their peers in offending and substance misuse is highly complex and challenging. In this context, it is hardly surprising to find that optimism, trust, and loyalty are essential features of relationships which should be active and participative, purposeful, 'pro-social' and explicit in their negotiation of roles, boundaries and mutual expectations.

If and when such relationships can be established, being desistance-focused in terms of intervention would mean different things in different cases, as the discussion above suggests. It would seem likely, however, that it would require a focus on aspects of each individual's motivation, attitudes, thinking and values which might help or hinder progress towards desistance. Drawing on the 'What Works' research, this is that part of the worker's task which would seek to build individual capacities or 'human capital'. However, the discussion above also suggests that it would be at least as important to work to access and support opportunities for change, for example around accommodation and employment, and, through these opportunities, to seek the development of the individual's 'social capital'. This underlines the importance of advocacy as a key professional task and skill.

From the research literatures around both desistance and rehabilitation, it also seems clear that, particularly in working with young people involved in offending, developing effective methods of working with families would be essential (Graham and Bowling 1995; Utting and Vennard 2000). Trotter's (1999) work provides a review of some related literature, some helpful practical guidance and a good starting point for further study in this connection. Where family situations have irretrievably broken down, innovative approaches to accommodating young people unable to remain at home would be required. Finding forms of accommodation that support processes of desistance through positive relationships with 'significant others' seems vital. In contrast, the associations between peer group problems, accommodation in group-care settings and persistence in offending, seem indicative of the limitations to what such forms of provision can offer in supporting reductions in offending.

Finally, the effectiveness literature suggests that as well as *using* research evidence, effective interventions *generate* research evidence. Thorough monitoring and evaluation are clearly implicated as being of key significance in developing effective practice. The complexities of these tasks are not to be underestimated (Merrington 1998; McNeill 2000) but clearer delineation of goals, objectives, methods and measures is vital. Making the 'logic' of the intervention explicit – stating why the plan is designed as it is as well as how and why it is expected to achieve change – is only the start of a process that must be supported by adequate resources and rigorous review. The brief outline offered above concerning desistance-focused assessment ought to assist in this process. In this model, a clearly articulated plan for promoting desistance would also represent, in terms of monitoring and evaluation, an explicit statement of an individualised hypothesis concerning what work is required with *this* person in *this* case to bring about reduction or cessation of offending *and* why that work is necessary and appropriate.

The desistance research also underlines why a commitment to seeking the views of people involved in offending and their families is as important as more quantifiable indicators of progress. Only with such qualitative data can more comprehensive understandings of what works and why it works be developed. Studying the outcomes of supervision in the absence of data both about its processes and about extraneous changes in the lives of offenders leaves what has been termed the 'black box' of probation supervision unopened (Farrall 2002: 3–4). To these methodological concerns we might add ethical reasons for seeking and heeding the views of offenders. If, as seems to be the case, embarking on the journey towards desistance is perilous and difficult for the people concerned, then we need to learn more *from them* about what might persuade them to desist and about the support that they need to see their decisions through.

SUMMARY OF KEY ISSUES

- This chapter discusses emerging research about how and why people 'desist' or stop offending.
- Links between age, gender and desistance reveal that while life transitions (like getting a job, finding a partner or starting a family) create opportunities to desist, young men often struggle to grasp these opportunities. 'Desisters' tend to have been more confident and determined at the outset about changing; for them, new attainments create an over-riding interest in 'going straight'. Thus, desistance relates not only to events in offenders' lives, but also to what these events mean to them.
- Desistance-focused probation practice requires thoroughly individualised assessment, focused on the inter-relationships between desistance factors, which build towards clear plans to support change. It requires engaging, active and participative relationships characterised by optimism, trust, and loyalty, as well as interventions targeted at those aspects of each individual's motivation, attitudes, thinking and values which might help or hinder progress towards desistance. Crucially, it also requires work to access and support opportunities for change, for example around accommodation and employment. Finally, such practice requires approaches to evaluation which are themselves engaging since it is vital to learn more from offenders about what persuades them to desist and about the support that they need to see their decisions through.

ACKNOWLEDGEMENTS

A shorter version of this chapter entitled 'Beyond "What Works": How and why do people stop offending?' has been previously published as a briefing paper by the Criminal Justice Social Work Development Centre for Scotland (this and other briefing papers can be accessed at **www.cjsw.ac.uk**). I am grateful to the local authority which funded the original research project (reported more fully in McNeill and Batchelor 2002), from which this paper is derived and, in particular to its Head of Criminal Justice for assistance throughout the project. The research project was undertaken along with my colleague from Glasgow University's Department of Sociology, Susan Batchelor. I am also grateful to Janet Jamieson for introducing me to the desistance research and to Stephen Farrall for providing further expert advice and assistance.

References

Burnett, R. (1992) *The Dynamics of Recidivism: Summary Report.* Oxford: Centre for Criminological Research, University of Oxford.

Burnett, R. (2000) 'Understanding criminal careers through a series of in-depth interviews', *Offender Programs Report*, 4, 1–16.

Ditton, J. and Ford, R. (1994) *The Reality of Probation: A Formal Ethnography of Process and Practice.* Aldershot: Avebury.

Farrall, S. (2002) *Rethinking What Works with Offenders: Probation, Social Context and Desistance from Crime.* Cullompton: Willan.

Farrall, S. and Bowling, B. (1999) 'Structuration, human development and desistance from crime', *British Journal of Criminology*, 17, 252–267.

Flood-Page, C., Campbell, S., Harrington, V. and Miller, J. (2000) *Youth Crime: Findings from the 1998/99 Youth Lifestyles Survey* (Home Office Research Study No. 209). London: Home Office.

Graham, J. and Bowling, B. (1995) *Young People and Crime* (Home Office Research Study No. 145). London: Home Office.

Jamieson, J., McIvor, G. and Murray, C. (1999) *Understanding Offending Among Young People.* Edinburgh: The Scottish Executive.

McIvor, G., Jamieson, J. and Murray, C. (2000) 'Study examines gender differences in desistance from crime', *Offender Programs Report*, 4, 5–9.

McNeill, F. (2000) 'Defining effective probation: Frontline perspectives', *Howard Journal of Criminal Justice*, 39, 382–397.

McNeill F. and Batchelor, S. (2002) 'Chaos, containment and change: Responding to persistent offending by young people', *Youth Justice*, 2, 27–43.

Maruna, S. (2000) 'Desistance from crime and offender rehabilitation: A tale of two research literatures', *Offender Programs Report*, 4, 1–13.

Maruna, S. (2001) *Making Good: How Ex-convicts Reform and Rebuild their Lives.* Washington, DC: American Psychological Association.

Merrington, S. (1998) *A Guide to Setting Up and Evaluating Programmes for Young Offenders*. London: Institute for the Study and Treatment of Delinquency, King's College.

Prochaska, J. O. (1984) *Systems of Psychotherapy: A Transtheoretical Analysis*. Chicago: Dorsey.

Rex, S. (1999) 'Desistance from offending: Experiences of probation', *Howard Journal of Criminal Justice*, 38, 366–383.

Roberts, C., Baker, K., Merrington, S. and Jones, S. (2001) *Validity and Reliability of ASSET: Interim Report to the Youth Justice Board*. Oxford: Centre for Criminological Research, University of Oxford.

Trotter, C. (1996) 'The impact of different supervision practices in community corrections: Cause for optimism', *Australian and New Zealand Journal of Criminology*, 28, 29–46.

Trotter, C. (1999) *Working with Involuntary Clients: A Guide to Practice*. London: Sage.

Trotter, C. (2000) 'Social work education, pro-social orientation and effective probation practice', *Probation Journal*, 47, 256–261.

Uggen, C. and Kruttschnitt, K. (1998) 'Crime in the breaking: Gender differences in desistance', *Law and Society Review*, 32, 339–366.

Utting, D. and Vennard, J. (2000) *What Works with Young Offenders in the Community?* Ilford: Barnardo's.

10

ESSENTIAL SKILLS IN WORKING WITH OFFENDERS

Jonathan Hopkinson and Sue Rex

INTRODUCTION

The Probation Service in England and Wales has gone through many changes since it emerged from the Police Court Missionaries at the beginning of the last century. Since the 1980s, these changes have been marked by the growth of centralised accountability and a less individualised relationship between probation officer and offender – the first marked by the Statement of National Objectives and Priorities (SNOP) (Home Office 1984), National Standards (starting with community service in 1989) and the introduction of a National Probation Service in April 2001. We have also seen the probation order made a sentence of the court (Criminal Justice Act 1991) and the removal of the requirement for the offender's consent to a community sentence (Crime (Sentences) Act 1997).

From the perspective of one of us, a long-serving probation officer, the background of the employees of the Service has also changed over time. Police Court Missionaries came from structured and evangelical backgrounds. In the 1970s staff were often drawn from former servicemen and salesmen. The early 1980s saw a growth in the employment of university graduates, and more recently the intake to the Service has become increasingly diverse.

Throughout all these changes, some elements of the core skills remain unchanged. Risk assessment has always been a key feature, as courts, and latterly prisons, have been asked to release offenders back into the community on trust. There have been many changes to the form of supervision but the underpinning balance of Care and Control has continued to be a key feature – ever since the supportive-directive typology originally applied to social work more generally by Mayer and Timms (1970). Probation staff have always had to maintain a level of optimism about the potential for change tempered with some realism about the prognosis for change.

The nature of the relationship between offender and probation officer used to be governed by the injunction 'Advise, assist and befriend'. Despite changes to the purpose of the Service, engaging with the offender remains critical for most successful interventions. This process has been described as 'Joining' and 'Achieving a Therapeutic Alliance' by family therapists.[1] Moving from a medical model to a more justice-based construct, the idea returns in the concept of 'Legitimacy', as explored later in this chapter. Supervisory practices have moved from a casework model to a case management system in which the offender has contact with a range of staff who undertake specific tasks. However, successful intervention continues to rely on our ability to respond to individuals' needs – and on collaboration between officer and offender. The engagement of the offender is a key element in ensuring that collaboration. This will require an approach that is flexibly responsive to the offender's needs and to the context of the interaction. How to achieve such an approach is the subject matter of this chapter. We start with a consideration of the overarching idea of responsivity, before moving to various aspects of practice, and a discussion of various techniques that may help a probation officer engage an offender in a process of change.

RESPONSIVITY

Responsivity is one of the key principles to have emerged from the 'What Works' literature – that the programme or intervention should match the learning styles of offenders. It is also the principle that has perhaps caused the most difficulty and confusion for practitioners. It is sometimes interpreted as meaning that offenders should be selected on the basis of their ability to respond to the methods deployed by the programme rather than that programmes should be designed that are responsive to the learning styles of different offenders. There is also tension between the responsivity principle and another key 'What Works' principle – that of Programme Integrity. The latter requires that the methods used should relate to the aims of the programme, that adequate resources should be available, and that staff should be appropriately trained and supported. This is often interpreted as requiring strict adherence to the Programme Manual. It can create difficulties if an exercise does not seem

---

[1] See Ryan and Carr (2001) on the value of circular questioning to the establishment of a therapeutic alliance in a family setting. This technique can be adapted for other settings where an offender has a strong reference group.

appropriate for or to work with a particular group of offenders, or an offender has experienced a crisis (such as a loss of accommodation) which seems more pressing to him or her than the programme exercise.

We know from the available research (summarised by McGuire 1995) that the learning styles of most offenders require active, participatory methods of working, rather than a didactic mode, on the one hand, or a loose, unstructured, 'experiential' mode, on the other. The least effective methods have been found to be non-directive counselling (which seems to provide an insufficient sense of direction for change), and confrontation (as in deterrence-based programmes such as 'scared straight', which seem to be overdidactic and alienating).

Responsivity is reflected in several of the criteria used by the Joint Prison and Probation Accreditation Panel (2002) to accredit programmes for use with offenders (see the Panel's Second Report for a summary of the accreditation criteria). These include:

- **Effective methods:** that the programme uses methods proven to work – the Panel has approved cognitive-behavioural methods and structured therapeutic communities for people with drug or alcohol addictions or other patterns of anti-social behaviour
- **Skills-oriented:** that the programme teaches skills for offence-free living – these include literacy, numeracy, how to find work, make and keep relationships and general problem-solving
- **Engagement and motivation:** that the programme encourages a positive response – motivation should be assessed at the selection stage and built throughout the programme. There should be positive commitment from staff, and the content and methods of teaching should match the way the participants learn best and motivate them to want to learn to change
- **Continuity of programmes and services** – that the programme is integrated into the overall plan for the offender's sentence and supervision (for example, the offender should be able to make a smooth transition between prison and community-based programmes and build on their progress).

The last two are especially crucial to the question of responsivity. The aspirations behind these criteria are worthy – it would be difficult to disagree that offenders should be motivated to change and that there should be an integrated supervision plan surrounding attendance on a programme. However, they create expectations that pose real challenges for practitioners. So let us take a closer look at what is involved in each.

The criterion on **Engagement and motivation** addresses the various points at which this issue impinges on practice. At assessment, considerations include levels of literacy, intoxication or reduced alertness from drugs/alcohol, or learning difficulties. At this stage, potential problems should be identified and offenders either excluded or arrangements made to enable them to learn. Adequate motivation should be assured either through selection/exclusion through motivational tests, or through programme elements designed to enhance motivation. The assessment tools that we shall refer to later in this chapter are clearly relevant here, as is the technique known as Motivational Interviewing (see also Chapter 8 of this book). However, the criterion also allows for the possibility that offenders will be excluded; this implies a need to make difficult judgements as to whether a particular offender has the resources – or can be adequately motivated – to get through a programme.

In relation to programme delivery, the criterion states that pre-programme preparation should be specified; this will be the responsibility of the case manager. In addition to achieving a 'pro-treatment' environment, the programme should involve structured methods that engage offenders' active participation. The criterion envisages that a range of methods will be used to maintain interest and accommodate a variety of learning styles; that positive and negative incentives will be used selectively; and that the materials used should be appropriate to the age, gender and culture of participants (drawing guidance from research into the responsivity of different groups).

When it comes to the staff delivering the programme, the criterion specifies that they should be well-trained, competent, and motivated. They should use an appropriate 'style' – one that is 'confident, warm, sensitive to the needs of participants, fair, set consistent standards, not condone or collude with abusive attitudes and behaviours and model the kinds of attitudes which offenders should emulate'. Opportunities to reinforce learning should be created outside the programme, and a supportive community developed (including work with family, friends and home community to promote support and involvement rather than hostility, indifference or ignorance towards the programme).

The criterion on **Continuity of programmes and services** addresses how case management in the probation service can provide clear links between the programme and the management of supervision overall. For example, there should be explicit guidelines on the roles of case managers and programme delivery staff, covering enforcement and breach, and the reinforcement of learning and motivational work. Effective arrangements should be laid down for liaison, handover and communication between programme staff and other staff. These should include a three-way meeting, and reports by delivery staff for the case manager, at the end of the programme and reports for each review required by National Standards. For their part, case managers should have a clear understanding of the aims and objectives of the programme, and either the skills to undertake reinforcement and relapse prevention or the ability to refer to staff with these skills.

The criterion lays down similar requirements on through-care in the prison service to ensure that progress made in prison is reinforced by rehabilitative efforts in the community. For example, individual objectives should be identi-fied at the end of the programme for the offender to pursue to strengthen and build on the progress made in the programme, which should apply both inside and outside prison and be reviewed in a report by a supervising probation officer at the end of the licence.

So what are the implications of these principles for different areas of prac-tice? We now consider that question, starting with assessment before turning to supervision planning and case management.

ASPECTS OF PRACTICE

Assessment

Ideally, the process of change begins with an accurate assessment of the change required to meet a realistic goal, agreed between the officer and offender, and an analysis of the steps that might achieve this. As noted above, an approach that is responsive to the offender's need and context will be more effective in gathering information to aid assessment, but also if the process is meaningful for the offender he or she will be more motivated to undertake the process of change. Community Justice Standards have been developed which relate to assessment. These are a part of a much wider range of standards under-pinning National Vocational Qualifications.[2]

Unlike the Police Court Missionaries, who had to rely on subjective judge-ment and faith, we now have the benefit of a body of research evidence to assist us. This has been drawn on to improve on clinical assessments of the likelihood of re-offending made by probation officers. Initially, 'second generation' tools, such as the Offender Group Reconviction Score (OGRS), were developed to provide an actuarial estimate of the proportion of offenders with a particular profile who will be reconvicted. Such approaches produce a structured analysis relying on 'static factors' that summarise past behaviour patterns. They provide a simple actuarial assessment of the group's prognosis rather than that of any one individual who falls within the group.

'Third generation' assessments have now been developed that can take into account changes in individual circumstances or 'dynamic' factors, such as employment or substance misuse (Raynor 2001). Examples of these more refined instruments can be found in the 'Offender Assessment System' (OASys)

---

[2] The relevant standards are: D102 Process information relating to individuals' offending beha-viour; D103 Assess individuals' offending behaviour and prepare sentencing proposals; D204 Develop plans to manage the risk of harm of releasing and resettling offenders in the community following custodial sentences.

and the 'Spousal Assault Risk Assessment' (SARA) used in cases of domestic violence (Kropp *et al.* 1995). We can also use other tools such as psychometric tests (for example, Beckett, Beech and Fisher 2001) to help analyse an offender's attitudes in comparison with a non-offending control group, or the normal range of responses from other offenders. The 'Risk Matrix 2000' (Thornton *et al.* 2002) for assessing sex offenders combines information from static, dynamic and attitudinal sources. Despite these refinements, we still cannot predict an offender's responses with 100 per cent accuracy. The significance of psychometric test results can be open to more than one interpretation, and they are never completely watertight. The best results are achieved through 'triangulation' – a process that uses all available sources, including static, dynamic and attitudinal information in conjunction with the officer's clinical judgement of the individual through face-to-face interview. Skilful assessments will cite evidence from all these sources and analyse the relationship between them.

The level of assessment required will depend on what is being assessed and the accuracy needed. Several assessment tools have shorter screening versions, which can be used to identify offenders who require more detailed assessment using specialist tools. There are screening tools for literacy and other basic skills, for example, and SARA has a screening assessment version. This is helpful in enabling a case manager to identify when to seek specialist help from employment, educational or medical sources.

Assessments are prepared at several stages of contact with an offender, and their purposes vary accordingly. At the court stage the assessment will be largely based on information obtained from the offender at a time when he or she is more likely to try to present himself or herself well to reduce the risk of punishment. Offenders will tend to deny culpability, minimise the seriousness of their actions, justify their behaviour and underestimate the risk of further offending. The court, contrariwise, will want a reliable assessment of the risk of re-offending, the likelihood of serious harm to the community and the prospect of intervention to reduce these risks. The probation officer can use assessment tools to give a baseline, taking account of the effect of the court process, in interpreting the offender's responses. Assessment tools can also give the probation officer confidence in challenging the offender's self-assessment: e.g. 'We know that 75 per cent of people in your situation will re-offend. What evidence can you give me to suggest that you are one of the 25 per cent who do not re-offend?'

The situation is similar when preparing a report for a Parole Assessment. The offender will be very keen to suppress any evidence that they are likely to fail in the outside community. This is reinforced by the institutional experience where disclosure can be seen to militate against progression through the system. Officers will have the benefit of a closer observation of the offender's behaviour than is usually available in the community. This is a double-edged tool, as offenders' behaviour in custody may not be a reliable indication of their behaviour in the community. Some offenders flourish in an institutional setting but not outside it. Other offenders appear to show poor coping skills in the institution, but are responsive to freedom. Risks may change from one setting to another.

Supervision planning

National Standards governing the supervision of offenders in the community require the preparation of a supervision plan within 15 working days of the commencement of supervision (Home Office 2000, para. C10). This plan will incorporate assessments of the risk of re-offending, potential harm to the community, harm to staff and self-harm. The plan also incorporates a statement of the process seen as required to achieve the objectives of supervision. The objectives are more likely to be achieved if offenders actively participate in, understand and agree with the proposed plan. In the long term it will be the actions of the offender that will prevent relapse.

The Probation Service also contributes to Sentence Planning, by which the Prison Service determines the progress of prisoners through the prison system and their preparation for eventual release. The government's intention is to enhance the links between the Prison Service and the Probation Service in pursuit of the 'seamless sentence' (see Home Office 2001), partly through the use of OASys as a common assessment tool. Although this is now being implemented in the Probation Service, the Prison Service has delayed its introduction and is (at the time of writing) preoccupied with the recent sharp increases in the prison population. In this context, the expectations of the Probation Service's contribution to Sentence Planning in Prison are not always clear or easy to deliver. At least in theory, however, a service working in the community has a different perspective on risk and should have information about the environment into which the prisoner will eventually be released.

Gathering information about the home environment and local community requires a more active, less office-based approach than the Service has employed in recent years. Although National Standards require officers to undertake home visits (Home Office 2000, para. D13), the emphasis on frequency of contact in practice encourages an office-based approach. Home visits provide an opportunity to study the locality in which the offender lives. They may give insights into patterns of activity in the community. Offenders will behave differently on their own turf. Their homes may give clues about their attitudes and interests. Their family, friends and neighbours can either support the offenders' attempts to avoid relapse, or they may collude with offenders' denial of the need to change, or even actively encourage criminality.

Multi-Agency Public Protection Panels have been set up following the Crime and Disorder Act 1998 (section 115) and the Criminal Justice and Court Services Act 2000 (sections 67 and 68). These panels are intended to develop collaboration between different agencies in cases where the risk of harm to the public posed by offenders in the community is extremely high. The panels convene Case Conferences along similar lines to Child Protection Conferences. Probation officers and other practitioners contributing to these panels will be expected to pool information, to produce a more accurate assessment of risk and to develop a coherent strategy of risk management. In these circumstances, offenders must be made aware that the confidentiality of their contact with the Service is limited.

Trust and good communication are essential to risk management as well as interventions aimed to create positive change. Offenders who are unwilling to engage in formal programmes can be managed by restriction of liberty such as electronic monitoring or custody. However, the risk is more likely to be reduced when some form of agreement is negotiated with the offender, acknowledging the agency's concerns about the risk he or she poses, defining the parameters of liberty and engaging the offender in joint management of the restrictions placed on him or her.

Case Management

Case Management is a relatively new term in the Probation Service. It has been used loosely in a variety of ways, leading to some confusion about its meaning. On the basis of experience as a probation manager, the common models of Case Management can be characterised as:

- **Factory processing,** by which officers can assess large numbers of offenders and refer them on to others for specific interventions but retain little involvement
- **Modular involvement,** by which officers assess the offender, before embarking on one of a range of structured programmes, which they themselves deliver
- **Specialist roles,** by which officers assess offenders and refer them to a specialist programme. They then prepare them for this programme, support them during it and work with them afterwards to reassess any additional needs.

We believe that the last model is preferable, and accords more closely with 'What Works' principles as enshrined in the accreditation criteria discussed above. However, it demands a large investment of time, and will be hard to sustain without adequate resources. When workloads are high, the factory model is more likely to dominate, but it is far less effective.

Various resources are available in reaching an understanding of what is meant by Case Management. The Probation Inspectorate has defined the principal Case Management tasks as: 'Manage People, Manage Activities, Manage Information, and Manage Quality' (Chapman and Hough 1998: 45). More recently, Case Management has been described in Occupational Standards.[3]

As discussed above, offenders' participation in a programme requires activity from the case manager at various stages. In preparing offenders for a programme there are a number of very practical tasks to complete. Offenders need clear information about the nature and rules of the programme that they are about to attend. They also need practical information about times and transport arrangements. Problems that might interfere with attendance need to be resolved. As mentioned in the earlier discussion of responsivity, offenders need to be motivated to attend and to be willing to learn from the programme.

During the programme the case manager needs to monitor the offender's progress and be ready to anticipate problems that could interfere with his or her engagement. At times, case managers may need to act as advocates to ensure that offenders' needs are appropriately met. After the programme has been completed, case managers need to help offenders reflect on what they have learned in the programme, to reinforce the learning and to help them apply it. There is also an opportunity to reassess other unmet needs. At this stage, there is room for considerable creativity in the case manager's approach – rather differently from the pre-programme preparation stage where the focus is more prescribed.

So what techniques are available to a case manager to help engage offenders in programmes and other interventions to help them achieve positive change and move away from offending? In exploring that question, we start with Motivational Interviewing and various approaches that the case manager can use to promote communication and learning. We then turn to pro-social modelling and the important question of how offenders might be encouraged to comply with programmes and other requirements. Throughout, our intention is to introduce the reader to a variety of resources rather than to provide a comprehensive account of the different techniques and approaches to which we refer.

---

[3] References to Case Management can be found in the following Standards: D102 Process information relating to individuals' offending behaviour; D103 Assess individuals' offending behaviour and prepare sentencing proposals; D202 Plan, supervise, enforce and review sentences in the community; D204 Develop plans to manage the risk of harm of releasing and resettling offenders in the community following custodial sentences; D302 Enable individuals to change their offending behaviour; D304 Contribute to the implementation of groupwork programmes to address offending behaviour; E203 Contribute to the prevention and management of abusive and aggressive behaviour; E409 Enable individuals to understand and address their difficulties; F102 Promote people's equality, diversity and rights; F307 Develop one's own knowledge and practice.

PROMOTING CHANGE – TECHNIQUES

Engaging offenders in change

'Motivational Interviewing' (MI) is a useful technique to help engage offenders in the process of change required by their participation in a programme. It is based on the following key principles:

- The ability to express empathy
- The ability to develop discrepancy
- The ability to avoid arguments
- The ability to 'roll' with resistance
- The ability to support efficacy

MI needs some practice to be delivered naturally and effectively. The techniques involved are described in detail in Miller and Rollnick (1991). A shorter, practical handbook is Ruth Mann's (1996) guide to applying the technique to work with sex offenders. Although this book has a specialist focus, MI is well-explained and easy to adapt for other types of offences.

Much of the work of the case manager will be to engage the offender at all stages and to encourage the development of trust and respect. One way of achieving this is by some self-disclosure. This can help to achieve the 'Warmth, Empathy and Genuineness' described in Rogers (1951: 348–349). Disclosure has to be handled with care and must always be truthful. It has the effect of reducing the distance between officer and the offender. It makes the officer more human but also more vulnerable. Some officers may be very successful in engaging offenders, but at a cost to their sense of professional identity, and risk being drawn into collusion. This can lead them to be overprotective of the offender or move into inappropriate personal relationships.

Another way of engaging offenders' attention and reducing defensive responses is for offenders to look at their problem in the third person. Offenders can reflect on their dilemmas by listening to a scenario, watching a dramatic representation or using a computer program. Interactive computer programs are available from organisations such as Passada (1999) or Geese Theatre (1998). Officers can invent scenarios similar to offenders' situations and help them to consider the consequences of certain actions. Some workers use symbols and metaphors effectively to help offenders visualise and imagine their situations in a fresh light. Family therapists have used this technique and it is adaptable for use in probation work (Cade 1982).

Using dramatic techniques can help offenders imagine change over time. With two or more chairs in a room, offenders can be asked to view one as their present situation and the others as the goals that they wish to achieve. They can then be asked to define the steps that they need to take to achieve their goals. This exercise can also be approached pictorially. Priestley and McGuire (1985: 65–66) use a picture of a ladder on which offenders set out the steps towards their goals.

We know that individuals understand and view the world in different ways. The way in which offenders see the world is important. Unless we understand the meaning of words and ideas for them there is a danger of failed communication. Kelly's (1995) Construct Theory can help us to be aware of the potential for differences in understanding between individuals. It is, however, unlikely that there will be sufficient time to employ a full analysis of the individuals' personal constructs. Nevertheless, close observation can give the officer hints about the way in which an offender perceives the world. The officer's approaches and use of language can be adapted accordingly.

Cultural upbringing can significantly affect the preferred pattern of verbal communication. Hofstede (2001), through research in 70 countries on four different communication variables, has observed statistically different cultural patterns of communication between 40 of these countries. Sensitivity to cultural differences in verbal and non-verbal communication patterns can help reduce the risk of officers making inappropriate assumptions. For example: a Sikh offender on a cognitive-behavioural programme struggled with the use of the word 'I' because of a cultural expectation that he should refer to his family and wider community. It also can give pointers about the acceptability of direct communication.

There have been a number of attempts to describe or categorise differences in conceptual understanding, and to assess differences in learning styles (see, for example, Watkins *et al.* 1998; Gast and Taylor 2002).

Promoting pro-social behaviour

The earlier discussion of the conditions necessary to support programmatic intervention with offenders, including the need for a 'supportive community', recalls the need to attend to offenders' social environments if they are to be encouraged to move towards crime-free lives. Reviewing the literature on aftercare services, Haines (1990) concluded that what counts in prisoners' resettlement is the social environment to which they return, and the support of family and friends, and a situation that fosters law-abiding attitudes and behaviour. Interviewing men released from prison, Burnett (1994) found that they often prevaricated between criminal behaviour and avoiding offending, and kept their options open, so that the absence of a job or shortage of cash might easily push them back into crime.

The literature on offenders' 'criminal careers' reveals that moving away from offending is a complex process. Studying self-reported offending among 14–25-year-old men and women, Graham and Bowling (1995) found that 'normative' processes play a part in people's movement away from crime. They conducted life-history interviews with people who had stopped offending, which, they argued, showed that offenders do not simply stop offending because they acquire partners, children, employment and economic independence, but because they make a fresh start, find some direction or meaning in life, or learn that ultimately crime does not pay.

This raises the question how the changes described by the people whom Graham and Bowling (1995) interviewed come about. Can practitioners supervising offenders in the community contribute to these normative processes? Possibly they can, by incorporating into their practice a set of techniques known as 'pro-social modelling', which seems to have aroused some interest in the UK. The Probation Inspectorate's Effective Practice Guide described pro-social modelling as 'a necessary input for effective programme delivery' (Chapman and Hough 1998: 49–50), a view that seems to have informed statements in the accreditation criteria about the style of delivery that should be adopted by staff delivering programmes (see above).

Christopher Trotter's research in Australia is known for providing the most thorough exploration of pro-social modelling (Trotter 1996, 1999; also see Chapters 8 and 9 of this book). According to Trotter, pro-social modelling 'involves the practice of offering praise and reward for . . . pro-social expressions and actions . . . [Also] the probation officer becomes a positive role model acting to reinforce pro-social or non-criminal behaviour' (Trotter 1993). In other words, the offender is given a definite lead (hence 'modelling' rather than non-directive counselling), and this is done in a constructive and positive way, rather than through negative threats (hence, 'pro-social' rather than deterrence). Entwined in these practices are elements of reinforcement through encouragement and reward, and modelling through positively exemplifying the desired behaviour.

Trotter's study found that the breach and reconviction rates of offenders supervised by Community Corrections Officers (CCOs) assessed (on the basis of questionnaires completed by probationers and an analysis of case files) as using 'pro-social' methods were significantly lower than similar groups of offenders. He also claimed a strong statistical relationship between pro-social modelling and lower rates of recidivism, which was sustained over a four-year follow-up period (Trotter 1996).

'Pro-social modelling' is not an entirely new concept to probation practice (indeed, elements have been found in social work practice more generally ever since the 'supportive-directive' typology originally developed by Mayer and Timms 1970). Collectively, British research specifically on probation suggests that probationers want supervision to be a 'purposeful' experience, and appreciate probation officers' showing respect and concern for them. Significantly, they seem more ready to accept a certain amount of encouragement and direction from supervisors who do so – though practitioners may not always realise that this is the case.[4]

Because it concerns the manner in which offenders are supervised or programmes undertaken with them, pro-social modelling clearly encompasses a broad set of practices that can be used in a wide range of circumstances. Unfortunately, this flexibility carries with it the difficulty of identifying what concrete supervisory practices the approach actually involves, and what makes it distinctive. Even then, although the idea might be admirable in theory, sustaining the intricate practices required to deliver pro-social modelling may be quite difficult. In Trotter's work with Australian CCOs, the kinds of techniques practitioners were described as developing (being punctual and reliable; being polite and friendly; and being honest and open) may not seem particularly novel or sophisticated to British probation officers. Recognising these kinds of difficulties, Trotter (1999) has used case scenarios to illustrate the use of pro-social modelling in different settings, arguing that research shows that the use of the approach can be strengthened through training and awareness. He has also emphasised the need for practitioners to focus on positives and to be open and explicit about their role and the goals they are pursuing, to ensure that pro-social modelling is distinguished from 'moralising' and remains sensitive to differences of gender, race and culture.

Between October 1997 and October 1999, the Institute of Criminology participated in a pilot project with the Cambridgeshire Probation Service aimed at incorporating principles of pro-social modelling into probation practice and assessing the impact (see Bottoms and Rex 1998). Unfortunately, staff movement, and other implementation difficulties, together with incomplete data, meant that findings were inconclusive.[5] However, the project did provide some opportunities for practitioners to develop their understanding of the concept of pro-social modelling and how it might translate into specific practices. Some of that learning took place in a preparatory two-day workshop in which probation officers, who had volunteered to participate, developed ideas for applying pro-social modelling to their practice.

---

[4] See Rex (1999), citing Ditton and Ford's (1994) conclusion that a recidivist at the turning point might need active encouragement and the finding of Sainsbury, Nixon and Phillips (1982) that probation officers massively underestimated the importance of their encouragement to probationers.

[5] Only three project probation officers upon whom the evaluation could be based had been involved from the outset and had attended all the training (four of the original recruits were transferred to other posts, and another five probation officers joined the project having received a personal briefing) – this illustrates the difficulties (and dangers) of implementing a project with a selected group of staff. In interviews, participants sometimes saw the practice of the ideas as quite elusive, and pointed to external pressures and countervailing trends which impeded the use or impact of pro-social modelling (see Rex and Crosland 2000).

Subsequent interviews revealed some underdevelopment of the principles in practice. One example was in encouraging pro-social behaviour through the use of rewards, where there was a heavy emphasis in the workshop on the simple acknowledgement of progress. Other opportunities to reward probationers were identified: early termination; reduction in frequency of appointments; setting time aside to address particular problems; home visits; and advocacy. In discussing their practice afterwards, however, it was positive feedback and praise that project probation officers emphasised; they perceived limitations in what else they could offer probationers, and in the scope for identifying positive achievements in some people's lives.

Promoting compliance

It is quite obvious that any work can only be effective if offenders actually attend the programme or other intervention. Accordingly, the accreditation criterion on **Engagement and motivation**, referred to above, states that attendance and completion rates will be used as direct evidence of participants' responsiveness to the programme. This raises the question how offenders can be encouraged to comply with community-based programmes (an issue that does not arise in quite the same way in a custodial setting). In addition to the negative incentive of the threat of enforcement action under National Standards, it has been argued that positive incentives are required to persuade offenders to turn up (see Bottoms, Gelsthorpe and Rex 2001: para. D4 in Appendix).

Bottoms (2001) explores the relationship between effectiveness and compliance in relation to the delivery of community penalties, and distinguishes four main kinds of compliant behaviour:

- *Instrumental/prudential compliance* (based on self-interested calculation), brought about, for example, because of the disincentive of enforcement or the incentive of early termination for good progress
- *Normative compliance* (based on a felt moral obligation, commitment or attachment) encouraged, for example, by causing an offender to reflect on the distress caused to the victim of his or her crime
- *Constraint-based compliance* (derived from some form of constraint or coercion), brought about, for example, by the physical restrictions imposed by electronic monitoring
- *Compliance based on habit or routine*, for example, the use of cognitive behavioural programmes to achieve an altered way of thinking and altered behavioural routines.

One form of normative compliance discussed by Bottoms (2001) in some detail is legitimacy, as developed by the political theorist David Beetham (1991).

Here, compliance with a rule is secured because that rule has been promulgated by a person or body with legitimate authority, acting in a proper way to exercise that authority. Legitimacy requires, not just formal legality, but also that office holders – such as probation officers – 'act fairly and that they can and do justify what they do to those who are affected by their decisions and practices (such as offenders and their families), thus heightening the likelihood that their authority will be assented to' (Bottoms 2001: 102). Bottoms draws empirical support for this point from Tyler's (1990) study of Chicago citizens' encounters with the police and courts, from which Tyler concluded that people are generally more concerned with issues of *procedural fairness* and with the *manner* in which they are treated than they are with the outcome of the case. He also cites support for the proposition that the legitimate use of authority can promote longer term compliance with the law from Paternoster *et al.*'s (1997) study of interventions in cases of domestic violence, in which the fairness or otherwise of the conduct of the arresting officers seemed to have consequences for arrestees' subsequent compliance with the law.

The Cambridgeshire pilot project on pro-social modelling described above encompassed principles of legitimacy, which were seen to complement pro-social modelling (see Bottoms and Rex 1998). In the context of the Cambridgeshire pilot, the way in which probation officers used their authority was seen as exemplifying what kinds of behaviour they were seeking to encourage in the people they supervised. As such, it was seen to enhance the 'modelling' aspect of pro-social modelling, and as helping to explain why a practitioner using this approach might hope to exert a positive influence on offenders.[6]

SUMMARY OF KEY ISSUES

- The probation officer's original brief was to 'advise, assist and befriend'; over time the Service has become equipped with better risk assessment tools and a curriculum of predominantly educative programmes. However, engaging with the offender remains critical if intervention is to be successful, as acknowledged in the accreditation criteria used by the Joint Accreditation Panel. The importance of seeking an active collaboration with offenders, and of being responsive to their needs and different learning styles, arises at all stages of supervision. Here, various resources are available to help case managers achieve that kind of engagement – screening and assessment tools and psychometric tests; Motivational Interviewing, dramatic and other techniques.

[6] See Rex (2001) for a discussion of how probation officers developed legitimacy in their supervisory practices.

- There are general approaches too, that may help supervising officers promote compliance, cooperation and change. Modelling appropriate behaviour remains a key component of the role of the probation officer, its efficacy recently reinforced by the availability of empirical evidence. Indeed, in offenders' responses to pro-social modelling, either within a group or in one-to-one supervision, it is still possible to recognise Rogers' 'hypothesis . . . that group members identify with their leader and in the process internalise some of their attitudes and behavioural patterns' (Rogers 1951: 348).

References

Beckett, R. C., Beech, A. and Fisher, D. (2001) *Adult Sex Offender Assessment Battery*. (Unpublished).

Beetham, D. (1991) *The Legitimation of Power*. London: Macmillan.

Bottoms, A. E. (2001) 'Compliance and community penalties', in A. E. Bottoms, L. Gelsthorpe and S. A. Rex (eds) *Community Penalties: Change and Challenges*. Cullompton: Willan.

Bottoms, A. E. and Rex, S. A. (1998) 'Pro-social modelling and legitimacy: Their potential contribution to effective practice', in S. A. Rex and A. Matravers (eds) *Pro-Social Modelling and Legitimacy: The Clarke Hall Day Conference*. Cambridge: Institute of Criminology, University of Cambridge.

Bottoms, A. E., Gelsthorpe, L. and Rex, S. A. (eds) (2001) *Community Penalties: Change and Challenges*. Cullompton: Willan.

Burnett, R. (1994) 'The odds of going straight: Offenders' own predictions', in *Sentencing, Quality and Risk: Proceedings of the 10th Annual Conference on Research and Information in the Probation Service*. University of Loughborough, Birmingham: Midlands Probation Training Consortium.

Cade, B. (1982) 'Some uses of metaphor', *Australian Journal of Family Therapy*, 3, 135–140.

Chapman, T. and Hough, M. (1998) *Evidence-Based Practice: A Guide to Effective Practice*. London: Home Office.

Ditton, J. and Ford, R. (1994) *The Reality of Probation: A Formal Ethnography of Process and Practice*. Aldershot: Avebury.

Gast, L. and Taylor, P. (2002) *Responsivity in Practice – Ideas for Engaging Learners*. Birmingham: University of Birmingham.

Geese Theatre (1998) *Lifting the Weight*. Available at: http://www.geesetheatre.com/CDROM.html

Graham, J. and Bowling, B. (1995) *Young People and Crime* (Home Office Research Study No. 145). London: Home Office.

Haines, K. (1990) *After-Care Services for Released Prisoners: A Review of the Literature*. Cambridge: Institute of Criminology, University of Cambridge.

Hofstede, G. (2001) *Culture's Consequences: Comparing Values, Behaviors, Institutions and Organizations Across Nations* (2nd edn). Thousand Oaks, CA: Sage.

Home Office (1984) *Statement of National Objectives and Priorities*. London: Home Office.

Home Office (2000) *National Standards for the Supervision of Offenders in the Community*. London: Home Office.

Home Office (2001) *Making Punishments Work: Report of a Review of the Sentencing Framework for England and Wales*. London: Home Office.

Joint Prison and Probation Accreditation Panel (2002) *What Works – Towards Effective Practice, Second Annual Report 2000–1*.
Available at: http://www.homeoffice.gov.uk/cpd/probu/probu.htm

Kelly, G. A. (1995) *The Psychology of Personal Constructs*. Norton: New York.

Kropp, P. R., Hart S. D., Webster, C. D., Eaves, D. and Belfrage, H. (1995) *Manual for the Spousal Assault Risk Assessment Guide*. Vancouver: British Columbia Institute on Family Violence.

McGuire, J. (ed.) (1995) *What Works: Reducing Reoffending – Guidelines from Research and Practice*. Chichester: Wiley.

Mann, R. (ed.) (1996) *Motivational Interviewing – Negotiating Behaviour Change*.
Available at: www.NOTA.co.uk

Mayer, J. E. and Timms, N. (1970) *The Client Speaks*. London: Routledge & Kegan Paul.

Miller, W. R. and Rollnick, S. (1991) *Motivational Interviewing: Preparing People to Change Addictive Behavior*. New York: Guilford Press.

Passada (1999) *Lifeskills and Lifestyles* (Passada Software in partnership with Cambridgeshire Probation Service).
Available at: www.passada.co.uk

Paternoster, R., Brame, R., Bachman, R. and Sherman, L. W. (1997) 'Do fair procedures matter? The effect of procedural justice on spouse assault', *Law and Society Review*, 31, 163–204.

Priestley, P. and McGuire, J. (1985) *Offending Behaviour: Skills and Stratagems for Going Straight*. London: Batsford Academic and Educational.

Raynor, P. (2001) 'Community penalties and social integration: "Community" as solution and as problem', in A. E. Bottoms, L. Gelsthorpe, and S. A. Rex (eds) *Community Penalties: Change and Challenges*. Cullompton: Willan.

Rex, S. A. (1999) 'Desistance from offending: Experiences of probation', *Howard Journal of Criminal Justice*, 38, 366–383.

Rex, S. A. (2001) 'Beyond cognitive behaviouralism? Reflections on the effectiveness literature', in A. E. Bottoms, L. Gelsthorpe, and S. A. Rex (eds) *Community Penalties: Change and Challenges*. Cullompton: Willan.

Rex, S. A. and Crosland, P. E. (2000) *Project on Pro-social Modelling and Legitimacy: Findings from Probation Order Supervision, Report to Cambridgeshire Probation Service*. Cambridge: Institute of Criminology, University of Cambridge.

Rogers, C. R. (1951) *Client Centred Therapy*. London: Constable.

Ryan, D. and Carr, A. (2001) 'A study of the differential effects of Tomm's questioning styles on therapeutic alliance', *Journal of Family Process*, 40, 67–77.

Sainsbury, E., Nixon, S. and Phillips, D. (1982) *Social Work in Focus*. London: Routledge & Kegan Paul.

Thornton, D., Mann, R., Webster, S., Blud, L., Travers, R., Friendship, C. and Erikson, M. (2002) 'Distinguishing and combining risks for sexual and violent recidivism', a paper presented at the New York Academy of Sciences Conference on Understanding and Managing Sexually Coercive Behavior.

Trotter, C. (1993) *The Supervision of Offenders – What Works: A Study Undertaken in Community Based Corrections*. Melbourne: Social Work Department, Monash University and the Victorian Department of Justice.

Trotter, C. (1996) 'The impact of different supervision practices in community corrections: Causes for optimism', *Australian and New Zealand Journal of Criminology*, 29, 29–46.

Trotter, C. (1999) *Working with Involuntary Clients: A Guide to Practice*. London: Sage.

Tyler, T. R. (1990) *Why People Obey the Law*. New Haven, CT: Yale University Press.

Watkins, C., Carnell, E., Lodge, C., Wagner, P. and Whalley, C. (1998) *Learning about Learning*. Warwick: The National Association for Pastoral Care in Education, Institute of Education, University of Warwick.

11

ENFORCING SUPERVISION AND ENCOURAGING COMPLIANCE

Carol Hedderman

A BRIEF HISTORY OF ENFORCEMENT

Supervision in place of custody or following custody is inherently conditional. For example, the United Nations (1951: 4) described probation as consisting of:

> . . . the conditional suspension of punishment while the offender is placed under supervision and is individual guidance or 'treatment'. (Quoted in Harris 1995: 4)

As Harris (1995) points out, providing similar services without sanction would not be probation, it would be social work; noting that even the etymology of the word probation supports this as *probatio* means proving oneself and *probator* translates as 'an approver'.

The conditional nature of such supervision is apparent from the Probation Service's inception in the UK and elsewhere. The power to return non-compliant offenders to court was available to Police Court Missionaries working in London between 1872 and 1907 (King 1958; Dersley 2000). At that time, offenders had to consent to supervision and the 1907 Probation of Offenders Act made it clear that such consent was deemed to include accepting a return to court if their behaviour was unsatisfactory. The court could then impose another penalty for the original offence or impose a fine while allowing supervision to continue. Dersley (2000) reports that, by the end of the first year, less than 5 per cent of those on probation had been recalled. At least part of the reason for this low rate was that the criteria for judging breach were poorly defined. Subsequent legislation and guidance through the first half of the twentieth century did little to clarify this. Instead, in the Probation Rules of 1949, supervisors were positively encouraged to use their discretion about the number of appointments set, based on a consideration of individual offenders' circumstances and progress. Resorting to formal breach proceedings was generally seen as a last resort, although in a very few cases it was acknowledged that early breach might be used as a short sharp shock to get an offender to comply (King 1969). As Dersley (2000) notes, this approach fitted well with prevailing concerns about how to handle the sometimes conflicting demands of acting as an officer of the court, ensuring that the court's wishes were carried out, while trying to create a positive relationship of trust with the offender. Willis (1981), in one of the few studies carried out prior to the Criminal Justice Act (CJA) 1991 and the introduction of National Standards, argued that both probation officers and offenders were more concerned with employment and financial and domestic problems than with control. Fielding (1984) also suggests that supervisors may have been reluctant to breach because it could be interpreted as a measure of their own inability to engage and reform the offender.

By the 1980s the atmosphere had changed in that probation, which had largely been viewed as a branch of social work up to that point, began to go out of fashion. This was partly due to a misunderstanding of research by Martinson (1974) which was interpreted as showing that 'Nothing Works', although he actually concluded that the evidence base was too flawed to be able to draw conclusions about what was effective. As Vennard, Sugg and Hedderman (1997: 2) notes, Martinson's own caveats:

> ... tended, however, to be overlooked by those who saw in the article strong empirical support for the rejection of a treatment approach and for return to a just deserts perspective, in which the principle of appropriate and proportionate punishment is paramount in the sentencing decision.

This fitted well with the then Conservative government's rejection of explanations of crime which involved references to offenders' circumstances. Offenders were characterised as 'wicked' rather than 'misguided' and expected to take moral responsibility for their own actions. Nevertheless even those who doubted the rehabilitative power of community supervision continued to value it for its value in keeping the prison population – and costs – down. However, expectation of what supervision should focus on began to change.

Supervisors were encouraged to police attendance in an effort to bolster public and sentencer confidence in non-custodial options and overcome their image as 'soft options'. Failing to breach for non-compliance was viewed as a sign that supervisors were siding with offenders rather than working in the broader public interest. The concern was that this would lead to a decline in the use of non-custodial sentences. Indeed, Lloyd (1991) suggests that this was behind the decline in the use of Community Service (now Community Punishment) Orders through the early 1980s. Following the introduction of

National Standards for Community Service[1] in 1989, he notes a trend towards tougher enforcement, with supervisors breaching after three rather than four absences. The number of orders terminated for breach also increased. As these changes were accompanied by an increase in the use of Community Service, it is reasonable to conclude that there was a link. However, Lloyd also warned that overly tough enforcement might have the opposite effect to that intended, as sentencers might be discouraged from using the orders if they were asked to deal with too many trivial breaches. He also expressed concern about the way an overzealous use of breach and revocation might affect the prison population.

The start of the 1990s brought two important changes to the enforcement context. First the CJA 1991 which was enacted in 1992 determined (among other things) that:

- custody should be reserved for the most serious offences or to protect the public from serious (violent or sexual) harm;
- courts could impose a mix of probation and community service in a new 'Combination Order' (now the Community Punishment and Rehabilitation Order); and
- community sentences were not just to be seen as alternatives to custody but as sentences in their own right.

Second, National Standards covering not only Community Service but other types of order and supervision on licence were introduced in 1992.

In the run-up to these changes and shortly after they were introduced, commentators began to speculate how they would affect practice. Drakeford (1993: 299–300) advocated a 'minimalist approach' in which breach was to be treated as a response of last resort. He pointed to the way the Standards allowed room for professional judgement and argued that local guidance should encourage this to be used particularly for offenders with chaotic lifestyles. Broad (1991) was also concerned that the move towards standardisation might have unfortunate and unintended effects, warning that it might lead to officers failing to adequately investigate the reasons for non-attendance in their rush to breach. He also predicted that issuing local guidelines would promote these effects. In contrast, McWilliams and Pease (1990: 22) were concerned that while seeking to limit the exercise of discretion, local codes of practice would actually serve to drive the use of discretion underground. Thus decision-making would become both more arbitrary and less easy to scrutinise. They argued

---

[1] These Standards required offenders to be breached or warned in writing following a first incident of non-compliance. At a second failure, the case was to be referred to a Senior Probation Officer for a decision about breach. The offender was to be breached after three failures in all cases.

that statutory control had always been part of the probation officers' role and that the officers '. . . who collude with the evasion of court-mandated control give the opposite communication to that required'.

Possibly the most important change brought in by the 1992 National Standards was that the government specified how many appointments which should be made ordinarily and the minimum number which might be where this could not be achieved. In other respects, the Standards were drafted in such a way as to regularise rather than eliminate the exercise of professional judgement in dealing with absences and other failures to comply. An examination of how probation and community service staff viewed the Standards found that they were considered 'helpful in ensuring fair and consistent enforcement practice, and allowed them to use discretion where necessary. However, it was also clear from their replies that probation staff sometimes employed National Standards loosely . . .' (Ellis, Hedderman and Mortimer 1996: 54). Unusually, this study also considered how officers encouraged compliance, including setting more frequent appointments,[2] cancelling hours worked when an offender on community service had turned up but behaved badly, revoking early for good behaviour, setting appointments to coincide with other important regular events (usually signing on). Despite Drakeford's (1993) contention that the notion of constructive breach was a fallacy, all of the 89 officers interviewed drew a distinction between breaches where the intention was to reinforce respect and encourage compliance, and those with a recommendation to revoke. They described using the latter where the order has become unworkable due to repeatedly poor attendance or the offender had otherwise withdrawn his or her cooperation.[3] In either case the officers cautioned that whether breach actually served to discipline or punish was not entirely within their control:

> . . . there is little point in the Probation Service reacting swiftly to breach proceedings if, when an offender fails to answer a summons, the police are slow to enforce the resulting warrant, or the case takes so long to come to court that the order has been completed. (Drakeford 1993: 52)

Even before Ellis, Hedderman and Mortimer had completed their research, the government had decided to publish revised National Standards (1995) which considerably curtailed supervisors' discretion about when to breach and how to respond to first and second failures to attend. It also published *Strengthening Punishment in the Community* (Home Office 1995). As its name implies, this Green Paper discussed how community sentences might be used

---

[2] It should be noted that some officers thought this simply doubled an offender's opportunities to fail.

[3] Respondents explained that offenders were rarely breached for anything other than failure to attend, partly because this was the most common form of non-compliance but also because it was easiest to prove.

to deliver punishment and deterrence as well as rehabilitation (Hedderman, Ellis and Sugg 1999).

National Standards were further revised in April 2000, so that there are now very few circumstances in which an absence may be regarded as acceptable and virtually every case in which more than one unacceptable absence occurs will go to court for a breach hearing. One of the main reasons for the revisions was that Probation Inspectorate ('Quality and Effectiveness') reports which scrutinised individual areas' performance on a common set of measures, criticised one area after another during the 1990s for failing to offer appointments in line with National Standards, or to enforce them rigorously. In some cases Chiefs were even said to have simply decided not to require staff to work to a particular requirement. By 1998 the service had been criticised by the Home Affairs Select Committee on Alternatives to Custody, who expressed concern about the laxity with which orders were being enforced.

By that point, the extent to which cases were breached on or before a third unacceptable absence had been made a Key Performance Indicator (KPI), with a target of 90 per cent. However, there was a lack of clarity about how rates should be calculated when breach was initiated more than once in relation to a single order. This made it possible to generate breach rates of more than 100 per cent, making the results nonsensical. Making breach a KPI also implied that the government's concern with enforcement was purely managerial.

By the time National Standards 2000 were introduced, new pressures were in operation. The 'Nothing Works' debate had been informed by the 'What Works' literature (see Vennard, Sugg and Hedderman 1997) leading to a belief that 'Some things work for some people some of the time'. A consistent finding from the literature is that those who fail to complete programmes have worse reconviction results than those who complete and usually worse than control groups.[4] This difference is partly due to selection effects, in that those who are least likely to re-offend are also those who are most likely to complete. However, we also know that offenders can be persuaded, cajoled and coerced into a programme with beneficial effects (see Edmunds *et al.* 1999, for an example relating to drug offenders). To this extent National Standards might be seen as supporting effective practice. However, the idea that programme delivery should incorporate notions of 'pro-social modelling' was also being strongly advocated (Chapman and Hough 1998). Derived from the work of Trotter (1993), pro-social modelling assumes that positive reinforcement is more effective in securing not only offenders' attendance at programmes but also their active and willing participation. Thus supervisors are expected to praise and reward offenders displaying appropriate, non-criminal

---

[4] See, for example, the National Probation Directorate's (2000) summary of results from a recent evaluation of the 'Think First' Programme.

behaviour, rather than using negative sanctions to deter non-compliance. The then Chief Inspector suggested that seen from this perspective National Standards also:

> ... belong to offenders who should know what is expected of them and what action will be taken if they fail to comply with the requirements but also what they can expect from the probation service in the way they are being supervised. (Her Majesty's Chief Inspector of Probation 1996, quoted in Her Majesty's Inspectorate of Probation 2000)

However, aside from offering advice about the number of appointments offenders will be offered, the Standards say nothing about the standard of help an offender might reasonably expect or how compliance might be rewarded. They are also couched in terms which focus on prohibiting poor behaviour rather than reinforcing appropriate conduct.

Currently then, National Standards are expected to promote a variety of objectives. They are expected to promote compliance while also, serving to limit discretion, making decision-making more transparent and accountable, measuring officers' (and areas') performance, promoting confidence in community penalties to ensure that courts make use of them, setting probation apart from social work, and discouraging collusion between supervisors and offenders. There is a natural tension between at least some of these. In particular, as discussed below, allowing fewer failures before breaching and reducing supervisors' discretion about when to breach may promote public and sentencer confidence, but at the same time it reduces the options and time a supervisor will have to actively encourage compliance. With very limited discretion supervisors may be able to wield a stick, but have few positive inducements with which to promote compliance.

RECENT IMPROVEMENTS IN ENFORCEMENT

In 1999, responding to the then Home Secretary's complaints about poor enforcement, the Association of Chief Officers of Probation (ACOP)[5] moved to improve it. Part of the action plan was to arrange for an independent audit of the way court orders and post-release licences were enforced throughout England and Wales. This was supervised by the current author. The results (Hedderman 1999) set a baseline from which to measure subsequent changes in practice, following new guidance from ACOP on enforcement and recording

---

[5] ACOP was disbanded on 1 April 2001 when the new National Probation Service was established. The Association was a Professional Association of Chiefs and Assistant Chiefs. It functioned as an informed pressure group and was frequently consulted on changes in legislation and practice by government and the media.

enforcement action. Six months after the first audit, ACOP commissioned a second round of the audit. This showed improvements on most measures, including:

- more timely first appointments;
- a higher proportion of offenders on probation being offered 12 or more appointments; and
- an increase in the proportion of offenders on probation, community service (CS) and post-release licences being dealt with in line with or in excess of National Standards requirements at a first, second or third unacceptable absence.

Although there was still variation between areas, the extent of variation had narrowed on most measures and the trend towards tougher enforcement was a general one.

While the results were still some way short of meeting the KPI target of 90 per cent of appropriate cases being breached by a third unacceptable absence, they suggested that improvements could be made without further instruction or guidance from the Inspectorate or the government.

The current National Standards 2000, which came into force on 1 April 2000, clarified some 1995 Standards and made others more stringent. One of the most important changes was the requirement that, for offenders on court orders, breach should be instigated as a result of a second unacceptable failure to attend rather than a third, with the first failure being responded to by means of a final (red) warning letter.[6] Other changes included:

- requiring that offenders be informed of the time of their first appointment before they leave court;
- changing references to the first 'three months' of CRO and CPO supervision to '12 weeks'[7] and some clarification of the number of appointments to be made in licence cases;
- distinguishing more clearly between a first CPO appointment for assessment, for which the deadline is five working days from sentence, and for first work placement, which should be made within ten working days;
- making it clear that non-attendance at an appointment with a partner organisation should be dealt with in the same way as a failed probation appointment;[8]

---

[6] National Standards 2000 stated that the letter should be 'yellow', but this was amended to 'red' by Probation Circular 24/00.

[7] Previously areas were free to interpret 'three' months as 12 weeks, a quarter of a year (13 weeks) or even calendar months.

[8] Circular 24/00 amended this requirement to refer only to appointments that are of a similar frequency and duration to appointments with a supervising officer.

- providing more specific guidance about the limited range of circumstances in which absences may be considered acceptable; and
- regarding absences as unacceptable unless proved otherwise.

All of the then 54 services (which became 42 areas within the new National Probation Service) took part in each round of the audit. This involved providing details of appointments made and attended and responses to non-attendance over the first three months for probation and community service orders and post-release licences initiated in March 1999 ($N = 10,008$), the first half of September 1999 ($N = 4386$) and September 2000 ($N = 8924$) respectively. As the audits represent only a sample of cases active in each year, estimates are inevitably subject to some sampling error. As a cautious guide, differences of at least 2 percentage points in the results of the second and third audits may be considered statistically significant.

Cases sampled in all three rounds of the audit were found to be alike in terms of the offences for which offenders had been sentenced, age, sex, ethnicity and type and length of supervision. This makes comparisons between different rounds of the audit meaningful as they are not distorted by being based on very different mixes of cases. It also confirms that areas did not 'fix' their returns to generate more favourable results.

When compared to the results of the second audit, the results of the third audit show:

- the proportion of first appointments that were set in the timeframes required by National Standard rose from 82 per cent to 90 per cent;
- possibly as a consequence of the new requirement to notify offenders of first appointments before they leave court, attendance at first appointments went up from 81 per cent to 85 per cent;
- the new requirement to offer a first placement session within 10 working days to those on CS was achieved in 74 per cent of all CS cases and 85 per cent of cases where a first assessment appointment was made within 5 days;
- the proportion of probation cases in which offenders were offered 12 appointments was virtually unchanged at 75 per cent. However, the proportion of cases in which services offered more than 12 appointments went up from 50 per cent by 6 percentage points;[9]
- the newly clarified Standard of nine appointments in the first 3 months was met or exceeded in about the same proportion (80 per cent) of licence cases;

---

[9] These figures cannot be calculated for Community Service as the Standards specify the number of hours to be worked rather than the number of appointments.

- the percentage of offenders who attended all their appointments or had an acceptable reason for being absent rose from 46 per cent to 53 per cent.

Under the National Standards 1995, offenders were allowed up to two unacceptable absences before being breached. An overall compliance rate can be generated by adding together cases which had no unacceptable absences with those which involved less than three. This shows that the compliance rate for offenders in the second audit was 78 per cent. Judged by 1995 Standards, the compliance rate in the current audit would have been 84 per cent.

The more stringent National Standards 2000 require that offenders on court orders are only allowed one acceptable absence before being breached, although those on licence may have two. Calculated on this basis 73 per cent of offenders in the third audit complied. The comparable figure for Audit 2 (i.e. if National Standards 2000 had been in place) was 67 per cent.

The third audit showed that 71 per cent of offenders were dealt with at least as severely as National Standards 2000 require at a first unacceptable absence whereas 77 per cent of those in the second audit were dealt with as the 1995 Standards require. The proportion of cases in which no action was taken remained at around 10 per cent while the use of measures which are less than National Standards require (e.g. a verbal or written reminder) rose from 7 per cent to 15 per cent. This means that while performance may not have improved to the level required by the 2000 Standards, performance in relation to the 1995 Standards was maintained.

About two-thirds of responses to a second unacceptable absence were at least as severe as the relevant set of Standards required in the second and third audits. However, the proportion of cases in which less severe action (as opposed to no action) was taken trebled (to 9 per cent). If cases in the third round were judged by 1995 Standards, this means that performance levels were either being maintained or improved on.

Fifty-six per cent of offenders on licence were breached on their third unacceptable absence as National Standards 2000 require. Overall, half of all those with a third unacceptable absence were breached or recalled at this stage compared with nearly two-thirds of comparable cases in the second round (see Table 11.1). The percentage of cases in which no action was taken or information was missing both nearly doubled. Together these results indicate a decline in both performance and record-keeping. However, only 7 per cent of cases in the third audit got as far as a third unacceptable absence without having been breached or recalled compared to 21 per cent in the second audit.

Overall, the results of the third audit suggest that while the stricter enforcement standards required by National Standards 2000 had not been achieved, performance had been maintained and in some instances improved in relation to 1995 Standards. In particular, compliance had gone up.

Table 11.1 Responses to a third unacceptable absence

	Audit 2 (%)	Audit 3 (%)
No action taken	7.5	12
Action taken		
Less severe than NS requires	2	11
Formal warning letter (NS 1995)	6	–
Formal warning letter (NS 2000)	–	3
Final warning letter	16	11
Breach initiated	62	50
Not clear what, if any, action taken	6.5	13
Three unacceptable absences	923	651
% of total sample	21%	7%
Total sample	4386	8924

FORGING A LINK BETWEEN ENFORCEMENT, COMPLIANCE AND EFFECTIVE PRACTICE

However restrictive, the simple existence of National Standards is unlikely to promote confidence in community penalties. Promoting confidence requires that the Standards are complied with, otherwise, as the Lord Chief Justice (2001) has noted:

> . . . offenders may receive custodial sentences because the judiciary does not believe there is any credible community alternative.

By showing that the Probation Service is working to ensure that offenders are seen at least as frequently as National Standards require, and takes action when attendance falls off, the results of the second and third audits may have enhanced the credibility of community sentences and thus encouraged their use. As programme completers generally outperform non-completers, the fact that the third audit showed improvements in attendance suggests that National Standards may assist in the delivery of effective work. However, in promoting compliance, there is obvious value in a graduated response running from reminding offenders of the terms of their orders through initial and final warnings. Punishing non-compliance by substituting a custodial sentence should be reserved for those who have shown themselves to be unwilling to comply despite efforts made to assist and encourage them to do so. Each revision of the National Standards has reduced the number of failures an offender is permitted and sought to increase the chances of an order being terminated. However, the implications this may have for selection effects do not seem to have been thought through. The likelihood is that this may lead to those offenders who are most in need of effective supervision being breached and resentenced before they have a chance to be transformed into 'completers'.

Bottoms (2001) suggests that compliance may come about in response to a constraint or coercion; because of habit; through a calculation of self-interest; or because of a feeling of moral obligation. National Standards are almost entirely geared to ensuring compliance through constraint or coercion. They make passing reference to encouraging attendance to become a habit; for example, by making appointments coincide with 'signing-on' days or making first appointments before the offender leaves court. But there is much more scope to 'design out' non-attendance by employing ideas adapted from situational crime perspective (Clarke 1997). Examples might include sentencers stressing the consequences of non-attendance when pronouncing sentence; and having agreed times and days of the week for first appointments so that its timing can be announced at the time of sentence (Hedderman, Ellis and Sugg 1999).

The Standards are also silent about encouraging compliance by rewarding it. Teesside's idea of providing breakfast to those attending a final programme session is one example, but Underdown (2001: 120) recommends that other stronger incentives might include 'reducing the restrictions or lessening the demands that the overall community penalty imposes'. He suggests that this might be accomplished by increasing the court's role in overseeing orders. Another option might be a graduated system of positive rewards which could be incorporated into National Standards (Hedderman and Hough 2000). These might range from awarding attendance certificates (the positive equivalent of a final warning letter) to early termination for good behaviour. What is novel about this suggestion is not the range of techniques – experienced practitioners will be able to think of many other options – but the idea that, like the breach system, routes to positive rewards should be spelled out and operated even-handedly and transparently. Any sign of arbitrary decision-making would bring the system into disrepute with offenders in much the same way that such decision-making is said to undermine sentencers' confidence in enforcement.

Encouraging offenders to appreciate 'what's in it for them' is another obvious strategy. Appealing at the outset to their self-interest by spelling out the help which can be accessed in relation to employment, education, accommodation, finances, child care, and transport may encourage attendance in a way that promising to work with them on their offending behaviour may not.

Encouraging compliance by making it normative is probably the most diffi-cult to achieve given that, by definition, offenders are given to rule breaking. However, Underdown (2001) suggests that 'Cognitive training programmes aim to improve cause–effect thinking and understanding of social obligation through values enhancement' (pp. 120–121). Recruiting the support of law-abiding family members as a sort of unofficial mentor might also be worth considering (Webster *et al.* 2001). Pro-social modelling techniques such as ensuring that sessions begin on time and that staff treat offenders with respect and courtesy may also encourage offenders into normative compliance. Trotter's (1999) work certainly suggests that it does so. This may also follow, as Underdown (2001) suggests, when attendance at cognitive-behavioural programmes leads to a better understanding of social obligations and changes in the values to which participants subscribe.

Conclusive evidence about the link between enforcement and reconviction is not yet available (Hedderman and Hearnden 2000). Some light will be shed on the link between the severity of enforcement and reconviction by a study based on cases in the second audit of enforcement discussed above, but this will inevitably continue its focus on enforcement. If the government's aim of putting 30,000 offenders through probation programmes by 2004 (Home Office 2001) is to be achieved, however, new research is needed which focuses on exactly how positive approaches to securing compliance 'work'.

SUMMARY OF KEY ISSUES

- National Standards were introduced in the 1980s in an effort to persuade sentencers and the public that that supervision in the community was not a 'soft option'. Subsequent revisions to the Standards have been intended to limit supervisor discretion in the light of evidence that officers were failing offer as many appointments as the Standards specified or to respond quickly or firmly enough with non-compliance.
- The results of three recent national audits show that the Probation Service is capable of stricter enforcement and that compliance rates have improved. These are positive developments in that they may encourage sentencers to use community penalties in place of custody. It may also mean that offenders stay in effective programmes long enough for their attitudes and behaviour to be affected.
- However, there are dangers in tightening up enforcement. Reducing the number of failures an offender is permitted and increasing the chances of an order being terminated could simply intensify selection effects and result in those offenders who are most in need of effective supervision being breached and resentenced before they have a chance to be transformed into 'completers'.
- An effective disciplinary system needs to provide a graduated response, including rewards for good behaviour. Punishing non-compliance by substituting a custodial sentence should be reserved for those who have shown themselves to be unwilling to comply despite such efforts made to assist and encourage them to do so. It is also important to note that conclusive evidence about the link between enforcement and reconviction is not yet available.

References

Bottoms, A. E. (2001) 'Compliance and community penalties', in A. E. Bottoms, L. Gelsthorpe and S. A. Rex (eds) *Community Penalties: Change and Challenges*. Cullompton: Willan.

Broad, B. (1991) *Punishment under Pressure: The Probation Service in the Inner City*. London: Jessica Kingsley.

Chapman, T. and Hough, M. (1998) *Evidence-based Practice: A Guide to Effective Practice*. London: Home Office.

Clarke, R. V. (1997) *Situational Crime Prevention: Successful Case Studies*. Albany: Harrow and Heston.

Dersley, I. (2000) *Acceptable or Unacceptable? Local Probation Service Policy on Non-compliance and Enforcement* (unpublished undergraduate (BA Community Studies/Diploma in Probation Studies) dissertation). Birmingham: School of Social Sciences, Birmingham University.

Drakeford, M. (1993) 'The Probation Service, breach and the Criminal Justice Act 1991', *Howard Journal of Criminal Justice*, 32, 291–302.

Edmunds, M., Hough, M., Turnbull, P. J. and May, T. (1999) *Doing Justice to Treatment: Referring Offenders to Drug Services* (Drugs Prevention Advisory Service Paper No. 2). London: Home Office.

Ellis, T., Hedderman, C. and Mortimer, E. (1996) *Enforcing Community Penalties* (Home Office Research Study No. 158). London: Home Office.

Fielding, N. (1984) *Probation Practice: Client Support Under Social Control*. Aldershot: Gower.

Harris, R. (1995) 'Studying probation a comparative approach', in K. Hamai, R. Ville, R. Harris, M. Hough and U. Zvekic (eds) *Probation Around the World*. London: Routledge.

Hedderman, C. (1999) *ACOP Enforcement Survey: Stage 1*. London: ACOP. Available at http://www.sbu.ac.uk/cpru

Hedderman, C., Ellis, T. and Sugg, D. (1999) *Increasing Confidence in Community Sentences: The Results of Two Demonstration Projects* (Home Office Research Study No. 194). London: Home Office.

Hedderman, C. and Hearnden, I. (2000) *Improving Enforcement – the Second ACOP Enforcement Audit*. London: ACOP. Available at http://www.sbu.ac.uk/cpru

Hedderman, C. and Hough, M. (2000) 'Tightening up probation: A step too far?', *Criminal Justice Matters*, 39 (April), 5.

Her Majesty's Inspectorate of Probation (HMIP) (2000) *Making National Standards Work: A Study by HMIP of Enforcement Practice in Community Penalties*. London: Home Office.

Home Office (1995) *Strengthening Punishment in the Community*. London: Home Office.

Home Office (2001) *Criminal Justice: The Way Ahead*. London: Home Office.

King, J. (1958) *The Probation Service*. London: Butterworth.

King, J. (1969) *The Probation and Aftercare Service*. London: Butterworth.

Lloyd, C. (1991) 'National Standards for Community Service Orders: The first two years of operation', *Home Office Research Bulletin 31*. London: Home Office.

Lord Chief Justice (2001) *The Woolf Report: A Decade of Change?* London: Prison Reform Trust.

McWilliams, W. and Pease, K. (1990) 'Probation practice and an end to punishment', *Howard Journal of Criminal Justice*, 29, 14–24.

Martinson, R. (1974) 'What works? Questions and answers about prison reforms', *Public Interest*, 35, 22–54.

National Probation Directorate (2000) *What Works? Newsletter* (Edition No. 4). London: Home Office.

Trotter, C. (1993) *The Supervision of Offenders – What Works: A Study Undertaken in Community Based Corrections*. Melbourne: Social Work Department, Monash University and the Victorian Department of Justice.

Trotter, C. (1999) *Working with Involuntary Clients: A Guide to Practice*. London: Sage.

Underdown, A. (2001) 'Making "What Works" work: Challenges in the delivery of community penalties', in A. E. Bottoms, L. Gelsthorpe and S. A. Rex (eds) *Community Penalties: Change and Challenges*. Cullompton: Willan.

United Nations (1951) *Probation and Related Measures* (Document E/CN.5/230). New York: United Nations.

Vennard, J., Sugg, D. and Hedderman, C. (1997) 'The use of cognitive-behavioural approaches with offenders: Messages from the research', in C. Hedderman, D. Sugg and J. Vennard (eds) *Changing Offenders' Attitudes and Behaviour: What Works?* (Home Office Research Study No. 171). London: Home Office.

Webster, R., Hedderman, C., Turnball, P. J. and May, T. (2001) *Building Bridges to Employment for Prisoners* (Home Office Research Study No. 226). London: Home Office.

Willis A. (1981) 'Social welfare and social control: A survey of young men on probation', *Home Office Research Bulletin 11*. London: Home Office.

12

PARTNERSHIPS IN THE PROBATION SERVICE

Judith Rumgay

INTRODUCTION

Within the past decade, partnership has become a major feature of Probation Service activity. The explosion of the partnership phenomenon onto the criminal justice stage has had particular implications for the probation service, which, uniquely, relates both to the agencies of the criminal justice system and to those of the multiple social support services that offenders require. Yet, much less attention has been paid to the role of the Probation Service in multi-agency activity as compared with that of the police. This emphasis of interest is probably due to the perceived power differential between these two agencies. However, the Probation Service alone has the pivotal quality, and long experience, of inhabiting both the criminal justice and the social welfare organisational realms.

One consequence of this dual existence has been to burden the Service with alternative meanings of the very term 'partnership'. It was first offered this caption for the development of contractual relationships with non-statutory organisations for the delivery of services to offenders, reflecting the move to purchaser–provider relations that characterised the health and social services during the early 1990s. More broadly, however, 'partnership' in criminal justice terms has come, over the same period of time, to connote the increasing number of multi-agency crime prevention, community safety and community development collaborations that are required for the implementation of social policy in an age of 'joined-up' government. The list of such enterprises is rapidly expanding, to embrace, for example, Drug Action Teams, Youth Offending Teams, Crime and Disorder Reduction Partnerships, Multi-agency Public Protection Panels, and Supporting People consortia for social housing.

Disconcertingly, the popularity of the partnership ideal, reflected in this burgeoning inter-agency activity, has grown considerably faster than the accumulation of knowledge about effective practice. In 1991, the report of the Home Office Standing Conference on Crime Prevention averred: 'The case for the partnership approach stands virtually unchallenged but also hardly tested' (p. 14). It is debatable how much better equipped we are, a decade later, to elaborate the principles of successful partnership in forms that may assist the proliferation of effective, rather than merely optimistic practice.

This chapter begins by setting out the complex policy framework within which the probation service has forged these multi-layered relationships with its statutory and non-statutory partners. It then moves to examine more deeply the meaning(s) of partnership, its theoretical justification and the hallmarks of successful partnership.

PARTNERSHIP AS POLICY

There are four discernible strands in policy for partnerships affecting the probation service: contracting for supervision services; community crime prevention; targeting of special groups; and coordinated social planning and provision.

Contracting for supervision services

The Probation Service's introduction to the notion of partnership as a formal policy intention, as opposed to a general proselytising for cooperative spirit between agencies with common clientele, followed the paradigm of changes in the delivery of health and social services initiated by the NHS and Community Care Act 1990. Within this framework, the statutory agencies of health and welfare were required to shift their role in service delivery from that of principal providers to becoming purchasers of services provided by private and voluntary sector organisations. Similarly, the Home Office's plans during the late 1980s and early 1990s for an expansion of community-based alternatives to imprisonment included the expectation that 'elements of a supervision programme could *and would* be provided by organisations and individuals outside the probation service' (Home Office 1990a, emphasis added; Home Office 1990b).

The Home Office initially facilitated the development of partnerships between probation areas and non-statutory organisations by providing financial support for local initiatives through a Supervision Grants Scheme (inevitably known as SUGS). It later devolved responsibility for both developing and financing the partnership enterprise to local probation areas (Home Office 1992). Implementation of the process was secured by the requirement for each area to submit its plans for committing expenditure of a minimum of 5 per cent of its revenue budget on partnerships with 'independent' sector organisations (Home Office 1993a–c). The proportion of the budget to be dedicated to partnership contracting was subsequently revised to 7 per cent, to include sums spent on accommodation schemes.

Community crime prevention

This narrow conceptualisation of partnership as contracting for specific services was reserved for the Probation Service alone among criminal justice agencies (Crawford 1999). Alongside it, a broader vision of multi-agency collaboration in crime-relevant fields of activity was emerging, in which the probation service would become an important contributor. During the 1980s, growing interest in crime prevention, as opposed to detection and prosecution, encouraged the expectation that a coordinated multi-disciplinary approach was more likely to prove successful than policing in isolation. Home Office initiatives to explore and promote the promise of partnerships in crime prevention included the establishment of its Standing Conference on Crime Prevention in 1985, the dissemination of good practice examples (e.g. Home Office 1990c), and the launching of the Safer Cities Programme, a major action research evaluation of crime-prevention projects with a partnership approach (Tilley 1992; Department of the Environment, Transport and the Regions 2000). Again, facilitation was followed by mandate. The government affirmed its faith in multi-agency collaboration in crime prevention in the Crime and Disorder Act 1998, which imposed a duty on local councils, in cooperation with police, probation and relevant others to formulate and implement a strategy for reducing crime and disorder in their localities. These collaborative groups were awarded the title of Crime and Disorder Reduction Partnerships.

Targeting of special groups

Specific groups of individuals involved in, or at risk of, involvement in crime have also been targeted for the multi-agency approach. First, in 1995, the Conservative government's drugs strategy moved significantly away from its emphasis on law enforcement to an integrated approach centring on the establishment of local Drug Action Teams. Notably, these groups were to be composed of the most senior representatives from health, social services, education, probation and police, in order to ensure their ability to implement policy and resource decisions agreed at inter-agency level within their own organisations (Lord President of the Council and Leader of the House of Commons, Secretary of State for the Home Department, Secretary of State for Health, Secretary of State for Education and the Paymaster General 1995).

Again, the Teams were charged with the duty of drawing up an action plan to tackle drugs problems in their areas.

Second, the Crime and Disorder Act 1998 imposed a duty on local authorities, acting in cooperation with the police and probation services to ensure the availability of youth justice services in their areas. Moreover, each area was required to establish Youth Offending Teams for the delivery of those services, which were to include practitioners from the police, probation, health, education and social services.

Finally, the Criminal Justice and Courts Services Act 2000 required police and probation services jointly to make arrangements for assessing and managing the risks posed locally by known sexual and violent offenders and others whose criminal histories suggested a potential danger to public safety. In so doing, they were required to negotiate the involvement of social services, health and local authority housing departments (Home Office 2001). These assembled groups became known as Multi-agency Public Protection Panels.

Coordinated social planning and provision

The partnership ideal has spread beyond the strict concerns of crime control to affect other areas of social policy, with similar implications for the probation service. An example of this is the Supporting People project for planning and delivery of social housing by multi-agency consortia through an integrated funding system. This initiative is of particular interest for the probation service in so far as it combines the social welfare intention to support vulnerable people with the potential for enhancing the role of housing organisations in reduction of neighbourhood disorder and anti-social behaviour. It thus throws the dual role of the Probation Service into sharp relief.

Thus, over the space of a decade, the Probation Service has become a participant in a range of activities in which inter-agency collaboration is required in policy and statute. While, initially, it might have appeared as one manifestation of the Conservative government's priorities of rolling back the state and introducing the methods of the marketplace into the functioning of public agencies, the partnership approach rapidly became a much more complex, diverse phenomenon. Its popularity has continued to expand unabated in the policies of Labour administrations. Its appeal lies in its promise to fulfil a number of policy goals for the resolution of social and crime problems, combined with the rationalisation of resource expenditure. The proliferation of these disparate policy meanings of partnership, however, appears to have been accompanied by a shift in perspective on the importance of particular contributors. While partnership was initially promoted to the probation service in terms of its relationships with non-statutory agencies, the voluntary sector's distinctive contribution to achieving wider, and, in the current climate of anxiety about crime, more pressing policy goals is currently poorly considered. Thus, when considering the Probation Service's future towards the end of this decade of partnership expansion, the Home Office 'referred to its partners almost exclusively as the statutory agencies of police, Crown Prosecution Service, prisons and local authorities, with barely a nod in the direction of 'those other local bodies which help to deliver public protection services' (1998: 11–12)' (Rumgay 2001: 127).

For the Probation Service, as we have seen, this complex partnership enterprise has entailed forging a range of inter-agency relationships that serve different policy purposes: contractual arrangements for service delivery by non-statutory agencies; community-wide strategies for risk reduction and support of vulnerable people; and targeting of specific groups of individuals for multi-agency monitoring and intervention.

THEORIES OF PARTNERSHIP

In the context of this proliferation of partnership activity, what meaning does the concept hold for those who are obliged to participate? So much of this effort has been policy driven that it frequently appears to be an atheoretical exercise in pragmatism rather than guided by any conceptual framework for understanding the partnership process. Yet, there are diverse perspectives on the meaning of partnership, ranging from the relatively cynical to the idealistic. Moreover, each perspective has implications for the partnership reality, in terms of the nature of the relationship between partners, the inclusion of participants in the collaborative process and the scope of the partnership project. This can be illustrated by exploring the dimensions of three alternative views: partnership as redistribution of responsibilities; partnership as system efficiency; and partnership as empowerment.

Partnership as redistribution of responsibilities

From the narrowest viewpoint, partnership may be interpreted as the redistribution of responsibilities: an exercise in which responsibilities of one, probably statutory, organisation are transferred to other, possibly voluntary or private sector agencies (Reid 2001). This may be considered a constructive response to appreciation of the particular expertise of alternative agencies, which may be purchased to secure additional specialised resources. It also offers a financial inducement to agencies that otherwise might regard offenders as too uncooperative and unmotivated, and their problems too complex to merit the expenditure of effort. A positive view of partnership as redistribution of responsibilities, therefore, focuses on its potential for importing additional skills and expertise to the 'host' organisation, which passes some of its service delivery functions to its partner.

One consequence of the partnership enterprise, particularly that part which concerns contracting for elements of offender supervision, has been the attempt to differentiate between 'core' (i.e. non-transferable) and 'non-core' (i.e. trans-ferable) activities of the probation service, which, as a statutory organisation, may be held solely accountable for the delivery of certain services. This has proved far more difficult than might be anticipated. To some extent, this definitional difficulty may be seen to be self-serving for an organisation that has been reluctant to yield its ownership of the wide range of activities encompassed by offender supervision (Rumgay 2000a). There are, however, real problems in any attempt to delimit the scope of the service's work to those functions that are required by statute (Smith, Paylor and Mitchell 1993). These are, in part, related to the problems of sustaining accountability in conditions of service fragmentation, particularly in times when the service is increasingly regulated by performance standards (Smith, Paylor and Mitchell 1993; Adams and Nelson 1997). They also, however, concern the paradoxical potential for a qualitative decline in the Probation Service's contribution to community well-being through a retraction of its focus to risk assessment, monitoring and enforcement, at precisely the time when greater participation in multi-agency partnerships designed to promote that very purpose is required (Smith, Paylor and Mitchell 1993; Rumgay 2001). Indeed, this perspective, by focusing on the importation of additional expertise, underplays the extent to which the process itself requires new management skills, broader appreciation of the social policy field as it affects partners and a re-direction of resources towards project support and maintenance in the 'host' agency (Rumgay 2000a; Reid 2001).

In the early years of the partnership enterprise, there was little evidence of the shift of probation officer activity from primary caseworker to case manager anticipated in Home Office policy (Cross 1997; Rumgay 2000a). This was probably due to a mixture of factors. First, the Probation Service largely con-trived to structure its partnerships in order to avoid encroachment on its tradi-tional territory by its new partners. Thus, in successful partnerships, probation officers perceived enhancements to their own practice rather than a constric-tion of their role in offender supervision (Rumgay 2000a). Second, there was little evidence that voluntary sector agencies aspired to the functions of the Probation Service. Rather, their motivation for entering into partnership was to improve the quality of their own services to a client group that was often difficult to reach (Cross 1997; Rumgay 2000a). Third, the required 5 per cent expenditure of probation area budgets on partnerships, particularly when limits were set on expenditure on each partnership, was unlikely to produce sufficient partner resources substantially to replace probation officer activity in supervision (Rumgay 2000a). To the extent that a move towards case management has taken place in more recent years, this is arguably due to more fundamental financial and policy pressures on the probation service to alter its traditional methods of delivering community supervision. If so, however, it may herald disappointment, since *effective* case management occurs in a broader context of system integration. Indeed, in the human services, '[c]ase management has enjoyed widespread acceptance and popularity because it has not been viewed as a systematic reform but as a function that can be incorporated into ongoing fragmented delivery systems . . .' (Moore 1992; Austin 1993: 451).

Moreover, the expansion of multi-agency partnerships in crime prevention and social care, via this model of responsibility redistribution, extends the potential for a blurring of boundaries between agencies. For example, in the context of increasing appreciation of the importance of poor housing strategies in the production of social disorder, how might we differentiate between activities undertaken to support vulnerable people in their homes and those which serve to monitor and control their potential for criminal behaviour? This is an increasingly complex issue at a time when 'anti-social' behaviour, which may fall short of criminal activity, has become a central concern of housing authorities. Questions of organisational accountability are further compounded when different functions, such as the provision and maintenance of housing, support and supervision of tenancies, and counselling for specific problems such as substance misuse, debt and unemployment are dispersed among several agencies. Not surprisingly, then, this understanding of partnership as transfer of responsibilities has evoked critiques of the processes by which government disperses central responsibility for social problems, and in particular the crime problem, to local level (Crawford 1999).

Partnership as system efficiency

An alternative perspective promotes partnership, not as a *cause* of service fragmentation but as a *solution*. On this view, fragmentation is endemic at all levels of public policy-making and implementation, from central government departments, through separate agency functions to service delivery (Locke 1990). The result is inefficiency, through incomplete coverage of some needs, unnecessary duplication of services for others, underutilisation of complementary resources and lack of overall coherence at a strategic level (Locke 1990). It is from this critique of existing fragmentation that partnership derives its intuitive promise, holding out the prospect of increased efficiency, effectiveness and comprehensiveness through integrated systems of community provision (Locke 1990; O'Looney 1997).

There are, however, a number of impediments to achieving this ideal. The most fundamental of these is the inertia of organisations and the individuals within them. General support for service integration is much easier to secure than service integration itself, because of the effort required to effect it: 'while most of us are in favor of making improvements, few like to make changes in their own worlds; almost all of us would prefer that someone else do the changing' (Armstrong 1997: 115). Indeed, effective system integration requires major investment in producing and sustaining change at policy-making, managerial and service delivery levels in participating organisations (Agranoff 1991).

More profoundly, there is considerable hesitation about the forms and intensity of inter-agency relationships that are required to satisfy the aim of partnership. A range of terminologies is applied to the activities that might encompass partnership, with little attention to their different nuances. These include, for example: liaison, in which agencies continue to function autonomously in respect of policy-making, priority-setting and resource allocation; coordination, in which agencies consult over policy issues, attempt to reduce duplication and occasionally take joint action; cooperation, in which policy and practice coherence is attempted, some resource sharing and joint funding is undertaken and information is shared on mutual interests; and consortium, in which several organisations join together in a programme of activity (Locke 1990). Elsewhere, the term 'collaboration' has been invoked to connote a shift from agency autonomy to a collective enterprise which, in its ideal forms, includes power-sharing, comprehensive planning, system change and commitment of resources to address the social and health problems of local communities (Harbert, Finnegan and Tyler 1997; O'Looney 1997; Reilly 2001).

While sloppy use of terminology may frustrate many of these commentators, it can be in organisational interests to preserve such vagueness. Notably, in their partnership plans, local probation areas advanced almost any form of inter-agency contact as evidence of existing partnerships. These 'partnerships' included, for example, communication, liaison, information-sharing, joint working, representation on crime-prevention groups and provision of community service placements (Rumgay 2000a). This appeared to exploit an ambiguity in Home Office guidance, which, notwithstanding the policy intention to introduce contracted elements of supervision, advised probation areas to 'embrace the full range of possibilities for partnership arrangements' (Home Office 1993c). Thus, the probation service seized the advantage of this definitional uncertainty to dilute the impact of partnership policy on its command of its traditional professional territory (Rumgay 2000a).

Moreover, perpetuation of agency isolation can bring its own savings, in so far as the failures of a poorly integrated service can be passed to another organisation. For example, school dropouts or drug users may move from educational or treatment services into the criminal justice system. In this way, costs may be 'exported' from one agency to another (Pumariega *et al.* 1997; Ambrose 2001). While a detached view would recognise such a process as inefficient and wasteful of resources overall (Pumariega *et al.* 1997; Ambrose 2001), to an underresourced and pressured organisation it may have an immediate appeal. And while system integration may produce savings in avoiding waste, underutilisation and duplication, all accounts of such initiatives testify to the substantial investment of professional time and resources required to achieve it (Armstrong 1997; Minicucci 1997; Rumgay 2000a; Folayemi 2001; Reilly 2001). In any event, there is an inherent tension between the competing views of system integration primarily as a means to cost-efficiency through elimination of waste and as a pathway towards comprehensive provision, which implies the generation of new services to fill gaps between existing ones (Hassett and Austin 1997).

Partnership as empowerment

At their most visionary, conceptualisations of multi-agency collaboration require the involvement of 'grassroots' community representatives in the collective enterprise, including their control over the forms that projects and services may take. This may occur at several levels. For example:

1   **Enhanced voluntary action**   Statutory organisations may seek to strengthen the capacity of small voluntary agencies to meet identified needs at local level. Partnership as empowerment in this sense was an ambition in the partnership plans of several probation areas (Rumgay 2000a). Indeed, the Probation Service has a creditable history as a founder of local voluntary initiatives to meet the needs, for example, of substance misusers, the homeless and crime victims (Rumgay 2000a). In some partnership projects, imaginative approaches have been taken to strengthening local agencies in ways that simultaneously enhance their accessibility to offenders (Rumgay 2000a).

    These forms of empowerment are limited by the relatively small funding capacity of local probation areas. However, very often these initiatives derive from the practical efforts of committed individuals within the Service at least as much as from organisational planning and expenditure. Moreover, empowerment by offering services 'in kind', in the forms, for example, of advice, advocacy and accommodation, has long played a valued role in the Probation Service's relationships with local agencies (Rumgay 2000a). Indeed, the contracting initiative provoked several voluntary agencies to declare their preference for these supports 'in kind' over money, particularly when insensitive handling by the Home Office of the potential for conflicts of interests threatened to disrupt established Probation Service representation on their management committees (Cross 1997; Rumgay 2000a).

2   **User participation in treatment** Alternatively, the individual users of specific services may be included in decisions about their personal treatment planning and delivery. One of the most elaborate examples of this approach is the US 'wraparound' strategy for integrated provision of support and treatment services to families of emotionally disturbed children. Defining characteristics of this approach include 'strengths-based', rather than deficiency-focused, assessment, community-based care wherever possible, and unconditional continuing care, alongside the family's right to refuse care proposals with which they disagree (VanDenBerg and Grealish 1996; Epstein *et al.* 1998; Osher and Osher 2002). While a number of studies suggest positive outcomes for the wraparound approach (Bruns, Burchard and Yoe 1995), proponents also acknowledge that many schemes which adopt the title fall short of these criteria (VanDenBerg and Grealish 1996; Epstein *et al.* 1998; Malysiak 1998).

3   **Consultation** More broadly, agencies responsible for particular services may establish local consultative groups of community members, with a view to negotiating their agreement on types, quality and delivery. An example of this approach is the requirement, since 2000, on local authorities to develop Tenant Participation Compacts, in which residents contribute to the design and delivery of housing services. The extent to which these arrangements have resulted in a redistribution of power between housing providers and their tenants is, however, contested (reviewed in Reid 2001).

4   **Coalitions** The most ambitious approach to partnership as empowerment involves the establishment of community development groups, or 'coalitions', with a broad aim to initiate a programme of improvement in the quality of health and social life, in which citizens are powerful participants in the collaborative process (Chavis *et al.* 1993; Berkowitz 2001; Wolff 2001a). Multi-agency, multi-faceted enterprises on this scale have been promoted as the way forward to ameliorating complex social problems, such as drug misuse, that defy single answers (Chavis *et al.* 1993; Klitzner 1993). Their sheer complexity, however, renders them difficult to analyse and evaluate, not least because of their dynamic, evolutionary nature, their adaptation to unique local community conditions and their interdependence with other community-wide strategies of health and social improvement (Klitzner 1993; Berkowitz 2001).

The Probation Service's record of successful facilitation of local voluntary effort is not matched by its involvement in these other types of empowerment through partnership. This has much to do with its focus on offenders, who are not easily empowered, and whose empowerment is not readily approved by conventional society. Indeed, user participation and influence is not a dominant feature of its practice (Rumgay 2000b). It has, however, been argued that a primary justification of its involvement in partnerships lies in the potential for linking offenders with opportunities that do not rely on criminal justice processes, enforcement and exclusion (Rumgay 2000a; 2001).

There is no inherent fault in any of these theories of partnership. Each is capable of improving provision for offenders and community safety. Rather, the Probation Service's implementation of these approaches has been mediated, at national and local levels, by three types of influence: emotional, by its organisational ideology; environmental, by public attitudes to crime and offenders; and structural, by the availability and responsiveness of potential partners. Moreover, as this brief overview indicates, the problems of partnership lie less in its chosen theoretical form, than in the complexities of implementation. These are widely underestimated (Reilly 2001), obscured by the optimistic assumption that, since partnership is self-evidently beneficial in its effects, good will between agencies will suffice to bring it into being along with its benefits. Successful partnership is undoubtedly possible, yet little attention has been paid to equipping the service with the particular knowledge and skills it needs to accomplish it, leaving individuals largely to trial-and-error processes of learning by discovery (Rumgay 2000a).

SUCCESSFUL PARTNERSHIP

The preceding discussion has illuminated the complexity and difficulty of the partnership enterprise for those who are required to implement it. There is, however, a growing literature on the characteristics of successful partnerships, which shows an encouraging similarity across different fields of endeavour. Studies commonly focus on particular themes: leadership; clarity; process; and conflict resolution.

Leadership

Successful partnerships have been found to owe much to their championship by particular individuals (Rumgay 2000a; Reilly 2001). Such champions invest considerable time and personal effort in the development and support of the project, including promoting its utilisation and assisting partners in their transition to partnership status (Rumgay 2000a). In the field of technological innovation, championship qualities have been summarised thus: 'to inspire and enthuse others with their vision of the potential of an innovation, to persist in promoting their vision despite strong opposition, to show extraordinary confidence in themselves and their mission, and to gain the commitment of others to support the innovation' (Howell and Higgins 1990: 320; see also Weber and Khademian 1997). This study found champions to have the personal

qualities of risk-taking and innovativeness and the skills to articulate a compelling vision of an innovation's potential value to the organisation and to
express confidence in others to participate effectively in its introduction.

Personal commitment is a hallmark of the project champion (Howell and
Higgins 1990; Armstrong 1997; Rumgay 2000a). Indeed, it has been argued
that it would be impossible to 'create' a champion through institutional
assignment, since the requisite personal qualities are activated only by self-
appointment (Howell and Higgins 1990). Be that as it may, some organisational features appear to enhance the likelihood that leaders, such as project
champions, will come forward. For example, Rumgay's (2000a) study of partnerships between the Probation Service and voluntary sector substance misuse
agencies revealed that self-appointment was characteristic of the championship
role. Yet, some probation areas clearly operated in ways that encouraged and
supported championship. It has been argued that such role-taking should be
fostered by human services seeking to improve levels of practitioner support
for effective programmes of intervention (Corrigan 1995).

Perhaps ironically for the Probation Service, which has recently moved
to a strongly centralised structure, it has been observed that *de*centralised
decision-making authority characterises innovative organisations (Shin and
McClomb 1998). This has important implications for partnerships, which
are necessarily adapted to local conditions (Rumgay 2000a). Management
leadership styles that encourage organisational change and leadership have
been observed to include articulating a mission to which staff will subscribe
(Austin 1993; Armstrong 1997) team-building and staff development (Austin
1993; Shin and McClomb 1998), and managing the external environment
through building relations with outside organisations (Austin 1993; Menefee
1997).

Clarity

Problematic partnerships between the Probation Service and voluntary sector
agencies are often marked by poorly defined aims, objectives, professional
roles and relationships (Rumgay 2000a). Wolff (2001b) advises that goals
and objectives must be 'concrete, attainable and, ultimately, measurable'
(p. 176). Lacking these qualities, partnerships may be easily side-tracked by
time-consuming crises and issues, the relevance of which to the project aims
are questionable. Successful partnerships are those in which each partner's
contribution to the enterprise, roles of and relationships between staff at management and field levels, and lines of communication and decision making are
clearly established and understood (Rumgay 2000a; Wolff 2001b).

An early study of probation officer perspectives on community crime prevention, revealed much uncertainty as to the nature and value of the service's

potential contribution (Sampson and Smith 1992). Officers perceived their concerns with 'quality of life' issues as a tangential issue for others, particularly the police, who understood prevention primarily in terms of situational measures such as target hardening and surveillance. It is possible that the probation service's more recent focus on risk management has provided it with a clearer sense of its contribution to crime prevention groups. Moreover, the formation of collaborative Drug Action Teams, Youth Offending Teams and Multi-agency Public Protection Panels and the emergence of cooperative initiatives in supported housing for offenders has potentially helped to broaden partner agencies' conceptualisations of crime prevention to illustrate the Service's strengths. Whether or not that is an accurate surmise, a more recent study found probation representatives were rated second only to the police in their perceived helpfulness in multi-agency crime prevention fora (Department of the Environment, Transport and the Regions 2000).

Process

It has been observed that in many problematic partnerships between the Probation Service and voluntary sector agencies, implementation has been simply devolved to staff at ground level after the contract was secured (Rumgay 2000a). This leaves staff in ignorance, and suspicious, of the intended purpose and nature of the relationship with partners. Several commentators point to the necessity of a clear plan for operationalising the stated goals of partnership. Such plans may well be complex, since successful implementation may require the development of an internal infrastructure that is capable of supporting the partnership, staff willingness and competence in using the partnership opportunity, and collaborative relationships both with partners themselves and with organisations that are potentially helpful to the partnership enterprise (Austin 1993; Armstrong 1997; Reilly 2001; Wolff 2001b).

Partnership development has a tendency to focus disproportionately on the initial phases of collaborative formation and agreement on long-term aims. However, in the total collaborative exercise, the initial exercise in goal-setting is followed by specifying concrete objectives, operationalising those objectives to render them measurable and preparing an action plan for implementation (Harbert, Finnegan and Tyler 1997). Wolff (2001b) further cautions that the focus on action must be conscientiously maintained, avoiding the potential for multi-agency collaborations to deteriorate into an exercise that primarily serves the internal needs of partners. Such ongoing focus on delivery, rather than internal partnership functioning may be achieved by setting concrete, proximal objectives by which progress may be measured, rather than relying exclusively on ultimate, global ambitions (see, for example, Hyde, Burchard and Woodworth 1996; Harbert, Finnegan and Tyler 1997).

Conflict resolution

Managing conflict has emerged as an important issue, even for partnerships that are generally working successfully (Rumgay 2000a). However, one study found that 'when inter-professional difficulties arose at successful partnerships, they were isolated issues, swiftly resolved, and did not rankle. At problematic partnerships, multiple difficulties were experienced, which were pervasive, poorly resolved and persistent' (Rumgay 2000a: 95).

There are numerous potential sources of conflict in the context of inter-agency relationships. These range from relatively simple issues, which could be remedied with aforethought, to deeper, more complex antagonisms, which may appear intransigent. For example: ignorance about the functions, services and constraints of a partner organisation may encourage a focus on problems and shortcomings rather building good practice (Northmore 2001); similar terms may have very different meanings for different professions (Armstrong 1997); practices that are deemed appropriate in one professional context may be denigrated in another (Minicucci 1997); expertise may be unrecognised (Bennett and Lawson 1994); there may be uncertainty, anxiety or rivalry over 'turf' boundaries (Armstrong 1997); or there may be a clash of perspectives on the nature of particular problems, treatment approaches or ethical issues (Bennett and Lawson 1994). Weber and Khademian (1997) further suggest that multi-agency collaborations are particularly vulnerable to conflict when the task confronting them is complex, there are time and resource constraints on the negotiations and participants are playing for high stakes.

The ethos of partnership, at least as it idealised, tends to operate to suppress the overt expression of conflict (Crawford 1999; Wolff 2001a). This may have the negative consequence of encouraging inappropriate and ultimately unsatisfactory tactics of conflict avoidance or management (Griffiths 1997; Crawford 1999). Alternative perspectives encourage strategies of 'conflict trans-formation' (Deutsch 1994; Chavis 2001), in which areas of conflict are used as opportunities for constructive change.

A central consideration in conflict resolution is the motivations of participants to remain at the negotiating table. Key to this perspective is the realisation that negotiation occurs when organisations recognise their interdependence. Were it not for this appreciation of mutual need, dissatisfied participants would simply withdraw (Rubin 1994). For many organisations, including the probation service, the increasing number of statutory requirements to engage in multi-agency partnerships has imposed mutual interdependence upon them, whether or not it is a valued aspect of professional life. More deeply, however, mutual interdependence is seen to involve awareness that certain problems cannot be solved, or could be solved only through greater time and resource expenditure by organisations acting in isolation (Weber and Khademian 1997; Reilly 2001).

Although the Probation Service is by no means itself immune to the kinds of inter-professional conflicts noted above (Rumgay 2000a), nevertheless, its long experience as a mediator between criminal justice and social welfare organisations suggests it has a capacity for facilitating conflict resolution. Indeed, its dual existence might be seen to confer a key role in assisting organisations with potentially competing values and operational styles to forge constructive relationships, since, importantly (Weber and Khademian 1997), it enjoys credibility with both law enforcement and human service agencies. There is now a literature that illuminates general principles of effective and durable conflict resolution. These include: resolving small conflicts before they escalate (Deutsch 1994); defining conflicts in concrete, specific terms that make them appear manageable rather than by appeal to broad, potentially irreconcilable principles (Deutsch 1994); expanding the available alternatives for resolution (Deutsch 1994); and standing firm on the results of negotiation (Weber and Khademian 1997).

CONCLUSION

At the time of writing, it seems highly unlikely that partnership is about to disappear as a policy 'fad', to be rapidly submerged by the onslaught of new fashions in ideas as to how criminal justice and social policy goals may be reached. Even were that to happen at some future date, the organisational legacy of the past decade of investment in partnership generation will not be readily demolished. Moreover, in an age in which professional specialisation is proliferating in response to the expanding knowledge base of separate disciplines, integration of services is crucial to the maintenance of coherence in social planning and provision (Halley 1997; Chavis 2001). Yet, despite the necessity of partnership involvement, both as a pragmatic response to statute and as a fundamental necessity for social problem-solving, little attention continues to be paid to equipping professional staff with the knowledge and skills which successful partnership demands. Rather, the partnership ethos encourages naïve faith in the capacity of good will to accomplish its aims. Moreover, for those who enter partnership in the expectation of savings in time, resources and expenditure, the reality will be disconcerting. Nevertheless, as this chapter has tried to show, a realistic, albeit daunting, appraisal of the challenges of partnership may illuminate the practical means to achieving its promise.

SUMMARY OF KEY ISSUES

- The chapter examines the rapid and complex growth in partnership activity in crime prevention, community safety and community development, with particular focus on the implications for the Probation Service.

- It identifies four significant strands in policy for partnerships: contracting for supervision services; community crime prevention; targeting of special groups; and coordinated social planning and provision.
- It then explores three alternative theoretical models of partnership: as redistribution of responsibilities; as system efficiency; and as empowerment. It is suggested that the problems associated with partnership activity have less to do with the model adopted than with the complexities of implementation.
- Qualities of successful partnership across a range of disciplines are found to involve common issues in leadership, clarity, process and conflict resolution.
- The chapter concludes with criticisms of the repeated neglect of staff preparation and training for the challenges of policy implementation and naïve misrepresentation of partnership as a means to achieving savings in time, resources and expenditure. It also, however, argues that successful partnership is both achievable and crucial to coherent social planning and provision.

References

Adams, P. and Nelson, K. (1997) 'Reclaiming community: An integrative approach to human services', *Administration in Social Work*, 21, 67–81.

Agranoff, R. (1991) 'Human services integration: Past and present challenges in public administration', *Public Administration Review*, 551, 533–542.

Ambrose, P. (2001) ' "Holism" and urban regeneration', in S. Balloch and M. Taylor (eds) *Partnership Working: Policy and Practice*. Bristol: Policy Press.

Armstrong, K. L. (1997) 'Launching a family-centered, neighbourhood-based human services system: Lessons from working the hallways and street corners', *Administration in Social Work*, 21, 109–126.

Austin, C. D. (1993) 'Case management: A system perspective', *Families in Society: The Journal of Contemporary Human Services*, 74, 451–459.

Bennett, L. and Lawson, M. (1994) 'Barriers to cooperation between domestic-violence and substance-abuse progams', *Families in Society: The Journal of Contemporary Human Services*, 75, 277–286.

Berkowitz, B. (2001) 'Studying the outcomes of community-based coalitions', *American Journal of Community Psychology*, 29, 213–227.

Bruns, E. J., Burchard, J. D. and Yoe, J. T. (1995) 'Evaluating the Vermont system of care: Outcomes associated with community-based wraparound services', *Journal of Child and Family Studies*, 4, 321–339.

Chavis, D. M. (2001) 'The paradoxes and promise of community coalitions', *American Journal of Community Psychology*, 29, 309–320.

Chavis, D. M., Speer, P. W., Resnick, I. and Zippay, A. (1993) 'Building community capacity to address alcohol and drug abuse: Getting to the heart of the problem', in R. C. Davis, A. J. Lurigio and D. P. Rosenbaum (eds) *Drugs and the Community: Involving Community Residents in Combatting the Sale of Illegal Drugs*. Springfield, IL: Charles C. Thomas.

Corrigan, P. W. (1995) 'Wanted: Champions of psychiatric rehabilitation', *American Psychologist*, 50, 514–521.

Crawford, A. (1999) *The Local Governance of Crime: Appeals to Community and Partnerships*. Oxford: Oxford University Press.

Cross, B. (1997) 'Partnership in practice: The experience of two probation services', *Howard Journal of Criminal Justice*, 36, 62–79.

Department of the Environment, Transport and the Regions (2000) *Partnerships in Community Safety: An Evaluation of Phase 2 of the Safer Cities Programme*. London: Department of the Environment, Transport and the Regions.

Deutsch, M. (1994) 'Constructive conflict resolution: Principles, training, and research', *Journal of Social Issues*, 50, 13–32.

Epstein, M. H., Jayanthi, M., McKelvey, J., Frankenberry, E., Hardy, R., Dennis, K. and Dennis, K. (1998) 'Reliability of the wraparound observation form: An instrument to measure the wraparound process', *Journal of Child and Family Studies*, 7, 161–170.

Folayemi, B. (2001) 'Case story #1: Building the grassroots coalition', *American Journal of Community Psychology*, 29, 193–197.

Griffiths, L. (1997) 'Accomplishing team: Teamwork and categorisation in two community mental health teams', *Sociological Review*, 45, 59–78.

Halley, A. A. (1997) 'Applications of boundary theory to the concept of service integration in the human services', *Administration in Social Work*, 21, 145–168.

Harbert, A. S., Finnegan, D. and Tyler, N. (1997) 'Collaboration: A study of a children's initiative', *Administration in Social Work*, 21, 83–107.

Hassett, S. and Austin, M. J. (1997) 'Service integration: Something old and something new', *Administration in Social Work*, 21, 9–29.

Home Office (1990a) *Partnership in Dealing with Offenders in the Community*. London: Home Office.

Home Office (1990b) *Supervision and Punishment in the Community: A Framework for Action*. Cm 966. London: Home Office.

Home Office (1990c) *Partnership in Crime Prevention*. London: Home Office.

Home Office (1992) *Partnership in Dealing with Offenders in the Community: A Decision Document*. London: Home Office.

Home Office (1993a) *CPO 23/1993: Probation Service Partnership Policy: Submission of Partnership Plans 1993–1994*. London: Home Office.

Home Office (1993b) *PC 16/1993: Probation Supervision Grants Scheme: Arrangements for Grants to Local Projects 1994–1995*. London: Home Office.

Home Office (1993c) *PC 17/1993: Partnership in Dealing with Offenders in the Community: Submission of Partnership Plans 1994–1997*. London: Home Office.

Home Office (1998) *Joining Forces to Protect the Public: Prisons-Probation, A Consultation Document*. London: Home Office.

Home Office (2001) *PC 44/2001: Criminal Justice and Court Services Act 2000: Sections 67 + 68, Guidance for Police and Probation Services*. London: Home Office.

Home Office Standing Conference on Crime Prevention (1991) *Safer Communities: The Local Delivery of Crime Prevention through the Partnership Approach*. London: Home Office.

Howell, J. M. and Higgins, C. A. (1990) 'Champions of technological innovation', *Administrative Science Quarterly*, 35, 317–341.

Hyde, K. L., Burchard, J. D. and Woodworth, K. (1996) 'Wrapping services in an urban setting', *Journal of Child and Family Studies*, 5, 67–82.

Klitzner, M. (1993) 'A public health/dynamic systems approach to community-wide alcohol and other drug initiatives', in R. C. Davis, A. J. Lurigio and D. P. Rosenbaum (eds) *Drugs and the Community: Involving Community Residents in Combatting the Sale of Illegal Drugs*. Springfield, IL: Charles C. Thomas.

Locke, T. (1990) *New Approaches to Crime in the 1990s: Planning Responses to Crime*. Harlow: Longman.

Lord President of the Council and Leader of the House of Commons, Secretary of State for the Home Department, Secretary of State for Health, Secretary of State for Education and the Paymaster General (1995) *Tackling Drugs Together: A Strategy for England 1995–98*. Cm 2846. London: HMSO.

Malysiak, R. (1998) 'Deciphering the Tower of Babel: Examining the theory base for wraparound fidelity', *Journal of Child and Family Studies*, 7, 11–25.

Menefee, D. (1997) 'Strategic administration of nonprofit human service organisations: A model for executive success in turbulent times', *Administration in Social Work*, 21, 1–19.

Minicucci, C. (1997) 'Assessing a family-centered neighbourhood service agency: The Del Paso Heights model', *Administration in Social Work*, 21, 127–143.

Moore, S. (1992) 'Case management and the integration of services: How service delivery systems shape case management', *Social Work*, 37, 418–423.

Northmore, S. (2001) 'Improving partnership working in housing and mental health', in S. Balloch and M. Taylor (eds) *Partnership Working: Policy and Practice*. Bristol: Policy Press.

O'Looney, J. (1997) 'Marking progress toward service integration: Learning to use evaluation to overcome barriers', *Administration in Social Work*, 21, 31–65.

Osher, T. W. and Osher, D. M. (2002) 'The paradigm shift to true collaboration with families', *Journal of Child and Family Studies*, 11, 47–60.

Pumariega, A. J., Nace, D., England, M. J., Diamond, J., Fallon, T., Hanson, G., Lourie, I., Marx, L., Solnit, A., Grimes, C., Thurber, D. and Graham, M. (1997) 'Community-based systems approach to children's managed mental health services', *Journal of Child and Family Studies*, 6, 149–164.

Reid, B. (2001) 'Partnership and change in social housing', in S. Balloch and M. Taylor (eds) *Partnership Working: Policy and Practice*. Bristol: Policy Press.

Reilly, T. (2001) 'Collaboration in action: An uncertain process', *Administration in Social Work*, 25, 53–74.

Rubin, J. Z. (1994) 'Models of conflict management', *Journal of Social Issues*, 50, 33–45.

Rumgay, J. (2000a) *The Addicted Offender: Developments in British Policy and Practice*. Basingstoke: Palgrave.

Rumgay, J. (2000b) 'Policies of neglect: Female offenders and the probation service', in H. Kemshall and R. Littlechild (eds) *User Involvement and Participation in Social Care: Research Informing Practice*. London: Jessica Kingsley.

Rumgay, J. (2001) 'Accountability in the delivery of community penalties: To whom, for what, and why?' in A. E. Bottoms, L. Gelsthorpe and S. A. Rex (eds) *Community Penalties: Change and Challenges*. Cullompton: Willan.

Sampson, A. and Smith, D. (1992) 'Probation and community crime prevention', *Howard Journal of Criminal Justice*, 31, 105–119.

Shin, J. and McClomb, G. E. (1998) 'Top executive leadership and organizational innovation: An empirical investigation of nonprofit human service organizations (HSOs)', *Administration in Social Work*, 22, 1–21.

Smith, D., Paylor, I. and Mitchell, P. (1993) 'Partnerships between the independent sector and the probation service', *Howard Journal of Criminal Justice*, 32, 25–39.

Tilley, N. (1992) *Safer Cities and Community Safety Strategies* (Crime Prevention Unit Series Paper 38). London: Home Office Police Department.

Weber, E. P. and Khademian, A. M. (1997) 'From agitation to collaboration: Clearing the air through negotiation', *Public Administration Review*, 57, 396–410.

Wolff, T. (2001a) 'Community coalition building – Contemporary practice and research: Introduction', *American Journal of Community Psychology*, 29, 165–172.

Wolff, T. (2001b) 'A practitioner's guide to successful coalitions', *American Journal of Community Psychology*, 29, 173–191.

VanDenBerg, J. E. and Grealish, E. M. (1996) 'Individualized services and supports through the wraparound process: Philosophy and procedures', *Journal of Child and Family Studies*, 5, 7–21.

13

VICTIM WORK IN THE PROBATION SERVICE: PERPETUATING NOTIONS OF AN 'IDEAL VICTIM'

Basia Spalek

INTRODUCTION

Probation work is currently undergoing a transformation as a result of the instigation of a victim-oriented approach to the management of crime. Developments within the 'victims' movement', such as the rise of the Victim's Charter in 1990, and the second Victim's Charter in 1996, have led to the incorporation of a victim perspective (see Home Office 1990, 1996). Recent policy documents and circulars issued by the Probation Service, such as the publication of National Standards 1995, Probation Circular 61/95 and guidance provided by the Association of Chief Officers of Probation (ACOP) and Victim Support highlight three areas in which victim-focused work is being applied. These consist of the need to help the victims of crime cope with their plight, the need to incorporate a victim perspective when dealing with offenders as a way of reducing crime, and the development of restorative justice strategies. While signalling a potentially positive focus for probation work, the development of a victim perspective has taken place rather quickly, with little consideration of the tensions and problems that can arise from attempting to respond to both victims' and offenders' needs simultaneously. The aim of this chapter is to present an account of victim work within the Probation Service, and to highlight and address possible problems that may arise. It is argued that although the Probation Service has attempted to respond to a victim-oriented approach, in the absence of an explicit rationale for work with victims an implicit rationale can be uncovered, one which causes some concern for the author here. It appears that the Probation Service views victims as consumers of a criminal justice system. As a result, victims are separated from their socio-structural context and the image of an 'ideal victim' is perpetuated.

RESPONDING TO VICTIMS' NEEDS: PROBATION AND THE VICTIMS' MOVEMENT

Crucial to developing an appreciation of the recent developments in the Probation Service in relation to its work with victims is an understanding of the wider context, in terms of an evolving victims' movement. Over the last 30 years or so in Britain, a 'victims' movement' has arisen, whereby a variety of different victim sub-groups, policy-makers and state agencies have striven to give legitimate recognition to victims' losses, and to improve their treatment by the criminal justice system (Mawby and Walklate 1994). Prior to this movement, it could be argued that the victim of crime was largely a 'forgotten actor' in the criminal justice system (Zedner 1994), since he or she was often marginalised by the trial process and the subsequent punishment of the offender, and little emotional and practical help was made available (Zedner 1994). An important aspect of the victims' movement has been a concern to document the process of victimisation, so as to use this information in order to respond effectively to victims' needs. Since the 1970s, researchers working in a number of different fields have carried out research studies looking at the impact of a wide variety of crimes, including robbery, burglary, assault and rape. These studies show that different types of crime have similar psychological, emotional, behavioural, financial and physical effects (Maguire 1982; Shapland, Willmore and Duff 1985; Mezey 1988; Lurigio and Resick 1990; Resick 1990; Indermaur 1995). Victim satisfaction with various agencies and processes of the criminal justice system has also been examined because of a recognition that victims are vital to the reporting and investigation of cases and are essential as providers of evidence in court (McCabe and Sutcliffe 1978; Mawby and Colston 1979). For example, in a study by Shapland, Willmore and Duff (1985), the level of victim satisfaction with the police was found to decrease as their case progressed through the criminal justice system, largely due to receiving insufficient information regarding their case. These results were confirmed by Newburn and Merry's (1990: 19–20) study which illustrates that the flow of information between the police and victims can be particularly poor. The issue of 'secondary victimisation' has also been raised, whereby victims of crime can be victimised further by agencies of the criminal justice system, through insensitive or harmful treatment (Maguire and Pointing 1988: 11).

For an agency whose work has predominantly been with offenders, the Probation Service has surprisingly been involved with victims since the early days of the victims' movement. Probation officers have played an important role in the development of Victim Support schemes, the first scheme being set up in 1974 as a result of inter-agency discussions about the impact of crime on individuals (Tudor 2002). However, the work with victims here did not have a significant impact on probation practice, with offenders continuing to constitute the main focus of attention. More recent developments in the victims' movement have had a much more pronounced impact on probation work. In 1990 the Home Office announced the introduction of a 'Victim's Charter'. This set out the services that victims should expect from the criminal justice system. The Charter introduced the requirement for probation services to make contact with the victims of offenders given life sentences, to inform them of the sentence and release from custody. At the same time, victims were to be given the opportunity to express their anxieties regarding certain aspects of the offender's release, which might be taken into consideration by decision-makers.

The effect upon probation practice of these requirements significantly increased after the publication of the revised National Standards for the Supervision of Offenders in the Community in 1995. These placed a duty upon probation officers to contact all victims of serious sexual and violent offences which resulted in a custodial sentence of four years and over, within two months of sentence (Tudor 2002). Probation Circular 61/95 was issued, which provided guidance for probation services about the arrangements for contact with victims of serious offences or their families. This applied not only to cases where offenders were sentenced to four years or more, but also to those cases where an offender given a shorter custodial sentence was being supervised, where the sexual or violent nature of the offence were such that the provisions of paragraph 13 of the National Standard applied. The Circular requires that probation officers provide information to the victim about the custodial process, and also that they obtain information from the victim about any concerns they may wish to be taken into account when the conditions (but not the date) of release are being considered.

In 1999, the HM Inspectorate of Probation (HMIP) undertook a thematic inspection into victim work in probation services. The report stemming from this inspection, entitled *The Victim Perspective: Ensuring the Victim Matters*, was published in 2000. This report resulted in the publication of Probation Circular 108/00, when victim contact work became statutory in April 2001. This was in response to the Criminal Justice and Court Services Act 2000, which under section 69 placed a new statutory duty on local probation boards to work with victims of crime. Under the Act, and according to the Circular, from April 2001, victim contact work must be extended to all victims of serious violent and sexual offenders who have been sentenced to one year or more in custody. This is likely to have a significant influence upon caseloads, and so the National Probation Service has indicated additional financial resources for this (see Probation Circular 62/2001).

The HMIP 2000 Victim Report indicates that the majority of probation areas have responded positively to the increased emphasis placed upon the victims of crime. Almost all areas have committee approved policy statements for victim contact work, most of which originated after 1996, illustrating how work with victims is at a very early stage. HMIP (2000) estimates that victim contact work has cost the probation service approximately £3.5 million (p. 15). Different areas have also adopted different models for their victim contact work. Most areas have used specialist staff, although in 11 areas victim contact work is carried out by the offender's supervising officer. The HMIP 2000 Report did not draw any conclusions regarding which model operates most effectively and found that in most areas, initial contact with victims is made by letter. However, the National Standard requirement for contacting victims within two months of the offender's sentence is often not met. Tracing victims can be a complex and time-consuming process, complicated by the issue of what people count as victims since indirect victims may need as much support as direct victims. There may also be one or more direct victims of a single criminal event, and in these cases probation areas will have to make contact with each victim, increasing their likely workload. At the same time, arrangements with the police to provide information for victim contact do not always work well, as in some probation areas, the HMIP 2000 Victim Report found that the information was arriving late (interestingly, HMIP found that only 19 probation areas had agreed protocols with the police). Where victims are contacted by the probation service, the HMIP 2000 Report found that almost all staff approach the initial interview in a sensitive manner and that most victims feel that the information given to them is helpful. Nonetheless, an issue that the probation service may have to consider in the future is what person is best suited to contacting victims, and what grade of staff should be involved here. Currently, initial interviews with victims are undertaken by a wide variety of people and grades of probation staff – including members of Victim Support schemes, specialist victim contact officers of PSO grade, specialist victim contact officers of PO grade and offenders' case managers.

As can be seen above, the Probation Service has incorporated victim-oriented work. Despite this, however, there seems to be no explicitly defined philosophy for work with the victims of crime. An implicit philosophy can, however, be discerned, one which links to the ethos of the wider victims' movement. Initiatives which have emerged out of the victims' movement essentially de-politicise victims, since they view victims as individual consumers of a criminal justice system, whose needs should be satisfied. Although the risk of victimisation has been documented as varying according to the race, class, age and gender of a person, the structural, social and historical processes which produce these regularities have not been questioned or explored (Mawby and Walklate 1994). This approach to victimisation is evident in probation practice. Similar to the increasingly individualised responses to offenders whereby social and economic circumstances which form the background to offending are marginalised as a result of the loss of the 'rehabilitative ideal' (Crawford and Enterkin 1999), probation work with victims incorporates a de-politicised, consumerist and individualistic notion of the victim. Victimisation is viewed as individual suffering which can be alleviated through effective communication and responses. Victims and their reactions have been effectively homogenised, through ignoring wider structures of race, gender and class that may have an influence upon the experience of victimisation. In 1996 the Association of Chief Officers of Probation (ACOP) put together a joint statement with Victim Support, giving guidance to local victim support schemes as well as to probation services. The purpose of this statement was to make sure that probation services were making use of the services that victim support schemes have to offer, and also to encourage these schemes to assist probation services. This clearly illustrates the individualised, 'victim as consumer' stance taken by the probation service, since Victim Support is uncritical of wider social structures which impact upon, and influence, victimisation. Other, more radical and politicised responses to victims, such as Rape Crisis and women's refuges, have thus been largely sidelined. The preference shown by the probation service towards Victim Support looks set to continue, since the National Probation Service publication *Victim Contact Work: Guidance for Probation Areas* (2001) has singled out Victim Support as an appropriate agency to whom victims can be referred.

It can be argued that viewing victims of crime as consumers, separated from their socio-structural context, is deeply problematic, since homogenising victims in this way limits the effectiveness and adequacy of victim initiatives. Crime survey data reveals that certain factors are associated with the likelihood of being victimised, suggesting that victims are not just people who happen to be in the wrong place at the wrong time, but rather some people are more likely to be victimised than others due to their class, race, gender and so forth (Davis, Lurigio and Skogan 1997). For example, lower-income groups are more likely than others to suffer a personal violent victimisation, including sexual assault, robbery or assault (Fattah 1989). Some surveys also suggest that people belonging to an ethnic group have high levels of victimisation. For instance, ethnic minority groups have been found to experience higher rates of victimisation in the case of crimes such as burglary, theft, assault and robbery (Mayhew, Elliott and Dowds 1989; Fitzgerald and Hale 1996). Moreover, the ability to cope with crime also varies with these factors, with people occupying a low socio-economic status having fewer resources to draw on in order to carry on with their lives in the aftermath of a crime (Young and Matthews 1992). These findings illustrate how important it is to consider wider factors influencing victimisation so that initiatives can be developed which cater to the specific needs of victims, taking into account victims' broader socio-structural circumstances. The future of probation work with victims, however, is likely to become more standardised and less likely to include a consideration of the victim's particular set of circumstances, due to the introduction of a National Probation Service and the movement towards centralisation and consistency of approach between different probation areas. As stated previously, the HMIP 2000 Report highlights that there are currently a wide variety of different models of victim contact work. However, the report indicates that in the same way that work with offenders is currently being designed to take account of effective practice principles, victim programmes can in the future also be designed to reflect 'effective practice'. In this way, it is likely that the current level of diversity among victim programmes will be reduced. Yet in the words of one woman, whose daughter was murdered, 'I wanted to demonstrate the complexity of the impact of murder . . . [there are] a variety of reactions and needs among individual members of families of murder victims' (Moreland 2001: 111). Thus, we need to respond to victims from a perspective that acknowledges their own specific reactions and needs, and one which takes into account the wider socio-structural context to their victimisation.

A further issue to consider when looking at contact work with victims is that the Probation Service may increase rather than decrease the harm suffered by the victim. Tension exists between responding to victims' needs and protecting offenders' rights. This tension has been acknowledged by Sir Graham Smith, HM Chief Inspector of Probation, when he states in the foreword of the HMIP 2000 Report that victim 'work is demanding and requires a high level of skill in balancing both the rights of the victim and the rights of the offender'. Offenders are entitled to know on what grounds their release conditions have been decided. This means that any concerns raised by the victim regarding the conditions of the offender's release may need to be disclosed to the offender. This may cause distress to the victim, and may result in increased hostility from the offender. Furthermore, victims' expectations may be raised about the level of influence that they have over an offender's release, expectations which cannot be fulfilled and which will therefore leave the victim feeling disappointed (Crawford and Enterkin 1999). In particular, victims of mentally disordered offenders at present have no right to receive information about the discharge of patients under the Mental Health Act, nor are they able to influence the conditions of discharge. However, a new Mental Health Act currently under proposal should make victim contact provisions (National Probation Service 2001).

PROBATION PRACTICE WITH OFFENDERS:
INCORPORATING THE VICTIM

A series of measures have recently been introduced, requiring probation officers to situate a victim perspective within their work with offenders. In the revised National Standards for the Supervision of Offenders in the Community, issued in 1995, priority was given to the protection of the public from re-offending (and from fear of crime) and also to the importance of considering the effect of crime on victims. Probation officers are thus to 'identify work to be done to make offenders aware of the impact of the crimes they have committed on their victims, themselves and their community' (paragraph 3.14) in supervision plans. When preparing pre-sentence reports (PSRs) the National Standards also require probation officers to make an assessment of the consequences of the offence, which includes an assessment of the impact of the crime on the victim. At the same time, PSRs should contain an assessment of the offender's attitude to the victim and the offence, highlighting evidence of acceptance or minimisation of responsibility, remorse or guilt. The HMIP 2000 Victim Report found that the percentage of PSRs in which there is an assessment of the offender's attitude to the victim and awareness of the consequences of the offence has improved since the 1997 HMIP survey of PSRs. However, the HMIP 2000 Victim Report highlights that the figures continue to be disappointing, particularly when taking into consideration the serious nature of the offences involved.

In terms of probation practice, an interview with the offender is key in establishing how remorseful he or she is with respect to the crime committed. Information supplied by the Crown Prosecution Service, including witness statements and police interviews, is also useful. In some areas victim personal statements are made and so these can be used to provide information about the consequences of the crime upon the victim. Guidelines issued by the National Association of Probation Officers advocate that PSR authors make direct contact with the victims of domestic violence. However, this approach has been criticised since it can result in the victim having to repeat his or her experiences to yet another agent of the criminal justice system, and might lead to the victim minimising the seriousness of the offence. At the same time, where home visits are organised, the offender may be present (Dominey 2002).

The PSR author is likely to assess offender awareness by directly asking the offender for their views about the offence. The probation officer may also ask the offender to generally talk about the experience of being a victim in order to see to what degree the offender understands the consequences of crime. Comments often featured in PSRs are that the offender demonstrates 'genuine remorse' or that conversely, the offender seems to regret the offence only in terms of having to appear before a court of law. The relationship of remorse to re-offending has not been researched, which means that it is not possible to say whether or not an offender who expresses remorse is less likely to re-offend than an offender who does not express remorse. Moreover, there is little indication of what 'expressing remorse' actually means. Some offenders will be apologetic for the crimes that they have committed only because they think that that is what is required of them and that it may mean a less severe punishment (Dominey 2002). Another problem for the PSR author is that establishing an identifiable victim may be problematic. Dominey (2002) uses shoplifting as an example, since the victim here may be a commercial organisation. Similarly, crimes such as drug possession for personal use and soliciting may not involve a victim. The probation officer therefore has to decide who qualifies as a victim, and this decision will be influenced by the officer's values (Dominey 2002).

The issues highlighted above indicate that although consideration of the victim in work with offenders seems a positive approach to tackling crime (as this signals a move away from viewing crime as an event which contains only an offender, since an offence typically also involves a victim), there are many problems to this approach. Implicit within the strategy adopted by the probation service is a view that the categories 'victim' and 'offender' are distinct. However, 'victim' and 'offender' may not necessarily be separate categories, but rather in some instances they may be interchangeable roles depending upon the circumstances of a particular incident at a particular point in time. There are cases where the victim and offender may change roles during the criminal event (see, for example, Fattah 1993). Polk's (1994) work clearly illustrates that in the case of male-to-male violence, the 'victim' is not necessarily passive, but rather has often played a contributory role, and may himself have a history of violent confrontations. Indeed, the characteristics which are associated with high risks of victimisation are similar to those associated with offenders: offenders and victims are disproportionately male, young, single, and urban residents of lower socio-economic status (Fattah 1989). This discussion raises the question of the extent to which probation work with offenders, with its heavy emphasis on the victim, will be able to deal with the intricacies inherent in some criminal events where the 'victim' and 'offender' are not so easily identifiable. It might be argued that the Probation Service is perpetuating the image of an 'ideal victim', who is passive and innocent (Davis, Lurigio and Skogan 1997). The image of an 'ideal victim' lies at the heart of the victims' movement and is evident in many of the victim initiatives that have been put into place. An 'ideal victim' is 'weak', 'passive' and is often associated with an ideal offender, who is dangerous (Christie 1986). As a result, the needs of many individuals who have been the victims of crime have not necessarily been responded to where those individuals have not gained 'ideal victim' status. According to Tudor (2002), for example, support services for young males are particularly thin, as are initiatives that are aimed at tackling the victimised pasts of many sexual and violent offenders. This discussion illustrates how problematic the label 'victim' actually is, and as such should be examined much more fully before being adopted by the Probation Service. Adopting a restorative justice approach might be one way of tackling the complexity behind some instances of victimisation, where the categories 'victim' and 'offender' may be interchangeable. The HMIP 2000 Victim Report describes how the Victim/Offender Mediation Unit in West Yorkshire probation service was approached by a local housing department to run a mediation pilot scheme with its tenants. The aim of the scheme was to enable the two people involved in a dispute to reach a resolution through a mediator. This approach acknowledged that both parties were likely to be both victim and offender. This brings us to the next strand of the Probation Service's approach to victimisation, that relating to restorative justice, and this will now be discussed.

RESTORATIVE JUSTICE AND VICTIM/OFFENDER PROBATION WORK

Restorative justice principles first began to influence probation work during the mid-1980s. The 1984 Probation Rules stated that 'it shall be part of the duties of a probation officer to participate in such arrangements concerned with the prevention of crime or with the relationship between offenders and their victims or the community at large as may be approved by the Probation Committee on the advice of the Chief Probation Officer (Rule 37 cited in Tudor 2002: 134). This requirement led to the development of four reparation pilot schemes, run by the Probation Service but part-funded by the Home Office. Despite the enthusiasm shown towards these reparation schemes by the probation service, the political climate quickly changed, and increasing numbers of offenders were incarcerated and socially excluded, and the Home Office stopped funding these reparation schemes. Nonetheless, some probation services continued to operate restorative justice practices, by funding the projects themselves (Tudor 2002).

More recently, during the 1990s, governmental interest in restorative justice approaches has been revived in Britain, alongside many other Western governments. Johnstone (2002) argues that a 'restorative justice movement' has gained ground, with the potential of challenging traditional criminal justice approaches to crime, and profoundly influencing the ways in which society responds to crime through influencing public perceptions of how we manage offenders. Traditional, adversarial approaches to criminal justice have the effect of disempowering victims, through marginalising their voices. At the same time, offenders are rarely given the opportunity to make amends for the crimes that they have committed. Restorative justice approaches can enable offenders to repair the psychological and material damage caused to the victim, and can play a role in reducing the victim's fear and feelings of powerlessness (Johnstone 2002). The Association of Chief Officers of Probation Position Statement 1996 indicated an intent to pursue victim issues within a framework of restorative justice. It argued that through adopting restorative justice principles, and by responding to victims' needs, the validity and authority of the Probation Service could be enhanced. At the same time, the statement maintained that restorative justice could lead to the improved rehabilitation of offenders, through engendering an increased awareness of the impact of crime on victims (Tudor 2002). Tudor argues that social work and counselling skills are needed for restorative justice. Working between victims and offenders is 'challenging and demanding and requires training, prior thought and strong support from management' (Tudor 2002: 138).

Significantly, the HMIP 2000 Victim Report looked at the development of restorative justice in the Probation Service. The report adopted a positive stance towards restorative justice, stating that the integration of restorative practices and the adversarial legal system to reinforce one another is desirable. The HM Inspectorate found that out of the eight probation areas that run mediation/reparation projects, only two had a policy or agreed statement on restorative justice. The report notes many examples of good practice, particularly focusing upon the work done by West Midlands and West Yorkshire probation areas, since these have been involved in direct work with victims since the 1980s, when they were involved in running pilot reparation schemes. The report concludes that in running mediation schemes alongside victim contact work, the opportunities open to victims increase, since victims can, for example, choose to meet the offender. Nonetheless, the HM Inspectorate of Probation does not fully embrace restorative justice principles, arguing that the extent of their incorporation into the criminal justice system is a matter of debate. It might be argued that restorative justice models have recently come under renewed threat as a result of the rise in street crime, and the subsequent social and political backlash which may lead to an increasingly punitive approach being adopted towards offenders.

CONCLUSION

This chapter has examined the recent developments in probation practice with respect to work with victims. The Victim's Charter 1990 and 1996, the publication of National Standards 1995, Probation Circular 61/95, guidance provided by the Association of Chief Officers of Probation (ACOP) and Victim Support, the HMIP 2000 Victim Report and Probation Circular 108/00 have provided the framework within which developments have occurred. The Probation Service clearly views victim work as a priority, and is seeking to incorporate a victim perspective at the core of its policy and practice. Advocates of the victims' movement will no doubt welcome the increased emphasis placed towards the victims of crime by probation areas, nonetheless some cautionary comments must be made. In adopting a de-politicised, consumerist notion of victimisation so quickly, the Probation Service has homogenised victims, thereby marginalising their social and economic circumstances. With the establishment of a National Probation Service, it is likely that victim work will increasingly become standardised in the form of effective practice principles for victims. As with effective practice principles with offenders, the adequacy of this work to incorporate diversity (race, class, gender, religion and so forth) is questionable. Moreover, a presumption that 'offenders' and 'victims' are distinct categories is also evident in the stance taken by the probation service towards victimisation. The ability of this rather rigid approach to cope with situations in which victim and offender may cross over also needs to be explored. It seems that ultimately, probation work with victims reflects values evident within the victims' movement. Although these values have led to an improvement in responses to victimisation for some victims of crime, they have also imposed limitations upon the ways in which we view victimisation. It is important that agencies of the criminal justice system consider these limitations before fully embracing victim-oriented approaches.

SUMMARY OF KEY ISSUES

- Over the last ten years or so, probation services have increasingly undertaken victim-oriented work, in response to the publication of the Victim's Charter, National Standards 1995, Probation Circular 61/95, and the publication of the HMIP 2000 Victim Report and Probation Circular 108/00.
- Three strands to the incorporation of a 'victim perspective' within probation work can be identified: the need to help the victims of crime cope with the emotional and psychological costs of crime, the need to incorporate a victim perspective when dealing with offenders as a way of reducing crime, and the development of restorative justice strategies.
- Nonetheless, little consideration has been paid by the Probation Service to developing a coherent philosophy for victim work.
- As a result, values underpinning the wider victims' movement have been incorporated into probation work. In particular, notions of an 'ideal victim', inherent within the victims' movement, have been incorporated by the probation service. This means that a de-politicised, consumerist notion of victimisation has been adopted, thereby homogenising victims and marginalising their social and economic circumstances.
- It is important for the Probation Service to consider the limitations imposed upon our understanding of victimisation by the perpetuation of an 'ideal victim' before fully embracing a victim-oriented approach.

References

Christie, N. (1986) 'The ideal victim', in E. Fattah (ed.) *From Crime Policy to Victim Policy: Reorienting the Justice System.* Basingstoke: Macmillan.

Crawford, A. and Enterkin, J. (1999) *Victim Contact Work and the Probation Service: A Study of Service Delivery and Impact.* Leeds: Centre for Criminal Justice Studies, University of Leeds.

Davis, R., Lurigio, A. and Skogan, W. (eds) (1997) *Victims of Crime* (2nd edn). Thousand Oaks, CA: Sage.

Dominey, J. (2002) 'Addressing victim issues in pre-sentence reports', in B. Williams (ed.) *Reparation and Victim-Focused Social Work.* London: Jessica Kingsley.

Fattah, E. (1989) 'Victims and victimology: The facts and the rhetoric', *International Review of Victimology*, 1, 43–66.

Fattah, E. (1993) 'The rational choice / opportunity perspectives as a vehicle for integrating criminological and victimological theories', in R. Clarke and M. Felson (eds) *Routine Activity and Rational Choice: Advances in Criminological Theory* (Volume 5). New Jersey: Transaction Publishers.

Fitzgerald, M. and Hale, C. (1996) *Ethnic Minorities: Victimisation and Racial Harassment: Findings from the 1988 and 1992 British Crime Surveys* (Home Office Research Study No. 154). London: Home Office.

HM Inspectorate of Probation (2000) *Thematic Inspection Report – The Victim Perspective: Ensuring the Victim Matters.* London: Home Office. Available at: http://www.homeoffice.gov.uk/hmiprob/themvict.htm

Home Office (1990) *Victim's Charter: A Statement of the Rights of Victims of Crime.* London: Home Office.

Home Office (1996) *The Victim's Charter: A Statement of Service Standards for Victims of Crime.* London: Home Office.

Indermaur, D. (1995) *Violent Property Crime.* Leichhardt, NSW: Federation Press.

Johnstone, G. (2002) *Restorative Justice: Ideas, Values, Debates.* Cullompton: Willan.

Lurigio, A. and Resick, P. (1990) 'Healing the psychological wounds of criminal victimisation: Predicting postcrime distress and recovery', in A. Lurigio, W. Skogan and R. Davis (eds) *Victims of Crime: Problems, Policies and Programs.* Thousand Oaks, CA: Sage.

McCabe, S. and Sutcliffe, F. (1978) *Defining Crime.* Oxford: Blackwell.

Maguire, M. (1982) *Burglary in a Dwelling: The Offence, the Offender and the Victim.* London: Heinemann.

Maguire, M. and Pointing, J. (eds) (1988) *Victims of Crime: A New Deal?* Milton Keynes: Open University Press.

Mawby, R. and Colston, N. (1979) *Crime and the Elderly: A Report Prepared for Age Concern.* Bradford: Bradford University.

Mawby, R. and Walklate, S. (1994) *Critical Victimology.* London: Sage.

Mayhew, P., Elliott, D. and Dowds, L. (1989) *The 1988 British Crime Survey* (Home Office Research Study No. 111). London: HMSO.

Mezey, G. (1988) 'Reactions to rape: Effects, counselling and the role of health professionals', in M. Maguire and J. Pointing (eds) *Victims of Crime: A New Deal?* Milton Keynes: Open University Press.

Moreland, L. (2001) *An Ordinary Murder*. London: Aurum Press.

National Probation Service (2001) *Victim Contact Work: Guidance for Probation Areas*. London: Home Office.

Newburn, T. and Merry, S. (1990) *Keeping in Touch – Police–victim Communication in Areas* (Home Office Research Study No. 116). London: HMSO.

Polk, K. (1994) *When Men Kill: Scenarios of Masculine Violence*. Cambridge: Cambridge University Press.

Resick, P. (1990) 'Victims of sexual assault', in A. Lurigio, W. Skogan and R. Davis (eds) *Victims of Crime: Problems, Policies and Programs*. Thousand Oaks, CA: Sage.

Shapland, J., Willmore, J. and Duff, P. (1985) *Victims in the Criminal Justice System*. Aldershot: Gower.

Tudor, B. (2002) 'Probation work with victims of crime' in B. Williams (ed.) *Reparation and Victim-focused Social Work*. London: Jessica Kingsley.

Young, J. and Matthews, R. (1992) 'Questioning left realism', in R. Matthews and J. Young (eds) *Issues in Realist Criminology*. London: Sage.

Zedner, L. (1994) 'Victims', in M. Maguire, R. Morgan and R. Reiner (eds) *The Oxford Handbook of Criminology*. Oxford: Clarendon Press.

14

HUMAN RIGHTS AND THE PROBATION VALUES DEBATE

Mike Nellis and Loraine Gelsthorpe

INTRODUCTION

The values of community, citizenship, social inclusion and human rights, and the balance between cohesion and difference and between equality and diversity . . . can all be either sustained or undermined by the way in which a country arranges and runs its criminal justice system. (Parekh 2000: xvii)

There seems to be a hiatus – to put it optimistically – in the understanding of what probation values are, or might be. Time was when it would have been easier to say, although throughout the history of the Probation Service such values were never formally codified. The basic facts of that history are well-known; but interpretations of what were good or bad ethical developments in the Probation Service continue to vary. What is striking about the present period is that while there is much of high intellectual quality being written about the kind of normative stance needed by the Service, focusing on citizenship (Faulkner 2002), civil liberties (Fulwood 1999), humanity (Lacey 2002), human rights (Hudson 2001; Scott 2002) and community justice (Harding 2000), very little of it informs the official ethical vision set out in *A New Choreography*, the mission statement of the National Probation Service (NPS). There is no clear overarching moral principle, or integrated set of moral principles, which succinctly captures what the new Service stands for. The value of 'victim-centredness' is well to the fore in *A New Choreography*, but the logo/strapline of the NPS (on its adverts and letterheads) highlights 'enforcement, rehabilitation and public protection'. These are clearly not incompatible, but it is not unreasonable to want a more synthesised statement in which primary and secondary (or derivative) values are expressed in proper relation to each other. If, as the new service evolves a clearer sense of its values emerges, all well and good; we will indeed look back on the present moment as a hiatus, a period of transition. If not – or if the Probation Service is merged with prisons to become a single Correctional Service – we may look back on the present as the point at which the possibility of distinct probation values began to fade. This chapter will begin with a brief history of probation values, explore the limited impact which anti-discriminatory values have had on the sentencing of women and ethnic minorities and question the potential of human rights as a means of revitalising anti-discriminatory concerns. It will end with a sketch of a possible way forward.

CHANGING PROBATION VALUES

The term 'advise, assist and befriend' – the legal aim of probation supervision from the inception of probation in 1907 to the Criminal Justice Act 1991 – became a kind of shorthand for the social work values to which the service laid claim throughout most of its twentieth-century history. Under the rubric of social work, the emphasis varied over time, from the spiritual (saving souls/ character building), to the therapeutic (providing treatment) to the pragmatic- ally political (providing alternatives to custody), although elements of all these survived in Service culture well into the 1970s. What they perhaps all had in common was a humanistic underpinning, a belief that rehabilitation was a moral good above all others in criminal justice, a sense that offenders should be individualised and treated as people, with respect and care, and helped rather than coerced to change – a process in which the discretion, skill and experience of the individual professional were of vital importance.

The language, and arguably the nature, of social work/probation values changed in the 1980s following severe internal criticism (by a rising younger generation of staff and trainers) of the limitations of an individualised approach to helping, which ignored the structural disadvantages and injustices experienced by the troubled and troublesome people who became the clients of social workers, failings which were sometimes perpetuated and exacerbated by the helping agencies themselves. The new values were expressed negatively, as 'anti-discrimination' and 'anti-oppressiveness', and drew on particular understandings of 'anti-racism' and feminism (recast as 'anti-sexism') that had roots in political movements and events outside social work. Disablism, heterosexism and ageism were duly added to the list of institutionalised forms of discrimination which social work sought to challenge. The Central Council for Education and Training in Social Work (CCETSW), a variety of social work academics and practitioners, and the National Association of Probation Officers (NAPO) in particular fashioned and promoted 'anti-discriminatory values' to an extent that they became part of the defining public identity of social work, attracting the criticism from conservative media, and eventually government, that social work had become too politicised, too oppositional, too 'politically correct'. A more muted stance (and language) was demanded of them. In truth there was far less consensus within social work than its more audible, most dominant, voices might have implied to the wider world. There were disputes about the fit (or lack of it) between the 'old' and the 'new' social work values, disputes about whether a model of anti-racism predominantly derived from African–Caribbean concerns adequately reflected or expressed Asian interests, and disputes about the appropriateness of restricting professional discretion, and coercing staff commitment to particular versions of anti-racism, in the name of countering discrimination.

As these arguments raged in the 1990s the Home Office thrust a new and fateful element into the mix: was probation 'social work' at all? Was it not essentially punishment? The government easily wrongfooted the Probation Service by demanding that it speak a moral language adequate to the challenges posed by contemporary crime – something that neither the 'new' nor 'old' versions of social work values had done sufficiently well. Worried about where an emphasis on punishment (and particularly 'just deserts') might lead, some sought to reaffirm social work values in a slightly more sophisticated way (Williams 1995). Others (Nellis 1995) settled for a break with the prevailing concept of social work but sought to reaffirm the deeper humanistic tradition behind it in a language that was morally serious about crime, drawing on discourses about community safety, penal reductionism and restorative justice, whose normative and discursive potential the Service had neglected. Yet others pressed, successfully as it turned out, for a reaffirmation of rehabilitation in terms of the burgeoning 'What Works' movement, as described by Peter Raynor in Chapter 5, although, as David Garland (2001) has pointed out, the contemporary meaning of rehabilitation in official policy differs from earlier versions because it is now merely one of several means to the end of control, not an end – a human ideal – in its own right, and pursued more coercively.

The best that can be said of the Probation Service as the millennium turned, as the new training arrangements (which separated probation training from social work) began to take root, as the organisation became centralised and as the names of familiar orders were changed (in community service's case, rather pointlessly – see the final chapter) was that it was learning to sound as though it was an organisation committed to dealing constructively with crime, which recognised the full spectrum of concern, fear and anger that characterised the public mood towards offenders, and the felt need for safety and protection. Traces of the social work traditions remained in its discourse – neither respect for persons nor the desire to challenge discrimination evaporated completely – and although the Service (and the Home Office) felt more comfortable articulating 'what works' than 'what's right' (some New Labour formulations elided the two), it was hard to deny that some discursive progress, at least, had been made.

VALUES AND *A NEW CHOREOGRAPHY*

A New Choreography failed to take thinking about values forward in a coherent fashion. It promoted an eclectic mix of moral commitments (victim awareness, rehabilitation of offenders), scientific aspirations (empiricism) and organisational imperatives (partnership; continuous improvement). Among the list is the rather vague slogan 'responding and learning to work positively with difference in order to achieve diversity'. A deeper understanding of what this particular value might mean is provided by Stretch Objective seven in *A New Choreography*, 'valuing and achieving diversity in the NPS and the Services it provides' (NPS for England and Wales 2001: 33). The essence of this is 'simple justice – no-one should be excluded from the NPS or the services it delivers because of their gender, race or ethnicity, religious beliefs, disability or sexual orientation' (p. 33), but it is clear that the primary emphasis is on staffing and promotion targets for particular categories of people, the assumption apparently being that services for minorities will be more easily improved if a more diverse staff group – at all levels of the service, and in the Probation Boards – can be created.

Within the diversity agenda, *A New Choreography* concentrates primarily on race and gender (as will this chapter), with disability earmarked as the next priority. The Service is congratulated on its 'good track record in recruiting minority ethnic staff', to a level in excess of the proportion in the national population, and (at 9.9 per cent in December 1999) above the Home Office's own race equality target of 8.3 per cent. Within this figure, Asian people – a tremendously broad category – remain underrepresented, at 1.5 per cent of the workforce (p. 34). In respect of women, the proportion of female probation officers has increased from 40 per cent in 1989 to 56 per cent in 2000 – at which point 71 per cent of trainees were women. There were 17 women chief officers (out of 54) prior to the reorganisation of the Service on 2001, now there are 18 (out of 42) (p. 35). All this ostensibly signifies an improvement in equality of opportunity within the Probation Service itself; whether it has translated into the provision of a better service – better justice – for the disadvantaged and oppressed, or had an impact on penal policy – which were its rationale – is something of a moot point. No independent research has ever been done to assess the actual (as opposed to the presumed) impact of anti-discriminatory and anti-oppressive discourse – its unintended as well as its intended outcomes – on the culture and practice of the Probation Service.

Take, for example, the issue of women offenders. It has long been recognised – and it is still accepted by criminologists – that women commit fewer, less serious crimes than men, and have shorter criminal careers, and yet, in England the numbers of women imprisoned have grown rapidly to 4425 (Home Office 2002a), with further increases anticipated (Gelsthorpe and Morris 2002). Even Prison Inspectorate reports have lamented the lack of adequate community provision for women (e.g. HM Inspectorate of Prisons 1997). The idea that Britain imprisons too many women, and that probation officers could do more to supervise them in the community, was recognised as 'the heart of the matter' by proto-feminists in the 1960s (Field 1966), and affirmed ever more strongly by successive generations of feminist and women-centred criminologists (Smart 1976; Carlen 1990; Gelsthorpe and Morris 1990). Worrall (2002: 137) rightly remembers 'the tide of accusations of sexual discrimination in the criminal system' in the 1980s and 1990s and the way that it 'caught the imagination' of women trainees (in particular) on social work/probation courses. While it would be unreasonable to claim that a significant reduction in custody for women was wholly within the gift of the probation service acting alone, it is not unreasonable to ask why this knowledge (which was not, of course, only disseminated in the probation service), coupled with the increasing 'feminisation' of the probation workforce, had so little impact on the process-ing of women offenders. Was it eclipsed by, or mistakenly confused with, the rather more simplistic and technocratic anti-sexism promoted by social work education's regulatory body, CCETSW, in the same period? Despite its *apparent* strength within the probation service something neutralised the force of feminist criminological critique, and even if, without a proper historical analysis of what went wrong, it is hard to identify specific factors, it is difficult to disagree with Worrall 'that the Service has missed opportunities to remain a major player in the lives of women offenders' (p. 136). In respect of the most recent shifts in Service practice – towards an over-reliance on cognitive-behavioural programmes developed mostly with men in mind – she is even more pessimistic, doubting 'whether [the Service] does in fact have anything to offer' women offenders (see also Kendall 2002).

A similarly dispiriting tale can be told about anti-racism in probation and the situation of Black offenders, and is in fact half told by *A New Choreography* itself, drawing on an Inspectorate report on race equality (HM Inspectorate of Probation 2000). From the early 1980s onwards, the Probation Service demonstrably showed more commitment to addressing racism within its own organisational structures than other criminal justice agencies, and arguably met with more success, than, say, the police, in terms of recruiting Black staff and in terms of sensitivity to racial discrimination in the prosecution and sentencing process. Social work courses, CCETSW and the NAPO were instrumental in achieving this. Bowling and Phillips' (2002) recent summary implies there was perhaps less research on racism in criminal justice than on sexism, but even so, it would be hard to deny the extent which the Service tried to be anti-racist. And yet the Inspectorate's investigation, while complimentary in small respects, still showed 'a great deal of inconsistent and poor practice', raised basic questions about the quality of report writing and supervision (p. 35) and demanded yet more change – an intensification of what had gone before – to eradicate institutional racism. Undoubtedly, there remains a case to answer, for while probation practice in dealing with White racist offenders may have improved significantly (one aspect of getting anti-racism right), Black men, and especially Black women, offenders are still disproportionally represented in the prison population (where racism remains rife). The ethnic profile of the Service may itself have changed, and the culture of the Service become more self-consciously anti-discriminatory, but this has not translated into better justice for Black offenders on any significant scale.

Implicitly, at least, there does seem to be a recognition that the particular discourses of anti-discrimination, anti-oppression, anti-racism and anti-sexism that pervaded social work/probation in the 1990s had severe limitations (or perhaps have just outlived their usefulness in changing the ethnic and gender profiles of the probation workforce). *A New Choreography* simply dissolves them all into a rather nebulous 'diversity' agenda, and remains committed to the assumption, surely questionable by now, that if diversity issues are got right *within* the organisation, this will automatically lead to structural improvements in service delivery to disadvantaged 'client groups'. It shies away from characterising diversity values in *negative* terms; the prefix 'anti' is avoided, despite the obvious utility of a value position which states what one is against *as well as* what one is for. Conversely, it relies upon the same micro-managerialism – detailed policies, procedures and instructions – to carry diversity issues forward as the older discourses relied upon, which, as some postmodern contributors to the value debate now point out, had the paradoxical effect of making anti-oppressive demands themselves seem oppressive and stultifying.

What might be the way forwards from the blandness of *A New Choreography*'s characterisation of values? Some commentators such as Hudson (2001) and Chouhan (2002) have seen in human rights and the idea of a 'human rights culture' a way of reinvigorating the anti-discriminatory discourses of the 1990s, of reinventing them without the features that, in some eyes, discredited them or limited their potency. Not only would a human rights approach permit an emphasis on respect for difference (the heart of diversity), it would also enable challenges to the excesses of managerialism (understood as an expression of state power); crucially it would do so in a vocabulary that was shared across the criminal justice system, which the earlier discourses, being much more probation/social work specific, never were. Given that the increasing integration of the criminal justice system and the homogenising of principles which underpin it make agency-specific values more difficult to articulate, there is a *prima facie* case for at least exploring the potential of human rights to the moral imagination of the Probation Service.

HUMAN RIGHTS: A NEW MORAL DISCOURSE?

The Human Rights Act 1998 was implemented on October 2000 in England, *parts of it* (relating to criminal trials) having been implemented five months earlier in Scotland. It incorporates the European Convention on Human Rights into British law and rebalances the relationship between the individual and public authorities (the state) in a way that several commentators have assumed will have significant implications for probation practice although curiously, in the definitive guide to the Act's implications for criminal law probation receives no mention (Cheney *et al.* 2001). It seems reasonable that statutory rights to liberty and security, to a fair trial, to no punishment without lawful authority, to freedom of expression, to privacy and family life, not to mention freedom from torture will have implications for criminal justice. New and existing legislation will have to be scrutinised for compatibility with the Convention (as indeed, had been happening prior to the Act's implementation). National Standards, sex offender orders (possible post-release restrictions of liberty) and electronic monitoring may be subject to challenges, so might professional practices such as risk assessment and breach action, and any decision based on what offenders *might do* as opposed to *actually have done*. It needs to be remembered that not all the 'new' human rights are absolute; some are subject to qualification if they 'conflict with national security, the prevention of crime and public safety' (Wallace 2000: 53) – rather loose terms at best, but which rightly remind us that the modern formulation of human rights originated in the Western response to the Holocaust, as a set of binding principles which repudiated totalitarianism. They are nowadays understood to protect and secure redress for crime victims from offenders, as much as to protect offenders (and victims) from an overweening state. The NPS's own resource pack addresses the empowering-the-state aspect of the Human Rights Act early on:

Importantly . . . the Act strengthens the position of the public authorities in many respects, in that it gives public authorities a duty to protect the rights of individuals, and to balance the rights of one individual or group against those of another individual or group. An obvious area of work where that helps the probation service to carry out its public protection duties is that it enables us to take action to disclose – in a proportionate way – information about people who present a risk to others. Whilst this may interfere with their rights under Article 8 of the Convention, provided that the Service can show that it is acting in accordance with its duty in a manner that falls within the exceptions set out in Article 8.2, a challenge to its actions is unlikely to be successful. It is that duty of a public authority to balance conflicting demands that gives us a new and invigorating authority to carry out our work. (National Probation Service 2001: 8)

John Scott (2002), the Chief Officer most involved in mapping the implications of the Human Rights Act for the Probation Service, has argued cogently and enthusiastically for the transformative potential of the legislation, although it is clear that he mostly sees it as giving impetus and legitimacy to existing forms of good practice. Openness and community involvement, the recognition that offenders are citizens, participation in partnerships with statutory and voluntary agencies, investing in staff and taking note of international developments in human rights are all portrayed as ways of taking the human rights agenda forward. Susan Wallace (2000: 55), a Scottish criminal justice social worker, argues even more stridently. She believes that the Act 'necessitates a total cultural change' in probation (which is worrying in its implication that human rights were not intuitively respected before). She is on slightly firmer ground in suggesting that the Convention become 'a central plank of ethical practice' in the sense of *reinforcing* traditional 'core values such as respect, honesty and openness', but it was of course open for practitioners to practise in this spirit before the advent of the Human Rights Act. What exists now is the possibility of enforcement in domestic courts, and if that helps to heighten practitioners' sense of offenders as people it may well sharpen and improve practice.

Nonetheless serious conceptual problems begin to arise at this point. Does the credibility of human rights depend on a prior sensibility which understands why and how they matter, or does the enshrinement of human rights in legislation create and sustain the sensibility? Even if one allows, as one reasonably might, a dialectical relationship to operate here, the question remains of what other moral resources, what other values, inform that sensibility and infuse themselves into the idea of human rights? For Michael Ignatieff, an internationally recognised commentator on human rights issues, this is the key issue, and one we neglect at our peril. An abstract commitment to rights, important as it is on the overall spectrum of human concern, is not in itself sufficient to kindle and sustain respect, decency and mutuality in ordinary day to day interactions; 'we all know people', he ruefully notes, 'who combine high flown commitment to rights with low down disregard for all the actual human beings who stand in their way' (Ignatieff 2000: 40). He invites us to acknowledge human rights as something 'on the outermost arc of our obligations', but which are only 'as strong as our innermost commitments' (p. 41), in essence

as a residual system of entitlement that people have irrespective of citizenship, irrespective of the states in which they happen to find themselves. Human rights are the rights men and women have *when all else fails them*. (p. 36, emphasis added)

The Probation Service and its partner organisations surely exist to ensure that 'all else' does not fail them. That does not deny the importance or necessity of human rights, but it locates them further in the background, behind tangible citizenship rights within a given state, and makes them dependent on what Ignatieff calls 'innermost commitments'. Of what might these commitments consist for probation officers? What insights into contemporary developments in crime control, and what moral and political knowledge might inform them? We will attempt a brief answer to these questions in the concluding section of this chapter. Meanwhile let us acknowledge, with Ignatieff, the best that can be said for human rights as a resource for sustaining ethical ideals and moral sensibilities:

> Yet we need to think of rights as something more than a dry enumeration of entitlements in constitutional codes, as more than a set of instruments that individuals use to defend themselves. Rights create and sustain culture and by culture we mean habits of the heart. Rights create community. They do so because once we believe in equal rights, we are committed to the idea that rights are indivisible. Defending your own rights means being committed to defending the rights of others. (p. 125)

Ignatieff's strength is his ability to understand how rights-talk, properly understood, can celebrate and reconcile a kind of moderated individualism with the pursuit of the communal or common good, a reconciliation which is self-evidently vital to social harmony in the complex, multicultural societies generated in the later twentieth century. He grasps that a key virtue of human rights is that without denying or disrespecting difference they ultimately appeal to universal qualities – against the tendency of some anti-discriminatory and anti-oppressive discourse to engage in 'categorism', to exaggerate Otherness and mistrust, and to foster social division and conflict. The emphasis on commonality, the denial of extreme Otherness, we might add, is particularly important in regard to offenders, who are so often scorned, demonised and projected beyond the human pale; some may well be, but most are not, least of all those who appear routinely on probation caseloads.

> The test of human respect always lies with the hard cases – . . . the prisoner who has shown no respect for others and now asks for respect from us; the uncontrollable adolescent whose behaviour seems to cry out for coercive restraint. To give these human beings the benefit of informed consent, the rule of law and such autonomy as they can exercise without harm to others is proof that we believe in human rights.
>
> Yet human rights alone are not enough. In extreme situations, we need extra resources, especially humour, compassion and self-control. These virtues in turn must draw on a deep sense of human indivisibility, a recognition of us in them and them in us, that rights doctrines express but in themselves have no power to instill in the human heart. (p. 39)

There is more. Ignatieff fully recognises that while rights-talk *can* contribute to social solidarity and community cohesion, it is rarely sufficient in itself to create and sustain a sense of mutuality and belongingness. He understands too that it can be glib to portray rights as an adequate answer to discrimination in the face of structural inequalities which reinforce it, and that enforcement and precedent-setting often depends on judges who are aligned too closely with existing power bases. He sombrely notes that a thinned-out conception of rights can in fact coexist with a divisive, sometimes lethal, emphasis on Otherness ('our' rights at the expense of 'theirs') and be used to shore up sectional interests: rights-claims alone, without the enrichment of a compassionate sensibility 'can be used to justify evil as well as good' (p. 52). In a specific probation context Gelsthorpe (2001: 161) has warned that human rights, while obviously useful and desirable, are best understood as backstops, attempts to limit harm rather than intrinsic galvanisers of good practice.

The general pertinence of these lines of argument has long been recognised by certain jurisprudential scholars in Britain, whose doubts that the Human Rights Act would make a significant impact on prevailing trends in criminal law and penal policy went unnoticed by those in probation who have envisaged human rights as a way of revitalising their ethical concerns. Conor Gearty (1998) has repeatedly shown how the meaning of human rights in Western democracies has been pared down and interpreted conservatively, to augment prevailing distributions of wealth and power, rather than 'in the service of humanity'. He complains of 'a lack of intellectual direction that has allowed the idea of "human rights" to be efficiently plundered', robbed of its subversive edge and democratic potential. Writing on the second anniversary of Britain's Human Rights Act Francesca Klug (2002) considers that it has thus far won few friends and, certain individual champions apart, has little actual support in government. She points out that it has not prevented oppressive legal developments in respect of asylum seekers and terrorist suspects; in the same spirit, she might have added that the recent White Paper, *Justice for All* (Home Office 2002b) – which will have fateful implications for the Probation Service – has been widely criticised for its assault on some time-honoured rights of due process, including jury trial and the presumption of innocence. The steady attenuation of offender's *citizenship* rights – connecting breach to benefit cuts, for example – has already affected probation practice and it would be unfortunate if the advent of ostensibly 'loftier' *human* rights were used to obscure this. The incorporation of the Human Rights Act into British law, formal landmark that it was, is not in itself evidence that an era of *enhanced* civil liberties is being ushered in, or that a democratic deficit is being addressed. There is, as a respected union leader has said, observing socio-legal developments in the aftermath of 9/11, a contrary view:

we didn't say that we would support the government undermining our liberty, our freedom, and our democracy, and we didn't say that we would declare war on Islam. There's a creeping totalitarianism which is emerging here and the rights of citizens are being incrementally taken away. (Bill Morris, quoted in *The Guardian*, 9 September 2002)

THE FUTURE OF PROBATION VALUES

Our primary aims in this chapter were to note the hiatus in thinking about probation values – the gap between available good ideas and official take-up of them – and, while not being entirely hostile to it, to dampen enthusiasm for the burgeoning belief that human rights discourse represents a kind of ethical salvation for the Probation Service. Nonetheless, having identified the limitations of earlier conceptions of probation values and discouraged over-confidence in a human rights perspective we feel obliged to offer a sketch of what probation values might be, of what the Service might yet stand for (see Gelsthorpe 2002 for the idea of 'educative values'). One of us has elsewhere suggested that probation values can usefully be redefined in terms of the principle of 'community justice', whose key components are the creation of community safety, the reduction of custody and the promotion of restorative justice. All three can be understood as aspects of what used to be called 'anti-oppressive practice', a concept which need not be restricted to the contexts of race and gender in which it originated (Nellis 2001a).

All three ideally need to be articulated in more detail than we have space for here, but the key idea in each case is as follows. First, to the extent that crime and the fear of crime blight citizens' lives, and sometimes damage the quality of life in whole communities, working to reduce the incidence of crime – a core probation task – can easily be characterised as anti-oppressive. Second, the avoidance of imprisonment – when community penalties could secure requisite levels of public safety, at less cost – ultimately reflects the democratic imperative to keep restrictions of liberty to a minimum: more immediately it can result in less damage to offenders and increased chances of social reintegration. Although policy-makers in recent years have played down the contribution which probation might make to the reduced use of custody, key figures in the criminal justice system, including Martin Narey, the Director-General of the Prison Service, and Lord Woolf, the Lord Chief Justice (himself a champion of human rights) continue to affirm its importance, and the penal reform network has repeatedly demonstrated that it is a feasible ideal. Both Carlen (2002) and Gelsthorpe and Morris (2002) have recently reiterated the specific case for reducing the use of custody for women offenders with even greater intellectual cogency than before. Third, to the extent that hitherto neglected crime victims need empowerment within the criminal justice system, this is best pursued within the framework of restorative justice, which seeks to give due weight to the needs, rights and interests of both victims and offenders – lest the strident, media-magnified voice of angry crime victims itself contributes to more oppressive legal and penal developments.

There is, in fact, a race and gender dimension to all these aspects of community justice, in the sense that there are ongoing political and professional concerns about women's safety and about racial violence, about the excessive or disproportionate use of custody for women and African–Caribbean offenders, and about the roots of much restorative justice thinking in non-Western cultural traditions. Aspects of the first two elements are highlighted by The Runnymede Trust's Commission on *The Future of Multi-ethnic Britain*. Their report (Parekh 2000), a masterpiece of politically committed scholarship which informs all the themes of this chapter, should be the touchstone of all near-future debate on race and ethnicity in criminal justice generally, and probation in particular. The eradication of racial discrimination in criminal justice agencies is central to its more general aspiration to foster a convivial multi-culturalism and to avoid the divisive, rift-ridden future it fears if this goal is not consciously pursued. Unlike the versions of anti-racism which took root in social work/probation in the 1990s, it plays down – albeit without ever doubting the virulence of racism – categorism (a polarisation of simplistic Black and White perspectives) and the fostering of a never-the-twain-shall-meet sense of Otherness as a solution to it. Rather like a novel which has been widely read in the same period, Zadie Smith's (2000) *White Teeth*, Parekh favours a more empirically informed emphasis on 'hybridity', recognising the manifest entwining and mutual accommodation of cultural and ethnic traditions in contemporary Britain, and seeing in them a source of hope. The value and virtue of difference and diversity is never lost, but it is always understood that this should not be celebrated and pursued to the extent that the possibility of community cohesion is irrevocably undermined. Parekh understands the importance of human rights as 'ground rules', but, like Ignatieff, does not believe that rights-talk is sufficient in itself to heal divisions or foster community cohesion (see Berkeley and McLaren 2002).

The last element of our sketch of the future of probation values requires that attention be paid to the dangers of managerialism – to the loss of humanity that its disciplines can entail (Nellis 2000). The new public management has been inextricably connected both to the rise of market forces and to the centralisation of state power, managerial strategies having been the means by which 'the centre' exerts detailed, almost real-time control over the periphery, on matters where 'the periphery' (as with local probation services) once had the autonomy to deal adaptively and creatively with varied local circumstances. Managerialism is about competition and market testing, about setting targets and performance indicators, about auditing and continuous improvement, about hierarchy and the 'right to manage' rather than participatory democracy, and about contracting-out and privatisation. It is respectful neither of professional knowledge nor – most tellingly – of a person's innermost commitments (i.e. loyalties outside or above the specific mission of the organisation); it simply requires the performance of a specified task, in a set way, by a set time; as Faulkner (2002: 47) puts it, employees' 'identities and values are . . . merged into a common grey culture of performance, management and quantitative measurement'.

No policy in criminal justice has been untouched by this. Indeed, one of the paradoxes of the versions of anti-racism and anti-sexism that were promoted in the Probation Service in the 1990s was their inadvertent legitimation of greater managerialism; tighter regulation of discretion throughout the hierarchy, rather than the education of hearts and minds, as the primary means of reducing discrimination. The Parekh Report is wiser in this respect (as in many others), recognising that certain forms of governance and organisation can subvert the very reforms they purport to carry forward. 'Increases in accountability', it notes, 'can be accompanied by an increase in direction by central government, diminished influence of elected local government, and an absence of any significant or effective sense of local ownership' (Parekh 2000: 140), with even less chance of minority voices being heard at local level. There are wider lessons to be learned here. Overcentralisation, excessive direction, and the micro-management of intrinsically local processes, leading to loss of authentic local ownership and commitment, certainly affect the Probation Service. There is no end in sight: as McLaughlin (2001: 170) notes, 'a viable post-managerialist vision has yet to be articulated by critics'. The political dangers of managerialism remain unrecognised so long as it is thought of as nothing more than a neutral tool for the achievement of certain social ends. It is, as diverse theorists have convincingly shown (Bauman 1989; Glover 1999) a profoundly misconceived – and arguably inherently oppressive – way to create and maintain social order; what begins ostensibly as a means invariably becomes an end – a rule-ridden regime – in itself. Michael Ignatieff locates the real source of order (and social peace) in multicultural democracies in an entirely different sphere, which returns us to the 'innermost commitments' of ordinary people:

> The precondition of order in a liberal society is an act of the imagination: *not* a moral consensus or shared values, but the capacity to understand moral worlds very different from our own. We may be different, but we can imagine what it would be like *to be each other*. (Ignatieff 2000: 138, emphasis in the original)

There is a slender hope here. We can indeed imagine this – but imagination is not formed in a vacuum, it depends on how people are socialised and educated, on the intellectual possibilities that particular milieux offer them.

Empathy and mutual recognition may to a degree be intuitive, but they come more 'naturally' to some than others – and there are various ways in which they may actually be discouraged, stifled and trained out of people until, as the poet Yeats (1961) once put it, there is '[m]ore substance in our enmities [t]han in our love' (p. 231). An emphasis on categorism – regarding individuals as exemplars of an imagined ethnic or political community whose Otherness (as opposed to difference) is exaggerated, seriously weakens empathy. So too does an impersonal managerialist emphasis on performance; all that matters then is that a functionary accomplishes the task, meets the target, regardless of their personal feelings and sensibilities. So too does an overemphasis on specialist expert knowledge, a professional-knows-best attitude which fails to enlist the subject of professional attention in the process of change and rehabilitation. To the extent that all these processes impinge on, or exist within, the new Probation Service, we may be in danger of dissipating the very qualities which give rise to the idea of common (if differentiated) humanity. Bernard Williams (2000), a leading British philosopher, sets this danger in a broader context, with higher education particularly in mind:

> We run the risk, in fact, that the whole humanistic enterprise of understanding ourselves is coming to seem peculiar. For various reasons, education is being driven towards an increasing concentration on the technical and the commercial, to a point where more reflective enquiry may come to seem unnecessary and archaic, something that at best is preserved as part of the heritage industry. (p. 496)

Where does this leave probation training? The possibility that such training would shift towards a 'concentration on the technical' was registered at the outset of the separation from social work, and has been mooted repeatedly since (Ford and Sleeman 1996; Bhui 2001). There may still be more scope for reflective enquiry than critics think, but the danger of drifting away from it is undoubtedly real, and Williams' warning should certainly be pondered. Probation training *must obviously* equip trainees to perform the practical tasks that the job requires, but if this is all that is required there is little point locating the programmes in universities, whose essential contribution to vocational education is surely to 'bring more things into view' (Barnett 2000) – to draw on 'overarching knowledge' not easily accessed in the Probation Service itself (Nellis 2001b). Whatever else it does probation training should offer a deeper, broader and more sophisticated understanding of values than is available in *A New Choreography*, even if its list is used – reasonably enough – as a starting point. Those who teach values to probation trainees must themselves know enough to recognise the failings of the earlier discourses of anti-discrimination and anti-oppressiveness, and to see both the strengths and weaknesses of the human rights perspective. They must also understand the full range of intellectual resources on which they might draw to develop a viable moral imagination for the probation service in a new century. See, for example, Margalit (1996) on decency; Glover (1999) on humanity; Parekh (2000) and Sacks (2002) on difference and multiculturalism; Clear and Karp (1999) on community justice, as well as the penal philosophy of Anthony Duff (2001, 2003), explored by Sue Rex in Chapter 3. Perhaps in this way the hiatus we noted at the outset will be overcome.

SUMMARY OF KEY ISSUES

- This chapter has sought to question the state of debate on probation values. While noting that *A New Choregraphy* continues to present the Probation Service as a value-based organisation, its own values are, to say the least rather bland. It seems to recognise that, for a variety of reasons, there can be no easy return to the anti-discriminatory values of the 1990s, which appear, at least in respect of gender and race, to have had a far greater impact on the demographic profile of the service itself, than on services for Black and women offenders.

- The 'diversity agenda', to which *A New Choreography* subscribes, is similarly focused, and may be similarly limited.

- The chapter then takes up the idea of human rights, which some commentators have seen as a resource for revitalizing probation values. While not disputing the importance of human rights to criminal justice *per se*, we doubt the potency of something as remote and abstract as legal rights-of-last-resort to function in this way, and suggest a different starting point.

- Probation values need to be conceptualised and articulated as normative statements by which the Service and its officers can stand, and which address the penal challenges of the day. Promoting community safety, promoting restorative justice and opposing the unnecessary use of imprisonment seem to us to be the starting point for new debates on probation values.

References

Barnett, R. (2000) *Realizing the University in an Age of Supercomplexity*. Buckingham: Open University Press.

Bauman, Z. (1989) *Modernity and the Holocaust*. Cambridge: Polity.

Berkeley, R. and McLaren, V. (2002) 'The emerging "Community Cohesion" agenda', *Vista*, 7(3), 241–245.

Bhui, H. S. (2001) 'New probation: closer to the end of social work?', *British Journal of Social Work*, 31, 637–639.

Bowling, B. and Phillips, C. (2002) *Racism, Crime and Justice*. Harlow: Longman.

Carlen, P. (1990) *Alternatives to Women's Imprisonment*. Milton Keynes: Open University Press.

Carlen, P. (ed.) (2002) *Women and Punishment: The Struggle for Justice*. Cullompton: Willan.

Cheney, D., Dickson, L., Skibeck, R., Uglow, S. and Fitzpatrick, J. (2001) *Criminal Justice and the Human Rights Act 1998*. Bristol: Jordans.

Chouhan, K. (2002) 'Race issues in probation', in D. Ward, J. Scott and M. Lacey (eds) *Probation: Working for Justice* (2nd edn). Oxford: Oxford University Press.

Clear, T. and Karp, D. (1999) *The Community Justice Ideal: Preventing Crime and Achieving Justice*. Oxford: Westview.

Duff, R. A. (2001) *Punishment, Communication and Community*. Oxford: Oxford University Press.

Duff, R. A. (2003, forthcoming) 'Probation, punishment and restorative justice', *Howard Journal of Criminal Justice*.

Faulkner, D. (2002) 'Probation, citizenship and public service', in D. Ward, J. Scott and M. Lacey (eds) *Probation: Working for Justice* (2nd edn). Oxford: Oxford University Press.

Field, X. (1966) *Under Lock and Key: A Study of Women in Prison*. London: Max Parrish.

Ford, P. and Sleeman, S. (1996) 'Educating and training probation officers: The announcement of decline', *Vista: Perspectives on Probation*, 1, 14–22.

Fulwood, C. (1999) 'Civil liberties and social control in the community', *Vista: Perspectives on Probation*, 5, 4–14.

Garland, D. (2001) *The Culture of Control: Crime and Social Order in Contemporary Society*. Oxford: Oxford University Press.

Gearty, C. (1998) 'No human rights please, we're capitalists', *The Independent on Sunday*, 13 December 1998.

Gelsthorpe, L. (2001) 'Accountability: Difference and diversity in the delivery of community penalties', in A. E. Bottoms, L. Gelsthorpe and S. A. Rex (eds) *Community Penalties: Change and Challenges*. Cullompton: Willan.

Gelsthorpe, L. (2002) 'Recent changes in youth justice policy in England and Wales', in I. Weijers and A. Duff (eds) *Punishing Juveniles: Principle and Critique*. Oxford: Hart.

Gelsthorpe, L. and Morris, A. (eds) (1990) *Feminist Perspectives in Criminology*. Milton Keynes: Open University Press.

Gelsthorpe, L. and Morris, A. (2002) 'Women's imprisonment in England and Wales: A penal paradox', *Criminal Justice*, 2, 277–301.

Glover, J. (1999) *Humanity: A Moral History of the Twentieth Century*. London: Jonathan Cape.

Harding, J. (2000) 'A community justice dimension to effective probation practice', *Howard Journal of Criminal Justice*, 39, 132–149.

HM Inspectorate of Prisons (1997) *Women in Prison: A Thematic Review*. London: Home Office.

HM Inspectorate of Probation (2000) *Towards Racial Equality*. London: Home Office.

Home Office (2002a) *Occupation of Prisons, Remand Centres, Young Offender Institutions and Police Cells in England and Wales 31st August 2002*. London: Home Office.

Home Office (2002b) *Justice for All* (CM 5563). London: Home Office.

Hudson, B. (2001) 'Human rights, public safety and the Probation Service: Defending justice in the risk society', *Howard Journal of Criminal Justice*, 40, 103–113.

Ignatieff, M. (2000) *The Rights Revolution*. Toronto: House of Anansi Press.

Kendall, K. (2002) 'Time to think again about cognitive behavioural programmes', in P. Carlen (ed.) *Women and Punishment: The Struggle for Justice*. Cullompton: Willan.

Klug, F. (2002) 'Human rights: A common standard for all peoples?' in P. Griffith and M. Leonard (eds) *Reclaiming Britishness*. London: Foreign Policy Centre.

Lacey, M. (2002) 'Justice, humanity and mercy', in D. Ward, J. Scott and M. Lacey (eds) *Probation: Working for Justice* (2nd edn). Oxford: Oxford University Press.

McLaughlin, E. (2001) 'Managerialism', in E. McLaughlin and J. Muncie (eds) *The Sage Dictionary of Criminology*. London: Sage.

Margalit, A. (1996) *The Decent Society*. Cambridge, MA: Harvard University Press.

National Probation Service (NPS) (2001) *Human Rights Act 1998: A Resource Pack for the National Probation Service*. London: NPS.

National Probation Service (NPS) for England and Wales (2001) *A New Choreography: An Integrated Strategy for the National Probation Service for England and Wales – Strategic Framework 2001–2004*. London: Home Office.

Nellis, M. (1995) 'Probation values for the 1990s', *Howard Journal of Criminal Justice*, 34, 19–44.

Nellis, M. (2000) 'Taking oppression seriously: A critique of managerialism in social work/probation', in I. Paylor, J. Harris and L. Froggett (eds) *Reclaiming Social Work: The Southport Papers Volume 2*. Birmingham: Venture Press.

Nellis, M. (2001a) 'Community values and community justice', *Probation Journal*, 48, 34–38.

Nellis, M. (2001b) 'The new probation training in England and Wales: Realising the potential', *Social Work Education*, 20, 416–432.

Parekh, B. (2000) *The Future of Multi-ethnic Britain* (A report from The Runnymede Trust). London: Profile Books.

Sacks, J. (2002) *The Dignity of Difference: How to Avoid the Clash of Civilisations*. London: Continuum.

Scott, J. and Ward, D. (1999) 'Human rights and the Probation Service', *Vista: Perspectives on Probation*, 5, 106–109.

Scott, J. (2002) 'Human rights: A challenge to culture and practice', in D. Ward, J. Scott and M. Lacey (eds) *Probation: Working for Justice* (2nd edn). Oxford: Oxford University Press.

Smart, C. (1976) *Women, Crime and Criminology*. London: Routledge & Kegan Paul.

Smith, Z. (2000) *White Teeth*. London: Hamish Hamilton.

Wallace, S. (2000) 'Responding to the Human Rights Act', *Probation Journal*, 47, 53–55.

Williams, B. (ed.) (1995) *Probation Values*. Birmingham: Venture Press.

Williams, B. (2000) 'Philosophy as a humanistic discipline', *Philosophy*, 75, 477–496.

Worrall, A. (2002) 'Missed opportunities? The probation service and women offenders', in D. Ward, J. Scott and M. Lacey (eds) *Probation: Working for Justice* (2nd edn). Oxford: Oxford University Press.

Yeats, W. B. (1961) 'The second coming', in *Collected Poems of W. B. Yeats*. London: Macmillan.

15

ELECTRONIC MONITORING AND THE FUTURE OF PROBATION

Mike Nellis

INTRODUCTION

Electronic monitoring (EM) developed slowly and experimentally in England and Wales, initially under a neoliberal Conservative government, latterly (since 1997) under the more managerial New Labour (Lilly 1990; Nellis 1991, 2000; Fay 1993). Given its inauspicious beginnings, few would have predicted then the situation which pertains now, where England leads the world in its proportionate use. Each phase of EM's expansion was, to begin with, triggered by acute government anxiety about rising prison numbers and prison overcrowding, but it has arguably acquired a momentum independent of such merely pragmatic considerations, which will eventually contribute to a transformation in what have traditionally been understood as 'alternatives to custody' or 'community penalties' – if not necessarily to a significant reduction in prison use. This chapter will explore the possible implications of EM for the future of the Probation Service.

The history of EM, in England, briefly, is this. It was used experimentally to enforce bail curfews in 1989–90 and then, again experimentally, to enforce a hitherto underused sentence, the curfew order, in 1995–6, the latter going national in December 1999. A discretionary early release from prison scheme, Home Detention Curfew (HDC), was introduced for the over-16s, with immediate national effect, in January 1999; 10–15-year-olds were made eligible for curfew orders in February 2001 and for bail enforcement in April 2002. From May 2002, a multi-component package of measures including EM, 'Intensive Supervision and Surveillance' (ISSP) could be given to young offenders at risk of custody. The maximum length of a curfew order for the over-16s is

245

six months, for the under-16s, three months. On 31 May 2002, the total number of offenders who had been tagged since EM's inception stood at 68,046, the vast majority of these (51,913) being on HDC. The current number of people tagged at that point was 4403 (Toon 2002).

Further uses of EM are anticipated, and already legislated for. The Criminal Justice and Court Services Act 2000 permitted the electronic monitoring of *any requirement* of a community penalty (at the court's discretion) – since making EM integral to the very nature of community penalties. Alongside the existing curfew order, an exclusion order is planned, aimed at offenders who pose a nuisance or a danger to particular victims (who are given home-based alarms sensitive to the offender's tag), and requiring him or her to stay away from certain places at certain times. As with curfews, exclusion orders can be used as a stand-alone penalty, or in conjunction with other measures. The Act also made provision for EM to be imposed where offenders are released from custody, not 'early' (as in HDC) but at their official release date – in essence making EM integral to all post-release supervision, including that of lifers. It anticipates the coming of tracking technology and establishes the power of the Home Secretary to 'to monitor electronically *the movements* of such offenders whilst subject to post-release supervision' (Home Office 2000: 7, emphasis added). Some of these developments are being piloted, but there have been implementation delays even at this stage.

Beyond this, governments, monitoring companies and professionals and academics in the criminal justice field continue to speculate on the future of EM in the broadest sense, not just in terms of new technologies such as Global Positioning by Satellite (GPS) (which is one way of enabling tracking, and is already a small-scale reality in the USA; Renzema 1998) but also in terms of the offender types who may be particularly suitable for monitoring. Released sex offenders (a group about whom there remains massive public/ media concern) are continually spoken of in this respect, although such has been the severity of the alarm about them that having initially been eligible for HDC, they were subsequently excluded from it. Nonetheless, tracking tagged sex offenders during some of the extended supervision period (English law allows up to 10 years) continues to surface in debate, although no concrete plans have yet been made.[1] The American Amitai Etzioni (1999: 74), for example, has proposed establishing isolated towns for released sex offenders

---

[1] The Shadow Home Secretary, Oliver Letwin, announced on BBC radio (*Today*, Radio 4, 20 September 2002) that he would encourage the Home Office to examine the potential of the satellite tracking of released sex offenders, based on apparently successful trials in Florida. On the same morning, by way of a reminder of tagging's limitations, *The Guardian* newspaper carried a small sidebar reference to a tagged 16-year-old boy in London who had subsequently been charged with murder.

to whom the mainstream community will not permit reintegration: 'Confinement could be achieved, if preferred by the residents, by the use of electronic bracelets rather than barbed wire and armed guards.' For a variety of reasons, both pragmatic and principled, such ideas are unlikely to be well-received in England, even now. Many aspects of EM have, in fact, been cause for unease in the English probation service (see, for example, McCulloch 1997), and to understand why it helps to begin at the beginning.

EM AND PROBATION: A CONFLICT BEGINS

When the idea of EM was first mooted in a government document – a Green Paper called *Punishment, Custody and the Community* (Home Office 1988) – few people in the social work/community penalty field knew what it was, or were aware of the process by which the Home Office had been persuaded of its merits. Harry Fletcher, Assistant Director of the National Association of Probation Officers (NAPO), was among the best informed. He knew that the Offender Tag Association had been formed in England by former journalist/ prison visitor Tom Stacey (in 1982) to promote the technology, and had been encouraging the Home Office to take note of North American developments, but initially had difficulty persuading NAPO itself that this should be attended to. Once the Home Office endorsed it Fletcher was sufficiently forewarned and forearmed to put both them and Stacey on the defensive, arguing that 'tagging' – Stacey's term for EM – was wholly incompatible with the social work traditions of the probation service, that it would be irrelevant to the often chaotic lives of many offenders, that it would not be cost-effective, and that it would be an unduly tough measure which, on the basis of the past proliferation of alternatives to custody, would not reduce the prison population.

Stacey proselytised actively for EM in the mid- and late 1980s, and never disguised his irritation with NAPO's reaction to it, although his often gratuitous hostility towards the Probation Service was hardly designed to win him allies. He saw EM as a palpably stronger and more effective way of supervising offenders in the community whether on bail, on a sentence or as a means of early release from prison. His ideal was the tracking of people's movements rather than the monitoring of people's presence in their own homes but he accepted at the time that the technology for the former was not yet available. Tagging was something 'different in kind from any penalty in history' and would 'manifestly deter, discipline and provide genuinely verifiable surveillance' (Stacey 1989: 19). 'It in no way upstages the role of the social worker', he wrote, 'but what it will do is verify, entirely neutrally, whether the offender is adhering to the conditions of his sentence and thus take all the snooping and checking off the shoulders of the social worker'. He regretted that this ingenious resolution of social work's longstanding care and control dilemma with offenders was not more widely welcomed, criticised 'vested interests' in the welfare professions and penal reform network for opposing the tag and was particularly saddened that he and they could not unite to reduce the use of imprisonment. Stacey – despite his otherwise conservative political outlook – had as great a personal animus towards prison as the liberal/left professionals and activists who were opposing tagging, and he felt that they were refusing a gift-horse.

Stacey's bold 'prophesy that over the next half century the tag will reduce imprisonment, by over 50 per cent, for offences which usually mean custody today' was naïve. Nonetheless he has won many of the arguments that social workers and probation officers ranged against tagging at the time, namely that it would not be used disproportionately against Black offenders, or in favour of middle-class offenders with homes and phones; that the technology was dependable; that its use was cheaper than prison; that there was some American evidence for its effectiveness; and that it would not *inevitably* be netwidening. Many of his social work critics had an exaggerated concept of the damage that EM might do to civil liberties and human dignity, and in claiming that EM unjustifiably invaded the privacy of the home neglected to set this against the fact that prison invaded the privacy of the person even more – and that many offenders would prefer EM (as indeed proved to be the case). NAPO's attempt to show that EM violated the European Convention on Human Rights on three grounds came to nothing (see Fletcher 1990). NAPO, however, has been proven right about EM's inability to reduce the use of custody, simply because during the period in which its use has been expanding the prison population has risen to an all-time high. The introduction of a new technology was certainly consequential for some offenders, but did not transform the terms of penal debate.

Supporters of EM may of course say that this is a premature judgement, and that with the proper reform of community penalties EM will yet play a part in reducing the use of imprisonment. Perhaps – the most recent White Paper *Justice for All* (Home Office 2002a) seemingly entertains a small reduction in prison use through a transformation in the way in which offenders 'in the community' are supervised. EM is integral to it, but not symbolically prominent. For a variety of reasons it now seems unlikely that EM will develop in England as an adjunct to social work or probation in the way that it has in some other European countries. The time when that could have happened is probably past. EM in England has been developed by government as a private sector initiative, something separate from the probation service rather than integrated with, or embedded in it. If anything, the public/private division has deepened over time, with probation and EM developing on parallel tracks. Furthermore, the ethos of social work (humanistic ways of working) is declining in criminal justice and a way of working which is best characterised as control and surveillance is in the ascendant. Possibly we are seeing a shift in criminal justice from a humanistic to a managerialist-surveillant paradigm, in which EM displaces and supersedes social work, in which social work becomes secondary (and perhaps even optional) to surveillant and regulatory purposes, and in which private sector organisations eventually become more important than the existing public sector ones. There is certainly renewed union concern about the creeping 'privatisation of the probation estate', starting, it seems, with hostel facilities (*NAPO News*, April 2002: 1). |

PROBATION SERVICE HOSTILITY TO EM

This institutionalised separation was probably inevitable given the political conditions prevailing at the time EM was first introduced. The Home Office was attempting (rather cogently) to press changes on the Probation Service to move the emphasis from 'social work with offenders' to 'punishment in the community'. The probation service had a long tradition of (at least initially) resisting anything which did not fit its narrow concept of social work, and repudiated all connotations of punishment. The only non-governmental supporters of tagging – the Offender Tag Association (OTA) – were outside the network of penal reform organisations whose views probation respected. Even the Police Federation and the Magistrate's Association were sceptical of EM, and the national press were, at best, lukewarm. Given these factors, it is perhaps unsurprising that the bodies which formally represented probation managers and practitioners – the Association of Chief Officers of Probation (ACOP) and the National Association of Probation Officers (NAPO) – were confident in their opposition to EM, which, although it was only one facet of the overall 'punishment in the community' initiative became emblematic of all that the probation service felt it was resisting: Fletcher (1990: 11) characterised it as 'pure punishment'.

The Home Office was initially open to the Probation Service running EM schemes themselves, but service intransigence (augmented by the more influential magistrates) increased the likelihood that government would involve the private sector to implement it. It is possible, given the political climate in the late 1980s and early 1990s, that the government would have championed commercial providers in any case (as it was beginning to do for prisons, in part to circumvent the hostility of prison officers to reform of prison management) but Mair (2001), one of EM's original Home Office researchers, is clear that it was indeed service attitudes which prompted the Home Office to go private (p. 172).

NAPO's stance was unfortunate because the actual attitude of working probation officers may have been more tolerant and open-minded than the bodies representing them. In a 1987–8 snapshot of probation practice, drawn from interviews with 62 randomly sampled officers (in four probation areas) 31 officers indicated acceptance of it, while only 20 resisted it as unethical, something to resign or get sacked over (Boswell, Davies and Wright 1993: 166–167). One of the first officers to write on tagging, Andrew Wade (1988), expressed cautious support for using it as alternative to custody, while warning strongly against likely netwidening. And while the chief probation officer who then chaired ACOP was wholly hostile to EM (Read 1990), the overall views of chief officers in this period are hard to gauge. At least one, James Cannings (1989), recognised that EM could not be disinvented, conceded that it was 'one piece in a large jigsaw puzzle' pertaining to crime reduction and argued that it should at least be experimented with as a form of intensive supervision. Interestingly – and presciently – he envisaged it as a means of structuring release from custody rather than as a sentence, and more interestingly still, he did not anticipate the involvement of the private sector.

Home Office researchers were hard pressed to present the 1989–90 EM/bail trials as a major success (Mair and Nee 1990). Stacey complained that bailees were a less than ideal group to judge it on (because time spent remanded on the tag, unlike a remand in custody, was not subtracted from any subsequent custodial sentence), and argued that only its use as a sentence would be a proper test of its potential. NAPO, and indeed other penal reform organisations, were mostly delighted by the apparent failure of the first scheme in 1989–90, and within two years were assuming that the whole idea of EM had been dropped. When an experiment with curfew orders was mooted in the mid-1990s NAPO insisted to policy-makers that it would 'not act as a deterrent for many offenders who by and large lead chaotic lives, may have mental health problems, may have problems with drink or drugs, are disorganised, are unemployed and tend to have unsettled home lives' (NAPO 1994). It publicly portrayed tagging as a gimmicky irrelevance to serious work with offenders, but behind this stance were deeper fears about the undermining of social work, and the growing influence of the private sector.

ACOP recognised that Home Office support for probation was at a particularly low ebb in the mid-1990s, feared being marginalised, and adopted a more conciliatory approach than NAPO. Dick Whitfield (1995), their lead officer on tagging, conceded that tagging *could* work in conjunction with probation input, but still questioned its cost-effectiveness. Another chief (Wargent 1995) said he would find it acceptable if it was targeted on high- rather than low-seriousness offenders released from prison. After the initial Home Office research on the curfew order trials had appeared ACOP were forced to concede more ground, although by then Whitfield was becoming a genuine supporter of the integrated approach to its use favoured in Sweden and the Netherlands. Magistrates in the trial areas were becoming more supportive, offenders found it irksome but not as bad as prison, and embarrassingly, probation officers in one area had been 'at best equivocal and at worst obstructive' (Mair and Mortimer 1996: 29). In early 1997 ACOP drew some positive lessons from a review of the international evidence on EM and welcomed the Home Office research, noting that 'successful completion rates have generally been good and while the range of cases has been too wide to draw conclusions, levels of compliance have been higher than expected, including offenders with chaotic lifestyles, including drug abusers'. It emphasised the importance of linking EM to 'other supervision programmes' as a means of 'reducing prison pressures' (ACOP 1997).

Rather surprisingly, no direct challenge was made to the dominant role of the private sector in EM's provision. It is possible that ACOP believed the commercial dimension of EM's provision would be checked by the incoming New Labour government, which, although not hostile to EM itself, had indicated in opposition that it would end the practice of *prison* privatisation. It reneged on this, however, and was thus unlikely to oppose privatisation in EM. New Labour's Home Detention Curfew scheme, which facilitated the early release of short-term prisoners – greatly increased the scope of the commercial provider's work. It also had the effect of increasing probation contact with tagged offenders who palpably valued being let out a few weeks or months early, even on the semi-freedom of the tag. This tended to make probation officers more aware of the tag's potential, and to win support for it (Nellis and Lilly 2000). Other factors also affected this change of mood. A new, younger generation of probation officers, less tied to the old social work ideals, more open to new technology in general, were willing to see EM entwined – where necessary and appropriate – with rehabilitation, rather than kept separate from it (Farooq 1998; Mann 1998). At this moment in time – although NAPO remains hostile to EM – probation officers in England would probably be willing to incorporate EM into their work, not least because they recognise the dangers of consolidating the private sector presence in criminal justice.

NEW LABOUR: DISPLACING PROBATION?

New Labour's plans for probation, however, are rather ambiguous. In the name of 'modernisation' it has been extending reforms – more managerialism, more central control, less professional or local discretion, greater emphasis on enforcement and punishment – that began under their Conservative predecessors. Creating the National Probation Service (NPS) epitomises this. An emphasis on coercive rehabilitation (usually accredited, group-based re-education programmes) remains but in essence, old-style probation officers cultivated slow processes of inner change in offenders in a fairly individualised way, while new-style probation officers galvanise rapid processes of compliance with external requirements in a fairly standardised way. The paradox of this tougher approach is that the Service is working with less serious, lower-risk offenders than a decade ago (with some significant exceptions post-release, in contexts like Multi-Agency Public Protection Panels).

The simultaneity of change in governance, structure and ethos has produced a turbulent and demoralised organisation – and this strained situation will not be the endpoint of organisational and cultural change. The pressure of centralised, hierarchical control is felt at all levels of the service. Most officers have unwieldy caseloads, with little time for personalised welfare work. Service is individualised, but in a limited and routine way. Sufficient numbers of offenders for accredited programmes have been hard to find, and tight enforcement requirements means that too many are breached before completing them. There is almost certain to be underperformance in terms of tight government targets set for 2004. Experienced people are leaving the Service and are being replaced by inexperienced people, whose training may or may not have placed emphasis on humanistic ideals. A culture focused on targets and procedures – even without the rhetoric of punishment – makes such ideals hard to uphold, and as Fionda (2000: 187) warns, 'the logical end to the managerialist argument lies well beyond the limits of humanitarianism'. It is quite possible that community supervision will become an unappealing, impossible job for decent self-respecting, creative people, and hence more suited to unreflective functionaries and computerised surveillance systems.

Is this being too speculative? Although, in practice, both curfew orders and HDC have been underused in terms of initial Home Office expectations (Walter, Sugg and Moore 2001), there is a sense in which EM has already been normalised in English criminal justice, by becoming integral to the very concept of supervising offenders in the community. New Labour's flagship legislation, the Criminal Justice and Court Service Act 2000 (which created the NPS), made EM available across both the range of community penalties and of post-release supervision. It legislated for tracking tagging in anticipation of tracking technology being perfected soon, one use of which will be for victim protection. A future is clearly being envisaged in which many more offenders experience EM as a matter of course, although – and this is the paradox of the new White Paper – it has become (almost) discursively invisible by dint of being incorporated discretely into new multi-ingredient supervision packages with names like 'Custody Plus', 'Custody Minus' and 'Community Custody Centre'. Formal attention is not being drawn to it. This mirrors the way in which EM has already been embedded in the ISSP projects, and it may reflect Home Office recognition that EM by itself does not seem to the public and the media to be a particularly punitive penalty.

Rhetorically at least, New Labour has committed itself to 'evidence-led policy and practice'. Does the development of EM exemplify this? Simplistically, yes, insofar as the Home Office has only proceeded with national roll-out after carefully researched trials (except in the case of HDC). But this has not been research into 'effectiveness' as such, more into the attitudes of those involved in its implementation and on the receiving end. As both Schmidt (1998) and Whitfield (2001) point out, evaluating the effectiveness of EM is bedevilled by continuing ambiguity as to its purpose: augmenting other community penalties, reducing custody, reducing recidivism. Schmidt concluded her overview of accumulated research by admitting that EM had cost–benefits and that it did not worsen public safety but that there was no clear and decisive evidence that it reduced post-programme recidivism, whether used solo or with other measures. Lobley and Smith (2000; see also Smith 2001) concluded after evaluating the Scottish EM trials that it would not be a cost-effective measure to introduce to Scotland – but the Scottish executive went ahead with it anyway. Whatever it is that drives the expansion of EM in Britain it is certainly not research into its proven effectiveness – it seems to be set apart from the criteria which otherwise govern that activity. At no point has research into EM been integrated with the research into effective practice which informs the accredited programmes in which, in both the Prison and Probation Services, government is placing so much faith. Nor are statistics on curfew orders contained in the annual *Probation Statistics* (Home Office 2002b), because the monitoring companies are considered the supervising authorities. This split may simply exist because of a silo mentality within the Home Office research and statistic streams, but it lends credence to the idea that EM is a separate development, something which is being encouraged to flourish at a distance from traditional providers of community penalties, and independently of the accredited programmes.

Even though some of its manifestations are now being hidden in sentencing packages, the growth and expansion of EM has to be seen, analytically, as part of an emerging surveillance culture – the intersecting, as yet haphazardly connected technologies and strategies which comprise the 'surveillant assemblage' (Haggerty and Ericson 2000). This, combined with the official loss of faith in humanistic intervention, gives EM a significant momentum. The culture of managerialism – the monitoring by one means or another of tightly specified requirements – strengthens it further, by creating a climate more favourable to instruction-and-oversight rather than to discretionary human responses. 'Managerialism gives a boon to technical controls that display some kind of elective affinity to it' notes Scheerer (2000: 251), seeing just such an affinity between 'managerialism and electronic monitoring'. This affinity arguably has three aspects, all derived from the way in which monitored curfews and exclusion orders provide more reliable means of achieving managerialism's inherent need for meticulous control than welfare professionals relying only on offender's unmonitored promises. First, a curfew with EM produces verifiable control-at-a-distance and in real-time in a way that probation officers cannot accomplish – EM is a 'just-in-time'-control, the equivalent of the post-Fordist 'just-in-time production' of goods. Second, it reflects and extends the growing reliance on computerised data – 'virtual files' – and computer-assisted decision-making in the criminal justice system – in this instance yielding clear, precisely timed, usable evidence of compliance/non-compliance. Third, it entails sur-veillance via the body (it is corporeal presence which registers – or not – in the monitoring centres) rather than control via the mind (appeals to reason, con-science, self-interest, truth-telling); the emerging voice-verification systems are a more sophisticated form of biometric surveillance which can dispense with the wearing of a tag.

EM: THE COMMERCIAL DIMENSION

Every expansion of EM further entrenches the private sector as a player in the British criminal justice system. This remains an extraordinarily understudied area, given the shifting ownership of some of the service providers and the fact that they are demonstrably participants in 'the commercial corrections complex' (Lilly 1992; Lilly and Knepper 1993). Securicor Custodial Services (a subsidiary of the main Securicor organisation, and already a provider of court escort services and immigration detention centres) was contracted for two of the curfew order trials; Geographix (a small independent organisation that had hitherto specialised in the electronic tracking of earthmoving equip-ment and boats) was awarded the third. Geographix's was subsequently taken over by Premier (a consortium organisation which included the US Wackenhut Corporation and a provider of prisons in England). When HDC and Curfew Orders were rolled out nationally in England and Wales, Securicor gained the contract for the north, Premier for the Midlands and London, and GSSC Europe (a subsidiary of the USA-based General Security Services Corporation) for the south. GSSC Europe was subsequently taken over by an indigenous British security company, Reliance. In May 2002 the Wackenhut Corporation's worldwide operations were bought out by Group 4, already a provider of court escort services, prisons and immigration detention centres in England. This altered the composition of the Premier consortium, and made Group 4 the world's largest security company.

The medium- and long-term ambitions of these organisations remains opaque to crime policy researchers in a way that those of public organisations do not. Limited information is available from websites, publicity and official histories (see, for example, Underwood 1997). Securicor, for example, seeks to 'globalise its core product range – in this case integrated justice services' and see themselves as 'leaders in the electronic monitoring market internationally' (www.securicor.com 5 May 2002). In Britain, Securicor employs one former probation officer in a middle management position, promoting EM. GSSC (now Reliance) employed three former probation staff (two managers and a retired officer). In conversation (16 May 2002), one of these managers noted the difficulty of engaging the newly formed National Probation Directorate in dialogue about the future of monitoring but at the same time noted that their organisation wanted to be seen as more than a mere security company and had ambitions to be taken seriously as a player in the criminal justice system. Perhaps because of their probation backgrounds these men were clear that EM's 'best' future – including tracking – was as a component in intensive rehabilitation programmes, not primarily as a stand-alone penalty. Whether more senior people in the organisation agree, however, is harder to ascertain. What is already clear is that each of the private sector providers is employing a growing number of monitoring staff (in control centres and in the field), who are being trained by the Custodial Care National Training Organisation (soon to be combined into a larger body with responsibility for police and probation training as well). The seeds of a new occupational group in the criminal justice system are possibly being sown here – separate from probation and youth justice – a group who may wish, or be directed, at some point in the future to encroach on the territory of existing groups.

There is no reason to believe that the commercial organisations involved in EM will promote a reduced use of custody, as, worldwide, many of them are also involved in its provision. 'Integrated justice services' readily encompass both prison and its alternatives, with commercial organisations benefiting from *both* the government's disillusion with traditional community penalties and its continuing responsiveness to popular punitive demands for increased imprisonment.

POPULAR PUNITIVISM AND THE LIMITS TO TAGGING

Popular punitivism – the vengeful sentiments expressed by certain sections of the public, the media and politicians in Britain (Bottoms 1995) – will undoubtedly constrain the development of EM for the foreseeable future. Contrary to the views of both supporters and opponents EM has not been seen by the British press as a significantly draconian punishment (the obvious corollary of this being a lack of anxiety about its civil liberty implications). At best, it has been portrayed as suitable for low- to medium-risk offenders, at worst as totally useless, a penalty easily evaded by the deceitful offender. The media derided Home Office attempts in February–March 2002 to extend HDC and to introduce EM as a pre-trial measure for young offenders; the emphasis in press and TV coverage was on how easy it was to re-offend while on the tag. All this is something of a paradox for those early probation critics who anticipated that EM would be seen (and wanted it to be seen) as 'pure punishment'; instead the popular media see it as something *analagous* to probation, just another 'soft' community penalty, another 'liberal' excuse for not using imprisonment.

EM does possess some of what might be regarded as the conventional attributes of punishment – it restricts liberty and regulates an offender's time. But it is as equally well-characterised as a surveillant form of control which enables real-time pinpointing and locatability in a way no other community controls have done before. Therein, however, lies the symbolic difficulty with EM, in both its curfew, and perhaps especially its forthcoming tracking form – for pinpointing and locatability are more commonplace experiences in the post-modern world (mobile phones, data trails etc.), something we have come to regard as a convenience rather than as a threat to our freedom. Now that a rudimentary technology is available some British parents are even considering implanting tags in their children in order (hopefully) to safeguard them from abduction (*The Observer*, 8 September 2002), a benignly intended use of tracking which might further weaken the image of tracking as something punitive *per se*. It is true that there is a difference between making oneself voluntarily locatable to family, friends and colleagues (although the data trails left by credit card transactions, and the recording of our movements by CCTV in public spaces are hardly something to which we *actively* consent) and having one's right to geographical privacy temporarily removed by a state agency (see Richardson 2002 for a taggee's perspective on intrusiveness). Nonetheless, the kind of pinpointing facilitated by EM is now simply a spot on a continuum of locatability created by information and communication technology (ICT), in which we are all to a greater or lesser degree implicated. EM, therefore, even in its tracking form, may never 'feel' distinctive enough, never 'other' enough, to be perceived by the law-abiding public as a particularly painful experience; it is punitive to a degree, but it is not the visceral, volatile, ostentatious imposition of pain characteristically desired by popular punitivists (O'Malley 1999).

Thus, although tagging may conceivably be 'toughened up' in the future, there is no reason to think that monitoring technology in its present form will significantly displace prison, as Stacey envisaged. Prison, for all its failures as a rehabilitative institution, remains a demonstrably viable means of incapacitation and a potent symbol of exclusion and censure. EM mirrors imprisonment to a degree (though not as much as its critics claim) but not sufficiently to displace it as a form of containment. However, precisely because it is not tainted with a humanistic ethos it can arguably withstand 'critique' by popular punitivism somewhat better than probation, and for this reason will probably displace probation with lower-seriousness offenders.

CONCLUSION

The precise development of EM in England has been shaped by the micro-politics of penal reform and professional self-interest, on the one hand, and by deeper, underlying shifts towards surveillance as a form of real-time control, on the other. Government has bowed to public and sentencer pressure for increased use of imprisonment. It initially reinvented probation as a form of attitude-changing groupwork but is now seeking to blur, almost completely, the distinction between community and custodial penalties. EM has undoubtedly intensified the actual level of control over offenders in the community, but it has never been integrated with the reinvented form of probation. There is arguably a greater degree of integration in the way in which EM has been introduced for young offenders – as an aspect of 'intensive supervision and surveillance' – which may well be a precursor of the new multi-ingredient penalty for adult offenders being promoted in *Justice for All* (Home Office 2002a). What is happening here, though, is not the kind of rapprochement between EM and 'social work' so eloquently championed by Whitfield (1997, 2001) but a transformation in the nature of offender supervision, in which surveillance will play a greater, if not necessarily more overt part. Perhaps, in England, we would have arrived at this point anyway, but with hindsight it can be seen that the Probation Service, while not mistaken in insisting upon an overarching humanistic approach to offenders, nor in demanding healthy debate about a prospective new penalty, was mistaken to reject EM so comprehensively at the outset, because it gave an additional incentive to government to involve and empower the private sector, whose ambition to develop 'integrated justice services' may yet have fateful consequences for probation itself.

SUMMARY OF KEY ISSUES

- Electronic monitoring (EM) must indubitably be understood as a form of surveillance, and not just as a new form of community penalty. It is likely to become a more common and more important element of offender supervision in the future, largely because of the way in which it has been embedded in the Criminal Justice and Court Services Act 2000, and because of a general sense in the Home Office, and nowadays among some in the penal reform world, that its potential remains underexploited. Research on EM's effectiveness remains equivocal; it may only produce minor gains in terms in terms of crime reduction, but its expansion to date does not seem to have been soley dependent on research results. Ideological factors and the crisis of prison numbers have been just as important.

- The original promoters of EM made rather grandiose claims for the potential of EM, in terms of both its capacity to discipline offenders and to reduce the use of imprisonment. The Probation Service and the penal reform network made rather exaggerated criticisms of its actual civil liberty implications – although it does have some – but were right to demand evidence of its effectiveness and to worry about the wider implications of the growth of a surveillance culture. The expansion of Home Detention Curfew has won greater support for EM from probation officers, but they rightly remain worried about the present role and possible future ambitions of the commercial organisations which administer it.

- Some writers, while always mindful of the dangers, hope for a creative rapprochment between EM and social work/probation in England, as has arguably developed in Sweden and Holland. The present government's apparent plans for the Probation Service – the blurring of traditional distinctions between community and custodial penalties – make this unlikely. The humanistic (social work) elements of probation are in decline, and we may be moving towards a managerialist–surveillance paradigm in offender supervision, which would give significant impetus to various forms EM – tagging, satellite tracking, and voice-verification systems), perhaps at the expense of probation.
- The commercial organisations that promote and provide EM, and prisons, are a wild card in penal policy, whose longer-term ambitions are hard to fathom. Further privatisation of the probation service cannot be discounted. Paradoxically, the single greatest constraint on the development of EM is the mentality of 'popular punitivism'. Contrary to the expectations of both those who promoted it, and those who criticised it, as a 'tough' punishment, EM has not been perceived as 'tough' by the public or the media, rather it has been seen as another 'soft' alternative to a deserved custodial penalty. Nonetheless, EM is not itself tainted by humanistic considerations, and can with skill be packaged as something tougher and altogether more controlling than probation, which is even more vulnerable to the critique of 'popular punitivism'.

References

Association of Chief Officers of Probation (ACOP) (1997) *Position Statement on Electronic Monitoring*. Wakefield, Yorkshire: ACOP.

Boswell, G., Davies, M. and Wright, A. (1993) *Contemporary Probation Practice*. Aldershot: Avebury.

Bottoms, A. E. (1995) 'The philosophy and politics of punishment and sentencing', in C. Clarke and R. Morgan (eds) *The Politics of Sentencing Reform*. Oxford: Clarendon Press.

Cannings, J. (1989) 'Electronic monitoring – A chief probation officer's perspective', in K. Russell and R. Lilly (eds) *The Electronic Monitoring of Offenders*. Leicester: Leicester Polytechnic Law School Monograph.

Etzioni, A. (1999) *The Limits of Privacy*. New York: Basic Books.

Farooq, M. (1998) 'Probation, power, change', *Vista: Perspectives on Probation*, 3, 208–220.

Fay, S. J. (1993) 'The rise and fall of tagging as a criminal justice measure in Britain', *International Journal of the Sociology of Law*, 21, 301–317.

Fionda, J. (2000) 'New managerialism, credibility and the sanitisation of criminal justice', in P. Green and A. Rutherford (eds) *Criminal Policy in Transition*. Oxford: Hart.

Fletcher, H. (1990) 'Leg irons or liberators?', *NAPO News 16* (December 1989–January 1990), 10–11.

Haggerty, K. D. and Ericson, R. V. (2000) 'The surveillant assemblage', *British Journal of Sociology*, 51, 605–622.

Home Office (1988) *Punishment, Custody and the Community*. London: HMSO.

Home Office (2000) *Guide to the Criminal Justice and Court Services Act 2002*. London: Home Office.

Home Office (2002a) *Justice for All* (CM 5563). London: Home Office.

Home Office (2002b) *Probation Statistics England and Wales 2000*. London: Home Office.

Lilly, J. R. (1990) 'Tagging reviewed', *Howard Journal of Criminal Justice*, 29, 229–245.

Lilly, J. R. (1992) 'Selling justice: Electronic monitoring and the security industry', *Justice Quarterly*, 9, 493–503.

Lilly, J. R. and Knepper, P. (1993) 'The corrections–commercial complex', *Crime and Delinquency*, 39, 150–166.

Lobley, D. and Smith, D. (2000) *Evaluation of Electronically Monitored Restriction of Liberty Orders*. Edinburgh: Scottish Executive Central Research Unit.

McCulloch, C. (1997) 'Electronic monitoring of offenders – A task for probation?' *Vista: Perspectives on Probation*, 3, 12–19.

Mair, G. (2001) 'Technology and the future of community penalties', in A. E. Bottoms, L. Gelsthorpe and S. A. Rex (eds) *Community Penalties: Change and Challenges*. Cullompton: Willan.

Mair, G. and Mortimer, E. (1996) *Curfew Orders and Electronic Monitoring* (Home Office Research Study No. 163). London: Home Office.

Mair, G. and Nee, C. (1990) *Electronic Monitoring: The Trials and their Results* (Home Office Research Study No. 120). London: Home Office.

Mann, S. (1998) *Probation Perspectives on the Curfew Order with Electronic Monitoring*. Norwich: University of East Anglia Probation Monographs.

National Association of Probation Officers (NAPO) (1994) *A Briefing on the Criminal Justice and Public Order Bill 1994 – schedule 9 – section 35 – Curfew Order*. London: NAPO.

Nellis, M. (1991) 'The electronic monitoring of offenders in England and Wales: Recent developments and future prospects', *British Journal of Criminology*, 31, 165–185.

Nellis, M. (2000) 'Law and order: The electronic monitoring of offenders', in D. Dolowitz, R. Hulme, M. Nellis and F. O'Neill (eds) *Policy Transfer and British Social Policy: Learning from the USA?* Buckingham: Open University Press.

260 Mike Nellis

Nellis, M. and Lilly, J. R. (2000) 'Accepting the tag: Probation officers and home detention curfew', *VISTA: Perspectives on Probation*, 6, 68–80.

O 'Malley, P. (1999) 'Volatile and contradictory punishments', *Theoretical Criminology*, 3, 175–196.

Read, G. (1990) 'Electronic monitoring is a costly distraction', *The Magistrate*, September, 13.

Renzema, M. (1998) 'Satellite monitoring of offenders: A report from the field', *Journal of Offender Monitoring*, Spring, 7–9.

Richardson, F. (2002) 'A personal experience of tagging', *Prison Service Journal*, 142, 39–42.

Scheerer, S. (2000) 'Three trends into the new millennium: The managerial, the populist and the road towards global justice', in P. Green and A. Rutherford (eds) *Criminal Justice in Transition*. Oxford: Hart.

Schmidt, A. K. (1998) 'Electronic Monitoring: What does the literature tell us?', *Federal Probation*, 62(2), 10–19.

Smith, D. (2001) 'Electronic monitoring of offenders: The Scottish experience', *Criminal Justice: The International Journal of Policy and Practice*, 1, 201–214.

Stacey, T. (1989) 'Why tagging should be used to reduce incarceration', *Social Work Today*, 20 April, 18–19.

Toon, J. (2002) *Electronic Monitoring in England and Wales*, paper presented at the 'Will Electronic Monitoring Have a Future in Europe?' workshop. Max Planck Institute, Freiburg, Germany, 13–15 June.

Underwood, S. (1997) *Securicor: The People Business*. Oxford: CPL Books.

Wade, A. (1988) *The Electronic Monitoring of Offenders*. Norwich: University of East Anglia Social Work Monographs.

Walter, I., Sugg, D. and Moore, L. (2001) *A Year on The Tag: Interviews with Criminal Justice Practitioners and Electronic Monitoring Staff about Curfew Orders* (Home Office Research Findings No. 140). London: Home Office.

Wargent, M. (1995) Letter to *Justice of the Peace* (23 December).

Whitfield, D. (1995) Letter to *The Daily Telegraph* (26 August).

Whitfield, D. (1997) *Tackling the Tag: The Electronic Monitoring of Offenders*. Winchester: Waterside.

Whitfield, D. (2001) *The Magic Bracelet: Technology and Offender Supervision*. Winchester: Waterside.

16

THE END OF PROBATION?

Mike Nellis and Wing Hong Chui

It has become commonplace to observe that the Probation Service – indeed the criminal justice system generally – is caught in a process of constant, rapid change, although surprisingly little thought has been given to the human and practical implications of this (Nellis 2002). Is there an optimum pace of change, in which there is time to establish and consolidate new ways of working at ground level in the way anticipated by policy-makers, before a new round of laws and policies demands newer things still from those on the ground? Despite New Labour's commitment to evidence-led policy and practice, which is partly rhetorical and partly substantive (Savage and Nash 2001), no answer has been forthcoming to this, in criminal justice or any of the other fields of policy which are similarly affected. In the view of one probation officer, any attempt at an answer – any attempt to claim the time for the task – risks exposing the dubious reason why policy changes so fast in the first place:

> The root of the probation service's difficulties, and those of the police and prison services, is snap-of-the-fingers policymaking that springs more from tabloid editorials than from an understanding of criminal justice. (Quoted in *The Guardian*, 2 August 2002)

There is truth in this picture of gestural politics – of politicians responding to 'popular punitiveness', needing to show the public that 'something is being done' – even if it is not the whole story (Bottoms 1995; Garland 2001). The various changes which produced the organisational and political framework in which the probation service currently works were detailed in Chapter 1, and most of the subsequent chapters have elaborated on the possibilities for best practice within that framework. Between them this amounts to specifying the theories, conditions and skills needed to carry forward the effective practice initiative, coupled with a constructive critique of the initiative aimed, not at replacing it, but at augmenting and improving it. After such a momentous period of change, a modest approach of this kind seems sensible. Ward, Scott and Lacey (2002) and Raynor and Vanstone (2002) have recently argued in similar terms. Broad strategies, and some alarmingly detailed demands, have been specified at the centre, but the challenge still remains to make it all work in practice. There is some continuity, of course, at least with the recent past – not everything began anew on 1 April 2001 – but the pressures on staff at all levels of the National Probation Service (NPS) have been onerous, to say the least.

Yet even as the NPS was being created, it was understood that further changes would be coming, many of which would be critical for probation because they were in part an attempt to resolve the long-standing problem of low public confidence in community sentences and in the operation of the criminal justice system more generally. The Halliday Review of Sentencing (Home Office 2001b) and the Auld Review of Courts (Lord Chancellor's Department 2001) were rightly claimed by government as the most significant in their field for 30 years, with far-reaching implications for criminal justice in Britain. In addition, a comprehensive enquiry on the resettlement of offenders by the Social Exclusion Unit (SEU) (2002), a unit within the Office of the Deputy Prime Minister, was clearly indicative of the ascendancy of resettlement – with its implied critique of how prison and probation services currently work together on this – on the political agenda. Although the ensuing reports were in part consultation documents, they were also indications of intent by government, expressions of commitment to change that had already been signalled in their Ten Year Plan (Home Office 2001a). A White Paper, *Justice for All*, based on the Halliday, Auld and SEU Reports appeared in July 2002.

This concluding chapter will speculate on the future shape and mores of the 'Probation Service' – the speech marks, connoting provisionality, are deliberate – in the light of *Justice for All* (Home Office 2002). It will also draw on observations from the new Chief Inspector of Probation, Rod Morgan, in his first annual report, which gives some insight into the way that management and practice has unfolded – and what still remains to be done – since the NPS was created.

JUSTICE FOR ALL: NEW SENTENCES

The White Paper proposes root and branch reform of the criminal justice system but contains few surprises because it draws on detail in ideas and proposals that were articulated in the Halliday and Auld Reviews. This section will focus specifically on proposals about 'community sentences'. The White Paper's case for change in sentencing is premised on the idea that the present arrangements are untenable, complex and unwieldy – and that the public have no confidence in the criminal justice system as a result (Home Office 2002: para. 5.2). Some of the reforms are predicated upon the perceived limitations of community penalties themselves, others on the manifest limitations of short custodial sentences, which, while suitably punitive, are of insufficient length to include interventions aimed at changing the prisoner's behaviour. Echoing Halliday, it seeks to put the 'sense back into sentencing', and to make all sentences effective at reducing crime. Sentencing is explicitly defined to include the traditional repertoire of measures available to courts but also not just to encompass the supervision and follow-up which has traditionally been called aftercare, throughcare or resettlement. Herein lie the seeds of a transformed understanding of the long-established distinction between community and custodial penalties. All the new sentences, perhaps with the exception of the first, are named in straightforwardly punitive terms to emphasise their conceptual – and sometimes actual – connectedness to imprisonment, rather than probation. Halliday's concept of 'the seamless sentence' – while honoured in spirit – is clearly too bland to be the public name of a new sentence.

A customised community sentence

The trend in sentencing policy over recent years has been towards specific and differentiated sentences. Paradoxically, *Justice for All* departs from this, proposing a generic non-custodial sentence akin to the suggestion mooted in an earlier White Paper (Home Office 1995). This would end the traditional distinction between probation and community service (or community rehabilitation and community punishment as they have been known since 2000) once and for all and offer sentencers 'a menu of options which can be combined to form a single sentence' (Home Office 2002: 5.21), according to need and risk. These options could include 'compulsory unpaid work, offending behaviour programmes, education and training, drug treatment and abstinence requirements, intensive community supervision, curfew and exclusion restrictions, electronic monitoring of compliance, residence requirements and participation in restorative justice schemes'.

Custody Plus

This sentence will be served partly in custody (a maximum of 3 months), and partly in the community, for a maximum of 12 months. The community part, rather than being considered as aftercare, will be an integral part of the sentence and consist of rigorous rehabilitative requirements and restrictions. The two parts will, in theory, flow seamlessly together and failure to comply with any community element will make a return to custody likely. Consecutive sentences of custody plus will be possible, permitting a maximum of 6 months in custody and a total sentence length of 15 months.

Custody Minus

This is, in effect, a reworking of the earlier suspended sentence, which has fallen into abeyance. It allows a sentencer to give a custodial sentence and suspend it (withhold its implementation) for a period of up two years on condition not only – as in the past – that the offender remain law-abiding, but that he or she undertake a demanding programme of activity in the community (comprising any of the measures available in the customised community sentence). Breach will lead to immediate imprisonment – the activation of custody – except in exceptional circumstances. The sentence will be reviewable by sentencers at any stage, and conditions might be strengthened or relaxed depending on progress.

Intermittent custody

Variations on this idea – temporary spells of custody phased over a stretch of time – have been suggested before, but have never got beyond the Green Paper (Home Office 1984) stage, essentially because they were deemed administratively complex (see Shaw and Hutchison 1984 for the earlier debate). Whether, in practice, the problems identified then can be overcome now remains to be seen, but *Justice for All* proposes that some offenders will be given a sentence whose 'custodial' element is served at weekends and whose community element is served during the week. Hypothetically, it will allow offenders to maintain employment and domestic responsibilities (assuming they do not have them at weekends). It is aimed at non-dangerous offenders and is considered 'especially effective for women offenders who have children'; the result may be 'fewer children growing up in care or starting life in jail'. The term 'custodial' in this context has interesting connotations. It encompasses existing open prisons, but also an entirely new idea, a network of 'community custody centres' which would restrict liberty and enable offenders to work, learn and maintain family ties. Their provisional name represents the ultimate blurring of the traditional distinction between 'community' and 'custody', and to complicate matters further it is envisaged that they will be set up within prison perimeters as part of a multi-functional, campus-style site. This will include various levels of security classification (a system which may itself change), so that changing from one level to another need not, as now, entail moving between different parts of a region or a country, perhaps impeding the resettlement process. When not in the centres, the White Paper adds, offenders could be tagged or subject to voice-verification – clearly locating electronic monitoring, in this instance, at the lower end of the seriousness spectrum.

ORGANISATIONAL CHANGE

Given the enormous effort put into the creation of the NPS, and the belief, even by some working within it, that this represented a strengthening of the Service's position in government, its future would seem to be assured for the foreseeable future. But is it? New Labour indicated soon after coming to office, with the setting up of the Prisons-Probation review (Home Office 1998), that it favoured a single correctional service combining both probation and prisons. This met with sufficient opposition, and the Home Office seemingly channelled its energies into a less drastic alternative, a centralised probation directorate parallel to the already centralised prison directorate. Nonetheless, a great deal of effort has been put into developing policy in tandem and the generic term 'correctional services' (meaning the Prison Service, Probation Service and Youth Justice Board (YJB)) has become a commonplace of Home Office discourse. Strategic planning is already undertaken by the Correctional Service Board, which comprises the Minister for Community and Custodial provision, the heads of the prison and probation directorates, and the Chair of the YJB.

Is a merged Prison and Probation Service, which would in effect bring to an end the already fading idea of probation as a distinct activity in the criminal justice system, still an option? James Cannings (2002: 51), a former Chief Probation Officer and an astute observer of probation politics, has recently observed that the future of the present probation arrangements, for all their apparent solidity, will depend on how well they are deemed to have met current challenges in 2004: 'How chairs, chiefs and boards react to . . . changes in the next few years will determine whether they last or whether they will turn out to be a half way stage to something rather less flexible'. Both Halliday and *Justice for All* are in fact non-committal on the issue, lending support to the idea that policy will depend on what transpires in the next two years. But, drawing on reports from the Prison and Probation Inspectorates, and that of the SEU (2002) on resettlement, the White Paper paints a dismal picture of the consequences of prison and probation being separate agencies, and implies that the present division of labour is unsatisfactory:

> Work is often duplicated, or more commonly not carried out or followed through. Those receiving prisoners or ex-prisoners cannot assume that the work which should already have been carried out in prison, has been undertaken. Work begun in prison (on drugs, offending behaviour or education and training) is currently rarely followed through in the community. (Home Office 2002: para. 6.10)

In addition a proposed 'national rehabilitation strategy' (proposed by the SEU, taken up by the White Paper) will require greater integration of prison and probation, as will the specific, individualised 'going straight contract' anticipated for 18–20-year-olds, a particularly skill-deficient group who make up a large proportion of the prison population, and 42 per cent of all offenders. The sentence of Custody Plus will require 'a change of infrastructure to make it possible' (Home Office 2002: para. 5.29) and with this in mind the White Paper looks beyond itself to 'a major independent review of the correctional services' which will be established at some as yet unspecified point in the future. This may not be far away: 'the government wants to promote closer collaborative working between the prison and probation services and will be looking at various models for achieving this' (p. 6.27).

Whether this includes full merger is uncertain, but even if it does not, more joined-up work in criminal justice is certain. The growth of joint working has proceeded haphazardly since the late 1970s and in the government's view was accelerated by its own Ten Year Plan in 2000. Joined-upness includes coterminosity of geographical jurisdictions, shared performance targets across all agencies, (e.g. in regard to delay, and rights of defendants, victims and witnesses) and shared information and communication technology (ICT) across agencies. All of these things are considered essential for case management (the tracking of cases through systems and across agencies). Problems of both collective and individual performance remain, and accountability structures need streamlining. Central to their resolution are new national and regional bodies to oversee delivery of criminal justice services. A National Criminal Justice Board comprising the most senior political and executive figures, accountable to a Cabinet committee, will head this up. Forty-two Criminal Justice Boards, with responsibility for local delivery, will report to the National Board.

Within this new framework, specific configurations are likely to become more prominent and powerful. Multi-Agency Public Protection Panels (MAPPPs) were established in April 2001 to enable police and probation to jointly assess and supervise sex offenders released back in the community. Continuing public concern about sex offenders will guarantee that MAPPPs are one of the main ways in which the probation service registers with the public (Kemshall and Maguire 2002). *Justice for All* proposes to enlarge the agency membership of these bodies and produce even better pooling of resources, to include the Prison Service, electronic monitoring providers, social services, housing and employment. Most controversially – although it is part of a more general desire in the White Paper to involve the public more in criminal justice policies – independent lay members will be appointed to strategic local groups overseeing and directing these arrangements, in the presumed hope that this will help assuage public anxiety about the management of sex offenders (Home Office 2002: para. 6.37).

THE CENTRAL AND THE LOCAL

The NPS was a *de facto* centralisation of what had hitherto been a localised service, albeit one which had become progressively more subject to Home Office direction and whose local boundaries were only haphazardly related to the prevailing structures of local government. Traditional arguments about the importance of local discretion in crime control have been losing force for some time across the criminal justice system, usually on the grounds of a need for a more standardised and consistent performance, and *Justice for All* does nothing to reaffirm them. Such discussion as there is about local auto-nomy surfaces in regard to the reform of the magistracy, where the tradition of decentralised discretion has lasted longest (much to the chagrin of central government, who have not always found the magistrates responsive to their vision of sentencing). The White Paper ostensibly concedes the importance of local justice, and welcomes the volunteers who become magistrates as 'a great strength of the justice system' (Home Office 2002: para. 9.21). But the traditional argument that local magistrates are by definition 'accountable' to the local communities from which they are drawn, informally reflecting the wishes and standards of those communities, is questioned. A more conven-tional managerial style of accountability is offered, in the form of new local boards with representatives from the judiciary, the local authority, court user groups and victim support organisations. The rationale is this:

> Local flexibility cannot be used to excuse wide variations in performance. Local services will need to satisfy clear national standards in performance, financial reporting and meeting national policy aims. Areas which perform well will earn greater flexibility and autonomy. (Home Office 2002: para. 9.25)

There is a confusion here. Local flexibility is being subordinated to a national blueprint, with autonomy granted only to those local agencies that most conform to national requirements! This impugns the very concept of local flexibility, although rhetorical requirements ensure its continued use. The key worry about the imposition of standardising managerial structures on the lower courts is that they will deter people from becoming magistrates; in the past it was precisely the element of public service, the investment that was being placed in their character and the autonomy of the job that made it appealing to many people (at least White middle-class people). The White Paper already notes 'problems of recruitment of lay magistrates in some areas' (para. 7.22), albeit without speculating on causes.

In respect of the Probation Service there are already anxieties that the strong local dimension enshrined in the Criminal Justice and Court Services Act 2000, and given expression through the 42 Probation Boards, is not working out as intended. There is a sense in which the local Boards are being used merely as agents of the National Probation Directorate (NPD), and some are acquiescing in this. In the view of the Chief Executive of the Probation Boards Association (formed out of the erstwhile Association of Chief Officers of Probation and the Council of Probation Committees) something rather more robust and autonomous was both envisaged, and is urgently required, if effective practice is to be tailored to local circumstances (Wargent 2002).

Tactfully, the Probation Inspectorate lends support for this, portraying localisation as 'an aspect of diversity' (Her Majesty's Inspectorate of Probation (HMIP) 2002: 9). It is not at all clear in *Justice for All* that this is the Home Office view. Cannings (2002) suggests that in the run-up to the 2000 Act the Probation Boards were actually a *reluctant* concession made by centralisers – rather than a principled commitment to localisation (as others saw it) – a site of authority beyond the control of the NPD, and (ideally) better dispensed with. The White Paper's proposed 42 Criminal Justice Boards, with responsibility for local delivery across a range of agencies, would report to the envisaged National Criminal Justice Board. It is difficult to see how the existing Probation Boards, serving only one agency, could fit in with such arrangements; without being named explicitly they seem to be encompassed by the following criticism:

> there are many interdepartmental and interagency bodies at national and local level that work with potential uncertainty in their role and/or their relationship with one another. These groups have developed in a piecemeal way over time and often have overlapping membership and terms of reference. They also lack, at times, the authority to commit to collective recommendations or decisions, particularly at local level. (Home Office 2002: para. 9.9)

VICTIM-CENTREDNESS AND RESTORATIVE JUSTICE

Under New Labour decisive moves have been made to make the criminal justice system more responsive to the needs of victims, and indeed, victim-centredness has become a cornerstone of the Probation Service's stated value system. *Justice for All* makes clear that there is still a long way to go. In part its very title reflects this. It buys into the idea that there is some truth in victims' perceptions that the criminal justice system is biased in the favour of offenders rather than victims and witnesses. Such perception legitimates and invites considerable institutional change. The White Paper proposes an independent commissioner for victims and witnesses, backed up by an advisory panel to champion victims' interests. A national strategy for victims is promised for the future – beyond what is in the White Paper itself – and a code of practice which specifies what victims can reasonably expect from all the criminal justice agencies with whom they are in contact. Better communication is promised to victims about both general and particular issues – victims' representation on local boards and MAPPPs, on the one hand, use of ICT to keep them informed of 'their' case, on the other. The most immediate procedural consequence for the NPS of the White Paper's proposals are probably the requirement to bring mentally disordered offenders within the scope of victim contact work – currently there is no obligation to inform victims of their release from hospital as there is for offenders from prisons.

Ostensibly, this increases the importance of reparation and restorative justice in crime policy. The White Paper proposes pilot schemes whereby prisoners can make amends to victims out of their pay. More restorative justice schemes are promised. Halliday, Auld and the SEU all sought to raise the profile of restorative justice – one to augment the effective practice agenda, one to clarify its relationship to sentencing and one to promote reparation within prisons. All three were agreed that the distinctive purpose of restorative justice was 'to ensure that offenders are unable to avoid the consequences of their actions and that victims' voices are fully heard' (SEU 2002: 84). *Justice for All* promises a national restorative justice strategy (on which a consultation document was promised later in 2002). The aim will be to create consistent, standardised restorative possibilities at all stages of the criminal justice process, for all age groups. Particular emphasis will be given to restorative justice for young people (something which is already well in hand in the YJB), in schools as well as the criminal justice system, and to specific techniques which seem effective in reducing offending.

All this is, in the main, to be welcomed. There is nowadays no possibility of undertaking constructive work with offenders that does not also take account of the needs, rights and interests of crime victims. That is as it should be. The danger – and this is why 'victim-centredness' is such a dangerously elastic term – is that a climate will inadvertently be created in which the sense of harm done to victims, and the shame and scorn which attaches to 'perpetrators', will make it ever more difficult to acknowledge the needs, rights and interests of offenders, and to reintegrate them into mainstream society. A balance is needed, which it will be hard to hold steady.

IMAGE AND LANGUAGE

The idea that the Probation Service has had an inadequate public profile, that its work has been inadequately understood and insufficiently appreciated has been a recurrent theme in discussions of probation's future over the past decade (Nash 2000). Rod Morgan makes it central to his argument in the 2001–2002 report: 'more must positively be done to raise the profile of the probation service with the public at large and sentencers in particular' (HMIP 2002: 5). He recommends that the NPD, the Boards and the local areas need to develop better media strategies and to use their imaginations from wall plaques to celebrate offenders on community service to the creation of improved public facilities, success stories (with both victims and offenders) in local papers, the badging of vehicles used by community service organisers. These are variations on suggestions that have been made before, and while not easy to quarrel with, they perhaps beg the question of why such obvious things have never seemed easy to do in the past. The local and national media – press, TV and radio – are at best an ambivalent friend of the Probation Service. The price of 'trumpeting' its successes, as Morgan recommends, may well be a corresponding difficulty in keeping its inevitable occasional failures and embarrassments out of the public eye – and in the field of criminal justice media-framed failures tend to make bigger and more lasting impressions than successes.

Nonetheless, serious thought has been given in recent years to the ways in which good practice in community-based work with offenders can be communicated to others, by penal reform organisations, by the probation service and by government itself. Much of this has been stimulated by Payback, an organisation set up in 1999 to demonstrate ways of improving the public understanding, and credibility, of community penalties. While it cannot claim to have had a direct influence on debate or policy Payback has left a legacy of new thinking which, while in no way guaranteed to bring about success, cannot be ignored by anyone interested in promoting community penalties (and reductions in custody). It has commissioned research into attitude change in criminal justice (Bowers 2002), advised the Halliday review, commented on various agencies' existing media strategies, sought to sensitise media organisations to their portrayals of offenders and victims and contributed to the establishment of its successor campaign, *Rethinking Crime and Punishment*. In essence, Payback has argued that the twenty-first century penal reform lobby needs to adopt – or extend – strategies and techniques akin to those of commercial marketing rather than continuing to rely on traditional discourses of social justice and compassion for the disadvantaged. Such an approach is itself not without difficulties – it may appear cynical or frivolous, and it runs the risk of downplaying moral considerations in a field where they badly need to be reaffirmed – but as Payback's evaluator concludes, it is 'the notable and perhaps unique achievement of Payback over its very short life . . . to place such questions firmly on many influential people's agendas' (Grimshaw 2002; see also Chapman, Mirlees-Black and Brawn 2002).

The Inspectorate believes that the most significant need for improved communication is with sentencers, both magistrates and judges, particularly as some older mechanisms of communication, for example Probation Liaison Committees (whose efficacy was variable) have been closed off by recent legislative changes. Sentencers in Britain, compared to other jurisdictions, have a wide repertoire of sentences at their disposal and – perhaps for good reason, given the remorseless pace of change – may have inadequate knowledge of their potential. Sentencers' knowledge of the effectiveness debate may also be patchy, and at present they have the discretion to ignore what they do not like. They need to be won over, not only to ensure justice for the offenders who appear before them, but also because they are still, although less so than in the past, significant opinion leaders in their local communities.

While recognising, post-Halliday, that it may not be possible to turn the clock back, Rod Morgan suggests as tactfully as he can that the recent controversial name changes from 'probation' to 'community rehabilitation' and 'community service' to 'community punishment' may not have been as advantageous as policy makers hoped (and as critics warned at the time). Morgan is further struck by the fact that so many of those who work in the criminal justice system, including sentencers, continue to use the old terminology which was at least broadly understood. It is doubtful that public knowledge and confidence has been increased by the changes, of which few people outside the criminal justice system are aware (HMIP 2002).

He singles out 'community service' as a term which might 'with advantage, continue' (not least because those on community punishment orders are still sent to community service projects!). 'Probation' is perhaps, less defensible, however, despite its embeddedness in the discourse of current criminal justice employees. *Justice For All* does seem determined to eradicate it from criminal justice discourse, only ever using the term to name the organisation, never to refer to a sentence or a form of practice. The proposed alternatives notwithstanding, this at least has the merits of honesty. Both the nature of practice with offenders in the community and the values underpinning it have changed considerably in recent years, and arguably there are limits to the elasticity of the term 'probation' that once described them so aptly. A large part of the reason why probation interests fought so hard to retain the name in the run-up to the Criminal Justice and Court Services Act 2000 was an almost talismanic belief that if the name was retained something of the humanity that it had traditionally stood for would also be retained. This was partly understandable and partly commendable – the term 'probation' has undeniably honourable connotations – but its supporters were reluctant to face up to the possibility that, after a century (over which its meaning evolved in any case) it may no longer be the most compelling or persuasive term with which to promote humanistic ideals in community-based work with offenders.

Set against the language which the Home Office wants to use – in which that most elastic of all terms, 'punishment', is always prominent – it may in one sense seem prudent to stick with what one knows, with what worked before. But if the very retention of old language – language which sounds as though it is addressed to the problems of the past – can actually work to ensure that the more punitive discourses become and remain dominant, if humanistic values and responses are to be retained, strengthened and developed, they may need to be articulated in new or at least modified ways. Compassion, rehabilitation, justice and personalised care need not be forsworn in work with offenders, but there is no point hankering naïvely or nostalgically for the lost simplicities of social work, or all the words that once gave expression to them. This seems to be the conclusion being drawn by some North American commentators:

> Probation is dead. At least that is the verdict of numerous, recent reports on the state of the art in community corrections. For instance, Maloney, Bazemore and Hudson (2001) argue that probation has 'gone the way of the Edsel' in terms of performance and reputation, and like the Ford Company's infamous failure, probation needs to be retired. Most important, they not only advocate the end of traditional probation practice (which they say is based on the 'rather bizarre assumption that surveillance with some guidance can steer the offender straight') but also dispensing with the 'brand name' of probation (which they rightly argue is a vague and uninspiring term) . . . They suggest that a far more fitting name for probation should be *community justice*. (Maruna 2002: 159–160)

The public language in which concern *about* crime, and concern *for* victims and offenders is expressed does matter. Coarse, simplistic language will coarsen and oversimplify actual responses and drown out the more sophisticated conversations – exemplified by the chapters in this book – necessary to a proper understanding of crime and what it takes to reduce its many manifestations (Nellis 1999). 'Community justice' does, on reflection, seem to have potential as an orienting term for work with offenders outside prison, encompassing much of the good work that is already developing, and may well be a fitting replacement for 'probation'. It is in essence about just ways of creating safety at local level. In that sense it accords with efforts to preserve and strengthen a 'strong local' dimension in crime control, appropriate to the circumstances of particular places and communities. It insists upon justice as the moral heart of all work with victims, offenders and communities, something which all local people have a stake in – and in that sense anticipates the central moral message of *Justice for All* – although attention always needs to be paid to what exactly 'justice' means. Various attempts have already been made in England to give substance to the concept of 'community justice' (Harding 2000; Nellis 2000, 2001c; Williams 2002). Nellis in particular has sought to develop it as a concept which can revitalise a commitment to the reduced use of custody, a matter on which most recent official publications are worryingly silent but which remains democratically desirable in general (democracy embodies a presumption against the restriction of liberty, permitting it only as a last resort – see Stern (1998)) – and professionally feasible to key players in contemporary probation politics.

MORALE IN THE PROBATION SERVICE

Processes of rapid change have tangible consequences – not always intended – both for the people who introduce and for those who undergo them. Conventional managerial wisdom – if such it can be called – seems to place no limit on the scope and pace of change with which probation staff are expected to cope, although a recent study of 'retention and recruitment' in the public sector generally (Audit Commission 2002) suggests this is deeply mistaken. Although it has rarely surfaced in criminological or policy discussion, there is an ongoing question about stress and morale in the Service, to which perhaps, only the union, the National Association of Probation Officers, pays attention. High levels of absence through sickness in the Service may be indicative of either or both, and these absences are now of such significance that the NPD is explicitly committed to reducing them. Staffing levels are low in some parts of the country, creating impossible pressures on those remaining. The Chief Inspector doubts if morale is as low as is sometimes claimed, but agrees that 'these issues are difficult to gauge' (HMIP 2002: 11). But anecdotal accounts certainly remain worrying. Although some staff are unhappy about the perceived departure of probation from its social work roots – and some have left the service for this reason – this is by no means the only complaint. Many probation staff have in fact been won over to the new philosophy and the new 'effective' practices, and are prepared to invest in them. It is the managerial issues which perturb them, as indicated by this officer:

> I think the group work courses we run – programmes in managing anger or thinking in a different way – are a great initiative but due to a lack of staff these days, offenders are on waiting lists to get on these programmes. On top of that, the psychometric tests we've been told to carry out to assess people before and after they take these courses are just gathering dust. . . . Each test can take up to three hours and they are good . . . but there is no money to interpret the results. So there the tests sit, done, but never scored. (Experienced officer, quoted in *The Guardian*, 2 August 2002)

In addition there is also a sense in which the reconfiguring of the Service as a centralised organisation has left it self-absorbed, preoccupied with its own internal processes, unresponsive to external agendas:

> I fear we are seeing the probation service fall in on itself . . . The appointment of manager upon manager has led to a bureaucratic organisation serving itself rather than the business it is in. (*Ibid.*)

While not necessarily accepting this, the Inspectorate does tactfully suggest that the Service is perhaps 'not as good as it might be at recognising the innovative, dedicated and effective work which probation staff deliver week in, week out'. There is also an additional worry that the new Service, racked by change, may not live up to the expectations of the officers who have come through the new training courses (separated from social work in 1997; see Nellis 2001a). High caseloads, excessive managerialism, lack of opportunity to give the best of oneself and limited communal resources may mean that trainees' enthusiasm for the Service is short-lived:

> It was my dream to obtain a professional qualification and put something back into society. Idealistic maybe, but idealism has been the defining quality of the public sector. Now I want nothing more than to get out. In my town – vibrant, successful, expanding – there is no housing for high-risk offenders, no treatment for prolific drug users and inadequate policing. . . . Many colleagues have gone on long-term sick from the pressure. . . . Tough on crime, tough on the causes of crime. It rings a bit hollow to those of us who work on the frontline with little or no idea what to do. (Newly qualified officer, quoted in *The Guardian*, 2 August 2002)

Not all trainees feel the same way (see Jarvis 2002), but there is a latent warning here. A managerial culture in which staff are reduced to being minions who merely follow procedures from this or that manual (Nellis 2001b), who are technically informed but insufficiently thoughtful, coupled with a climate of unceasing change in which nothing is ever consolidated, will ultimately produce an organisation whose culture is uncongenial to decent and creative people – and in which the vision of documents like *A New Choreography* and *Justice for All* will remain aspirational and unrealised, precisely because practice never consolidates. The documents will, literally, claim *more than is humanly possible on the available time scales*. The reassurance that they ostensibly offer (that in crime control terms something is being done) will be utterly chimerical, more substantive on the printed page than it will ever become in everyday life. The *human and personal* consequences of ever-accelerating, ever more prescriptive change are largely absent from criminological writing on the probation service – it portrays change as if it were merely an abstract process of policy implementation, and ignores probation officers' existential realties (although see Eadie 2000). This absence reflects the larger problem of 'missing persons' – the impoverished, thinned-out conception of personhood which Douglas and Ney (1998) believe weakens much contemporary social theory (including administrative criminology). Accounts of change in probation, or indeed any area of criminal justice, which fail to grasp the breaking points of the staff who are compelled to undergo it – as the Audit Commission (2002) at least tried to do – will probably misunderstand what the future of community-based work with offenders is likely to be.

This book was obviously put together with trainee probation officers particularly in mind and it is to be hoped that it will be widely used by them, their teachers and their immediate supervisors (practice development assessors). *If adequate space and time are given by policy-makers to well-trained, committed* and hard-working staff – and it is a bigger 'if' than we would like it to be – then, as the preceding chapters were intended to show, effective crime-reducing practice is possible. Such work may not in future be called 'probation' – and that may be no bad thing – but if it continues to respect the person-hood of both staff *and offenders*, it could still be more than worthy of the humanistic tradition from which 'probation' grew.

References

Audit Commission (2002) *Recruitment and Retention*. London: Audit Commission.

Bottoms, A. E. (1995) 'The philosophy and politics of punishment and sentencing', in C. Clarkson and R. Morgan (eds) *The Politics of Sentencing Reform*. Oxford: Clarendon Press.

Bowers, L. (2002) *Campaigning With Attitude: Applying Social Psychology to Criminal Justice Communication*. London: Payback.

Cannings, J. (2002) 'A walk around the lake', *Vista: Perspectives on Probation*, 7, 46–52.

Chapman, B., Mirlees-Black, C. and Brawn, C. (2002) *Improving Public Attitudes to the Criminal Justice System: The Impact of Information* (Home Office Research Study No. 245). London: Home Office.

Douglas, M. and Ney, S. (1998) *Missing Persons: A Critique of Personhood in the Social Sciences*. Berkeley: University of California Press.

Eadie, T. (2000) 'From befriending to punishing: Changing boundaries in the probation service', in N. Malin (ed.) *Professionalism, Boundaries and the Workplace*. London: Routledge.

Garland, D. (2001) *The Culture of Control: Crime and Social Order in Contemporary Society*. Oxford: Oxford University Press.

Grimshaw, R. (2002) *The Impact of 'Payback': The Campaign for Community Penalties*. London: The Centre for Crime and Justice Studies.

Harding, J. (2000) 'A community justice dimension to effective probation practice', *Howard Journal of Criminal Justice*, 39, 132–149.

Her Majesty's Inspectorate of Probation (HMIP) (2002) *Annual Report 2001–2002*. London: Home Office.

Home Office (1984) *Intermittent Custody* (CM 9281). London: HMSO.

Home Office (1995) *Strengthening Punishment in the Community*. London: Home Office.

Home Office (1998) *Joining Forces to Protect the Public: Prisons–probation – A Consultation Document*. London: Home Office.

Home Office (2001a) *Criminal Justice: The Way Ahead* (CM 5074). London: Home Office.

Home Office (2001b) *Making Punishments Work: Report of a Review of the Sentencing Framework for England and Wales*. London: Home Office.

Home Office (2002) *Justice for All* (CM 5563). London: Home Office.

Jarvis, S. (2002) 'A critical review: Integrating knowledge and practice', *British Journal of Community Justice*, 1, 47–64.

Kemshall, H. and Maguire, M. (2002) 'Community justice, risk management and the role of Multi-agency Public Protection Panels', *British Journal of Community Justice*, 1, 11–28.

Lord Chancellor's Department (2001) *A Review of the Criminal Courts of England and Wales*. London: Home Office.

Maloney, D., Bazemore, G. and Hudson, J. (2001) 'The end of probation and the beginning of community justice', *Perspectives*, 25, 22–30.

Maruna, S. (2002) 'Afterword: In the shadows of community justice', in T. R. Clear and D. R. Karp (eds) *What is Community Justice?: Case Studies of Community Justice*. London: Sage.

Nash, M. (2000) 'Deconstructing the probation service – The Trojan Horse of public protection', *International Journal of the Sociology of Law*, 28, 201–213.

Nellis, M. (1999) 'Politics, probation and the English language', *Vista: Perspectives on Probation*, 4, 233–240.

Nellis, M. (2000) 'Creating community justice', in S. Ballintyne, K. Pease and V. McLaren (eds) *Secure Foundations: Key Issues in Crime Prevention, Crime Reduction, and Community Safety*. London: IPPR.

Nellis, M. (2001a) 'The new probation training in England and Wales: Realising the potential', *Social Work Education*, 20, 416–432.

Nellis, M. (2001b) 'Taking oppression seriously: Critique of managerialism in social work/probation', in I. Paylor, J. Harris and L. Froggett (eds) *Reclaiming Social Work: The Southport Papers II*. Birmingham: Venture Press.

Nellis, M. (2001c) 'Community values and community justice', *Probation Journal*, 48, 34–38.

Nellis, M. (2002) 'Community justice, time and the new National Probation Service', *Howard Journal of Criminal Justice*, 41, 59–86.

Raynor, P. and Vanstone, M. (2002) *Understanding Community Penalties: Probation, Policy and Social Change*. Buckingham: Open University Press.

Savage, S. P. and Nash, M. (2001) 'Law and order under Blair: New Labour or Old Conservativism?' in S. P. Savage and R. Atkinson (eds) *Public Policy under Blair*. Basingstoke: Macmillan.

Social Exclusion Unit (SEU) (2002) *Reducing Re-offending by Ex-prisoners*. London: SEU.

Shaw, R. and Hutchison, R. (1984) *Periodic Restrictions Of Liberty*, papers presented to the 17th Cropwood Round-Table Conference. Cambridge: Institute of Criminology, University of Cambridge.

Stern, V. (1998) *A Sin Against the Future: Imprisonment in the World*. Harmondsworth: Penguin.

Ward, D., Scott, J. and Lacey, M. (eds) (2002) *Probation – Working for Justice* (2nd edn). Oxford: Oxford University Press.

Wargent, M. (2002) 'Leading backwards from the front', *Vista: Perspectives on Probation*, 7, 38–45.

Williams, B. (2002) 'Editorial: The meanings of community justice', *British Journal of Community Justice*, 1, 1–10.

INDEX

absences 185, 189–90
accountability 130, 163, 201, 267
accredited programmes 64–7, 133, 141
ACOP *see* Association of Chief Officers of Probation
actuaries 113–17, 167
adoption studies 21
age 147, 149–50, 156
anti-social behaviour 201
appointments 188–9, 191
argumentation, avoidance of 135–6
Asian people 230
assessment
  actuarial 167
  Assessment, Case Recording/Management and Evaluation (ACE) system 118, 119–20
  change 167
  Community Justice Standards 167
  desistance-focused probation practice 156–8, 160
  essential skills 167–9
  Offender Assessment System (OASys) 118–20, 124, 167–9
  Offender Group Reconviction Score 167
  Parole Assessment 168–9
  psychometric tests 168
  re-offending 167
  risk assessment 118, 119–20
  Risk Matrix 2000 168
  sex offenders 168
  Spousal Assault Risk Assessment (SARA) 168
  third-generation 167–8
  time for 168
Association of Chief Officers of Probation (ACOP)
  electronic monitoring 249–51
  Probation Boards Association, merger with 2
  Probation Inspectorate 8

restorative justice 223
risk assessment 111
supervision, enforcement of 186–7
victims 214, 218, 223
attendance rates 176
attitudes
  change 131–2
  desistance-focused probation practice 150–2, 158–9
  pre-sentence reports 97, 220
  supervision 83
  victims 220–1
audits 186–90, 192
Auld Review 262, 269
Australia 50, 51, 174–5

bail 101–2, 245, 250
behaviour *see* cognitive-behaviouralism
  behavioural and attitudinal change 131–2
  ethical 130
  modelling 178
  theories of 23–4
best practice guidelines 61
biological theories of crime
  adoption studies 21
  contemporary ideas 21–2
  definition 20
  DNA 23
  early theorists and theories 20
  environmental factors 22
  eugenics 23
  genetics 19, 21, 22–3
  neurotransmitters 22
  race 21
  somatotyping 20
  twin studies 21

CAFCAS (Children and Family Court Advisory and Support Service) 11
Care and Control 163

case management
  definition 171
  effective practice 131, 142
  essential skills 164, 166, 170–1
  factory processing model 170
  modular involvement model 170
  monitoring 171
  Motivational Interviewing 172
  participation of offenders 171
  partnerships in the Probation Service
      200–1
  research 84–5
  specialist roles 170
  unmet needs 170
  What Works movement 170
categorism 238, 240
Central Council for Education and
    Training in Social Work 228, 231
centralisation 1, 6–7, 10, 267–8
change
  assessment 167
  attendance and completion rates 176
  behavioural and attitudinal change
      131–2
  compliance 176–7
  effective practice 131–3
  essential skills 172–7
  offenders in, engaging 172–3
  Motivational Interviewing 172–3
  National Standards 176
  Probation Service 261–2 ʼ
  probation values 228–30
  procedural fairness 177
  promotion of, techniques for 172–7
  pro-social modelling 173–6, 177
Children and Family Court Advisory and
    Support Service (CAFCAS) 11
Church of England Temperance Society
    4–5
citizenship 236
coercive rehabilitation 58
cognitive-behaviouralism 24–6
  desistance-focused probation practice
      153
  effective practice 129–30, 132–3,
      141–2
  Relapse Prevention 137
  risk assessment 112
  Straight Thinking on Probation (STOP)
      80–1
  What Works 66, 68–9, 78–9
communication
  acceptance of responsibility 49–50
  community penalties 48–50, 52

community punishment orders 48
  consequentialism 49
  cultural upbringing 173
  decision-making 49
  Motivational Interviewing 173
  probation orders 48
  proportionality 48, 49, 50
  punishment 48–50, 52–3
  retribution 48, 49
  risk assessment 170
  verbal 173
  victims 216–19, 268–9
Community Justice Standards 167
community justice 237, 272
community penalties 262 *see also*
      particular orders (e.g. community
      rehabilitation orders)
  Community Justice Act 1991 97
  customised 263
  decline in use of 182
  desert theory 8, 45–6
  effective practice 129, 142
  electronic monitoring 246, 248
  image 270
  Justice for All White Paper 263–5
  language 271
  Motivational Interviewing 136
  names of, new 12–13
  National Standards 96
  Payback 270
  penal welfarism 44–5
  pre-sentence reports 97
  proportionality 44, 45, 47
  public protection 46
  Punishment in the Community initiative
      7–8
  rehabilitation 40
  restorative justice 51–2
  retribution 44–5, 52
  risk assessment 123
  seriousness of the offence 45–6
  statistics 45–6
  supervision, enforcement of 182
community punishment and rehabilitation
    orders 12
Community Punishment and Rehabilitation
    Service 10
community punishment orders 12
community rehabilitation orders 12
community service orders 77–8
completion rates 176
compliance
  change 176–7
  constraint or coercion 191

compliance (*continued*)
  effective practice, links with 190–2
  encouraging 184
  legitimacy 177
  links with 190–2
  National Standards 186
  normative 191–2
  promotion of 186
  rewarding 191
  supervision, enforcement of 184,
    189–92
conditioning 23–4
conferencing 50, 51
conflict resolution 208–9
consequentialism
  community penalties 39–41
  deterrence 39–40, 42
  Halliday Report 42
  incapacitation 39, 40, 42
  punishment 38–42, 46–7, 52
  rehabilitation 39, 40–2
  re-offending 41–2
  retribution 52–3
  utilitarianism 38–9
  What Works 41–2
Correctional Policy Framework 56
Council of Probation Committees (CPC)
  2, 8
counselling 223
crime prevention 43
Crime Reduction Strategy 60–2
crime, theories of 19–37
  biological theories 19, 20–3
  critical and feminist theories 29–33
  psychological theories 23–6
  sociological and environmental theories
    26–9
  transnational crime 34
Criminal Justice Act 1991
  aims of 97
  community penalties 97
  deserts movement 96–7
  National Standards 95–8
  Probation Service 95–8
  risk assessment 111
  social enquiry reports, renaming of 97
  supervision, enforcement of 183
Criminal Justice and Court Service Act
  2000 1, 10, 198, 252, 257
crimogenic needs
  effective practice 141
  lifestyle 117–21
  pre-sentence reports 220
  pre-trial investigations 98

  risk assessment 117–21
  Social Exclusion Unit 63
  What Works 63
Crisis Intervention
  autonomy, restoring 139–40
  coping 138–40
  effective practice 131, 138–40, 142
  impact, period of 139
  post-traumatic period 139
  recoil, period of 139
critical theories 29–31
  critical criminology 27, 29, 30, 31
  definition 29
  early theorists and theories 30–1
  knowledge and power 30
  Left Realism 30, 32
  marginalisation 30
  National Deviancy Conference 30
  New Criminology 30, 32
Crown Prosecution Service 220
curfew orders 241–2, 245, 250–6, 258
custodial sentences
  alternatives to, promotion of 77
  avoidance of 237
  community justice, use of term 272
  Custodial Care National Training
    Organisation 255
  incapacitation 40
  Intermittent Custody 264–5
  probation values 237
  release from custody 216, 219, 246
  research 77
  risk assessment 109
  supervision, enforcement of 190
  youth justice 77
Custody Minus 264
Custody Plus 263–4, 266

decentralisation 206
desert theory
  community penalties 45–6
  Community Justice Act 1991 96–7
  hybrid theories 46–7
  punishment 47
  retribution 8, 43, 44
  risk assessment 123
  seriousness of the offence 45
desistance-focused probation practice
  146–62
  age 147, 149–50, 156
  assessment 156–8, 160
  attitudes 150–2, 158–9
  avoiders 151
  cognitive-behaviouralism 153

desistance-focused probation practice
(*continued*)
  converts 151
  decision-making 153
  desisters, categories of 151
  earners 151
  effective practice 159
  engagement 158–60
  evaluation 158–60
  female offenders 149
  gender differences 149–50, 156
  hedonists 151
  interventions 152–60
  life transitions 149–52, 160
  male offenders 149–50
  maturational theory 147
  motivation 150–2
  narrative theories 148
  non-starters 151
  persisters, categories of 151
  planning 156–8
  probation officers, relationship with
    152–3
  problem-solving 153
  pro-social behaviour, reinforcing 153
  pro-social modelling 153–4
  reasoning 153
  rehabilitation 146–8, 159
  reinforcement 153
  relationships 152–6, 158–9
  research 147–9, 153–61
  role clarification 153
  social bonds theories 147–8
  social ties 153
  social work 154
  supervision 152–3
  survivors 151
  theoretical perspectives 147–9
  What Works movement 148, 159
  young offenders 149–50, 153, 156
deskilling and deprofessionalisation
  120–1
deterrence 39, 42
Diploma in Probation Studies 13–14
discrimination
  human rights 236
  probation values 227, 229–31, 238,
    240–1
  race 238
  risk assessment 115, 121
  sex 231
diversion 6, 102
diversity 230–2, 238, 241
DNA 23

domestic violence
  pre-sentence reports 220
  Solution-Based Approaches 141
  Spousal Assault Risk Assessment (SARA)
    168
  victims 220
Drug Action Teams 197–8

ecological theories 27–8, 29
effective practice 129–45, 262
  accountability 130
  accredited programmes 141
  behavioural and attitudinal change
    131–2
  case management 131, 142
  change, achieving 131–3
  cognitive-behaviouralism 129–30,
    132–3, 141–2
  community penalties 129, 142
  compliance 190–2
  crimogenic needs 141
  Crisis Intervention 131, 138–40, 142
  cycle model 132–2
  desistance-focused probation practice
    159
  Effective Practice initiative 7, 118
  ethical behaviour 130
  meta-analysis 132
  Motivational Interviewing 131, 133–6,
    142
  Nothing Works 129
  probation officers, professionally
    development of 130–1, 142
  rehabilitation 60
  Relapse Prevention 136–8, 142
  research 81, 84–5
  risk assessment 118
  Solution-focused Approaches 140–1,
    142
  supervision, enforcement of 190–2
  training 131
  victims 219
  What Works movement 60–1, 68, 129
electronic monitoring 245–60
  Association of Chief Officers of
    Probation (ACOP) 249–51
  bail 245, 250
  commercial dimension 254–5, 258
  community penalties 246, 248
  Criminal Justice and Court Service Act
    2000 252, 257
  curfew orders 241–2, 250–4, 256
  Custodial Care National Training
    Organisation 255

electronic monitoring (*continued*)
  effectiveness of   248, 253, 257–8
  exclusion orders   242
  future of   246–7
  Global Positioning by Satellite   246
  history of   245–6
  Home Detention Curfew   245, 251,
    252–3, 255, 258
  Intensive Supervision and Surveillance
    245–6
  Intermittent Custody   265
  Labour Government   251–4
  limits of   255–6
  managerialism   252, 253
  National Association of Probation
    Officers (NAPO)   247–8, 249–51
  National Probation Service   251–2
  Offender Tag Association   249
  offenders, types of   246–7
  popular punitivism   255–6, 258
  privacy   248
  private sector involvement   251, 254–5,
    258
  Probation Service   252–4
    hostility to   249–51, 258
  release from custody   246
  Scotland   253
  sex offenders   246–7
  social work   247–9, 257–8
  statistics   246
  supervision packages   252
  surveillance   253–4, 257
  tracking   256
  training   255
  White Paper *Justice for All*   248
  young offenders   245–6, 257
enforcement of supervision   181–90
  absences   185, 189–90
  appointments   188–9, 191
  Association of Chief Officers of
    Probation (ACOP)   186–7
  audits   186–90, 192
  breach   181–3, 189
  community penalties, decline in use of
    182
  compliance   189
    constraint or coercion   191
    effective practice, links with   190–2
    encouraging   184
    normative   191–2
    rewarding   191
  conditional, nature of supervision   181
  consent of offenders   181
  Criminal Justice Act 1991   183

custodial sentences   190
  decision-making   183–5, 191
  effective practice, links with   190–2
  improvements, recent   186–90
  incentives   191
  Key Performance Indicators   185, 187
  licence, offenders on   189
  National Standards   182–6, 187,
    189–92
  Nothing Works approach   182, 185
  Probation Inspectorate   185, 187
  Pro-Social Modelling   185–6, 192
  reconviction   192
  rewards   191
  self-interest, appealing to   191
  What Works movement   185
Enhanced Thinking Skills Programme   66
environmental factors   22
environmental theories   26–9
essential skills in working with offenders
  accountability   163
  aspects of practice   167–71
  assessment   167–9
  Care and Control   163
  case management   164, 166, 170–1
  change, techniques for promoting
    172–7
  continuity of programmes and services
    165–6
  effective method   165
  engagement   165–6
  Joint Prison/Probation Accreditation
    Panel (JPPAP)   165, 177
  modelling behaviour   178
  motivation   165–6
  National Standards   163, 166
  Police Court Missionaries   163
  prison service, throughcare in the
    166–7
  probation officers, relationship between
    offenders and   164
  probation orders   163
  Probation Service   163
  programme delivery   166
  Programme Integrity   164
  rehabilitation   166–7
  responsivity   164–7
  risk assessment   163, 177
  Statement of National Objectives and
    Priorities (Home Office)   163
  supervision   85, 166, 169–70
  What Works movement   164
ethics   13, 130, 227–30, 233–7
ethnic minorities *see* race

eugenics 23
European Convention on Human Rights 233
European Excellence Model 12
exclusion orders 242

factory processing model 170
female offenders *see* women offenders
feminist theories 31–3
  contemporary ideas 31–2
  critical criminology 31
  gender theory 33–4
  needs of female offenders 32
  patriarchal society 31
  probation values 231
  sexual abuse 32
  stereotyping 33
  victimisation 33

gender *see also* women offenders
  desistance-focused probation practice 149–50, 156
  discrimination 231
  feminist theories 33–4
  managerialism 239
  probation values 230–1, 238
genetics 19, 21, 22–4
gestalt therapy 24–5
Global Positioning by Satellite 246
governance 10–12

Halliday Report 42, 262, 269
harm, risk of 110, 111, 116, 119, 170
high-risk offenders 109
Home Detention Curfew 245, 251, 252–3, 255, 258
home visits 169
housing 28, 29, 198, 201
human rights
  citizenship 236
  discrimination 236
  European Convention on Human Rights 233
  Human Rights Act 1998 233–6
  National Probation Service 233–4
  probation officers 235
  probation values 233–7, 240–1
  public authorities 233
  qualifications 233

image and language 269–72
IMPACT study 76
incapacitation 40, 42
incentives 176, 191

institutional racism 232
Intensive Supervision and Surveillance 245–6
Intermittent Custody 264–5
interventions
  desistance-focused probation practice 152–60
  partnerships in the Probation Service 206
  What Works 62–4, 70
interviews *see* Motivational Interviewing
investigations *see* pre-trial investigations

joined-up government 102–4, 195
Joint Prison/Probation Accreditation Panel (JPPAP) 41–2, 64–5, 165, 177
just deserts *see* desert theory
Justice for All White Paper
  electronic monitoring 248
  National Probation Service 267–8
  restorative justice 268–9
  sentencing 262–5

Key Performance Indicators 185, 187

language and image 269–72
Left Realism 30, 32
Level of Service Inventory – Revised (LSI-R) 118, 119–21
licence, offenders on 189
life transitions 149–52, 160
lifestyle 117–21
local areas 11, 202, 203
local authorities 197, 204
Local Probation Committees, replacement of 1
localised service 267–8

managerialism
  electronic monitoring 252, 253
  gender 239
  National Probation Service 274
  Probation Service 7
  probation values 238–40
  race 239
maturational theory 147
media 369–70
mediation 50, 222, 223
mentally-disordered offenders 219, 269
minorities *see* race
missionary phase 4–5
modelling *see* Pro-Social Modelling
modernisation of the Probation Service 8–10

modular involvement model 170
morale of the Probation Service 273
Morrison Report 94
motivation 150–2, 165–6 *see also*
    Motivational Interviewing
Motivational Interviewing
    accredited programmes, referral from
      133
    aims of 134–5
    argumentation, avoidance of 135–6
    case management 172
    communication 173
    community penalties 136
    definition 133–4
    discrepancy, development 135
    dramatic techniques 172–3
    effective practice 131, 133–6, 142
    National Standards 133
    pre-sentence reports 133, 136
    principles 172
    self-disclosure 172
    self-efficacy, supporting 136
    self-motivating statements 134–5
Multi-Agency Public Protection Panels
    (MAPPP)
    aims of 266
    case conferences 170
    pre-trial investigations 103
    risk assessment 111, 170
    sex offenders 111, 266
    Supervision Planning 170
    victims 269

NAPO (National Association of Probation
    Officers) 120, 228, 273
narrative theories 148
National Association of Probation Officers
    (NAPO) 120, 228, 273
National Criminal Justice Board 268
National Deviancy Conference 30
National Probation Director, creation of
    1–2
National Probation Directorate 267–8
National Probation Service *see also*
    Probation Boards
    absence of staff through sickness 273
    accountability 267
    aims of 12
    bail information reports 101–2
    CAFCAS 11
    centralised control of the 1, 10, 267–8
    civil servants, staff as 11
    composition 11
    configuration of the 10–14

creation of 1–18
Criminal Justice and Courts Services Act
    2000 1, 10
electronic monitoring 251–2
enforcement 12
ethical framework 13
European Excellence Model 12
governance 11–12
human rights 233–4
image 269–72
Justice for All White Paper 267–8
Labour Government 265
language 269–72
local areas, reduction in 11
localised service, as 267–8
managerialism 274
morale in the 273–5
National Criminal Justice Board 268
National Standards 1, 10
New Choreography, A 61–2, 227,
    230–3, 240–1, 274
new national priorities 12
new public management 10
organisation and structure, new
    11–12
Powers of the Criminal Courts
    (Sentencing) Act 2000 1
pre-sentence reports 97
priorities of 12
Prison Service, merger with 266
probation values 227, 230–3, 240–1
public protection 12
rehabilitation 12
re-offending 56
role of 10–11
social work 273
staff 11, 13–14, 262, 273–5
Statement of National Objectives and
    Priorities 10
stress 274
training 274
victims 219, 224, 269
vision framework 13
National Standards
    aims of 96, 186
    change 176
    community penalties 96
    compliance, promotion of 186
    Criminal Justice Act 1991 95–8
    decision-making 186
    essential skills 163, 166
    Motivational Interviewing 133
    National Probation Service 1, 10
    new public management 95–6

National Standards (*continued*)
  pre-trial investigations 98
  Probation Service 95–100
  revision 184–5, 190
  risk assessment 112
  social enquiry practice 96
  supervision, enforcement of 182–6,
    187, 189–92
  Supervision Planning 169
  victims 214, 216–17, 220, 223
  women offenders 96
National Vocational Qualifications 14
neurotransmitters 22
New Criminology 30, 32
new public management 7, 10, 95–6,
  238
New Zealand 50, 51
Nothing Works
  effective practice 129
  research 75–6, 80, 87
  supervision, enforcement of 182,
    185

Offender Tag Association 249
Offender Assessment System (OASys)
  118–20, 124, 167–9
Offender Group Reconviction Scale
  (OGRS) 114–17, 119, 167
offenders *see also* essential skills in
    working with offenders, sex
    offenders
  attendance and completion rates
    176
  attitude to victims 220–1
  attributes of 109
  background information 97, 99
  case management 171
  change, engaging offenders in 172–3
  Crown Prosecution Service 220
  high-risk 109
  mentally-disordered 216, 269
  pre-sentence reports, attitudes to 97
  probation officers, relationship with
    164
  problems of 56–7
  prolific, initiatives on 85
  remorse 220–1
  supervision, views on 83
  types of 246–7
  victims 220–2, 224
  What Works 69
organisational change 265–6
origins and development of probation
  4–14

Parole Assessment 168–9
partnerships in the Probation Service
  195–213
  accountability 201
  agencies of the criminal justice system
    195
  anti-social behaviour 201
  budget 196–7, 200
  case management 200–1
  coalitions 204
  championship 206
  clarity 206–7
  commitment 206
  community development groups 204
  conflict resolution 208–9
  consultation 204
  Crime and Disorder Act 1998 198
  crime prevention 197, 201, 206
  Criminal Justice and Courts Service Act
    2000 198
  decentralisation 206
  development 207
  Drug Action Teams 197–8
  empowerment, partnership as 203–5
  fragmentation, inefficiency of 201
  good practice 197
  Home Office 196
  housing 198, 201
  implementation 207
  intervention 206
  isolation of agencies, perpetuation of
    202–3
  joined-up government 195
  leadership 205–6
  local authorities 197, 204
  local probation areas 202, 203
  police 198
  policy 196–9, 202, 210
  popularity of 196
  pre-trial investigations 103–4, 105
  Probation Service 203–6
  process 207
  redistribution of responsibilities, as
    199–201
  risk assessment 198, 200, 207
  Safer Cities Programme 197
  social housing 198
  social planning and provision,
    coordinated 198–9, 209–10
  special groups, targeting of 197–8
  Standing Conference on Crime
    Prevention 197
  successful 205–9
  Supervision Grants Scheme 196

partnerships in the Probation Service
(*continued*)
supervision services, contracting for
196–7
Supporting People project 198
system efficiency 201–3
Tenant Participation Compacts 204
terminology 202
theories of partnership 199–205, 210
user participation in treatment 204
voluntary action, enhanced 203
voluntary sector 206, 207
Youth Offending Teams 198
Pathfinder projects 41, 42, 81–2, 87
patriarchal society 31
penal marking 103
penal pessimism 95
penal welfare 40–1, 44–5, 52, 93–4
persisters, categories of 151
police
partnerships in the Probation Service 198
Police Court Missionaries 163
Police National Computer, information
from 115
pre-trial investigations 98
Probation Service 198
profiling 26
risk assessment 115, 198
popular punitivism 255–6, 258
pre-sentence reports
aims of 97–9, 104–5
analysis of offences 98–9
attitude of offenders 97, 220
background information, exclusion of
97, 99
community penalties 97
conclusions 99–100
crimogenic factors 99
domestic violence 220
Motivational Interviewing 133, 136
National Probation Service 97
National Standards 220
Probation Service 98–100
proposals, inclusion of probation
officers' 97, 100
risk assessment 108, 112, 114, 122
social enquiry reports, renaming of 97
statistics 105
supervision 100
victims 220
pre-trial investigations 92–107 *see also*
pre-sentence reports
bail information reports 101–2
crimogenic factors 98

diversion 102
inter-agency collaboration 103–4, 105
joined-up working 102–4
mercy, dispensing 92
Multi-Agency Public Protection Panels
(MAPPP) 103
National Standards 98–102
penal welfare 93
police, collaboration with the 103
predictive scales 98
probation court reports, changing nature
of 93–4
Probation Service 92–3
public protection 100–1, 103
punishment 92
risk assessment 100–1
sentencing 92
sex offenders, penal marking of 103
status of offenders 92
values 102
Prison Service
essential skills 166–7
merger with National Probation Service
228, 266
Offender Assessment System (OASys)
169
prisoners, rise in numbers of 8
Prisons/Probation Review 9, 265
probation values 228
race 232, 238
Sentence Planning 169
throughcare 166–7
women offenders 231, 238
privacy 248
Probation Boards 1, 10
autonomy 11
governance 10–12
Local Probation Committees,
replacement of 1
localisation 267–8
National Probation Directorate 267–8
Probation Boards Association 268
Probation Inspectorate 268
supervision, enforcement of 185, 187
role of 10, 11–12
Probation Inspectorate
Association of Chief Probation Officers
(ACOP) 8
Council of Probation Committees (CPC)
8
image 270–1
National Probation Director, creation of
1–2
Probation Boards 268

Probation Inspectorate (*continued*)
  restorative justice   223
  role of   8
  victims   216–17, 220, 222, 223, 224
probation officers
  desistance-focused probation practice
      152–3
  effective practice   130–1, 142
  human rights   235
  offenders, relationship with   164
  professional development of   130–1,
      142
  professional status of   95, 104
  social work   5, 8, 40
  supervision, views on   83
  training   3, 5
  victims   216, 220
probation orders   40, 44–5, 48, 163
probation reports   94–5, 97–8, 104
Probation Service *see also* partnerships in
      the Probation Service
  centralisation   6–7
  change, implications of   261–2
  Church of England Temperance Society
      4–5
  Community Punishment and
      Rehabilitation Service, proposed
      change of name to   10
  conflict resolution   208–9
  controlling the   6–8
  creation of the   4–6
  Criminal Justice Act 1991   95–8
  Diversion from Custody   6
  electronic monitoring   249–54, 258
  essential skills   163
  historical context   93
  justice model   6
  managerialism   7
  missionary phase   4–5
  modernisation of   8–10
  National Standards   95–100
  new public management   7
  partnerships in the Probation Service
      203–6
  penal pessimism   95
  police   198
  pre-sentence reports   92–3, 98–100
  pre-trial enquiries   93
  public protection phase   8
  race   231–2
  rehabilitation   57–8, 60
  research   78
  restorative justice   6
  retribution   6

risk management   95, 198
supervision   7, 169
treatment phase   6
voluntary agencies   203
welfare phase   5–6
probation values   227–44
  Asian people   230
  categorism   240
  Central Council for Education and
      Training in Social Work   228,
      231
  changing   228–30
  community justice principle   237
  discrimination   227, 229–31, 238,
      240–1
  diversity agenda   230–2, 241
  feminist critique   231
  gender   230–1, 238
  human rights   233–7, 240–1
  imprisonment, avoidance of   237
  managerialism   238–40
  moral principles   227–30, 233–7
  National Association of Probation
      Officers (NAPO)   228
  National Probation Service *A New
      Choreography*   227, 230–3,
      240–1
  new public management   238
  pre-trial investigations   102
  prisons, merger with   228
  race   229, 230–2, 238
  rehabilitation   228
  sex discrimination   231
  social work   228–9, 231–2
  training   240
  victims   227
  What Works movement   229
  women offenders   230–1
procedural fairness   177
profiling   25, 26, 110
programmes
  accredited   64–7, 133, 141
  continuity of   165–6
  delivery   166
  Programme Integrity   164
  Programme Manual   164–5
  Reasoning and Rehabilitation
      Programme   66, 79
  Safer Cities Programme   197
  What Works   63, 164–5
prolific offenders   85
proportionality   43, 47, 52, 123
pro-social behaviour, reinforcing
      153

surveillance 253–4, 257
survivors 151
suspended sentences 44, 264

tagging *see* electronic monitoring
Tenant Participation Compacts 204
tracking 256
training
　Central Council for Education and
　　Training in Social Work 228, 231
　Custodial Care National Training
　　Organisation 255
　Diploma in Probation Studies 13–14
　effective practice 131
　electronic monitoring 255
　National Probation Service 274
　National Vocational Qualifications 14
　probation officers 3, 5
　probation values 240
　risk assessment 109
　social work 3, 8, 13–14, 84
transnational crime 34
treatment modality 63
twin studies 21

United States
　public opinion 2–3
　research 76
unmet needs 170

values *see* probation values
victim work in the Probation Service
　214–26
　Association of Chief Officers of
　　Probation (ACOP) 214, 218, 223
　attitude of offenders 220–1
　Charter 214, 216, 223, 224
　commissioner for, proposal for 268
　communication 216–19, 268–9
　consumers, as 217–18, 224
　contact 216–19, 269
　　costs of 217
　　staff, types of 217
　Crown Prosecution Service, information
　　from the 220
　domestic violence 220
　effective practice 219
　HM Inspectorate of Probation report
　　216–17, 220, 222, 223, 224
　'ideal victim' 221, 224
　impact of crimes 215
　interviews with victims 221
　mentally disordered offenders, release of
　　219, 269

Multi-Agency Public Protection Panels
　(MAPPP) 269
National Probation Service 219, 224,
　269
National Standards 214, 216–17, 220,
　223
national strategy for 268–9
needs of victims, responding to 215–19
offenders
　attitude to victims, of 220–1
　Crown Prosecution Service,
　　information from the 220
　interviews with 220
　remorse of 220–1
　victims, as 221–2, 224
policy documents and circulars 214,
　217–18, 223, 224
practice 220–2
pre-sentence reports 220
　domestic violence, contact with
　　victims of 220
　offenders attitudes to victims,
　　containing evidence of 220
probation officers 216, 220
probation values 227
race 218
release from custody
　expectations with regard to 219
　informed of 216, 219
　mentally disordered offenders 219
restorative justice 50–2, 222–3, 268–9
risk 217–18
satisfaction with agencies 215
sentences, informed of 216
serious offences 216
socio-economic status 218–19, 224
statements, victim personal 220
Victim Support schemes 216, 218
victimisation 33, 217–19, 224
Victim/Offender Mediation Unit, West
　Yorkshire 222
Victim's Charter 214, 216, 223, 224
victim's movement 214–19
voluntary action, enhanced 203
voluntary sector 203, 206, 207

Wales, Straight Thinking on Probation
　(STOP) project in 59, 80–2
welfare phase 5–6
What Works movement 7
　accreditation of offending behaviour
　　programmes 64–7
　best practice guidelines 61
　case management 170

What Works movement (*continued*)
   coding   79
   community base   63
   cognitive-behavioural theory   66, 68–9,
     78–9
   crimogenic needs   63
   desistance-focused probation practice
     148, 159
   doubts concerning   67–9
   effective practice   129
   Effective Practice Initiative   60–1, 68
   Enhanced Thinking Skills Programme
     66
   essential skills   164
   Home Secretary's Crime Reduction
     Strategy   60–2
   inconsistencies in probation practice
     60–1
   intervention   79
     principles of effective   62–4, 70
   Joint Prison/Probation Accreditation
     Panel (JPPAP)   64–5
   meta-analysis   59, 79–80
   New Choreography, A   61–2
   offenders, views of   69
   principles   62–4
   Probation Service, modernisation of the
     9
   probation values   229
   Programme Integrity   63, 164
   Programme Manual   164–5
   psychological criminologists   78
   race   64
   Reasoning and Rehabilitation
     Programme   66, 79
   reconviction data, reliance on   68
   rehabilitation   41, 52, 59–60, 69–70,
     79
   re-offending, reducing   56–73
   research   75, 78–80, 82–3, 86, 87, 165
   responsivity   63, 164–5
   risk assessment   111–12, 117
   Social Exclusion Unit   63
   supervision   67–8, 70, 185
   treatment modality   63
women offenders
   age   149–50
   community provision for   231
   desistance-focused probation practice
     149
   feminist theories   32
   National Standards   96
   prison statistics   231, 238
   probation values   230–1
   risk assessment   121
   sex discrimination   231
   social enquiry practice   96

young offenders
   age   147, 149–50, 156
   custody, promotion of alternatives to
     77
   desistance-focused probation practice
     149–50, 153, 156
   electronic monitoring   245–6, 257
   research   77
   restorative justice   50, 269
   Scotland   153
   supervision   7
   Youth Offending Teams   198

Pro-Social Modelling
  Australia 174–5
  desistance-focused probation practice
    153–4
  meaning 174
  pilot project on 175, 177
  research 174–5
  rewards 176
  supervision 175, 185–6, 192
psychological criminologists 78
psychological theories
  behavioural theories 23–4
  cognitive theories 24–6
  conditioning 23–4
  contemporary ideas 25–6
  definition 23
  early theorists and theories 23–5
  Freud, Sigmund 23
  genetics 24
  gestalt therapy 24–5
  profiling 25, 26
  rational choice theory 24–5
  recidivism 24
  risk assessment 25
  testing 25
psychometric tests 167
public authorities 233
public protection
  National Probation Service 12
  pre-trial investigations 100–1, 103
  Probation Service 8
  risk assessment 110–11, 122, 124
punishment
  communication, as 48–50, 52–3
  consequentialism 38–42, 46–7, 52
  definition 48
  desert principles 47
    community penalties and 45–6
    hybrid theories 46–7
  hybrid theories 46–7
  language 271–2
  pre-trial investigations 92
  proportionality 47
  Punishment in the Community initiative
    7–8
  rehabilitation 59
  restorative justice 50–3
  retribution 42–5, 46–7, 52
  theories of 38–55

race
  Asian people 230
  biological theories of crime 21
  categorism 238

discrimination 238
diversity 238
hybridity 238
institutional racism 232
managerialism 239
prison population 232, 238
Probation Service 231–2
probation values 229, 230–2, 238
research 85–6
risk assessment 121
Runnymede Trust's Commission *Future
    of Multi-Ethnic Britain* 238
social work 231–2
victims 218
What Works 64
rational choice theory 24–5
Reasoning and Rehabilitation Programme
    66, 79
recidivism *see* re-offending
reconvictions 68, 80, 114–17, 119,
    167
reducing re-offending
  Home Office's Correctional Policy
    Framework 56
  National Probation Service 56
  offenders, problems of 56–7
  rehabilitation 57
  What Works 56–73
rehabilitation 5–6, 8, 57
  aims of 58
  coercive 58
  community penalties 40
  definition 57
  desistance-focused probation practice
    146–8, 159
  Effective Practice Initiative 60
  essential skills 166–7
  Joint Prison/Probation Accreditation
    Panel (JPPAP) 41, 42
  National Probation Service 12
  national strategy, proposal for 266
  Pathfinder projects 41, 42
  penal welfarism 40–1, 52
  Probation Service 9, 57–8, 60
  probation values 228
  punishment 59
  Reasoning and Rehabilitation
    Programme 66, 79
  research 59
  restorative justice 52, 223
  retribution 59
  revival of 59
  Straight Thinking on Probation (STOP)
    59

rehabilitation (*continued*)
  What Works movement   41, 52, 59–60, 69–70, 79
reinforcement   153
Relapse Prevention   137, 138, 142
relationships   152–6, 158–9
release from custody   216, 219, 246
reoffending
  assessment   167
  reducing   56–7
  Relapse Prevention   136–8, 142
  research   82
  risk assessment   110, 115, 117
reports *see also* pre-sentence reports
  bail information reports   101–2
  changing nature of   93–4
  pre-trial investigations   93–4
  probation   94–5, 97–8, 104
  social enquiry reports   94–5, 97–8, 104
research   74–91
  case management   84–5
  community service orders   77–8
  custody, promotion of alternatives to   77
  design   76, 87
  desistance   82
  effective practice   81, 84–5
  future agenda for   82–6
  IMPACT study   76
  implementation   84–5
  lessons of, applying the   80–2
  Nothing Works, rethinking   75–6, 80, 87
  outcome-based   82
  Pathfinder projects   81–2, 87
  policy   84, 86, 87
  Probation Service   78
  prolific offender initiatives   85
  Pro-Social Modelling   174–5
  race   85–6
  reconviction rates   80
  rehabilitation   59
  qualititative   83
  quantitative   77, 82
  recidivism   82
  resettlement of prisoners   85–6
  Social Exclusion Unit   85
  social policy   85
  social work   77, 84
  standards   76
  Straight Thinking on Probation (STOP)   80–1
  supervision
    comparison of offenders and officers' views of   83
    personal skills   83–4
    prolific offenders   85
    systems instead of people, influencing   77–8
    United States   76
    What Works movement   75, 78–80, 82–3, 86, 87, 165
    youth justice   77
resettlement   85–6, 262
responsivity   164–7
restorative justice
  advantages of   222–3
  Association of Chief Officers of Probation (ACOP) position statement   223
  Auld Report   269
  Australia   50, 51
  community penalties   51–2
  conferencing   50, 51
  counselling   223
  empirical support for   51
  Halliday Report   269
  HM Inspectorate of Probation report   223
  Justice for All White Paper   268–9
  mediation   50, 223
  New Zealand   50, 51
  pilot schemes   222–3, 269
  policy statements   223
  Probation Service   6
  punishment   50–3
  rehabilitation   52, 223
  Social Exclusion Unit   269
  social work   223
  victims   50–2, 222–3, 268–9
  youth justice   50, 269
retribution   6
  community penalties   44–5, 52
  consequentialism   52–3
  crime prevention   43
  desert theory   8, 43, 44
  Probation Service   6
  proportionality   43, 52
  punishment   42–5, 46–7, 52
  rehabilitation   59
  suspended sentences   44
rewards   176, 191
risk and risk assessment   108–28
  actuarial methods
    clinical methods and   113–17
    evaluation of   115–17
    groups or populations of offenders   116–17
    Police National Computer, information from   115

risk and risk assessment (*continued*)
    race 121
    reconviction, assessing risk of
      114–15
    static factors, reliance on 117
    women offenders 121
  approaches to 112–21
  Assessment, Case Recording/
    Management and Evaluation (ACE)
    system 118, 119–20
  Association of Chief Officers of
    Probation (ACOP) 111
  attribute of offenders, as 109
  classification of risks 112
  clinical methods, actuarial methods and
    113–17
  cognitive-behaviouralism 112
  communication 170
  community penalties 123
  core tasks 108, 112, 124
  Criminal Justice Act 1991 111
  crimogenic needs, assessing 117–21
    instruments 117–19
    lifestyle 117–21
    problems and potential 119–21
  custodial sentences 109
  decision-making in practice 121–5
  defensibility 113
  definition of risk assessment 109–10
  desert theory 123
  de-skilling and de-professionalisation
    120–1
  dimensions of 109–10
  discrimination 115, 121
  Effective Practice Initiative 118
  equality principle 123
  evidence 111
  essential skills 163, 177
  false positives and negatives 122
  harm, risk of 110, 111, 116, 119, 170
  high-risk offenders 109
  Level of Service Inventory – Revised
    (LSI-R) 118, 119–21
  Multi-Agency Public Protection Panels
    111, 170
  National Association of Probation
    Officers (NAPO) 120
  National Standards 112
  Offender Assessment System (OASys)
    118–20, 124
  Offender Group Reconviction Scale
    (OGRS) 114–17, 119
  partnerships in the Probation Service
    198, 200, 207

  police 198
  Police National Computer 115
  pre-sentence reports 108, 112, 114,
    122
  pre-trial investigations 100–1
  Probation Service 95
    police and 198
  profiling 110
  proportionality 123
  psychological theories 25
  public protection 110–11, 122, 124
  reconviction, assessing risk of 114–17,
    119
  re-offending, risk of 110, 115, 117
  rise of risk in probation practice
    110–12
  Risk Matrix 2000 168
  sentencing 122–3
  sex offenders 116
    Multi-Agency Public Protection Panels
    111
    registration of 111
  social and political context 122
  Spousal Assault Risk Assessment (SARA)
    168
  supervision 119, 123–4
  training 108
  victims 217–18
  What Works movement 111–12, 117
  working with offenders 109–10
  workload 119–20
Runnymede Trust's Commission *Future of
  Multi-Ethnic Britain* 238

Safer Cities Programme 197
Satellite, Global Positioning by 246
Scotland
  electronic monitoring 253
  young offenders 153
self-disclosure 172
self-efficacy, supporting 136
self-motivating statements 134–5
sentencing *see also* community penalties
  effectiveness 271
  Halliday Review 262
  Justice for All White Paper 262–5
  parity 43
  pre-trial investigations 92
  probation orders 44–5
  proportionality 43
  risk assessment 122–3
  Sentence Planning 169
  Straight Thinking on Probation (STOP)
    81

sentencing (*continued*)
  Supervision Planning   169
  suspended sentences   44, 169
  terminology   371
  victims   216
seriousness of the offence   45, 216
sex discrimination   231
sex offenders
  assessment   168
  electronic monitoring   246–7
  Multi-Agency Public Protection Panels
    111, 266
  penal marking   103
  pre-trial investigations   103
  registration of   111
  risk assessment   111, 116
  Risk Matrix 2000   168
sexual abuse   32
social bonds theories   147–8
social enquiry practice   96
social enquiry reports   94–5, 97–8, 104
Social Exclusion Unit
  crimogenic needs   63
  research   85
  resettlement of offenders   262
  restorative justice   269
  What Works   63
social planning and provision, coordinated
  198–9, 209–10
social ties   153
social work
  Central Council for Education and
    Training in Social Work   228,
    231
  desistance-focused probation practice
    154
  electronic monitoring   247–9, 257–8
  morale   273
  National Probation Service   273
  probation officers   5, 8, 40
  probation values   228–9, 231–2
  race   231–2
  research   77, 84
  restorative justice   223
  sex discrimination   231
  training   2, 8, 13–14, 84
sociological and environmental theories
  26–9
  communities   28, 29
  contemporary ideas   28
  critical criminology   27
  definition   26
  early theorists and theories   27–8
  ecological theories   27–8, 29

housing   28, 29
  sub-culture   27
Solution-Based Approaches   140–1, 142
somatotyping   20
Spousal Assault Risk Assessment (SARA)
  168
Standards *see* National Standards
Standing Conference on Crime Prevention
  197
Statement of National Objectives and
  Priorities (SNOP)   7, 10, 163
statistics   3–4
stereotyping   33
Straight Thinking on Probation (STOP)
  59, 80–2
Streatfield Report   94
stress   274
study of probation, reasons for   2–4
sub-culture   27
supervision *see also* enforcement of
    supervision, Supervision Planning
  desistance-focused probation practice
    152–3
  electronic monitoring   252
  essential skills   85, 166, 169–70
  Intensive Supervision and Surveillance
    245–6
  offenders' views of   83
  packages   252
  partnerships in the Probation Service
    196–7
  pre-sentence reports   100
  probation officers' views of   83
  Probation Service   7
  prolific offenders   85
  Pro-Social Modelling   175
  research   83–4
  risk assessment   119, 123–4
  Supervision Grants Scheme   196
  What Works   67–8, 70
  women offenders   7
Supervision Planning
  aims   169
  harm, risk of   170
  home visits   169
  information gathering   169
  Multi-Agency Public Protection Panels
    (MAPPP)   170
  National Standards   169
  Offender Assessment System (OASys)
    169
  Probation Service   169
  Sentence Planning   169
Supporting People project   198